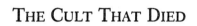

THE CULT THAT DIED

THE CULT
THAT DIED

The Tragedy of Jim Jones
and the Peoples Temple

by
GEORGE KLINEMAN
and SHERMAN BUTLER
and
David Conn

With Research by Anthony O. Miller

G. P. PUTNAM'S SONS   New York

The authors gratefully acknowledge the following publications, broadcasters and publishers for granting us permission to use excerpted materials and information:

The Associated Press.
Creative Artists Guild, Inc., for excerpts from tapes, 1979 Creative Artists Guild, Inc. All rights reserved.
Esquire Magazine, "Nine Places to Hide," by Caroline Bird, © 1961, Esquire, Inc.
The Indianapolis Star and *The Indianapolis News.*
The Guyana Chronicle, Georgetown, Guyana, S.A.
I-Team, KPIX-TV, San Francisco, "Portrait of a Madman," © 1979, Westinghouse Broadcasting Company, Inc.
KUKI Radio, Ukiah, California.
MCA Music, for "Joe Hill," by Earl Robison and Alfred Hayes, © 1938, renewed 1965, MCA Music, a division of MCA, Inc.
New West Magazine.
The Palladium-Item, Richmond, Indiana.
The Press Democrat, Santa Rosa, California.
Random House, Inc., for information from *True Tales From the Annals Of Crime and Rascality,* by St. Clair McKelway, © 1936, St. Clair McKelway and A. J. Liebling.
San Francisco Chronicle, for excerpts from Herb Caen, © 1977.
The San Francisco Examiner.
The Ukiah Daily Journal.
The Washington Post, © 1973, 1979.

Library of Congress Cataloging in Publication Data

Klineman, George.
   The cult that died.
   1. Jones, Jim, 1931-1978. 2. Peoples Temple.
I. Butler, Sherman, 1937-   joint author. II. Conn, David, joint author. III. Title.
BP605.P46K56 1980   289.9   80-13705
ISBN 0-399-12540-X

PRINTED IN THE UNITED STATES OF AMERICA

To Eileen,
who gave so much, and to Steve Katsaris.

Acknowledgments

Larry Lee Litke, an attorney for Alameda County, helped lay the keel for this book. He was a constant companion in times of great stress, and his steadfast support went unabated during those years of risk when few would have understood his role. Were that not enough, nine months before the holocaust, Litke brought to this project the literary talent of his good friend Sherman Butler.

To another Alameda County attorney, Ben H. Zuppan, I express my gratitude for his help and unsolicited counsel.

My thanks to Margot Ania Phillips for a variety of tasks, and to Elizabeth Jean Nelson, doctoral candidate in rhetoric at the University of Wisconsin, for her insights into the peculiar parlance of the Peoples Temple leader.

And I am ever grateful to my coworkers at Chevron Oil and to other friends who contributed documents, articles, and encouragement.

—David Conn

Foreword

The Cult That Died was first conceived, under a different title, in March of 1978. Following discussions with George Klineman and David Conn, Sherman Butler drafted a proposal and a chapter-by-chapter synopsis that, surprisingly, parallels the structure of the existing text with one exception: the tragic events of November 18, 1978. Work on the book became a race against time after June of 1978, when Klineman interviewed Deborah Layton Blakey and learned of Jim Jones's plans for a mass suicide. The authors were convinced that unless Jones were stopped, there would be a thousand rotting corpses in the jungles of Guyana.

In the five months between that interview and the massacre, the authors hoped they could get the book written and published before Jones carried out his plan; they talked—half-seriously—of hiring a pilot to drop copies on Jonestown. They were certain that once the truth was out in book form someone in Washington would intervene on behalf of the adults who were being held against their will at the jungle encampment and of the children too young to decide whether to die for an insane cause.

Klineman finished the original draft of chapter one in June. Butler edited and rewrote it. The initial response from publishers was favorable, but it soon became clear that the authors would have to complete more of the book before they could secure a contract. Eventually, Klineman wrote the original drafts of nine chapters, in addition to doing much of the research and interviewing. Butler wrote chapter five and the bulk of the final chapter. Finally, all eleven chapters were processed through Butler's typewriter until the authors felt they could pronounce the work finished. Conn conducted interviews for chapter eight and researched the connection between Peoples Temple and the Disciples of Christ.

Only four chapters were completed by November of 1978. Klineman was in Indianapolis retracing Jim Jones's steps when news of the massacre reached him. Of innumerable frantic phone calls between Indiana and California that week, one had a particularly significant—and salutary—effect on the book that now exists. Klineman called from Indianapolis and urged Butler and Conn to enlist the services of Anthony O. Miller, an investigative reporter and compulsive researcher who is responsible for much of the information contained in chapters three, four, seven, eight, ten, and eleven.

The authors of *The Cult That Died* toyed with the idea, following the example of e. e. cummings, of a "No Thanks" heading for a portion of these pages. The "Thanks" portion would certainly be genuine and long; the "No

Thanks" would go to those in the public sector who defied the weight of evidence and tried to convince us they never really had any association with the Reverend Jim Jones. These latter-day heroes boast and brag of turning down bribes, of confronting Jones with his crimes, but the facts show that Jones used them and their offices to wipe his feet or line his purse. The names we proposed in our vengeful fantasy would be those of public officials who told us there was "no benefit" in their speaking of their once close association with the preacher. They fed us erroneous information. They forgot or refused to return phone calls. Their stories changed each time we spoke with them. They are still at large.

Although the breadth of our forgiveness falls short of saintliness, we decided against the "No Thanks" acknowledgments and we offer instead our warmest thanks to the hundreds of people who have given us their time, freely and generously, toward the compiling of information for this book. We long ago lost count of the number of sources of information we have spoken with over the past year and three months.

The courage and devotion to truth of former Temple members who opened up their homes and consented to taped interviews deserve a conspicuous expression of our gratitude. Among these former members were people who, like ourselves, hoped naïvely that the book would be made before Jim Jones carried out his threat of mass suicide. The more of you we talked to, the more we were convinced of the urgency of the task before us. November 18, 1978, took us all by surprise, and made us question whether there wasn't more we could have done.

We owe a special thanks to Faith Worley, Ross Case, Steve Katsaris, Linda Dunn, and Tim Cahill, a contributing editor of *Rolling Stone* magazine, for sharing with us a wealth of materials and a mountain of trust. Others who hurried to the nearest Xerox machine for us or let us borrow their only copies of materials that contributed substantially to the book include John Barbagelata and Terry Francois, former San Francisco supervisors; Whitey and Opal Freestone; Joe Holsinger, former aide to Congressman Leo Ryan; Cecil and Georgia Johnson; George and Lena McCown; Rodger and Virginia Morningstar; and Nancy Shaw, director of the Indianapolis Human Rights Commission.

To Rob Fitz, our editor at G. P. Putnam's Sons, we extend our deepest admiration and thanks for his perceptive suggestions on the manuscript, his support and encouragement, and his unwavering good humor.

We gratefully acknowledge also some of our colleagues who work in the communications media who have gone out of their way to assist us: Suzanne Caster, *San Francisco Chronicle;* James Clancy, formerly of KTVU television; Charles Griffo of *The Indianapolis Star,* and the library staff there; Bob Klose, staff reporter, and Steve Hart, Ukiah Bureau Chief, *The* (Santa Rosa) *Press Democrat;* Warren Olney, NBC-TV, Los Angeles; Dick Reynolds, *The*

(Richmond, Indiana) *Palladium-Item;* and the I-Team, KPIX Television, San Francisco, for copyrighted material used in Chapter One.

The authors and a compulsive researcher could not have compiled, alone, the cornucopia of taped interviews, newspaper clippings, and documents that nourished this book. We are indebted to Eileen Klineman and Sheila Conn for assisting us in organizing the avalanche of materials that fell on us after the massacre. Eileen also edited and criticized early drafts.

There were others whose contributions should not go unnoticed: Don Clauder of Copytape in Santa Rosa worked long hours deciphering six reels of tapes smuggled from Peoples Temple, tapes that had been recorded and rerecorded at varying speeds, then spliced together; and Jim Russell helped educate the authors early on the complexities of finding a publisher. Finally, as an alternative to the "No Thanks" section we thought about, let us acknowledge those public officials—who shall remain nameless—who could not officially release the documents we sought. They mailed them, anyway, in plain brown envelopes.

George Klineman
Sherman Butler

Sebastopol, California
June 15, 1979

9

PASTOR JIM JONES
The most unique
PROPHETIC HEALING SERVICE
You've ever witnessed!
Behold the Word made Incarnate in your midst!
Hear his Divine Message of Apostolic Equality!
God works as TUMOROUS MASSES ARE PASSED in every service . . .
Before your eyes, THE CRIPPLED WALK, THE BLIND SEE!
SCORES ARE CALLED OUT OF THE AUDIENCE in each service and told the intimate (but never embarrassing) details of their lives that only God could reveal!
CHRIST IS MADE REAL through the most precise revelations
and the miraculous healing in this ministry of His servant,
JIM JONES!

—from a flyer advertising a Peoples Temple service, Embassy Auditorium, Los Angeles

I *

The Church in the Wildwood

The new '73 Pontiac wagon glides like a big boat through the wine country north of San Francisco to Redwood Valley, California. The driver checks his map and watches for the sign. He turns at a tree-lined road and follows it to an eight-foot chain-link fence topped with barbed wire. Behind the fence, an armed guard with close-cropped blond hair paces at the gate, a .38 police special in a holster on his hip. The guard squints at the unfamiliar wagon and reaches for his walkie-talkie.

"All right," he whispers, holding the transceiver close to his mouth. "Strange car coming up. Can you see it from the tower?"

"Can't see nothin' up here but the leaves in the trees," says the voice of his partner from the tower. "Be right down."

The man in the tower above the big chimpanzee cage clips his walkie-talkie to his belt and descends the steep stairs two at a time. At the bottom he meets the guard who's been circling the leader's house and together they step quickly toward the gate. They arrive just as the station wagon rolls into the driveway. They stop the car. The first guard squeezes through the gate and knocks on the driver's window.

"Is this Peoples Temple Christian Church?" the driver asks, bewildered. He is a pipe-smoking business type in a light-blue summer suit. His wife, holding the broad-brimmed straw hat that shades her summer dress, leans forward to hear the guard's answer. Both of them feel a little embarrassed and are not sure why.

The first guard answers in clipped tones. "Yeah. But meeting's closed today. Better leave," he says, "unless you got a membership card."

"This *is* Sunday," the woman protests. "We'd just like to go to church. If you don't mind."

"I'm sorry. Members only today. Now, would you please leave?" The guard sounds a bit annoyed.

"I don't think you understand," says the driver. "My wife and I just drove a hundred and ten miles up from San Francisco to hear Reverend Jones, and we're not about to . . ."

---

* A reconstruction of a typical Peoples Temple service, based on interviews, tapes, and documents smuggled from the Temple, and tapes of Jim Jones's voice.

"Look, mister, I can call one of the counselors, but they're just going to tell you the same thing I'm telling you."

The wife watches the guard with the pistol jog back toward the rustic church. "I think we'd better go, dear. I don't want anything to happen." The driver frowns in disgust and eases the big wagon down the shoulder and back on to the road. "Maybe this wasn't such a good idea after all," the woman suggests.

If anything were to happen, it would be her fault. It was all her idea to come to Redwood Valley. Her neighbor started talking up this great prophet of God named Jim Jones—"Father" to his thousands of followers in Redwood Valley, San Francisco, and Los Angeles—who has special powers of healing and divination. He knows things only God could know. He cures things only God could cure. He had even raised forty-three people from the dead; no one in his church ever died.

Well, she was going to see for herself; and now she and her husband are back on the highway in the sweltering heat, heading back home while the others in the parking lot are being admitted to the church. The others—most of them are black—mill around the door, where uniformed aides take names and conduct careful body searches. In line waiting to be searched and admitted are George and Lena McCown, a white couple from Willits. They have their membership cards, all right. They have some money in their pockets, too. They don't carry much else; they've been through the search before. Lena hates being pat-searched because she's afraid that the aides might decide to search her more carefully. She's heard about the restroom searches. People have to strip as if they were being booked into county jail. Not that she has anything to hide, but it's the principle of the thing.

Yes, the strip searches must be much worse than letting the Temple guards go through your purse, item by item, and although Lena hates it, she puts up with it. They have taken her fingernail files, tweezers, emery boards— anything that "could harm Father"—and sent them to Lost and Found, where they stayed lost. Well, no more. Today she left her purse at home.

George and Lena step up to the table and show their cards. They have to sign in. Everyone has to sign his or her name in the lower right-hand corner of a blank paper, one per customer. George and Lena have heard that Father can transform these signed blank papers into signed confessions of child molesting or family orgies or assassination conspiracies simply by typing in the appropriate words above the signature.

Then comes the search. The McCowns lean against the wall on the palms of their hands while the guards pat their clothing, feeling quickly and expertly for weapons. It's a little bit frightening, a little humiliating, an armed guard rummaging around your body like that.

Inside the main hall, with its rows of folding metal chairs, other aides whisk George and Lena away in opposite directions. Husbands and wives do not sit

14

together, and white people always sit next to black people. Doesn't matter who; Pastor Jones wants his flock to look like pepper and salt, black and white, all mingled. Father wants to create the right effect; his ministry is to all races, his congregation is a bouquet of skin colors, his followers are equal in the eyes of him and God.

The heat inside is not yet oppressive, and the odor of sweat is not yet as strong as the odor of cologne. Lena tries to get comfortable, but there's barely room to move; the chairs are too close together. She'd better move now, while she can, before the aides are patrolling the aisles making sure everyone is sitting up straight. So she fidgets, she stretches her legs forward, she turns to see who's there. She sees some familiar faces: there's Neva Sly, and Rick Cordell, and the Mertles; there's Corine Liggins all the way up from Los Angeles, and Phyllis Houston, and young Robin Wages. Most of the faces, though, are unfamiliar. They belong to members from San Francisco and Los Angeles, Sacramento and Oakland.

Lena turns her head back toward the pulpit where Father will speak. Fans overhead pull the odors and the heat up toward heaven; but with the temperature expected to be over a hundred by midafternoon, the odors and the heat will stay down below there with the congregation, down where the people can look toward the cooler glory of the wall-sized stained-glass window with the raised stage and the pulpit standing under the light of a four-pointed star, an incandescent icon behind Father, an electric cross bright enough to permit Father to wear his shades—constantly. Lena has seen Jim Jones only once or twice without his shades.

There's nothing special about Pastor Jim's shades. A sign on the pulpit explains carefully that

> Pastor Jones' robe is used.
> It covers his worn, modest
> clothing.
> He buys no new clothes!
>
> His are ordinary sunglasses
> which reduce distractions
> during Meditation!

Lena has heard that Father wears his shades because he has special power in his eyes, and for some reason she has never understood, Jim Jones is the only person in the Temple allowed to wear sunglasses. She found out the hard way. Once she had poison oak in her eyes and her doctor's orders were to wear sunglasses all the time. So she wore them to church and was ordered to take them off right away. She did. She was afraid if she didn't, one of the guards would knock them right off her face.

15

More people are filing in, and on the stage, to the right of the pulpit, the choir is assembling and the band is plugging in. Danny Pietila tightens the thumbscrews on his drumstands and adjusts the height of his stool. Lena likes Danny. He's a fair-haired local boy of seventeen who doesn't quite fit in. He's a real good drummer, that Danny, even when he's thinking—and that's all the time—about his Robin. She's fourteen and foxy. She thinks all the time about Danny, too. It's as if the beatings they've been getting mean nothing to them; they still "see too much of each other," against Father's orders.

The band plays the Temple as if it were a big, friendly club. After all, how many places can you play that have more than a thousand people, all listening as hard as they can? The band is really getting into the music, and Danny works out a complicated riff for "Something's Got A Hold of Me," a foot-stompin', hand-clappin' gospel number about a soul in the grip of Father's power. Danny's a bit nervous—it's the first song of the day—but as the choir marches into it, voice by voice, and the bass thumps out its line, Danny's smooth and funky as a catfish and soon the crowd is clapping to the gospel beat:

> Something's
> got a hold
> of me-ee (Oh, yes, indeed, I said)
> Something's (Something's)
> got a hold (got a hold)
> of me-ee (of me. Don't you know that)
> I went to a meeting last night (but my heart)
> but my heart wasn't right (Can't forget it, yeah)
> Something's (Something's)
> got a hold (got a hold)
> of me-ee (of me. O-o-o-oh . . .)

Yeah! Everybody's feeling good. Whatever fears walked in that door are lost in the spirit of the people all together.

> . . . It
> Must have been the Holy Ghost (Holy Ghost)
> Holy Ghost (Holy Ghost)
> Holy Ghost (Holy Ghost)
> Yeah! Something's . . .

People are still straggling in, and as they walk down the aisles to their steel chairs, it is apparent that something's got a hold of them. Lena gets caught up in it, too; she claps her hands, just like the person on her right, just like the

16

person on her left. Sporadic shouts of "Amen!" punctuate the song's phrases. Lena's a little surprised to hear a shout escape her own lips: "Amen!"

A young woman who's rarely seen at Temple services anywhere struggles toward a door carrying no less than five suitcases. The door is to the counseling room, on the north side of the hall next to the kitchen. Lena knows this room as the place the money goes—it is here the offerings are totaled after each service. Now it serves a different purpose.

The young woman sets two of the suitcases down on the tiled floor and opens the door. She is a member of the Temple staff. Some recall that she was once Father's personal secretary. A few even know her name: Linda Dunn— although they seldom see her anymore. She greets fellow staffer Sandy Bradshaw and they close the door quickly behind them. Like Linda, Sandy is young and attractive. Like Linda, who works as a clerk for a lumber company, Sandy has an outside job—she works for the Mendocino County Probation Department. Like Linda, Sandy works long hours for Jim Jones without pay.

The two women approach the conference table in the middle of the room. There sits Patty Cartmell in short black hair and long gaudy muumuu. She is a big woman. Her man-sized arms jiggle like gelatin whenever she pounds the table or shakes a finger to hurry her helpers, and the stern look on her face belies the myth that fat people are good-natured. She greets Linda unsmilingly, then returns to her task: overseeing the catalogs of personal information on people at the service. Father will use these slips of paper for his "revelations."

Linda sits down after hoisting one of the suitcases to the tabletop. She pops open the lid of the suitcase and starts sifting through the files inside. She checks the name list to see who is in attendance today and matches a name from her list with one of her files.

While Linda matches names with files, Sandy and Patty discuss a new member who has been talking to people on the outside. "I've got a good one on her," Patty tells Sandy. Sandy laughs and nods her head; it's comfortable to agree with Patty. Patty is the most dedicated worker on Jones's behind-the-scenes staff; she oversees the information gathering and trains each of the women selected for Jones's intelligence apparatus. Sandy helps Linda Sharon Amos with the files for the Ukiah area, which includes Redwood Valley, and Linda Dunn has Los Angeles. There are others, nine in all, who gather information in San Francisco, Fresno, Indianapolis, Seattle, Cincinnati, and anywhere else there are potential or active members.

The women remind themselves there is no time for chatting. Father has told them repeatedly that he has to have that material—something, anything—on every soul that enters the building, and he has to have it now. Otherwise they'll have to answer to Jack Beam, first of Jim Jones's assistant pastors.

17

Suddenly there is a knock on the door. The three women conceal the files under other papers on the table. "Come in," says Patty.

It's Wayne Pietila, Danny's older brother. Wayne is one of the guards who has a permit to carry concealed weapons. His special mission is to guard the cancers, but now he has come to pick up the papers for today's service. Wayne grabs the information sheets and hands Patty a few more names from the attendance list, then leaves the room.

Something's got a hold of Lena, in spite of herself. As the song comes to an end, she can see that every seat in the hall is filled. Over there in the aisle is Birdie Marable, strolling among the people with a box full of the paraphernalia of faith suspended from her neck like the tray of a cigarette girl. In Birdie's box are color photographs, blessed personally by Pastor Jim, showing him in various poses—pictures that will protect the faithful from traffic accidents, secure financial blessings, protect loved ones, and ward off evil spirits. The good health picture has been especially popular. Key chains and lockets with Father's image encased in plastic promise no greater mysteries than general good fortune, but the egg timer—a small hourglass with pink sand that takes two full minutes to empty, supported in a wood frame and graced with the image of Father's beaming face—has real power; it is to be set on the dashboard of the car before every trip, to time the believer's meditation on Father's love before the wheels start rolling down the highway. Birdie's sales pitch is slick and warm; she is a good salesperson, and she takes pride in doing her job well.

These icons of faith in Father range in price from a dollar sixty-nine to six dollars. On a good day, one service could gross a thousand dollars from the photographs alone. But that was another time, before everyone was well stocked. Today, it seems nobody wants pictures of Father to pray over or to stick in the pocket of a favorite coat or to clip to the car's visor on the trip to Detroit.

City black, bad and clean, Melvin Johnson glides up to the mike as the guitar whips out a Bo-Diddley lick and the saxophone sashays in, all bold nigger with shiny shoes, and Danny drives in hard with the bass and the organ in a hyped-up heartbeat thud-thud, thud-thud-thud, ecstatic martyrs all together, and Melvin Johnson sways and cuts into "Walk a Mile In My Shoes," a Joe South song that makes a plea for tolerance and understanding. Some of the young people in the audience remenber when "Walk a Mile In My Shoes" made the charts in 1970 and was played over and over again on the Top 40 stations until everybody had the words memorized. At Peoples Temple, young and old are singing along with the chorus and standing up and moving all the way to the end of the song.

*   *   *

18

The Reverend Archie Ijames, assistant minister, the only black man in the Temple hierarchy, steps up to the pulpit. He is silent for a moment while the people sit back down. He says, "You know how Father loves you." He says, "You know how he's your protector, how he takes care of you." He says, "I think it's time to take an offering."

Out come the buckets—not collection plates lined with red felt and shallow as a soup bowl, but deep buckets, the kind you get when you go to the Colonel for fried chicken. Danny's girlfriend, Robin, takes her buckets to the back of the hall, the very last row, and starts circulating them among the crowd. The buckets make their way row by row toward the front, where Robin and the others will hustle them to the counting room.

Vicky Moore watches her father stand up there and ask for money for this white savior who permits only one black man in his inner circle. Even if Archie is her father, even if he is among the privileged, she doesn't like all this talk of racial equality while she watches all the blacks in the congregation pour their money into buckets to be totaled and administered by a staff of whites. She's a tall, proud woman, and even though she's been involved with Peoples Temple as long as Archie has—since 1954 when she was fourteen—she keeps asking questions. That is, she kept asking questions until a few years ago. Then she became resigned.

This first collection doesn't amount to much—you can hear coins falling against the bottom of the bucket as far as the third row up. Lena just passes the bucket on; she's holding on to her dollars for the big offerings later. Down in Louisiana where she grew up she was taught real well to hold on to her money. No way are George and Lena going to give up 25 percent of their income to the damned church. Most members do, but they won't. The more the church gets, the more it wants. But offerings on a Sunday, well, that's a little different.

Up front, members are lining up to give testimonials on Father's powers. Lena even did it once. Just stood up and talked; no one had to ask her. She talked for at least a full minute, maybe more. It used to be that testimonials lasted an hour, but they've been cut down to about fifteen minutes.

A white woman—judging from her accent, she is from the Deep South—came up on the bus from Los Angeles to tell all the members how she used to have terrible headaches, headaches so bad she couldn't sleep, couldn't read, couldn't even think straight, until Pastor Jim prayed for her. And they went away.

"Praise Father!" shouts a man from the back, and several voices respond: "Amen!"

An elderly black woman with straightened hair is next. "I was havin' low pains. I was eatin' Tums an' Pepto-Bismo' all the time. I was havin' to take laxatives, too. Jim Jones knew it—in a revelation—an' he called me up in front of a thousand peoples in San Francisco. Jim Jones, he tol' me I had cancer of the bowels. He tol' me he would make me pass that cancer. He tol' me I would see that cancer befo' my very eyes.

"Marceline Jones, she take me in the res' room an' I pass that cancer. Marceline say, 'Here it come,' an' I hear it go plop into some plassic bag. Marceline pick up that cancer in tissue paper an' show ever'body in the congregation. I been praisin' the Lord an' Jim Jones ever since. I been singin' the praises of our healin' Father 'cause I ain't had no pain now in three weeks. Praise Father!"

"Praise Father!" returns the audience.

A young black man in T-shirt and jeans jogs toward the pulpit with a wire from the tape recorder in his hand. He waves his hand in the air. His excitement infuses his words from the start. "Hey! I'm going to tell you—we just had a miracle, about two minutes ago, right over there on that recorder, because we been having trouble with it all evening. One of us would have to sit over there and ground one of the wires so there wouldn't be a buzz on the tape.

"Well, I want you to know, when that noise was coming over there, we was putting aluminum foil up there, and then we got the warning from Jim to take it off." A breathless chuckle punctuates his phrases. "And let me tell you— that was a miracle, 'cause when we took that off, it started recording when Terry came up here. There wasn't a buzz on it. No one was touching it. And now it's running perfectly! Ho!"

A ripple of applause moves through the congregation. "I tell you," the man continues, "if you're lacking in faith, I don't know why—because that is so *true!*" The ripple of applause builds to a crescendo as the man leaves the pulpit. Thank you, Jim.

"All right, all right!" Melvin Johnson glides up to the mike once more. He breaks into his talk as if he had never left the stage. "I was just thinking . . . if I wasn't here, I'd be in the penitentiary. And it's because of Jim Jones that I'm not in the penitentiary right now, doing twenty-five to life." Melvin Johnson sighs deeply. "I got in trouble for narcotics. I'd been in trouble several times for it. This last time I got arrested for narcotics was three and a half years ago. And then Jim Jones came into my life, I finally got the break that I never got before, and he told me everything was going to be all right, and when I went to cool it—I stayed clean. You don't just clean up after five years of misery and bad attitudes. . . .

"Yes, I know, I know other folks want to talk." Melvin Johnson is not ready to relinquish the microphone. "But a lot of other things happened to me since I been here . . . all about Father's caring, you understand? You know, he cares about every little thing. Even when you don't know he's around—he's around."

"All right!" shouts someone in the congregation. "Praise Pastor Jim!" Melvin Johnson turns from the pulpit.

A thin black woman, frail and myopic, in thick, round glasses and a schoolgirl dress, bounds up to the microphone with long, exuberant strides. "One year and six months ago," she begins; she feels she has to shout even though she has a mike, "I came out of the hospital on crutches. My doctor told me I would never walk again, that I would go from crutches to a wheelchair. But I told him, I told him—I told him that God was going to make me walk again!" She pauses. A chorus of staggered "Amens" bubbles through the multitude. "And on Wednesday, my sister brought me to Redwood Valley for a service.

"Pastor Jim Jones called me out and asked me why I was on crutches. I told him I couldn't walk. He lay his hands on my crutches and someone took them away. I found myself standing alone without them. He told me to walk to him, and I repeated that I couldn't walk. He told me to stop looking at my feet, to walk to him." She pauses again, choked up a bit, and swallows. "All I know is—" She swallows again. "All I know is, I walked to him." She pauses one more time. There are tears on her cheeks. "My sister tells me I walked and ran all over the church crying, 'I can walk! I can walk!' but I can't remember everything that happened. I was too excited. I have been walking ever since." She swallows hard and shouts, "AND I WILL ALWAYS WALK! PRAISE FATHER! PRAISE FATHER! PRAISE FATHER!"

The people in Peoples Temple can't keep their seats. They stand and shout in unison, almost as if rehearsed, "Praise Father!" Applause fills the hall; it is a signal for the next offering, and Robin and the others whose job it is to pass the buckets get busy again. Up on stage, a black woman in a pink cashmere coat—she wears it despite the eighty-degree temperature inside—steps to the microphone. Beads of sweat form on her forehead as she gives her testimony in a shrill, nervous voice.

"I had something wrong with my throat. I couldn't swallow, but Pastor Jim took the trouble from my throat and made me well again. I'd gone to the doctor, but he said nothin' was wrong 'ceptin' my nerves. Pastor Jim knows about this and he calls out my name. I steps forward to the pulpit and Jim says I have a cancer. A nurse comes up to me with a bunch of Kleenex in her hands. Pastor Jim says I will pass that cancer, and the nurse reach down my throat to help it along."

The woman tries to hold back her tears and wipes her eyes with a red handkerchief from her coat pocket. "Suddenly, I feel the cancer on my tongue and I taste something so bad only the Devil could have put it in my body. It tasted so terrible I can still taste it today. It was rotten, like something dead, and there was blood all around it. Jim Jones cured me of cancer spit up and I signed a piece of paper that says he did. I'm talking the truth because the truth shall set us free! Praise Pastor Jim!"

"Praise Pastor Jim!" echoes the congregation.

A tall man in his forties approaches the microphone. He walks with an easy confidence and carries some papers in his hand. He is white, and just under the collar of his blue choir robe the dark tie and white button-down collars of his shirt are visible. As he waits for the applause to die down, he clears his throat. "I want to tell you," he begins, "of a testimony that we got in the mail."

His speech is clear, calm, and well articulated. "A Mrs. Nona Breton sent us an unusual testimony, an unusual blessing she received through her anointed photo of Pastor Jim. She wrote that she had been bothered by obscene telephone calls at night, after her husband had left for work. Now that's scary. Wow. She became frightened and nervous, afraid to answer the telephone after her husband left. It must have been night after night. Just imagine.

"Then she got an inspiration. She placed her anointed photo of Pastor Jim beside the telephone. The next time she received an obscene telephone call, she quickly placed the receiver down on the picture. She wrote that she did not receive one more call after that. Now, that's fantastic." He pauses. "How about that? Incredible, isn't it?"

His performance is effective. The collection buckets are moving across the rows, going from hand to hand. Robin waits at the end of a row and gets a bucket, then hands it to the person on the end two rows forward. She sees Lena McCown pull out a dollar bill and drop it in the bucket. Robin smiles at Lena. Robin likes her job better the closer it takes her to the front. Up there she can see Danny more easily. He's into his drumming. The band is playing again. As soon as this collection is finished, Robin can look at Danny again. First she must take the buckets to the counting room.

Danny's drums keep driving, through some up-tempo songs and some slow ones, then everything and everyone are silent for a moment while Marceline Jones, Jim's wife, steps demurely to the microphone. She wears a white gown with gold braid that makes her look to be the saintly maiden aunt of the sweet baby Jesus. Her light-brown hair is ratted, fluffed, and piled atop her head the length of her face; she could be a blond Nefertiti in her forties. The congregation applauds. "Praise Mother Marceline!" shouts a man in the rear of the hall, but no one echoes his impassioned chant. The man sits down and folds his hands in his lap.

The organist plays a slow roll, as somber and saccharine as the music in a funeral home, as the bass plucks out a serious, soulful pizzicato prayer. Mother Marceline closes her eyes and sings:

> Black baby, black ba-a-by,
> As you grow up
> I want you to drink
> From the plenty cup.
> I want you to stand up

22

Tall and proud.
I want you to speak up
Clear and loud,
My little black ba-a-by.
Black baby,
As the years roll by
I want you to laugh
With your head held high.
I want you to lift up
The justice code.
I want you to walk
Down freedom's road.
My little black baby.

There is hardly a dry eye in the house. There are tears in Marceline's eyes, too. Her agony for racial inequality twists her face ever so sweetly. The song she sings is a tribute to her own adopted black son, James Jones, Jr.

She leaves the pulpit and takes her seat. In a minute, the applause fades, but not before the Reverend Ijames assumes the pulpit, raises both arms in praise of Marceline, and implores, "Let's show our Glorious Mother how much we love Father! Dig deep, brothers and sisters, dig deep!"

Out come the buckets again.

The band and the choir prepare for one last song. This one is heavy gospel, roll-your-eyes-and-show-the-pink-hands gospel to save your very soul:

If you can hear him
He sometimes tells you
Who often knows not, knows not
Which wa-ay to turn.
But there is one
Who know the road
Who'll help us carry
Who'll help us carry
A heavy load . . .
Don't you know that
He's Able (He's Able) . . .

and Shirley Smith belts it out, "He's Able," and she and the choir exchange call and response, "He's Able," and the people sing it, too, "He's Able," because they know He's Able, and they know who He is.

He's a friend (to the friendless)
He's a father (to the fatherless)

23

He's a joy (in your sorrow)
He's your hope (for tomorrow)
. . . For surely He's Able
To carry you through.

He is life. He is hope. He is the joy we feel. He is approaching the pulpit this very minute. He is wearing a white robe. He is surrounded by guards wearing army surplus jackets, all alike. George recognizes the two guards in front as Jim McElvane and Rick Cordell, but he doesn't know the two men in back, nor the ones on each side of Pastor Jim. George wonders, too, whether Rick Cordell is carrying the pistol George has seen him carry before, down in Los Angeles. George wonders whether all six guards may have pistols under their army coats.

Father looks neither to the left nor to the right, as far as George can tell. It's difficult to see where Father is looking, with his eyes behind those shades. His cowboy-handsome face is all business as he marches briskly up the aisle from the rear of the hall. As he mounts the stage and approaches the pulpit, the applause drowns out the last chorus of "He's Able." Jim's businesslike face melts into a broad smile as he looks lovingly on his flock and the buckets fill with bills.

Father shakes hands with his lieutenants and steps up to the microphone. Here it comes, thinks Lena, as she wiggles a little to settle comfortably in her seat. She knows from experience that road ahead is long. The first time she came to a Temple service, Jim Jones preached for three hours, "just downing white people," she recalls. Lena kept wanting to leave, but the black woman who talked her into attending kept telling her to hush up—and they were, after all, good friends. Lena doesn't really remember why she went back again and again, only that today she is part of People's Temple and it seems she always will be.

Father speaks.

"This valley," he begins, his voice a twangy, midwestern drawl, a stage whisper that sounds like a hot wind rustling through dry cornstalks, "—this is a beautiful valley here. This is a beautiful valley in many ways. But I have seen things here that haven't the remotest connection with truth, I have heard people say things, and they frighten me. Certainly we have had harassment. Certainly we have endured things we don't like to endure. Do I have to tell you what they are? You know what they are. I don't have to focus on the negative things that attack our human service ministry, no. I know and you know that the good people in this beautiful valley far outweigh the negative people, isn't that right? Well, it has been a growth experience enduring all the negative things we've had to endure, and thank the Lord for the good people, the wonderful people we've met. We've met a group of wonderful people, a

24

group of Methodists in Sacramento, people I had never knew, who made a press conference telling of some of the good work they had known that we have done, and with our human service minsitry and our missionary work let me say we have done together some good work, people down in Sacramento, even as far away as they are from us—and other churches have done similarly—yet there are those who would vilify us, yet do they ever stop to think that one hundred and four students are being educated partially or fully in our dormitories in the terribly expensive fields of law and medicine? Yes, we have nine of our students who are studying to be medical doctors. Does this sound like magic? Does this sound like the occult? There is no magic in faith, and we certainly have no interest whatever in any kind of witchcraft or occultism. Each of our members go for annual checkups and the church pays their bills and we have nine of our students who are studying to be medical doctors and they are being fully sponsored by this church, by you and me, and those negative people are saying, 'We have so much money, we have so much money,' but do they ever stop to think? We have been successful in rehabilitating one hundred and twenty-seven people from hard-line drugs, youngsters in this community that once were troublemakers they are now making straight A's in college. It is an interesting fact that not once had one member of Peoples Temple been arrested for anything. They don't smoke, they don't use drugs, they don't imbibe in alcohol, they're good citizens, and those people, all those people out there, they wonder, How do we do it? Well, I am not God. If they mean as all men are sons of God or women are daughters of God in that they fulfill the requirements of love, well, yes, I do love constantly, I do care, and in that instance I can relate to that, but if they mean, if you mean, if you're speaking of the Creator of the universe, I am not so presumptuous. Please don't confuse me with that. And that's the Christ life; if you're going to live the Christian life, you're going to get persecution. A woman attacked us just the other day for our stand on abortion. Have we ever taken a stand on abortion? Well, a woman attacked us—I'm sure she was a conscientious woman, a wonderful woman, a responsible member of the community—about our stand on abortion. Well, I am not God. I do not say who should live and who should die, in or out of the womb. A woman's womb is certainly a part of her, a woman's body is certainly a part of her, and I do not take a stand. I am concerned about any form of human murder, and abortion, well, I just wonder, where are we going next? A life created in the womb, that is holy, that is sacred, holy and sacred as the love between the man and the woman who put that life in the woman's womb, and I tell you again, do not confuse me with the Creator for I am not He but I do know that life in the womb is holy and sacred as is the love that put it there, I do not decide should it live or should it die; I only know that love is sacred and holy and today we are going to talk a little bit about that love but we are not one for mincing

25

words, are we? Today we are going to talk about sex." He pauses for breath.

"All of you who have had sex in the past month, raise your hands!" Hundreds of hands wave in the air.

"All of you who have had sex in the past week, raise your hands!" Several hands go back down.

"And all of you who have had sex in the past two days, raise your hands!" Only a few hands remain in the air. Jim Jones looks around the room and begins calling out names.

"Tom Hunter,* when was the last time you had sex?"

Tom is sitting near the front. "Just last night, Father."

"Who'd you have sex with last night?"

"My wife."

"Did you enjoy it?"

"Yes."

"Did she enjoy it?"

"Ah—I think so."

"What did you do together?" Jones wants to hear some details. Tom Hunter is pretty bland. "I know some of you have done a lot more than that," Jim continues. "Who else will speak?"

The testimonies become increasingly bizarre. One woman stands up and tells of having sex with dogs. Another confesses to an experience with a horse. Father listens intently. George McCown represses a laugh; he knows if he doesn't keep a straight face, he'll be up there next. He's certain some of these stories have been arranged before the service, and that makes the scene even funnier to him. Why the hell would a woman want to tell people she'd done it with a horse?

Father listens with an infinitude of understanding to these tales of desperate women's kinky ways. All eaten up with sympathy, he comments in passing that he, Jim Jones, has "enough to satisfy every woman in this room. And I know you want to go to bed with me—but I'm not going to do it." In truth, he confides, sex is not that important to him, all the "whores, sluts, and bitches" in his congregation are unworthy of him, and furthermore all the men are homosexuals, latent or otherwise. "I am the only true heterosexual here," he reveals.

"But," preaches this man of the cloth, "instead of allowing the selfish thoughts of hatred, lust, and materialism to occupy my mind, I am dwelling solely on the ideas of life and health. By closing my mental doors to all but the holy thoughts of God/Good, I have become an instrument of His power, which is working through me to heal every affliction known to man." Thus, Pastor Jim explains, although they know him as Father, he is also the Son and the Holy Ghost. He is, in fact, the reincarnation of Jesus Christ. He may even be,

---

*Fictitious name.

26

according to some members, God Himself, although he denies that allegation frequently, often without waiting to hear it. "No, I am not God," he says. "Please don't confuse me with that."

While Father rambles on and on with his sermon, Lena squirms in her chair; George crosses his legs; Danny blinks his eyes to help him stay awake; Robin gets her collection bucket ready (no telling when there'll be another offering); and Birdie—well, Birdie listens and sighs as she hears Jim Jones saying, ". . . and Mary was no goddamned virgin . . ." Ooh-ee, how that man can carry on. She wonders how Jim can do it, how he can keep it up hour after hour, week after week. She wonders sometimes if Jim Jones hasn't gone clean out of his mind. And now this one! Some woman stands up and Birdie listens and begins to doubt her own ears. The woman is testifying to what a fantastic lay is this Jim Jones. He satisfied her as no man has ever satisfied her before. Birdie can't believe her ears. Another woman stands up and gives a similar story. Father beams from his pulpit. He blesses the congregation with the information that he, Jim Jones, has ten inches for any woman worthy of him. "Ten inches!" he repeats. There are no takers.

George McCown squirms in his chair. His bladder is full, but Temple rules prohibit members from leaving their seats to use the bathroom. To enforce the policy, guards are stationed at the bathroom doors. George crosses his legs—he wonders how in hell Father goes on so long without pissing—and hopes the six o'clock dinner break will come soon. He has no way of knowing the time unless he turns his head almost all the way around to check the clock over on the wall, but he doesn't want to be seen letting his attention slip away from Father, and he has long since given up his watch to the Temple. No material attachments, that's the rule.

Father rambles on and on about the Temple philosophy, which is based, he says, partly on Marxist socialism. "He who is really evolved," claims this man of God, "acts as an atheist, asking nothing from God: that is, asks nothing for himself. The most highly evolved person, he who is ready to leave this plane, acts as an atheist. He doesn't ask God for a thing. He lives a life of principle."

Father pauses for a sip of water. He points to the sky and asks angrily, "What's your sky-God ever done? Two out of three babies in the world are hungry. Misery is in every one of your homes. (That's right!) The only happiness you find is when you can come here and find the visions and see some of the uplifted and the miracles of help and the miracles of cooperation. (Yeah!) The only happiness you've found is when you come to this earth-god. (Yeah!) You prayed to your sky-God and he never heard your prayers. You asked and begged and pleaded for help with your suffering, and he never gave you any food. He never provided a bed. He never gave you a home. But I, the socialist worker god, have given you all those things!" (Yeah! Yeah! That's right!)

The congregation quiets down and Father holds up a thick family Bible. "I want to give you freedom. Whom the Spirit sets free, the Son sets free, is free in me. *(Yeah!)* That's what I've come to do—give you freedom, freedom to know that some of you used to live in utter terror to hold this"—he holds up the Bible—"this rite as though it were sacred. No! It's not sacred! And you won't die if you drop it." He drops the Bible. "You won't die if you stand on it." He stands on it. "You won't die if you jump up and down on it." He jumps up and down on it. "Nothing will happen to you. *(Yeah!)* I want you to find the living epistle which is rendered unto all men. I want you to realize that you must be the Scripture, that any other scripture before you and the word I'm now imparting is idolatry." *(Yeah! Yeah!)* Father continues in a calmer voice, "Because I am freedom. I am peace. I am justice. I am equality. I . . . am . . . God!" *(Yeah! Yeah! All right!)*

He carries on to warn his flock of the dangers of self-indulgence and violence. "Nihilism and hedonism have only succeeded in fragmenting all progressive movements in our country. Certainly we who affirm apostolic equalitarianism, and social and radical justice, have nothing whatsoever to gain from this insanity of violence, but could it enhance further the stranglehold of the military-industrial complex on the United States, which even President Eisenhower warned us in the early 1960s was a danger to our great country?"

Lena has heard Jim Jones speak on violence so many times she can almost repeat what he's going to say word for word. Her eyelids are getting heavy. She's been sitting in one place too long, hearing the same shit too many times, but she dare not go to sleep. If they catch her falling asleep, she may get called on the carpet and whipped. But they can't whip her mind, so she daydreams while Pastor Jim rasps on and on with his familiar phrases. She has to get her mind off the stifling heat and the muggy air that carries the odors of a thousand sweaty bodies.

"Nothing is less genuinely radical in America than violence, because we have been saturated with violence from the beginning of our history. Our murdering violence began with our efforts to dispossess and kill the American native, which we did in countless military campaigns. . . .

"Certainly there was blood and violence in our own revolution! Our national anthem glorifies it by mentioning the 'rockets and bombs bursting in air,' and our own so-called Christian civilization hatched such murderous schemes as the conquest during the Crusades and the horrifying persecutions done in the name of the church as revealed in Fox's *Book of Martyrs*. . . .

"Yes, violence is as common to our history as cherry pie."

Jim Jones slides from talk of violence to talk of revolution. The word excites Jim Cobb, a black teenager who fancies himself a Marxist militant. Cobb leaps to his feet and raises his clenched fist in salute. "Revolution!" he shouts.

"My friend," Jones looks toward Cobb, "the genuine radical is not one who acts on the premise that violence is something revolutionary in the American picture. No, the real radical is one who is engaged in a determined struggle to break out of the vicious cycle of violence that is part of our everyday life."

Jones also tells Cobb and others of his persuasion "that so-called revolutionary violence has not helped the students, the socially deprived blacks, whites, or browns in this country." Revolutionary violence, he says, "will only compound terror, repression, and dictatorship in America," and will serve only "the tyrannical hold of the rich and the super rich."

Lena's thinking of that first service she went to. Why do they keep coming back, she and George? What is it about Jim Jones that keeps drawing her back week after week until the wee hours of the morning? And George, he donates so much of his time to the church, driving and servicing the Temple buses. Part of it is fear of what will happen to her and her family if she does leave. She's heard stories of horrible things that have happened to people who have dropped out. Terrible accidents. Fatal diseases. Deaths.

Lena's attention snaps back to Father. He has suddenly raised his arm in the air and is pointing toward heaven. "I'm having a revelation," says Father. "There's a man in the audience who lives on Twenty-first Street in . . . in, let's see . . . in Seattle!"

Jones waits a moment for the man to respond.

"He has a dog. The dog's name is . . . CoCo. There's a red telephone in the dining room."

A tall, thin black man in his early twenties begins to rise from his chair. His face has a look of utter amazement.

"It's you, Robert Maddox!" Jones shouts, apparently guessing the man's name before he's even completely standing.

Robert Maddox* laughs nervously as he looks around at the wildly applauding crowd.

"You are Robert Maddox, aren't you?" says Father.

"Yes, I am."

Robert Maddox tosses his head back and laughs. "I can't believe this!" he says joyously. "Thank you, Father! Thank you!"

Before the applause and the shouting die down, Jones is inspired with another revelation, this one about a woman in Los Angeles who has a yellow cover on her toaster in her kitchen. She lives on Century Boulevard. She's been seeing a doctor regularly for stomach pains. The woman stands and Jones tells her to step forward. As she walks toward the pulpit, Faith Worley, a Temple nurse, follows her with a wad of tissues in her hand. Jim Jones tells the woman the Maalox she's been taking won't do her any good. Doctors can't help her, either; she has cancer.

The woman sobs uncontrollably. "Oh, Pastor Jim! Oh, Pastor Jim! Help me, Pastor Jim!"

* Fictitious name.

29

The woman cries fearfully. In her family, they pass young. Her grand-mother died of cancer; so did her aunt, and so did her mother. Then the disease crept through the ghetto, it seemed, taking people one by one. There was the man down the street who had it in his prostate; there was the woman downstairs who had to have both breasts cut. They all suffered terribly. They tried everything: pain pills, radiation therapy, apricot pits, the Hoxsey cure. They even tried Jim Jones's prayer cloths and special anointed oil, but they died anyway.

"Oh, God, you have to help me, Pastor Jim!" the woman pleads in genuine terror.

Jim Jones flashes a half smile and looks out toward the audience. "I shall help you. I shall heal you. I shall make you pass that cancer."

He places his hands on the woman's head.

He looks heavenward for just a moment.

"Heal! Heal! Heal!" he shouts, and Faith, the nurse, steps forward and thrusts her hand down the woman's throat. It's all in a day's work; Faith grew up in Peoples Temple, following her parents from Indianapolis when she was thirteen. The woman gags. Something that looks like a tumor, foul-smelling and covered with blood, falls out of her mouth and into the wad of tissues in Faith's hands. Blood runs down the woman's chin and she makes a horrible face, grimacing as if she had just bitten into a piece of rotten meat.

Elmer Mertle, Temple photographer—a curly-haired white man with deep-set eyes and a lanky frame—takes some quick shots of this event with his 35-mm camera, whose bright flashes make the healing seem a medical milestone.

The woman sobs. She wipes the stinking blood from her chin. Faith hands her a bottle of grape juice; she takes a few gulps to rinse out her mouth. The congregation is in a frenzy of excitement that could lift the roof. Tears stream down the woman's wizened black cheeks as she walks up to the pulpit and raises her arms high, hands open wide. "Praise Pastor Jim!" she shouts.

"Praise Pastor Jim!" returns the flock. "Praise Father!"

And the collection buckets make yet another round while Faith parades up and down the aisles holding at arm's length before her the wad of bloody white tissues with the stinking ugly tumor for all to see. "Don't get too close to it!" warns Father, all compassion. "Don't breathe it!"

When the excitement dies down, and everyone is seated again, and peace is restored in the Temple, Jim Jones offers a testimony of his own. He tells of how many people have been miraculously healed of growths, tuberculosis, ulcers, cataracts, emphysema, heart trouble, deafness, epilepsy, blindness, arthritis, and "incapacitation"—all under his guidance. While he is speaking, a Temple aide approaches the woman Jones has just healed with a release form:

I, ———, hereby agree and consent to the use of my name in radio broadcasts and other communications sponsored or otherwise influenced by Peoples Temple Christian Church or Jim Jones, its pastor, for whatever purpose said church or pastor sees fit. I further agree and consent to have my talents and performances (whether musical, testimonial, or whatever) reproduced and used in such radio and other communications as said church or pastor sees fit. I expect no remuneration whatever for such reproductions. I sign this freely and without duress because I believe in the human service work of Peoples Temple Christian Church.

To this document the woman signs her name and gives as well her address and telephone number. At the urging of an aide, she writes in:

I was healed of <u>cansor</u> spit up.

Jim Jones tells of the forty people he has raised from the dead—they showed no vital signs until he touched them—and . . . "Wait!" he interrupts himself. He is having another revelation. "There is someone in this part of the room," he says, pointing to the people at his right. "The mother had measles when she was pregnant with this person. He can't hear."

Jones pauses, one second, two seconds, then his arm straightens suddenly and his finger points to a man sitting in the second row near the aisle. "It's you, Brother!"

The man to whom Jones's finger dramatically points slowly rises from his seat. He seems old—his hair and beard are powdery white. His glasses are thick and sit crooked on his nose. He leans heavily on a cane. He smiles sheepishly, not sure of what's going on, as Jones reveals more.

"Since birth you have barely heard a sound." The man nods his head sadly. "Because you haven't heard, you also cannot speak, but—Edward Miller—you read lips."

Edward Miller hobbles up to the pulpit while Father explains that one of Edward's legs is shorter than the other. Edward is all hunched over. He wears a coat that is too long in the arms.

On the shoulders of this poor sheep Father mercifully lays his hands. "I am going to heal you now," Jones tells Edward Miller, looking him straight in the eye through his ordinary sunglasses. "I want you to stand up and turn away. I don't want you to read my lips. Now, Brother, you know who I am. I want you to raise your right arm. Raise your right arm, Edward. Raise your right arm."

Somehow, after the third request, Father's words register. Edward raises his arm.

"Now, Edward, I want you to place your hand on your head."

Edward complies while the crowd cheers.

"Now, Edward, I want you to turn back around."

Edward turns around slowly, as if he's not really certain of what Father requested, until he's facing Jim Jones again.

31

"Edward, with your voice, I want you to repeat after me—we know you have never been able to speak; do you hear me, Edward?—I want you to repeat after me, I want you to have faith, Brother, and say: GOD IS LOVE."

Edward tries, but the words catch somewhere in his throat.

"GOD IS LOVE."

Edward makes a few guttural sounds. He's trying, he's really trying.

"GOD IS LOVE," Father insists with all the power of faith.

Edward takes a deep breath and tries again. "G-G-God . . ."

"Have faith, Edward." Jones is almost grunting with Edward. "GOD IS LOVE."

"G-G-God . . . G-God i-i-is l-love. G-GOD IS LOVE!"

Father did it. The miracle has happened one more time. The moment is upon the people like a wave crashing on the rocks—you can see it coming, you can count the seconds, and then the mute speaks: GOD IS LOVE. And you know it's true.

It's all George can do to keep from wetting his pants.

The hall is pandemonium. People stamp their feet and clap their hands. Poor Edward nods his head and smiles.

"Now, Edward," says Father, "I want you to rid yourself of that cane." Jim takes away Edward's cane. The old man, whose one leg is shorter than his other, walks forward, slowly at first, then gradually quickening and evening his pace until, Praise Father, he struts proudly up and down the aisles. Loudly praising Pastor Jim with his new-found faculty of speech, he runs out the back door. He never returns to his seat.

Amid praises and hosannas, Jim Jones announces it's time to break for dinner, and the people stand up and stretch. George McCown dashes for the bathroom door, where already a dozen men are lined up awaiting their turns.

Lena McCown gets up and strolls over to join the line forming near the kitchen. George comes over and joins Lena for the meal. They have small portions that disappear too quickly. George's plate is empty and he's still hungry, but he knows from past experience that what you see—the first helping—is what you get. There are no seconds. Every time he's asked for seconds in the past, the food committee has told him there's none left. Much of the food, George knows, is set aside for the members who live in Temple communes. The men all live in one dormitory, the women in another. George and Lena once talked about making that kind of commitment, but not for long. They decided they'd rather keep their family together. They would have had to give up everything: property, kids, sex. Sex is absolutely forbidden among communal couples, who made the pledge at a Wednesday night catharsis meeting in 1971.

Danny Pietila and Robin Wages haven't really noticed the skimpy portions of food. They exchange glances as Danny returns to the stage and the band starts warming up, with the choir, to signal that the service is soon to resume.

Robin sighs and returns to her post, and George and Lena are just about to take their seats when the band launches into another gospel number that gets the people back in the mood. They go through three lively songs with the choir before Jim Jones and his guards walk up the aisle again at a brisk pace and a bouncing stride. Father is refreshed and ready to convert the world.

He begins his sermon with a catalog of the Temple's humanitarian services: the drug rehabilitation program, the Temple dining room that feeds hundreds of down-and-outers each week, the draft counseling service, the church-sponsored homes for senior citizens, troubled youth, and mental retards, the free legal assistance, the free medical clinic, the college scholarships, the vacation program for inner-city youngsters, the Temple animal shelter. He lists the contributions Peoples Temple has made to worthy causes, contributions that have won the church recognition in the *Congressional Record,* the *San Francisco Chronicle,* the *Indianapolis Times,* the *Ukiah Daily Journal,* and even the *Washington Post.* There were the Temple's contributions to various news media for support of First Amendment rights and the gifts to the widows of slain policemen.

Thousands of dollars from Peoples Temple help to fill the coffers of the Brotherhood, the Disciples of Christ, of which Peoples Temple is a member church. The Disciples of Christ has 1.3 million members throughout the United States, including former president Lyndon Baines Johnson, and of all the churches affiliated with the Brotherhood, Jones reminds his people, Peoples Temple has more members than any other congregation in the country.

Keeping all of its people clothed and fed, maintaining the Temple's present level of human service, Jones says, costs thousands of dollars each day. It is time, he says, for a love offering. It is time for each member to come up with a Fair Share Contribution. "Reach into the bottoms of your pockets and your purses," he says, "and your hearts." And the buckets pass around the hall again.

Another of Jones's inspired revelations gives way to another healing. Father lays his hands upon another woman, a victim of cancer of the lower tract, whom Temple nurses Faith Worley and Janet Phillips escort to the bathroom. A few minutes later, they emerge with a handful of tissues in which rests another bloody, visceral tumor they show quickly to the congregation, as before.

Time, also, for another "walking" miracle, this time for a woman in a wheelchair. She's old and feeble, and no one in the audience has ever seen her before. Like Edward Miller, she's shaky and wobbly at first, then she runs around the hall shouting praises. She, too, runs out and does not return to her seat.

When the cheering dies down, Father reminds his flock of his deep commitment to his ministry, his vow never to buy new clothing. He

33

admonishes everyone to follow his example, to give up those extraneous material things. And to help them make this meaningful decision, he calls ushers to collect the trinkets, aisle by aisle. Lena hears a disturbance a few rows back. She turns to see one of the ushers, a youth in his late teens, standing over a black woman in her late forties. Temple members on either side urge her to give up her watch.

"No way," she says.

"Give it up," Jones says from the pulpit.

"When Father says 'Give,' you better give," demands the usher. Others soon pick up the demand. "When Father says 'Give,'" they shout at her, "you better give!" The woman finally capitulates and surrenders her gold watch. Jones praises her from the pulpit and thanks her for her offering.

Jones changes abruptly to one of his favorite lectures: the evils of drinking and smoking. He is aware, he says, that there are those in the Temple who have violated the proscriptions against these bourgeois vices. "Everyone who's been smoking or drinking, stand up," commands the stern pastor. A few rise, twenty-five or thirty guilty souls. Lena does not, although she's been on a drinking binge that worried George enough to call in the counselors for advice. She's been smoking, too. She figures it's all right to remain seated because George has the assurance of the counselors that nothing will happen to her.

Jim Jones calls all those who are standing to the front. Blue carpets cover the steps leading to the pulpit, and the pulpit itself is surrounded by a metal railing a few feet away, in front and to the sides, with openings in front center and to the left and right to allow access. The guilty members line up facing the railing and their offended Father, awaiting his pronouncements.

Lena's relieved that she didn't have to stand, because she knows what's going to happen to the others. She's seen it time and time again, on Wednesday nights and sometimes on Sundays. Members who are guilty of infractions of Temple rules line up. There are so many rules, Lena can hardly keep them straight: no drinking, no smoking, no sex, no pictures of departed relatives, no funerals, no diamonds, no furs, no jewelry, no nice furniture, no new clothes, no pictures of Jesus in your home, no dancing except during services, no country-and-western music, no radio unless it's Jim Jones on KFAX; no vacations, no potato chips, no wigs, no Bonnie Hubbard products, no pork, no coffee, no tea, no new cars . . . No wonder the line is long. Everybody must be guilty of something. This line is just for drinking and smoking, and Lena knows what's going to happen to them. They are going to stand up there beside the pulpit. They are going to bend over and grasp the rail with their hands. They are going to get whipped.

Brother Rick Cordell rises to his feet and raises his hand.

Pastor Jim recognizes him. "You're on the carpet, Rick."

"Father, there's been drinkin' goin' on at the McCowns'."

"Thank you, Rick."

Bonnie Beck, another Temple counselor, rises to her feet and looks directly at Lena McCown. "You better stand up," she says menacingly.

"You'd better get up here with the rest of them, Lena," says Father.

Oh, is Lena hot. Oh, is she angry. Red-faced and double-crossed, she approaches the pulpit. She's mad as hell at George for telling the counselors. She's mad as hell at the counselors. Damn that George! He should know better than to trust them. Can't trust nobody around here. Well, by God, she won't try to cover up, the way some of them do. Lena McCown tells the truth.

"Is it true, Lena, that you've been drinking beer and smoking cigarettes? And that you didn't stand up when you were supposed to?"

"I ain't gonna tell no lie," she tells Father.

"Well," he laughs, "you're better than most people in this church. At least we don't have to force it out of you. Better step in line, Lena."

Lena joins the group at the front of the church and Father calls for volunteers to carry out the punishment. "I'll do it, Father," calls a voice from the back. "Let me do it," calls another voice. But Jones decides to let the Reverend Harry Williams be the one to whip this group of incorrigibles. The Reverend Williams steps forward. He is a proud and dignified black man with a white tuft of hair crowning his head and a narrow mustache. The look on his face betrays his feelings—he doesn't want to hit all those people with that two-inch-wide belt—but he always follows Jim's orders. He is a Baptist minister from San Francisco who joined People's Temple because he believes Jim Jones is a prophet of God; Jim did cure him of a heart ailment and restored his youthful vigor. He owes Father that much.

Merciful Father prescribes five whacks with the belt. The sinners understand that if they cry out or protest or fail to say, "Thank you, Father," afterward there will be more whacks.

One by one they step to the pulpit, where Jim Jones can look down on them while Harry swats away with the belt. After a few tentative whacks, the crowd tells Harry to hit harder, and he does, until his arm gets sore. Hitting nearly thirty people five times each amounts to a lot of swinging.

Now it's Lena's turn. She steps up and takes her first—Damn that hurts!—two whacks. Damn that sonofabitch husband!

Brother Cleave Swinney shouts from a few rows back, "Harder, Harry! You ain't hitting hard enough!"

That's all Lena needs. She pivots and faces Harry eye to eye. She seethes with anger.

"You better not hit me no harder than anyone else gets hit," she says defiantly. Her voice shakes.

Jim Jones throws his head back and laughs.

Whack. That's four. *Whack.* That's five. Lena stands there and takes them all, gripping the rail in front of her until her knuckles turn white and her ass burns like it's been stung by a thousand bees. Still, she manages to stand tall and look proud as she marches back to her chair—Oh. "Thank you, Father"—but she can barely sit down. She shifts gingerly on the steel chair, but it's no use trying to get comfortable. At least it's after 2:00 A.M. and the service is about to conclude. Up at the pulpit, Jim Jones, sapped and sweating, has a few announcements before he says good night, but the Holy Spirit has used him so severely that he can barely find the strength to form his parting words.

I was alienated as a child. I was considered the trash of the neighborhood because in those days they referred to you as white trash. I fell into the category of white trash because my parents ostensibly were light-skinned; my mother was, anyway. They liked my mother less, though, than my dad because she was unconventional, and not religious. . . .

The church fell into my lap. . . . I took this church. I remember I thought I was going to die a thousand deaths when I got up in that pulpit.

—Jim Jones, from the transcript of
an interview found at Jonestown
and published in
the *Guyana Chronicle,* December 6, 1978

II

Hoosier Beginnings

The people of Indianapolis view the South Side as an area distinctly separate from the downtown's towering war monuments, Gothic churches, and skyscrapers, and from the more affluent North Side's pleasant, tree-lined neighborhoods. This is not to say that the South Side doesn't have its share of pleasant neighborhoods, or that the North Side doesn't have its share of slums. On the South Side, however, are more slums—and more factories, more poverty, more storefront religion. Amid the broken-down homes and clapboard sheds are scores of temples, "tabernickels," and "meetin' places," hand-clapping and holy-rolling churches that cater to the spiritual needs of the neighborhood. "The Church that Calls the Crowds to Christ" reads a December 5, 1953, ad in the *Indianapolis News* for the West Morris Street Free Methodist Church, Vernon G. Dunckel, pastor. The Assembly of God at Drexel Gardens touts a REVIVAL with DIVINE HEALING by Evangelist David E. Garns of Baltimore, Maryland. St. Paul's Spiritualist Church on Washington Street—which marks the division of the North and South Sides— offers "messages" from not one but "six mediums of the church." Just across the North-South line, on West New York Street, the Holy Quietness Christian Spiritualist Church mixes healing with its messages from mediums.

Down in the South Side the word spread quickly about a twenty-year-old student minister, Jimmy Jones, who could preach the Bible—and preach it with fire. People took to Jimmy right away. He was a handsome young man whose forceful, confident manner was enhanced by his shiny coal-black hair and burning eyes. He preached the Truth in simple terms, with a youthful enthusiasm that lifted up the spirits of the meek, the lame, and the oppressed who flocked to hear him. His love for animals and his mature understanding of human crises touched the people, and touched them deeply; but never so deeply as did his love for the Lord.

This modern-day St. Francis moved among his followers as if he wore a halo, telling them repeatedly how he would, as a young boy, nurse fallen blackbirds back to health, or take in stray dogs and cats who roamed the streets near his boyhood home in Lynn, Indiana, or nurture these strays while he kept at home his raccoon, his goats, and his rats. Jimmy's first cousin,

Barbara Shaffer, confirms the tales of young Jimmy's deep and early love for animals; she grew up with him in Lynn.

Lynn, Indiana, is about sixty-five miles east of Indianapolis. When Jimmy lived there, its population numbered no more than nine hundred souls. Jimmy came to Lynn as a toddler, from Crete, a hamlet five miles to the east consisting of half a dozen farmhouses built around a grain elevator. On May 13, 1931, James Warren Jones was born to James Thurman and Lynetta Jones at one of those farmhouses. Within two years after little Jimmy's birth, they moved into a modest six-room house in Lynn. "They weren't real close," Barbara Shaffer recalls. "They more or less just existed together."

Despite his Quaker upbringing, Jimmy's father, James Thurman Jones, marched off to war in 1917 and got his lungs burned by mustard gas; for the rest of his life he couldn't walk half a block without losing his breath. The disability earned him a monthly check from the government when he was no longer able to push a shovel on a road construction crew. Years later, when Jimmy Jones talked to a reporter from *The* (Richmond, Indiana) *Palladium-Item*, April 6, 1975, he promoted his father to the position of construction engineer; but Mrs. Shaffer is certain her uncle was a laborer when he was forced to quit working.

James Thurman Jones was fairly tall, about five feet and ten inches, with the dark hair and olive complexion of his ancestors in South Wales. For all his pain and disability, Mrs. Shaffer recalls, her uncle rarely complained about his health. They would sit together for hours on the front porch. Their years together in Lynn followed close on the heels of the heyday of the Ku Klux Klan, of which Jimmy said his father was a member.

During the 1920s, when the population of Indianapolis was about 314,000, the Ku Klux Klan in that city claimed 38,000 members, counting women. Klan membership plummeted after 1925, when the Grand Dragon was arrested and convicted of a brutal rape and murder, and by 1928 Indianapolis—once the bastion of the Invisible Empire—counted fewer than 7,000 Klansmen.

At its peak, the movement spread throughout rural Indiana. According to George Southworth, a journalism professor who left Lynn in 1936, the local Klan used to burn crosses on a baseball diamond a half mile east of town. The only other excitement in town, Southworth recalls, was an occasional medicine show. The racist pageant culminated with a flaming cross lighting the field; it always drew a crowd, and Southworth was part of the audience that showed up to gawk. Although some of the Klansmen wore white sheets, Southworth recognized several pillars of the community by their voices and mannerisms. Most of them didn't even bother to wear sheets.

If James Thurman Jones had been a member of the Ku Klux Klan, he never spoke of his secret society in the presence of his family, and Southworth never saw him at a cross-burning. Although he was one hell of a "rough talker," he never once talked of the Klan, claims Mrs. Shaffer, nor did he ever make racist comments about blacks, nor did he slur Jews and Catholics. If James Thurman Jones was a Klansman, he was damned quiet about it.

His wife, Lynetta, was not so quiet. She rolled her own cigarettes and paraded down the streets of Lynn smoking them defiantly, flaunting her long, straight black hair along with her independence, flicking ashes and challenging the mores of the tiny midwestern town as no woman ever had before. Mistrustful and daring, she cursed with the ease of womenless men, and anyone who crossed Lynetta Jones was lashed by a tongue that put most men to shame for their verbal impotence.

Lynetta Putman was born April 16 in eastern Indiana, in a small settlement along the Wabash River, two years into the twentieth century. Nearly fifty years later, her son would tell his followers she was half Cherokee, hoping that her olive complexion and black hair would lend credence to the claim; but Barbara Shaffer flatly denies her aunt was anything but white. In any case, Lynetta Putman Jones seems to have been blessed with a determination and devotion to work commonly attributed to both Cherokee squaws and pioneer matriarchs, for, with her husband permanently unemployed, she worked long hours in nearby factories to support the family. She was never around when Jimmy came home from school, and her little boy roamed all over the neighborhood, pestering the big kids and swearing as much as he could. George Southworth remembers that once his mother made him chase little Jimmy out of the yard for using foul language; Jimmy had picked it up, undoubtedly, from Lynetta.

When Jimmy was about seven years old, he strayed less and spent time with Mrs. Myrtle Kennedy until Lynetta came home from work. Mrs. Kennedy was forty-two years old at the time, a deeply religious woman, and she took young Jimmy under her wing and gave him his first taste of fundamentalist Christianity in Lynn's Church of the Nazarene, where she taught Sunday school. George Southworth remembers Mrs. Kennedy taking Jimmy there every Sunday. Neither of Jimmy's parents attended church regularly or even occasionally; they were indifferent to the wonders of God, so Myrtle Kennedy became, in Jim Jones's words, his "second mother."

Those Sunday-morning church experiences with Mrs. Kennedy had a profound and immediate effect on little Jimmy. According to the first published article about Jimmy Jones—in the March 15, 1953, issue of *The Palladium-Item,* when Jimmy was a student pastor at the Somerset Methodist Church—Jimmy started spreading the gospel to folks who needed it most. He told reporter William B. Treml of a time when, at age seven, he befriended "a ragged, bearded tramp who found himself near a Lynn family's home in the gathering dusk of an early spring day." The story continues:

> A young boy saw the lingering tramp and approached him. The ragged stranger would not raise his eyes as the boy questioned him about his home and what he was doing in Lynn.

Finally, the tattered knight of the road muttered:

"I don't have a friend in the world. I'm ready to give up."

The boy, barely through his first year of school, looked at the tired, beaten old man and said firmly:

"What do you mean, mister? God's your friend and I'm your friend. And Mom will get you a job."

And "Mom," Mrs. Lynetta Jones, did just that. Mrs. Jones, who now lives at 1130½ East Main Street, recalled that the man went to work in a Lynn factory.

Little Jimmy's religious inspiration did not stop with encouraging hopeless wanderers of the depression; he was so inspired by ecclesiastical theatrics that he began conducting "pretend church" services for the neighborhood kids, often baptizing the others in a nearby creek. The pretend church was so popular that Jimmy soon was conducting funerals for the neighborhood's departed pets. The children would gather up the remains of their furry loved ones, take them to Jimmy, and prepare them for a decent and proper burial, in a wooden box whenever possible, wrapped in rags when no box could be found. Cousin Barbara always sang a song, and Jimmy would say a few words and read from the Bible. The verses he selected were not always appropriate, Mrs. Shaffer recalls, but that didn't seem to matter greatly to the other children, as long as Jimmy read from Holy Scripture. They seemed to understand the difficulty of finding verses fitting for the passing of dogs and cats, rats, and an occasional goose.

Jimmy and Barbara went to Washington Township School, a two-story building that housed grades one through five downstairs and grades six through twelve upstairs. They had separate groups of friends there; Jimmy ran around with the boys, Barbara with the girls, and they rarely played together. After school, however, Jimmy and Barbara got together frequently, since their homes were only a block apart. During one of his visits to Barbara's house, Jimmy borrowed her Bible to write a cryptic message: "I would bet you will die in your 70s."

Opal Muntchner used to teach at Washington Township School. She remembers Jimmy as a "very serious-minded boy" in his early teens. "I always felt he was much more grown up than other boys his age." Although she never had Jimmy Jones in her class, she remembers him well. "He was a rebel, that's for sure." He "aspired to leadership" and was "kind of a leader of a gang of boys." It was about this time—when he was fourteen, according to Mrs. Shaffer—that Jimmy started carrying a Bible with him everywhere he went; he took his religion more seriously than ever, shopped around for the True Word, switching from the Nazarene to the Pentecostal faith, then, during his high school years, to the Church of Christ.

Washington Township School saw Jimmy Jones through the eleventh grade; then his parents separated. James Thurman Jones moved into a room in

Waldron's Hotel in Lynn and died there three years later, age sixty-three, on May 29, 1951—one year before his son started preaching. Lynetta and Jimmy moved twenty miles south to Richmond, where Lynetta had worked several years assembling pistons and piston rings for the engines of automobiles and airplanes.

Jimmy enrolled at Richmond High School in the fall of 1948. He took seven classes there, joined the Hi-Y club, and graduated in January 1949 an average student—although he would in the future claim honors. Beside his photograph in the 1949 school yearbook is the notation: *Jim's six-syllable medical vocabulary astounds us all.* He must have picked up the medical lingo at his job.

Jimmy worked full-time as an orderly at Richmond's Reid Memorial Hospital, and fared much better in that town than he would have in Lynn. Had Jimmy stayed in Lynn with his father, he'd have faced a dismal job market; Lynn's major industry is casket making. Prospects in Richmond were considerably better.

At the hospital, Jimmy caught the eye of a student nurse. Marceline Baldwin was pretty, blond, and charming, with a delicate chin, a perfectly chiseled Nordic nose, and eyes brimming with kindness. She was four years older than Jimmy. They had to wait until he graduated from high school to get married, and tied the knot on June 12, 1949, at Richmond's Trinity Methodist Church. When Marceline received her certificate as a registered nurse from Reid's school of nursing, the young couple moved to Bloomington so Jimmy could continue his education at Indiana University while Marceline joined the nursing staff at Bloomington Hospital. Jimmy transferred to Butler University in 1951 to attend evening classes as a part-time student. He later described himself as a law student, but Butler University has no such program. The university has a prelaw program, but its rolls have no listing for a James Warren Jones. His curriculum generally was geared toward a degree in education, which he finally received ten years later, in 1961.

It was a busy time in the young couple's lives. Money was not abundant. Jimmy had to work in factories while he was taking his college courses, and he added to his burden by enrolling in a correspondence course to obtain standing as a Methodist minister. During this period Jones did battle with a major conflict: his work in the hospital had him aspiring to a career in medicine, and his lifelong ambition had always been to become a man of the cloth. In April 1952, Jimmy Jones found an inspired resolution to the conflict: he would become both physician and minister. A few months later, he started his practice as a self-ordained healing preacher.

In June of 1952, he was assigned his first student pastorate at Somerset Methodist Church, a simple, concrete-block building at 3320 South Keystone Street, Indianapolis. He provides a colorful account of how that appointment supposedly came about in a transcript of an undated interview found at Jonestown and published in the December 6, 1978, *Guyana Chronicle:*

I'm wandering down the street, stopped at a used-car lot, and I met a man, I find out he's a Methodist superintendent—and I think, oh shit, he is a religious nut. I started knocking the church, just raising hell, knocking the church. He said, "Why don't you come to my office?" He must have been a communist. . . . Here I am raving against the church, knocking the church, ridiculing God, all this shit and he says, Why don't you come to my office?" I thought, "You fucker, I'm not coming to your goddamn office." But I did. For some instinctive reason I went. He said, "I want you to take a church." I said, "You giving me a church?"

Jimmy lost no time getting his name known and respected in the neighborhood; by fall, he had organized a fund-raising drive among Protestant and Catholic children for a twenty-thousand-dollar recreation building. The young preacher was soon getting the attention he deserved. William Treml's 1953 article in the *Palladium-Item* spoke not only of Jimmy Jones's childhood compassion but also of his innovative approach to preaching:

In his program, Jones preaches no doctrine, but simply points out moral lessons taken from the Bible. His inter-community church has become acceptable to all denominations, and the knowledge that no group is discriminated against has aided greatly in winning new members.

One of the new members was won not by the knowledge that no group is discriminated against but by the church's powerful loudspeaker. Cecil Johnson was working in his backyard in 1952 when he first heard Jimmy Jones four blocks away. Cecil stopped what he was doing and listened. Jimmy Jones made sense, Cecil thought; the young preacher was "really on the ball." Cecil decided he wanted to hear more. He persuaded his wife, Georgia, to go with him to church and to bring her fifteen-year-old son by a previous marriage, David Scott, with them. David was having problems at home; perhaps Jimmy Jones could help.

When the family walked into the humble church on South Keystone, they felt immediately at home. "It was a very small church," David recalls, "and the people were very friendly and seemed to show concern about others. It's not like one of these big churches where they don't know each other. It was like one of those down-home churches." Cecil, Georgia, and David were convinced that the poor young pastor of this down-home church was the most sincere man they had ever met. He was so sincere, the church was so down-home, that Jimmy brought in horse troughs to baptize his numerous new converts. "I couldn't have thought more of him if he'd been my son," Cecil says to this day. They all treated one another as family; when Jimmy lost his

43

Bible—and he preached the Bible in those days—he was too poor to afford a new one, and Georgia Johnson gave Jimmy Jones her Bible so he'd have one to use in church.

Cecil liked Jimmy so much he agreed to serve on the church's board of directors. He drove the church's old Dodge bus. When the building needed repairs, Cecil was there to do them. When Jimmy needed to borrow a car that wouldn't fall apart on the highway—he sometimes made trips from Indianapolis to Richmond—it was Cecil's new 1952 Studebaker convertible. When Jimmy thought the church could use a child mascot, he chose Cecil and Georgia's two-year-old, Mickie. Jimmy let the little girl run up and down the aisles during services, and often he would preach from the pulpit with Mickie in his arms.

After Georgia talked to Jimmy about her problems with her teenaged son, the kindly student pastor treated David like a younger brother. They would sit together for hours in the pews of the church and talk about teenage conflicts. During one of these man-to-man talks Jimmy told David he had seen "a sign from Heaven" that David would become a minister. He wanted David to enroll in a seminary. A young man who craved a "feeling of belonging" couldn't hope for more assuring words. David started going to the youth meetings; he sang in duets during services. One day Jimmy took David and some of the youngsters in the church over to the Laurel Street Tabernacle, which had a tank beside the pulpit with access from a trap door in the stage. Jimmy dunked them, one at a time, completely under the water for several seconds while invoking the names of the Trinity. David emerged from the tank in mild shock, a new soul, his sins cleansed, dripping from head to toe.

At Somerset Methodist, every service had a little time set aside for silent prayer. Worshipers would rise from their pews and go forward to kneel in a group before the altar, each soul communing with its own inner voices. Few services passed without a memorable event during these silent prayers. David remembers that typically someone would start talking in tongues or dancing in the spirit, running and shouting down the aisles. Jimmy Jones translated, for those who possessed not the gift of interpretation, the tongue of the Lord so all might understand; and when the spirit touched Jimmy himself, and the Lord spoke through His humble servant, Jimmy did his own translating.

David Scott was among the few members of the congregation who never got the spirit, despite the young pastor's efforts. Nevertheless, the two young men remained as close as brothers. Once, when David had a date with a girlfriend and needed a car, he asked Jimmy if he could borrow his old, battered black Plymouth. Jimmy let David have it without hesitation, even though David had never driven before. He was just seventeen years old, and had enlisted in the navy only days before; it might be his last date for months. David took the car out to a gravel road and practiced steering straight and shifting gears until he could move the car without lurching. He picked up his girl. They jumped back in the car and headed straight to South Keystone Street, to the last service David ever attended at Somerset Methodist Church.

Jimmy's borrowed church on South Keystone underwent a complete metamorphosis during his tenure. Even the name changed from Somerset Methodist Church to Somerset Christian Assembly to reflect its inter-denominational nature, "connected with, but not a member of, the Assemblies of God," according to the *Indianapolis News*. Jimmy wanted to buy the church and break away from the Methodists, whose doctrine cramped his style. He had a dream, he often told his flock, of opening his first church. He was going to call it Peoples Temple. But the offerings he collected were barely enough to keep his family going.

Meager though his income was, Jimmy found room in his heart and his budget to adopt Agnes, a nine-year-old girl whom the courts had taken from the custody of an alcoholic mother. Agnes was the first of six children Jimmy and Marceline were to adopt over the years—their own son, Stephan, was not to be born until 1959—and many people saw the adoptions as evidence that Jimmy Jones was indeed a man who put his faith into action, despite the strain on his pocketbook.

With barely enough to support his budding family, Jimmy had to seek other resources to finance a new church. He embarked on one of the most innovative fund-raising ventures in the annals of religion. With the approval of his congregation, Jimmy started selling live monkeys from the parsonage on South Villa Street. The charming young minister became a door-to-door salesman and set out from his home with a smile on his face and a sample under his arm. Housewives on the South Side were surprisingly receptive. One of Jimmy's early customers was Edith Cordell, who not only bought a monkey but also joined Jimmy's church, along with her sons, Harold and Richard, and their families.

The monkey sales attracted the attention of the local press. Jimmy told a reporter from the *Indianapolis News* (December 5, 1953) that he got the idea of selling monkeys when he was at Indianapolis University, from a South American student who promised there was money to be made in the monkey business. Jimmy consulted reference books on the habits of primates and ordered his first—a female chimpanzee named Sugar—through the mails. Jimmy took to her right away and taught her to be a companion to the family dog. Sugar was trained to use the toilet. She could eat at the table with a spoon. She used to sit like a baby in Cecil Johnson's lap.

Jimmy went into the monkey business in a big way. He imported three dozen of them—mostly rhesus monkeys—from South America, Africa, India, and Thailand. He kept them in the garage attached to his parsonage on South Villa Street, and once when four of them got loose Jimmy got on the phone right away and called Cecil for help. When Cecil walked into the garage, the monkeys had already made a terrible mess. They clambered along the rafters,

45

scattered the hardware, and chattered defiantly while Cecil put on heavy gloves to guard against the bites, then rounded the beasts up one at a time and locked them back in their cages.

Jimmy told a reporter that, at twenty-nine dollars per monkey, the church was not making a large profit and had to depend on volume sales to raise enough money for the first Peoples Temple. He claimed a waiting list "as long as your arm" and was having trouble, he said, keeping up with the demand. Part of the problem was the high mortality rate in shipping. Jimmy was having them shipped year-round, and the tropical creatures just didn't adjust to the Indiana winters.

Jimmy Jones's monkey business made the front page of the *Indianapolis Star* on April 10, 1954, with a two-column photograph of Jimmy and his nervous little friends. Jimmy was down on his luck with the monkeys. He had just lost two expensive gibbons the previous week. He was about to lose a shipment of seven monkeys, delayed six days in transit, three of which were already dead on arrival in New York. He was in no mood to dicker when the crate arrived in Indianapolis with only four sickly monkeys, and the customs officials wanted him to pay the air freight bill—eighty-nine dollars—for all seven monkeys. Jimmy refused to pay the bill and, according to the *Star*, "abandoned [the monkeys] in the Customs warehouse here in the basement of the Federal Building." Customs officials attempted to revive the four remaining monkeys with a diet of bananas and brandy, but only two survived to be sold at auction. To those who knew Jimmy Jones, the story didn't quite fit the image of the young pastor whose compassion for living creatures was so deep, he told his people, that he couldn't bring himself to set a mousetrap or swat a fly.

Jimmy quit the monkey business and became a full-time preacher again. As the number of his followers increased, so did the income he received from their offerings. He gradually introduced miracle healings into his services, but he had to keep them low-key because he knew the Methodists wouldn't go for too much razzle-dazzle and he did not, at that time, have much experience in miracle-making. He was, however, an astute observer of how they were performed. David Scott remembers the time when Jimmy became bold enough to cure a woman of the arthritis that crippled her arms and hands. Jimmy leaned over the pulpit and placed his healing hands on the woman and prayed. He asked the congregation to pray with him. "Be healed!" he shouted. "In the name of Jesus Christ, be healed!" Jimmy bore down with his hands on the woman's head as he called for the demon to leave her body. The woman started crying. She raised her arms and started talking in tongues. With her arms upraised she started moving her fingers. She was healed.

Cecil Johnson credits Jimmy Jones and divine intervention for the lives of his daughter, Mickie, and stepdaughter, Charletta. Charletta came down with rheumatic fever and Jimmy rushed her to the hospital and sat at her bedside while Marceline held a special prayer service at the church, a silent but fervent meditation behind the curtains at the altar with about twenty believers. Charletta was in an oxygen tent; she was not expected to live through the night. The next morning, after Jimmy's night-long vigil, the girl was sitting up in her hospital bed and playing cheerfully. Although she wanted to go home, the doctor wouldn't release her without further tests. He couldn't believe Charletta had recovered so quickly.

Jimmy Jones was a man "who had no problems" when he was on South Keystone, David Scott remembers. That was before David enlisted in the navy; if he had stayed around, he'd have seen Jimmy grapple with the first crisis of his ministry. All those miracle healings and Jimmy's announced intentions to start an integrated church attracted an increasing number of black congregants. The church's original members, who were all white, said nothing directly about all the new Negroes—but the pot was definitely boiling. The discontent finally found expression in a dispute over who owned the church organ. Loretta Cordell was the church organist; she sat at the keyboard and played the traditional hymns while Jimmy led the services. She and the rest of the Cordells sided with Jimmy. But by late 1954, Somerset Christian Assembly fragmented into factions, members dropped out at an alarming rate, and Jimmy Jones decided to move on.

He and his remaining followers set out to find a new church. He kept spirits up with reminders of his dream of one day starting a Peoples Temple, a church where all of his flock could worship together free of pressure and prejudice, a church for the people. Until that day, though, Jimmy and his followers would have to meet in "borrowed" churches. Jimmy rented the Holiness Tabernacle at the corner of Hoyt and Randolph, in the middle of a rundown neighborhood near the railroad yard. Jimmy renamed this church, too, and the Holiness Tabernacle became the Community Unity Church. It was a tiny, wood-frame building with a heavy coat of white paint and, like most Pentecostal tabernacles, was simple in architecture and free of pretentious trappings.

Before long the little church at Hoyt and Randolph proved to be way too small; Jimmy packed 'em in until they flowed over into the street. Voices on the South Side spread the word that Jimmy Jones was the Prophet of God. People came to hear him speak, to bask in the calm holiness of his face, to witness firsthand the miracles worked by this young man with a bow tie and the half smile of a soul at peace with God and the world. His services were fiery and emotional. He made miracles happen like clockwork every Sunday afternoon. He turned water into wine. He wiped cataracts from the eyes; they made a snapping sound only the faithful could hear. He removed growths and goiters. He made the lame walk; scores of witnesses saw people rise out of wheelchairs and run up and down the aisles praising him.

The Community Unity Church congregation soon outgrew the humble building at Hoyt and Randolph, and Jimmy took his flock up the street a few blocks to larger quarters at the Laurel Street Tabernacle, where Jimmy had once shared the pulpit with its pastor, the Reverend John Price. Jimmy became an associate pastor there, although he also learned to see the advantages of having an unsettled church. The more he moved around, the larger his audience. There were bigger offerings and a wider array of potential converts, a greater pool of talent from which to recruit lieutenants for the struggle ahead. Jimmy was beginning to need something more than divine assistance with his miracles. It was after one of the larger meetings down on the South Side that Jimmy met and befriended a maintenance man named Jack Beam.

The two men took to each other immediately. While Jimmy came across as a kind and loving pastor, Jack had a more abrasive personality. Jack was as tall as Jimmy, a bit more husky, and a decade older. They traveled together to central Ohio for special healing services, plucking out tumors in Cincinnati, Dayton, Springfield, Hamilton, South Charleston, Mason, and Xenia, Jimmy calling from the pulpit for the cancers to pass, Jack Beam out in the audience laying hands upon the afflicted. In Jimmy's absence, Jack Beam always let everyone know that Jack Beam was running the show. "I always felt as if he was a hit man. . . . I never felt he was legitimate," says Virginia Morningstar. She and her husband Rodger saw Jack Beam spring into action at a meeting in Cincinnati. They saw him again in South Charleston, and soon they saw him everywhere that Jimmy preached.

Virginia first heard Jimmy preach in 1955 on WPFB, a Middletown, Ohio, radio station. He was a guest on the evangelist Eddie Wilson's show, which aired Monday through Friday at three o'clock in the afternoon. When Virginia heard Jimmy Jones on Wilson's radio program she was fascinated with his inspiring voice, impressed with his undeniable psychic powers. She heard him identify a car over the radio by make and model and year, then match the car to a license plate and driver. She decided to attend the very next miracle revival. It was to be held at one of Cincinnati's Pentecostal churches; Rodger decided to go along, too, even though he was skeptical.

At a table in the church office just off the foyer, Jimmy Jones was sitting cross-legged when Rodger and Virginia walked in, Virginia carrying their eighteen-month-old daughter in her arms. The baby was wearing a red cap with animal designs. As they entered the sanctuary, Virginia pulled off the cap and stuffed it in the sleeve of the baby's coat.

There must have been two hundred people there. All the seats were taken. People were standing up in the back, eager to see miracles and hear prophecies. Jimmy Jones gave them what they wanted. He made the lame walk, he talked in tongues, he went into trances and had psychic revelations. He had a revelation about a little girl, right there in the audience, who had a red cap with animal designs. Virginia became excited; she pulled the cap from the baby's coat sleeve and waved it in the air. Jimmy continued with his revelation: the little girl who wore that cap, he said, was suffering from a "urinary tract malfunction." She had a heart problem, too, he said. The baby had been restless at night, Virginia knew, but she had never suspected the restlessness might be due to a serious health problem—not until Jimmy Jones uttered his revelation. The Morningstars were amazed at Jimmy's knowledge of the red cap—how could he know when it was hidden in the baby's sleeve?—until later, when they remembered Jimmy sitting cross-legged on the table near the door, watching everyone who walked in.

These convincing demonstrations of his powers won Jimmy a loyal following in central Ohio. He followed a circuit of Pentecostal churches in six counties: Butler, Clark, Franklin, Greene, Hamilton, and Montgomery. He continued to hold services in Indianapolis, too, and everywhere he went he brought with him his miracles, his humility, and his truth.

One of the stops on this circuit was the United Holiness Church in South Charleston, where Virginia's father, Ross Swaney, was pastor. Ross Swaney had been affiliated with three denominations in his lifetime—first Methodist, then Nazarene, and Pentecostal. He admired spirited preachers like Jimmy Jones, but he didn't like the way Jimmy Jones muscled in and all but took over his church. Where Jimmy showed up to preach, a large number of followers from Indianapolis would also show up. They would drive for a hundred and fifty miles or more over the roads that crisscross dairy land and cornfields for Jimmy's revivals, and Rodger observed that they seemed to be the only ones Jimmy ever healed. The beneficiaries of Jimmy's powers were never the people Rodger knew at the United Holiness Church.

Rodger and Virginia recall a time when Jimmy was called upon to heal a woman who was, in truth, suffering from an advanced case of cancer of the stomach. Her abdomen was distended as if she were pregnant. Jimmy laid his hands upon the woman, prayed, and shouted "Heal! Heal! Heal!" There was a spark of hope in the woman's eyes for a moment, but it faded quickly. She sobbed quietly as she hobbled back down the aisle. "She didn't get healed," Jimmy said. He was right. She died the following day. She was the only person from South Charleston who ever approached the pulpit for healing, Rodger says.

In 1961, Pastor Ross Swaney was dying of cancer, paralyzed from the waist down. Jimmy sent an ambulance for the old man all the way from Indianapolis to South Charleston, and the ambulance took him all the way back, to a care home owned by Peoples Temple. When Edith and her sister Gertrude visited their father at the Temple care home, they were so appalled by the living conditions that they took their father out and brought him home to die with dignity. Jimmy Jones followed soon after to officiate at Ross Swaney's funeral. He took charge of Ross's church in South Charleston, but only for a short time; he had alienated too many people to stay around for long.

Between his circuit riding and his borrowed churches, Jimmy managed, by late 1955, to realize his dream. He had raised enough money through offerings and pledges—Cecil Johnson was among those who donated a hundred dollars to the cause—to buy the building at 1502 North New Jersey Street, and the first Peoples Temple Full Gospel Church opened its doors on the North Side of the city. Jimmy got busy as he never had before. He preached, on Sundays, a regular morning service at 10:45; he preached a miracle service at 2:30 in the afternoon; he preached an evangelistic service at 7:45 P.M. For the sincerely devout and for those who missed the Sunday meetings, he preached another service on Thursday evenings. Every Sunday morning before church, at eight o'clock, he preached on radio WOWO Fort Wayne for fifteen minutes. He also preached Sunday nights on WIBC Indianapolis.

One Sunday evening, Archie Ijames—a black, self-ordained Indianapolis minister—tuned in Jimmy's broadcast on radio WIBC. Archie, his wife, Rosabell, and his daughter Vicky were impressed with this white minister who offered an interdenominational, interracial church. They were even more impressed when they attended a service. "I don't claim to have all the answers," Jimmy told them, "but if you know anything that I don't know that I need to know, it's your duty to come and tell me. I'm doing the very best that I know. What more could you ask of any man?" When Jimmy learned that Archie was a Sabbatarian, he offered the use of Peoples Temple on Saturdays, but Archie's church declined. Jimmy invited the Sabbatarians to attend the regular Peoples Temple services on Sundays, and some of them did, along with their friends and relatives. Within two years, Jimmy doubled the size of his congregation and finally achieved his truly integrated church. He later appointed Archie assistant pastor.

The word about Jimmy Jones spread from neighborhood to neighborhood, all over Indianapolis—not without a little help from Jimmy himself. He was on the radio. He sold monkeys door to door. He and his growing legion of followers circulated a flyer bearing his picture and documenting his miracle healings; it also announced the radio program and the services. He called it "The Open Door to All Man Kind." With its bulk mail permit, "The Open Door" was soon spreading the word to other congregations. Fundamentalist churches throughout the city were buzzing with stories of miracles that just had to be true. At one of the Assembly of God churches, Opal Worley first heard the word in 1956. Opal served the Assembly as a preacher and interpreter for the deaf; she was valuable, and her pastor did not approve her going to Jimmy Jones's services, but she kept going anyway. For four years she went on Sunday afternoons and sometimes in the evenings. "They were good services," Opal recalls. "They were real good. He preached right out of the Bible, and he would speak in tongues and dance in the spirit. It was beautiful, really."

Opal took with her her seven-year-old daughter, Faith, a delicate girl with black hair and wide, brown eyes set deep with wisdom beyond her years. Faith was a serious girl who preferred the company of adults to that of children her own age. Something in her innocence spotted Jimmy Jones as a charlatan, a con artist, a faker; but Faith was intrigued. Although she knew the healings and the revelations were phony, she was fascinated by Jimmy's smooth showmanship, by the absolute confidence with which he pulled off his miracles and left the yokels gaping. Faith sat quietly in the audience and watched Jimmy's every move.

The Worleys—Opal, Wade, and their two daughters, Theresa and Faith—lived in a primitive house on the South Side, in a neighborhood settled first by hillbilly Kentuckians. There was no running water, only a hand pump at the kitchen sink; water for bathing had to be heated on the coal-burning stove. A well-worn path from the kitchen door led to a backyard privy. As Ward Worley's wages increased—he was a factory worker—the family was able to take advantage of the more civilized conveniences of city living. They moved several times over the next few years to homes on the South Side that featured all the modern conveniences, like running water and flush toilets.

Opal was a dreamer. She was half Indian; she grew up with the belief that God's works are manifest in the earth, that the earth and its people are in God and of God. To the deaf and the mute, she became the voice of Jimmy Jones, preaching with her hands as she had at the Assembly of God church earlier, speaking to a silent world of miracles that only God could have directed, celebrating with agile fingers the hope that this healing prophet had brought to Indianapolis. Opal's dedication, and the loyalty of her family, contributed in no small way to the success of Jimmy Jones.

Despite his success, Jimmy was restless. He wanted to create more than just another fundamentalist movement with himself at the center. He and Marceline traveled whenever they could to visit a wide array of faith-healing churches, spiritualist congregations, and off-beat sects, and the summer of 1956 found them in Philadelphia at the Divine Circle Mission, headquarters for the Reverend M. J. Divine—better known as Father Divine (God).

"I don't have to say I'm God," said Father Divine in the only public statement he ever made about his alleged divinity, "and I don't have to say I'm not God. I said there are thousands of people who call me God. Millions of them. And there are millions of them who call me the Devil, and I don't say I am God, and I don't say I am the Devil. But I produce God and shake the earth with it." Born sometime between 1865 and 1877 as George Baker, the son of a Georgia sharecropper and former slave, this modern-day deity claimed to have arrived on earth in a puff of smoke during the time of Abraham. A Georgia judge gave "John Doe, alias God" the choice between confinement to an insane asylum and a speedy departure from the state, and Mr. Alias God chose the latter. He settled in Harlem in 1915 and set about convincing thousands of people he was indeed God. Later, he founded the Kingdom of God movement, promoted himself from his 1908 rank as God in the Sonship Degree to Father

Divine, and placed Himself on its throne. His disciples—he called them Angels—turned over all their property, money, and possessions and lived communally, in a climate of total sexual abstinence (he said). Father Divine passed on to his reward in 1965, leaving a reputed twenty million followers and something more than half that number of dollars in assets.

Three years after the Joneses' visit to Father Divine's Philadelphia Heaven, Jimmy wrote a twenty-eight-page tract he describes as "an authentic, unbiased, and objective statement of my experiences with this group over the past three years." Jimmy handed out copies of the little booklet wherever he preached. It was not universally accepted. Virginia Morningstar received her copy in South Charleston and "something clicked" in her mind; she never went to Jimmy's services again.

In the little booklet, Jimmy stresses he is "not a follower nor an affiliate with any of [Father Divine's] organizations," then gives the following account* of how "a pastor of a large full gospel assembly was more consecrated to Jesus Christ by his contact with the Rev. M. J. Divine Peace Mission":

> Three years ago in midsummer, [I] frequented the Circle Mission church and training school at Broad and Catherine streets in Philadelphia, Pennsylvania, which is the shrine of the renowned M. J. Divine. My visit to one of their extensions was motivated by reading the book, *Manifest Victory* by Rufus J. Mosely, an early apostle of the Pentecostal message. Until the time of this reading I had been totally antagonistic towards the Divine sect. Mosely referred to Mr. Divine as his friend John, and he related many incidents of the life of our subject which indicated that he was an honest person. I had heard the usual opinions that it was supposed to be a harem run by a demonically possessed immoral person; in fact, I was almost wholly convinced that it was a complete fraud. I had always been extremely opposed to adulation or worship of religious leaders. In order to stop flesh exaltation which seemed to be developing in my own healing ministry I publicly insisted that no one even refer to me as Reverend. Naturally, one can imagine the revulsion I felt upon entering their church and hearing the devoted followers of Mr. Divine refer to him as Father.
>
> My apprehensiveness was intensified when I arrived at the hotel, which was operated by the followers and was recommended to me for accommodations by the hostess of the Circle Mission Church. The receptionist informed me that my wife and I could not occupy the same room. This requirement was presented to me in a rather cold, businesslike manner and it dismayed me to such a degree that I took

*Edited with some revisions in punctuation.

my wife and departed. We found accommodations in a downtown hotel. Temporariliy I became absorbed with other plans. I had to minister at Rev. John Douglas' church a short distance from Philadelphia. My wife and I decided that we would write off the Divinist as a bad experience and charge it to memory.

Jimmy gave little thought to Father Divine's movement for two days. During the evening of the second day, while he was dozing off, he had an inspiration to attend one of Father Divine's informal services, which were always held during lavish banquets.

This service constituted endless varieties of foods free to whoever desires to participate, and it is intermingled with two or three hours of song and praise to their "God."

It had to be the spirit of truth that stimulated me to return to their atmosphere because my every natural inclination was opposed to it. I was nauseated by what seemed to be personal worship to their leader. Nonetheless when I would pause to think and be fair in my judgment, I could not help but see a peace and love that prevailed generally throughout the throng of enthusiastic worshipers. Every face was aglow with smiles and radiant friendliness.

After the feast was over we were asked by one of the staff if we would care to testify. Although I still felt that I was in a hot bed of error, I see now as I reminisce that there was enough hypocrisy in me to keep me from revealing my true attitude toward them in my speech. I will mention more later how this group helped me become completely honest with myself and others at all times.

The sweet way in which I was introduced is worthy of your consideration. It went something like this: "Rev. Jones, we are happy to have you in our midst. We would be happy for you to speak volitionally according to your own understanding because this is a hall of democracy. We do not impose any of our religious convictions upon you." This kindness and tolerance greatly softened my spirit. Another thing that helped me very much on this occasion to remain peaceful was the reply that Rev. Divine gave to one of his followers who exhorted. This evidently educated and cultured woman had previously gone into a great explanation of how she had gone to one of the leading officials of her city and endeavored to inform him as to the diety of Rev. Divine. She said something to this effect: "Father, they didn't accept me or believe in you." Rev. Divine stood up and replied to her rather caustically, saying, "Sister, or dear, if you had done as much to get them to accept the Christ in you as you did your interpretation of me, they would have accepted both you and me."

53

This act of humility pacified me long enough for me to stay another day in the mission and I grew spiritually as a result of it. . . .

I know it will seem strange to you, dear reader, that a person could be benefited spiritually by people who propagate the teaching of the deification of a person, which we have always considered to be gross misconception. But I must honestly state the facts; as the Holy Writ declares: "give honor to whom honor is due."

Jimmy Jones was truly impressed by Father Divine and his Peace Mission. He has lofty praise for the "flower garden of integration . . . in all Peace Mission churches throughout the world." He also praises the Divinites for their "cooperative communialism," which, he says, fulfills the scriptural principle: "from each according to his ability, to each according to his need." The commune—which the balding, five-feet-two-inch Divine dubbed "Heaven"—so impressed Jimmy that he flatly declares, "I have never seen a demonstration of democracy comparable to this in any other religious circles." The Divine movement, he says, is a model for America:

> . . . The absolute challenge is before the United States—"we are our brothers keeper," and if we fail to unite in this premise and live together, scientists assure us that we will ultimately die together. The Divine movement is one of the healthy deterrents in America that is doing all within its resources to avert such an imminent catastrophy.

Jimmy was a keen observer of the Divine movement during his brief stay in Philadelphia. He was especially intrigued by the Divinite vows of celibacy, which defectors claimed did not apply to Father Divine. Jimmy investigated the charges that Father Divine was keeping a harem, and concluded:

> . . . Contrary to what has been circulated, these people—including their renown[ed] leader—live lives of total sexual abstinence. . . . I have [sat] for hours on different occasions and talked with Rev. Divine and his personal staff, and I can affirm they do not practice other than what they preach. I have never observed any indiscreet behavior from either sex in all of my contact with the fellowship. And I am known to have a rather keen discernment. . . .
>
> The conscientious followers readily admit that they have had their frustrations and oppositions to overcome in this area, but they do not succumb to this tendency. If a member indulges in the mortal plain, he immediately resigns from them. . . .

His observations of the Divinites' celibate life had a profound effect on

54

Jimmy. The experience, he writes, forced him to take a closer look at his own lustful thoughts, which he is "very carnally proud" to report are under control. The number of double entendres and Freudian slips in this narrative indicate a subtle wit—or suppressed desire:

> Instead of trying to remove adulterous and sexual thoughts that often came into my mind, I was always justifying the fact that overtly I had been such a good, moral man, but when I met a few hundred young Divine followers who had overcome the sexual plain extensively without the legalized social outlet of a husband or wife, I was pricked in my conscience. Although I have not personally . . . maintained a life of celibacy, I definitely believe that I was saved from disaster— which my thoughts would have ultimately and conclusively led to—if the example of the Rev. Divine constituants had not stimulated me to look at my own heart. I can thank the Christ today that I can say that I am free from the sexual thoughts for intervals of many days at a time. . . .

There is some hedging early in the tract—Jimmy does disagree with "their two basic premises that Rev. Divine is complete perfection caucated in human form and that they have attained the imortality of the body"—but Jimmy finally takes a firm stand in defense of the paunchy deity and his disciples:

> I want it understood that I am not comparing Rev. M. J. Divine or any of his followers to David in his iniquity. I see the plan of God for these people in the future! Many skeptics are too busy looking at the trees to see the forest. God has put this lovely flock on my heart. I think of them constantly and no man save the spirit of Christ could know the love and concern I have for them. I will give my life if necessary to save them from hurt or destruction by their enemies.

Jimmy credits the Divine Peace Mission for his decision to cast from his life the evil of installment buying. The Divinites, he reports, "believe it is wrong to borrow on the future or put oneself under bondage to material things," based on the biblical admonition to "owe no man anything but to love one another." Jimmy followed the advice, and financial miracles happened immediately in his life:

> . . . My newly found faith enabled me to pay off several holdings within a very few months. We paid one church off and immediately agreed to acquire a huge synagogue with the understanding that the sellers would hold the building and charge us no interest until we could pay cash for the structure.

The "huge synagogue" was the building at Tenth and North Delaware streets. Peoples Temple had definitely moved uptown. The building was located on the northern fringe of the inner city; Jimmy bought the impressive brick structure for fifty thousand dollars from Rabbi Maurice Davis in 1957. It was, at last, a respectable-looking edifice, with a decorative archway more than three stories high at the entrance, and it would seat about four hundred people per service. The stairs out front were wide and majestic; they elevated the seeker and the believer to three welcoming doors crowned by an enormous stained-glass window that bespoke magnificently the glory within. And at the front, inside, before the pulpit, burned an eternal flame, a reminder of the building's years of service as a synagogue, a symbol of hope for the faltering in spirit, a marker of the transports of the soul from heresy to Christ. Jimmy kept it lighted all the time.

Jimmy's habit was to stand just outside the doors and exchange pleasantries with his flock; occasionally he would talk with Faith Worley. She was a good student, a child to whom good grades came easily, hungry for knowledge and experience. Jimmy spoke to her of politics and brotherhood and the ways of the world; to her thirsty young mind, Jimmy Jones seemed to know just about everything. She was bright and inquisitive and Jimmy seemed to take a special interest in her development. Although Faith respected Jimmy's intellect, she didn't think much of his ministry. Despite his affection for her, she was sure that Jimmy knew she viewed him as some kind of con artist. They shared that little secret without ever speaking of it.

Faith's suspicions began when Jimmy would talk about his own health problems, right from the pulpit, so that his followers could know that he suffered, too. Faith asked him once, after a service, why, if he could heal others, he could not heal himself. The question made him uneasy. He was visibly irritated. Healing others, he said, so drained him that he didn't have any energy left for himself. It would be selfish to heal himself at the expense of healing others. Jimmy liked that explanation so much that he repeated it verbatim at subsequent meetings whenever the question came up.

Jimmy's reputation as a healer and prophet, and his credibility in Faith's eyes, reached a low ebb on May 10, 1959. It was on this day that four of Jimmy's followers and his four-year-old adopted Korean daughter, Stephanie, were killed. The group was on its way back from an exchange service at Elmwood Temple in Cincinnati, where Pastor Jones preached while the Reverend Eddie Wilson took Jimmy's place at Peoples Temple. The driver of the car, Mabel Stewart—church organist Loretta Cordell's mother—swerved across the white line to pass a station wagon. An oncoming car rammed the wagon broadside. Six people died—the five from Peoples Temple and an eighteen-year-old Greensburg man who was a passenger in the other car.

"It's a little hard to understand these things," he told the *Indianapolis Star*. "Those people were like my flesh and blood." He had had a premonition of

56

impending tragedy, he said, when Mrs. Stewart's car left the meeting in Cincinnati. "For some strange reason, I told them that some of our people will never be back. I don't know what made me say it."

Stephanie's death was "meant to be," Jimmy said at the Sunday service following the accident. It was destined so that he and Marceline could adopt another Korean orphan whose need was even greater than Stephanie's. "The only thing Stephanie needed to experience in this life," he said, "was to be a child." In fact, he continued, his premonition was not the only one about Stephanie's impending death; Marceline had one, too. She was in the living room at the exact moment the accident happened. She had picked up a photograph and looked at it. The photograph was of Stephanie.

The explanation Jimmy gave Loretta Cordell was different. Her mother, Mabel, died so that she could become one of his messengers in the spirit world. At last, he could prevent the automobile accidents of other Peoples Temple members because Mabel would now be available to him in his revelations. Later, Jimmy from time to time conveyed messages from Mabel to Loretta; and—to cover all the bases—he and Marceline adopted Suzanne, their second daughter from a Korean orphanage.

Jimmy let himself suffer ill health so he could save his energies for healing others. Jimmy let five Temple members drive away to their deaths so they could fulfill their destinies in the world beyond. Jimmy adopted a second Korean daughter because the mission of the first had been completed. There were in Peoples Temple those of little faith, who doubted the credibility of Jimmy's explanations; but they dared not speak. Doubters, malingerers, and those who failed to keep up their tithes were subject to home visits from the church's board of directors. Jimmy himself usually presided over these visits, assisted by Jack Beam and other board members. The interrogations and the verbal abuse often got brutal—especially when Jack Beam had the floor. The committees of interrogation knew best how to reach every individual in Peoples Temple, for Jimmy had requested, during services, that all his followers write down their fears and turn in the lists to Beam or Ijames or himself. As the number of followers grew, the committees stopped going to individual homes. Those who violated the rules would be notified by telephone that they would be brought before the board at a specified time and place. They rarely failed to appear. The subpoenas of the board were infinitely more fearsome than those of a court of law

If there were any lingering wounds from the interrogations committee's ego effacements, they weren't allowed to fester for long. At the conclusion of each service, while Loretta Cordell played the organ and the teary-eyed parishioners hugged one another in an effusive display of brotherly love, Jimmy stood at the pulpit, available for confessions. Transgressors were encouraged to come forward and kneel before Jimmy and confess not their sins but their ill feelings toward others. Jimmy would direct the supplicants to make peace with their adversaries by verbalizing their animosities. Once stated, the ill feelings would vanish in a tearful outpouring, to be replaced by gusty emotions of unity, brotherhood, and Christian fellowship.

Faith felt awkward about the confessions. She did her share, even though she was not particularly religious; she did not worship, nor did she pray; but she confessed, only because she was expected to confess, and her fascination with Jimmy compelled her to do so. She watched every move he made.

What got Faith involved in the church were the Sunday afternoon meetings Jimmy held to explain the church's doctrines. Usually about two dozen young people attended the meetings. Like a university teaching assistant covetous of a position in the department, Jimmy would lecture and pace, pace and lecture, scrawling words on the board and dropping names like Hegel and Marx, Engels and Lenin. He would pepper his talks with three significant words— *thesis, antithesis, synthesis*—and offer his students a recipe for dialectical materialism. The words sounded good; what was the name of the philosophy his students were living by? The bland pablum of I-am-an-American had no color, no flavor, no guts next to the definite pronouncements of the German thinkers. *Thesis, antithesis, synthesis.* "From each according to his ability, to each according to his need" was, according to Jimmy, a variation of the Gospel according to St. Matthew, chapter twenty-five. Jimmy laced his weekly discourses with the works of Thomas Paine, even the blasphemous ones attacking Christianity, and spiced the talks further with quotations from Mark Twain and a sampler of comparative religion.

Race? Class? Money? Hunger? All creations of the capitalist exploiters, they made artificial distinctions among the children of God. In the world of Jimmy's utopian vision, there would be no race or class distinctions, there would be no need for money, there would be no hunger or sickness or pain. Jimmy did his best to make his ideals reality. Mingled in the racially integrated congregation were the destitute and the homeless who were invited to attend services after they had dined at The Pantry, the Temple's free restaurant. Jimmy had set many of these unfortunates back on their feet, so that now they were indistinguishable from the rest of the congregation. More easily identified were the recent arrivals, with their tattered, smelly clothes and matted hair, who sat huddled in the rear right corner of the church. They were, for the most part, men without jobs, men replaced by automation, men who had never worked. There were a few women, too—abandoned wives and prostitutes whose bloom had faded—who talked more easily with the derelicts and winos they came in with than they could with the other women there. All these people were encouraged to mix freely with the congregation; usually they kept to themselves. There was no requirement that they show up for services in exchange for a meal, but they showed up anyway. When they became adequately motivated by the example around them, they could take advantage of the Temple's free employment service.

By 1961, The Pantry was feeding between 120 and 150 persons every day; this largesse was one of the things that attracted the Reverend Ross Case. He was pastor of the First Christian Church in Mason, Illinois, when he first met Jimmy Jones, in the summer of 1959. The Reverend Case was at a church camp a few miles south of Indianapolis when a young black woman, Beatrice Stafford, told him of her church's racially mixed congregation. She was a member of Peoples Temple. Ross had to see for himself. He was deeply disturbed that "eleven o'clock Sunday morning was the most segregated hour in America," and he hurried to Indianapolis, to Tenth and Delaware, where he met Jimmy Jones, Jack Beam, and Archie Ijames, and saw black and white worshiping together under the same roof. At last, he thought, the racial barriers have begun to crumble under the leadership of a courageous young preacher with a "quick, agile wit." The Reverend Ross Case wanted to join Peoples Temple immediately, but he felt compelled to continue at Mason City for two more years.

When his obligation in Illinois was completed, the Reverend Case joined Peoples Temple and became its minister of visitation. Brother Case would consult the "member cards" that Rheaviana Beam, Jack Beam's wife, prepared for him, and go out calling on members' homes as Jimmy's representative. Brother Case was happy to help in whatever way he could; among his other responsibilities were working in The Pantry and attending a class at Butler University to take notes—Jimmy had enrolled but didn't have time to go. Brother Case received a salary from the Temple for a short time, but the salary was too much a burden on Temple finances. Brother Case voluntarily surrendered his salary and took a job as a substitute teacher in the Indianapolis public schools, later teaching full-time at School 22.

Ross Case donated his time to Peoples Temple because the Temple was doing good works. Welfare agencies sent people in immediate need to The Pantry for emergency assistance. Alcoholics threw away their bottles and got religion. Race hatred was extinguished as blacks and whites worshiped together. Counseling was always available, with Jimmy or one of his assistant ministers, whenever crises occurred in Temple families.

One such crisis occurred in Opal's family. She had divorced Ward Worley and married Whitey Freestone. Jimmy himself performed the ceremony. The problem was not between Opal and Whitey, but between Whitey and Opal's daughter, Faith. It seemed best for Faith to get out of the home, and Jimmy Jones advised Opal that Faith should move into the parsonage, with him and Marceline and the kids, at least temporarily.

Faith was pretty excited about the prospect of living with the Jones family. She was extremely fond of both Jimmy and Marceline. Marceline was a nurse, which is the occupation Faith hoped to pursue, and Jimmy, of course, had been Faith's mentor ever since she was a little girl playing on the steps of her church. She looked forward to spending more time with her best friend (she

59

called him "Jim") and discussing politics and philosophy; she never bargained for his growing attachment to her. Before long, Jimmy took to inviting Faith into his private study for discussions that lasted often into the wee small hours. Invariably, the lights were dim and the strains of Johnny Mathis singing "Wonderful, Wonderful" could be heard playing softly in the background. Jimmy would sit close to her in the amber glow of the shaded lamp, but the only touches were gestures of friendship and caring.

All the time Jimmy was spending with Faith used to rile Lynetta. She was living with her son and daughter-in-law at the time; she hadn't changed her habits much from those of her years in Lynn. She cursed Jimmy damn near every time she passed him for paying too much attention to the pubescent girl. Lynetta was working as a corrections officer at the Indiana women's prison on New York Avenue, and she wasn't about to take no guff from nobody, especially her own son. No way. She'd come stomping into the living room with a hand-rolled cigarette dangling from her lower lip and shake her finger at Jimmy while she shrieked at him. "You leave that girl alone," she would say. "Don't let her listen to that shit. She needs her rest." There was never a hint that Lynetta had the least respect for what her son was doing with his life. After Lynetta finished cursing Jimmy for his attention to Faith, and she had left the room, Jimmy would tell Faith, "You're more intelligent than most kids your age." When it was time to go to bed, Jimmy would go up to Faith's room and tuck her in. Sometimes he sat on the bed and stroked Faith's arm gently with his hand. Faith felt uneasy about it, but she was convinced Jimmy's affection was purely paternal. As she dozed off to sleep, Jimmy would get up and close the door gently behind him and tiptoe not to Marceline's bedroom but downstairs to his study, where he usually slept.

Daily life in the Jones household was not the life of the peaceful loving couple that the public saw in Jimmy and Marceline. It was, in fact, almost exactly the opposite. Marceline often broke down in tears when she was screaming at the top of her lungs at the children. She was irritable much of the time because of the pain she suffered with her chronically troublesome back; she had frequently to numb it with pain pills, and several times had to go into traction. Jimmy told Faith that Marceline had mental problems, too; she was schizophrenic. Occasionally, when the household tensions became unbearable, Jimmy and Marceline would shut the door to the upstairs bedroom and scream and shout in there for what seemed to Faith an interminably long time.

Jimmy's temper found ways other than arguing with Marceline to express itself. One night at the dinner table Jimmy flew into a rage at James Jones, Jr., the family's adopted black son. Jimmy yanked his thick leather belt from around his waist and took Jimmy Junior into the downstairs bedroom and whipped him and whipped him and whipped him and whipped him. Faith remembers the incident vividly because it lasted so long.

Jimmy Jones deplored violence in any form, he told his congregation, and he loved every one of God's creatures, even mice and flies. There were times, however, he told his congregation, when only violent death can end suffering. Jimmy told his congregation of a rabbit he once had in his backyard. The rabbit had been mauled and maimed by his dogs. He couldn't stand to see the helpless creature suffering so. He picked up a rock and smashed its skull. At first, Jimmy told the story only to a few members; then he shared it with the entire congregation, dwelling with apparent relish on all the gruesome details. The story may have been true; it may have been a test.

Tests of loyalty were not infrequent, even in the early days, and Jimmy made sure no one ever knew whether his tales were tests or just talk. But there were other kinds of tests, too; Faith passed her first when she was only a child. Jimmy called her father, Ward Worley, up to the pulpit one day not long after some spiritualist minister—a woman who preached at a church in Indianapolis—told everyone she'd had a revelation. Her revelation was that Jimmy Jones was soon to start having revelations. One of his first was that Ward Worley was given to chewing tobacco. Now, Ward was a shy man, but he was honest; when he was asked a question, he told the truth. Yes, he told Jimmy, it was true; he did chew tobacco.

The juice from the tobacco had caused cancer of the stomach, Jimmy told Ward Worley. To prove it, Jimmy had both Jack Beam and Marceline come up and take a whiff of Ward's breath. Both of them said they smelled cancer. Then, for a confirming diagnosis, Jimmy called Faith to step forward and smell her father's breath. She didn't notice anything different about Ward's breath, nothing at all, but she knew she had a choice: she could tell them what she smelled, or she could go along with the program.

Faith chose to go along with the program. After the praying and the laying on of hands, Jimmy told Ward to drink from his glass of water, the one Jimmy kept at the pulpit to sip during services. Ward drank the water that had touched Jimmy's lips, and Jimmy once more summoned his team of diagnosticians to smell Ward's breath. Jack was first, then Marceline; the cancer was gone, they said. Then Faith smelled her father's breath again. Yes, she agreed, the cancer was gone.

Sometime later—Jack Beam was already well rehearsed as Jimmy's confidant, aide, and number-one assistant in the manufacture of miracles—Jack and Jimmy met the woman who was to become, after Jack Beam, Jones's most valuable and dedicated ally, Patty Cartmell. They were at a meeting in Columbus, Ohio, where Patty lived with her husband, Walter, and their two children, Michael and Patricia. Walter was a meek soul who absorbed a lot of abuse from Patty's vitriolic tongue. He was a jack-of-all-trades who earned his bucks as a baker, a cabinetmaker, a carpenter, a handyman. Patty was loudmouthed and chatty, far from meek; she cursed and swore in a way that rivaled Lynetta's. Patty was also an expert manipulator who had a photographic memory for details. She was sloppy in her personal habits, demonstrated a marked preference for frumpy used clothing with no shape, perhaps to conceal the fact that she was never less than fifty pounds overweight.

Patty drove all the way from Columbus to Indianapolis to attend Jimmy's services. She would chatter on and on with Jimmy about politics and social action, which seemed a prime obsession, for it occupied all her time. When she wasn't writing letters to senators and congressmen, she was walking door to door in Columbus gathering signatures on petitions for leftist causes. She was in her early thirties then, virtually bursting with political energy. Jimmy put her to work almost immediately as a member of the inner circle. She, Jack Beam, and Archie Ijames were an invincible team that backed up Jimmy wherever he went, whatever he did, however he spoke. They traveled together and planned strategy. When one would testify, the others would corroborate the story, no matter how outlandish it was.

It was Patty's job in the early days to fuel the emotional fervor of the meetings by talking in tongues, running around the church in a trance, and hollering praises of Pastor Jim. She sang the loudest and clapped the hardest, and her testimonies touched people's hearts as no cerebral palsy telethon ever had. Faith remembers a woman who looked very much like Patty Cartmell in disguise at the church at Tenth and Delaware. The woman was gray-haired and hunched over and all but blind. She sat in the back of the hall holding one eye open with her fingers. Jimmy called the old woman up to the front while he told the story of her tragic life and how her eyelids would not stay open without help. Jimmy healed this woman of her unique blindness, corrected the bend in her back so she could walk straight again, and she walked straight out of the door of the Temple praising Jimmy all the way down the aisle and no one ever saw her again.

Jack Beam's brusque manner, broad shoulders, and booming voice commanded attention, and he loved to preach when Jimmy would let him, even though his mind had not enjoyed the benefits of a university education, as Jimmy's had. Jack wanted to share the limelight with Jimmy during the healings and the miracles. Jimmy wanted him only as an assistant. Jimmy often let Jack open the services to get the spirit going; he started many meetings with a recitation of Jimmy's miracles. Countless times he told the story of how Jimmy, with the help of the Lord, of course, lifted a car from Jack's body, then popped his crushed chest back into shape. The others verified the tale.

Archie Ijames—everybody knew him as "A. J."—was, in addition to being the Temple's token black leader, often an unwitting assistant in miracle-making. He helped with the production of the weekly radio program. He contributed his carpentry skill to Temple projects. He was adept at recruiting new members, especially among blacks, for although he had only a seventh-grade education, he was intelligent. He was aware there were things going on in the church that he knew nothing about, but Patty, Jack, and Jimmy were not about to tell him.

Among the mysterious goings-on were spooky phone calls in the middle of the night. Typically, one of the members would be awakened by the ringing telephone and the caller would talk in tongues, then hang up. Jimmy learned of the strange calls in his revelations. He would summon those who had received such calls up to the pulpit and reveal to them, as it had been revealed to him, whether the caller's voice was male or female, whether the message was good or evil. Some few found hexes and skull-and-crossbones painted on their homes, and dead cats hanging in their garages. The forces of evil were clearly afoot, but Jimmy knew of their dark workings and did his best to chase the demons away. Invariably, the calls would stop, the hexes would disappear, and the faithful could sleep through the night.

Some parishioners received calls that were blatantly racist. "Niggerlover!" the caller would shout, then slam down the receiver. Racial tensions ran high in Indianapolis during the fifties and sixties. The racist calls got worse in February of 1961, when Jimmy was named executive director of the city's human rights commission—the first director to receive a salary for the job. Mayor Charles Boswell appointed Jimmy Jones to the seven-thousand-dollar-a-year post on the recommendation of a black superior court judge, Mercer Mance, who chaired the commission's personnel committee. "It was difficult to find anyone who would do the job that needed to be done," says Boswell. Boswell says he had no idea Jimmy was a faith healer when he appointed him to the post. Had he—or anyone on his staff—checked into Jimmy's activities at the time, he'd have seen no healings, nor any other kind of miracle. Just before he was named to the job, Jimmy declared a temporary moratorium on miracle-making. To Boswell, Jimmy was a popular, soft-spoken preacher with a social conscience and an interracial congregation.

Mysterious phone calls to the members may have abated, but whoever was calling found a new target in Jimmy himself. Jimmy told his followers he was getting telephone threats at all hours of the day and night. One caller spoke with a handkerchief over the transmitter and warned Jimmy that his children were in danger. "We know the paths your children follow to and from school," said the caller. Jimmy told his people also of the bus-stop incident. Marceline and James Jones, Jr., were waiting for a bus downtown when a woman spat on both of them. Unknown persons—Jimmy said they were racists—tossed rotten tomatoes and vegetables at the church at Tenth and Delaware, and once, during a service, a hail of rocks came crashing through one of the front windows. These reports of unrelenting harassment caught the attention of *Indianapolis News* columnist Bill Wildhack, August 11, 1961:

> The Rev. James W. Jones expected some unpleasant experiences when he agreed to serve as director of the city's Human Rights Commission.

He was not wrong. Nearly every mail brought letters reviling him. Then he was harassed by telephone both at the office and at home.

This form of tormenting has practically ceased, but it has been replaced by a more insidious and evil persecution.

He has become the victim of a letter-writing campaign. His name is forged to letters making insulting statements about minority groups. The letters are mailed to Negroes and others known to be interested in the problem of racial relations.

Recipients of the letters who know the Rev. Mr. Jones spot them immediately as the work of a crackpot, but many others take them seriously. He is bewildered, not knowing how to fight this form of vilification.

Jimmy turned some of the letters over to postal authorities, but the culprits, whoever they were, were never caught.

The terrorist tactics persisted throughout the year and a half that Jimmy was executive director of the human rights commission. Others in Indianapolis who had taken a courageous stand against racism were left pretty much alone. The announcement of Jimmy's appointment to the post was treated routinely by the papers, in articles buried on page 17 of the *News* and page 15 of the *Star*. Most people in Indianapolis didn't even know there was a human rights commission.

It took Jimmy only three months in his directorship to run afoul of Mayor Boswell and the commission. When the mayor was out of town, Jimmy wrote a newsletter reporting on his activities. "The Mayor didn't like some of the stories," according to the April 22, 1961, *News*, "and he says some of the commission members were also upset by them. From now on, proposed copy for the monthly newsletter will be submitted to the commission and Boswell for approval." Jimmy did not resign, nor even issue a public statement denouncing the gag order; rather, he quietly continued to do his job. He met with owners of downtown businesses and urged them to comply with civil rights laws forbidding separate restroom facilities. He convinced restaurant and movie theater owners to open their doors to blacks. According to Mayor Boswell, Jimmy did an effective job; but he was far from being the champion of civil rights he had his congregation believing he was.

Jimmy was so far from controversial with his activities with the human rights commission that throughout his tenure he attracted the attention of the press only three times: in the Bill Wildhack column about the hate letters; in the article about his hassle with the mayor over the newsletter; and in a story that ran in the June 15, 1961, *News* about a preliminary investigation into charges that only one motel in all of Indianapolis would accept blacks. Jimmy conducted the investigation himself after the Reverend C. T. H. Watkins, pastor of the Bethel African Methodist Episcopal Church and a member of the human rights commission, leveled charges of discrimination. Jimmy lost not a second; he picked up the telephone and called six motels around town. He concluded that the Reverend Mr. Watkins's charges were "an unfair blanket statement" against motel owners.

For some reason, this obscure, basically noncontroversial bureaucrat seemed to be the victim of a continual campaign of harassment, and a vicious campaign it was; but why? Members of the church at that time recall that Jimmy spoke constantly of his enemies, both privately and from the pulpit. He seemed to revel in his unpopularity. Faith Worley was at Jimmy's house when some of the harassing calls came. The phone would ring. Jimmy would pick up the receiver and listen for a minute, then hang up without a word. "Another one of those calls," he would sigh. Because of the nature of the calls, Jimmy insisted on answering the phone himself, but once he asked Faith to pick up the phone. Sure enough, it was someone calling Jimmy a "niggerlover." Once Faith walked into the living room unexpectedly and overheard Jimmy making what sounded like a threatening call. He had a handkerchief draped over the transmitter.

Late in 1961, Jimmy planted a new seed of fear. He had had a vision, he said, of a great holocaust that would devastate Indianapolis. Jimmy told only a few members at first, and the word spread throughout the congregation. Brother Case believed that the vision was a message from God, and he had no reason to believe otherwise. The Reverend Mr. Case had always been one to believe the words of a true Christian, and he believed at the time that Jimmy Jones was the epitome. The Reverend Case suggested to the Reverend Ijames that the church's leaders move the congregation to a safe place as soon as possible. Archie agreed with Ross Case, after some prodding, but when the two men approached Jimmy with the idea he just laughed and said he was not about to run away and hide from the inevitable.

Jimmy approached Ross a few weeks later to admit that he had changed his mind; he'd go along with the relocation idea, but he doubted that more than a hundred members could be persuaded to make the exodus. The January 1962 issue of *Esquire* magazine ran an article by Caroline Bird titled "Nine Places to Hide," and Jimmy picked it up to learn the safest locations in the world in the event of nuclear attack. The only alternatives seemed to be to build underground bomb shelters—a popular activity at the time—or to die. Jimmy showed the article to Ross Case, and the two leaders agreed to limit their selections to industrialized areas, lest they be forced to live like savages. The nine safe places: Eureka, California; Cork, Ireland; Guadalajara, Mexico; Mendoza, Argentina; the central valley of Chile; Belo Horizonte, Brazil; Tananarive, Madagascar; Christ's Church, New Zealand; and Melbourne, Australia.

Jimmy lost no time. He took a leave of absence from the human rights commission and the spring of 1962 found him in Mexico City. He wired

Archie Ijames to meet him there; Archie was thrilled at the prospect of flying. When he returned home, Archie informed the other pastors that Jimmy would be flying down to Georgetown, British Guiana (now Guyana, an independent state), where the people spoke English. Jimmy held meetings there. He later said he was impressed by the cleanliness of the black women, who daily washed their clothes in the creeks.

From British Guiana, it was only a short hop to Belo Horizonte, Brazil, one of the nine safe places. Jimmy and his family flew there and settled into a three-bedroom house while Jimmy scouted the area. He explored alternatives to Christianity and even attended voodoo rites. According to Bonnie Thielman, who knew Jimmy in Belo Horizonte, he was not, as he claimed in letters to Indianapolis, running an orphanage; he and Marceline were merely feeding impoverished children in their kitchen. The homeless waifs showed up at Jones's doorstep every day for dinner.

From Belo Horizonte, the Joneses moved to Rio de Janeiro, where Jimmy taught at the University of São Fernando for about a year. According to the São Paulo *Jornal da Tarde* for November 30, 1978, "Other sources reveal that Jim Jones, in fact, did some social work in Rio in the company of another North American, Jack Beam. . . ." Jones himself often told the story of how he allegedly financed an orphanage in Rio:

> The Brazilians had tried to make a go of this orphanage and school but they did not have any resources, and I became the principal food resource. So this ambassador's wife offered me a pile of money if I'd fuck her, so I did. There is nothing to compare with the kind of revulsion felt when you're lying next to someone you loathe. And I loathed her, and everything she stood for—for the arrogance of wealth, the racism, the cruelty. I puked afterwards, it was so bad. . . .

Jimmy was gone until late 1963, longer than anyone had anticipated. He wrote letters first asking, then demanding, the lion's share of the offerings. Then there was a long period with no word from Jimmy at all; rumor had it that he had died in Belo Horizonte. During his absence, Ross and Archie shared the pulpit with two other assistant pastors, Tom Dickson and Russell Winberg; but none of them had Jimmy's charisma, and his flock gradually wandered off to other pastures.

Meanwhile, the human rights commission was muddling through without an executive director. They gave Jimmy until July 1 to resume his duties or face dismissal. Jimmy responded—on August 18—in the form of a telegram from Belo Horizonte. It was addressed to Alex Kertis, city personnel director:

RECUPERATED. CONSIDERING POST HERE BECAUSE UNDERSTAND

The commission read the telegram as a formal resignation.

After he returned from Brazil, Jimmy turned his attention again to the
holocaust. At first, he was vague about the date, but eventually he broke down
and revealed when the catastrophe would occur: June 15, 1967. There were a
few doubters, but most of his members took him seriously. Ross Case took him
seriously because Jimmy's prophecy paralleled exactly a prophecy of
Nostradamus's. Ross was not about to wait for the laggards; he moved his
family independently of Peoples Temple and came to northern California in
June of 1963. Ross had learned from a newspaper called the *Humboldt
Standard,* published in Eureka, that the "safe zone" extended between Eureka
and Ukiah. That was a stroke of luck; Ross had made arrangements with
Archie's son, Norman, a pilot, to fly his family to California as soon as
possible. Norman's light plane couldn't handle the altitudes above the
mountains of the coastal range near Eureka. They could, however, go as far as
Ukiah, and that is where they landed.

Ross Case called the Eureka school officials right away, only to learn there
were no teaching positions open in the elementary school division for the year
1963–64. He called the Ukiah school officials and was offered a job
immediately. The Reverend Ross Case and his family settled permanently in
Ukiah, more than a hundred miles from the nearest likely nuclear target.
They built a bomb shelter in the backyard according to the plans prepared by
the Office of Emergency Preparedness. At last, Ross and his family were safe.

The Reverend Case had been having misgivings about Jimmy before he left
for California. Ross saw another side emerging during the hours he spent with
Jimmy; Jimmy seemed not to be the Christian Ross once believe him to be.
There were minor incidents. Once Ross was riding with Jimmy in his black
Cadillac and they drove by the house of a woman member who was having
emotional problems. "You know what she needs?" Jimmy asked as he wheeled
the big machine past the house. "She needs someone to screw her." Brother
Case was disturbed that a fellow pastor would use such language; he was
disturbed by the attitudes behind it. He was disturbed also by Jimmy's
suspicious nature, his constant vigilance against the unknown enemies of
Peoples Temple. Ross would have been perfectly content never to have seen
Jimmy Jones again.

Despite Jimmy's eccentricities, his penchant for theatrics, and his dubious
reputation as a healer and prophet, the Disciples of Christ—whose national
membership at the time was about two million—ordained him on February 16,
1964. Apparently the Disciples had investigated Jimmy's background only far
enough to see his good works, and, since the Temple had been affiliated with

the Disciples for nearly four years, it was only logical to ordain the church's founding minister after he took the required courses at Cleveland Bible College in Ohio.

Presiding over the ordination was the Reverend Edward J. Malmin. He had met Jimmy in Brazil and was appointed pastor of Peoples Temple when the two men returned. According to an announcement in the *Indianapolis Star,* Jimmy was to "represent the church in Brazil" following his ordination. He chose instead to remain in Indianapolis, where he continued preaching, both at the Temple and on WIBC radio.

The Sunday morning radio broadcast came to an abrupt and voluntary end in April of 1965. There was another siege of telephone calls that began when Jimmy defended Mahatma Gandhi on the air, claiming that Gandhi was a spiritual leader who had "accepted the teachings of Jesus." A minister had attacked the Indian leader and Jimmy disagreed, saying he "couldn't see a loving heavenly father condemning to hell persons because they wouldn't accept some Christian doctrines." Following the program, Jimmy told Bill Wildhack of the *News* (April 17, 1965), there came a flood of harassing calls to his home at all hours of the day and night. Wildhack saw the latest wave of hate calls as a logical result of Jimmy's stand against racism:

> The Rev. Mr. Jones has taken a prominent role here in the struggle for racial equality. He served as executive [director] of the mayor's Human Rights Commission and he has adopted children of Negro, Korean and Japanese ancestry.
>
> He says some nasty remarks were made on the phone concerning his views on racial matters, but these seemed secondary to the attacks on his theological views.
>
> One of the favorite tricks of the anonymous callers was to get one of the children on the phone and say:
>
> "Did you know your father is an anti-Christ, a Devil?"
>
> During this period, the radio station also received harassing telephone calls, a fact confirmed by an employee involved.
>
> So, worried about the possible effect on his children and to save the station the embarrassment, the Rev. Mr. Jones voluntarily stopped his broadcasts.

Jimmy neglected to tell Wildhack and WIBC that he and his followers were already making plans to leave Indianapolis for greener pastures in California.

Early in 1965, the Reverend Case went to Hayward, California, to visit Jack and Rheaviana Beam, who had moved there after they returned from Belo Horizonte. Jack was exhausted from his work in Brazil with Jimmy, and he told Ross that he was no longer sure that he wanted to dedicate his life to Peoples Temple. Jimmy would be coming out to visit him, Jack said, and he asked Ross if he'd like to know the date so they could have a reunion. Ross said he would.

Jack called Ross a few weeks later. Jimmy was here, he said. Ross drove down from Ukiah. During their reunion, Jimmy asked Ross why he had chosen Ukiah, and Ross explained that the city's location would protect it from radiation in the event of a nuclear blast in the Bay Area. Jimmy wanted to see Ukiah for himself.

He was impressed with what he saw. When he returned to Indianapolis, he told his followers that God had shown him Ukiah in a revelation and that Ukiah would be the next home of Peoples Temple. With the holocaust imminent, it was move now or perish. Jimmy demanded secrecy, however; those who were going to join him were not to tell anyone outside the Temple, not even members of their own families.

Jimmy called Ross Case during the planning stages and gave him a list of the names, ages, and occupations of the pilgrims. He asked Ross to try to find jobs and housing in the Ukiah area. A few members settled there in the spring of 1965, but most of the 145 refugees trickled in over the summer months, when the temperatures were up over a hundred degrees, and their cars, jammed with all their worldly goods, carried the dust of half the United States into the small town. These latter-day migrants to the valleys of California came in buses, too, carrying only a few suitcases full of belongings. They were the Cartmells and the Cordells, the Stahls, the Beams, the Pughs, the Ijameses, the Phillipses, the Wades and the Beikmans, the Addisons and the Freestones. Faith Worley rode in the Addison's car; she had a crush on Steve, and riding together in the back seat gave them a chance to get to know each other. A few, like Hyacinth Thrash, were in their sixties; pulling up roots wasn't easy, but the alternative, they believed, was certain death.

It may appear contradictory with the prophecy of ominous events ahead for America, but we want to win as many to truth for their own sake while the harvest is ripe. Remember well that Redwood Valley well may be a refuge in time of storm.

—*Peoples Temple Newsletter,*
July 1970

You could never relate to Jones, because no matter how much you tried to be like him, you were always cut down for trying to be like him.

—Grace Stoen, San Francisco, February 1979

III

A Safe Place

When Jim Jones and his followers made their westward journey to Ukiah, California, in the summer of 1965, they sought neither Eden nor the New Jerusalem; they sought only safety from the holocaust. Ukiah never resembled Eden, even in the days when the Pomo Indians gave it its name, which means "deep valley." And deep it is, flat as an Indiana cornfield nestled between two mountain ranges, the Coastal and the Mayacamas. The mountains on the west divert the cool Pacific breezes away from the valley during the summer, and a stroll through the town's sizzling streets is like a Cook's tour of Dante's Inferno. The dry heat sits heavily on the valley throughout the day and night and presses sweating backs to bedsheets, or causes drivers to pry their soaking shirts off the vinyl backs of carseats and stop at one of the fast-food palaces that squat along State Street.

Ukiah is the seat of Mendocino County. Its downtown area is dominated by a rectangular building three stories high, painted a pale shade of institutional green and looming nearly twice as tall as the buildings around it: the Mendocino County Courthouse. At the foot of its steps, in the shade of the magnolia trees, a single bench is the daytime home of a group of unshaven men who pass among themselves a variety of bottles cloaked in paper bags and smile benignly on one another, be they white, brown, yellow, or black, for there are no racist winos in the courthouse park. In addition to the courthouse regulars, there were in Ukiah in 1965 some ten thousand other souls, workers and businessmen, housewives and professionals, rooted citizens and mobile-home dwellers, who made up about 20 percent of Mendocino County's total population.

The migrants from Indianapolis blended easily—except for the blacks. The arrival of the hundred and forty or more newcomers—they trickled in a few at a time—would have been nearly imperceptible, except for the blacks. One black family—the Ijames family—was already settled in Ukiah when Archie Ijames's oldest daughter, Vicky Moore, decided to move up from Oakland after her marriage broke up. She saw rural Ukiah as a welcome change from the Oakland ghetto, especially for her two children. Acres of pear trees and vineyards in the valley offered pleasant, if monotonous, vistas, and the air was clean except for the pleasant, pitchy aroma of smoke from nearby sawmills. Vicky was assured by church officials that Ukiah was not racist, even though the blacks in the community constituted less than 0.5 percent of the population. She found when she arrived that most of the other 99.5 percent linked civil rights activism with anarchy, communism, and revolution. But some of the townspeople were friendly.

Among the friendly townspeople was reporter Kathy Hunter, wife of the managing editor of the *Ukiah Daily Journal*. She penned a front-page article on July 26, 1965, that introduced Jim Jones and his group of interracial pilgrims from the Midwest to the community. Mrs. Hunter quotes the Reverend Jim Jones explaining why the group chose Ukiah: "its forward-thinking, freedom from intolerance and spirit of civic responsibility" parallel the ideals of Peoples Temple. He neglected to mention the vision of holocaust and the selection of Ukiah as a "safe place." Mrs. Hunter describes Jim Jones as "a tall man in his mid-thirties who mixes considerable personal charm with a razor-sharp intellect and a deep compassion for his fellow man." She goes on to describe the group:

> Represented in the group and indicative of the substantial background of the membership are nurses, teachers, a pilot, a traffic engineer, an electronics man, salespeople and private businessmen. One of the newcomers has already purchased an apartment house, another has bought a Ukiah motel, and still another is negotiating the purchase of a rest home here.
>
> Far from being a closed, tightly knit group living in a communal existence, members of the church live their own lives as part of the community as a whole, held together only by their belief that all men—white, black, yellow or red—are one brotherhood.

The members of Jim Jones's church lived their own lives as part of the community under conditions something less than ideal. Housing in Ukiah was inexpensive, but it was not plentiful. Although everyone found homes or rooms to rent right away, those homes or rooms were considerably more crowded than the homes they left in Indianapolis. Opal Freestone shared her one-room kitchenette apartment with four other people, including an elderly woman who needed constant care.

There had been a relocation plan, however nebulous. Ross Case had already been there a couple of years when he received the members list from Jim, with the names of the pilgrims and their work skills to help find them jobs and housing. Like a good Christian, Ross made efforts; but his confidence in Jim Jones and Peoples Temple had long since begun an unreclaimable erosion. On one of Jim's early trips to Ukiah from Indianapolis, he stopped by Ross's home to discuss future plans for the church. "Would they go for any Buddhist or Hindu teachings here in Ukiah?" Jim asked his former assistant pastor.

"I wouldn't think so," Ross answered. He had hardly expected such a question from a fellow Christian. He had no idea what kind of church Jim had in mind when Jim responded, "That's all right. We'll have to have our own church, anyway."

That response, and the comment Jim made when they passed the house of the woman in Indianapolis who "needs someone to screw her," and Jim Jones's admission at that time that he always "felt dirty" after sex with his wife—Archie was in the car with Ross and Jim—had Ross Case nearly at the brink of a religious schism. What tipped Ross were the events of late February 1965 that began when he received a letter from Harold Cordell, dated February 18. The letter rambled on for six single-spaced pages of excerpts from Jim Jones's sermons on how the Bible "is dotted through and through with fabrications, inconsistencies and incongruities which insult the normal intelligence of readers." That comment didn't set well with Ross; he had majored in Bible at college, and was a scholar who could quote chapter and verse at the drop of a ribbon placemark. Ross was particularly ired at Cordell's claim that Jim Jones was "a prophet of the first degree whose prophecies *always come true* to the minute detail."

Cordell went on to speak of Jim Jones's humility. "He often speaks of his imperfection," Cordell wrote, "and warns us not to think of him as God or worship him." How, then, to explain the discussion Ross had with Archie Ijames after receiving this letter? And three other letters from Jim himself, expressing similar sentiments? Ross Case got in touch with Archie and made it clear that he did not agree with the new direction Peoples Temple had taken. Archie replied that it was no longer acceptable to have differences of opinion in the group. Ross recalls Archie saying, "For myself, I have come to the position that I must submit my mind completely to the mind of Jimmy."

Ross called Jim Jones and confronted him with these inconsistencies; Ross was especially disturbed by Archie's opting for total submission. Jones's answer might have been predicted: "Oh, Ross," Jim said, "I certainly wouldn't expect that of you." Ross knew better. He considered these apparent heresies for some time, and finally scribbled a note to himself on a small piece of paper:

Is James jealous of Jesus? Satan was, and it led to his downfall.

Ross stuck the scrap of paper in a jacket pocket and decided to break with Peoples Temple—this time for keeps.

It was shortly after that decision that Ross Case began to receive letters from Temple members urging him to return to the fold. There were subtle threats that Mrs. Case might get fired from her job at Mendocino State

Hospital. There were even hints that Temple members wanted to do terrible things to Ross, but were restrained only by Jim's mercy. Nevertheless, Ross wouldn't budge; he was the first of the group from Indianapolis to break successfully with Peoples Temple, and he made it stick.

Even when he was having his doubts about Jim Jones, he still made efforts on behalf of his old friend and former partner. A letter addressed to Christian Assemblies, Inc., had to do with the purchase of the Evangelical Free Church at the corner of Bush and Henry streets in Ukiah. Early in February, Jim Jones had asked Ross Case to begin negotiations for its purchase. Jones had a couple of corporations chartered in Indiana at the time, and he asked Ross to make the deal under the aegis of Christian Assemblies, Inc., rather than Wings of Deliverance, Inc. Jim and Marceline had used the latter corporation to buy and sell several properties in Indianapolis. "We're going to have to put it under Christian Assemblies," Jones told Case, "because Wings of Deliverance can't stand investigation." Whether the reason was that records had not been kept adequately or that Wings of Deliverance had been involved in some unsavory operations, Ross didn't know; nor did he ask. He started negotiations and Peoples Temple acquired the church at Bush and Henry.

The little church was the first of Jim Jones's real estate acquisitions. He and Marceline bought a two-story home in Redwood Valley, a tiny community seven miles north of Ukiah, and settled down as respectable members of the community. Jim preached and took care of the business of his little church and Marceline worked in the nursing education program at Mendocino State Hospital, an institution for the mentally ill, alcoholics, and drug addicts. Marceline participated in an innovative rehabilitation program for adolescents; she worked also in the geriatrics ward. Marcie, as she was known, was well liked and respected by her colleagues; although her husband was a preacher, she never once attempted to proselytize either her coworkers or her charges. The couple listed their Redwood Valley address when they applied for incorporation papers on July 30, 1965. Their new nonprofit corporation bore the name "Peoples Temple of the Disciples of Christ." Its stated purpose was only "to further the Kingdom of God by spreading the Word." Jim Jones was president and Marceline was secretary.

The cozy family corporation and its followers kept pretty much to themselves at their tiny church at Bush and Henry. Every now and then an outsider would wander in to the building during services, and everyone, including Pastor Jim—"Just call me Jim"—would "act churchy." They would sing the traditional hymns—"The Old Rugged Cross," "Rock of Ages," "When the Roll Is Called Up Yonder"—while Loretta Cordell pounded out majestic chords on the old organ, and the Reverend Jim Jones would preach from the Bible, and the spirit of fellowship would descend on the group like a flood of warm milk.

But when Pastor Jim was alone with his group, he became the Prophet of

God, the embodiment of the same spirit that found a home in Jesus Christ, heir of the gifts of tongues and interpretation, of miracles and healings, of psychic powers and revelations. He recounted the revelation in Indianapolis, the vision of a bright burning flash of white light, the harvest of death and devastation that would happen (he said now) on March 16 at 3:09 A.M. (he neglected to mention the year this time). He recalled how he had diagnosed and healed the breast cancer that was eating poor Hyacinth Thrash. He recalled how he had foretold the assassination of President Kennedy, and how, in precise detail, he had seen the imminent demise of Earl Jackson, Eva Pugh's first husband, well before it happened. There was more. Jim Jones had had a revelation about himself. God had told him that he was Jesus Christ reincarnated. Nobody said a word.

This reincarnation of Jesus may have had divine powers, but for some reason known only to God and Jim Jones, they did not extend to real estate dealings. Shortly after negotiations began for the church at Bush and Henry, Jim discovered that Christian Assemblies, Inc., had lost its legal standing as a corporation; through some oversight, Jones had failed to file annual reports with the Indiana secretary of state. The church deal fell through in November, 1965, and Jim Jones's lilies found themselves out in the field. They found a temporary home ten miles north of Ukiah at the Ridgewood Ranch, a religious colony owned by Christ's Church of the Golden Rule. The sprawling ranch, originally a sixteen-thousand-acre estate, had a dairy, a public camping area, a printing plant, a real estate office, a mobile-home park, a restaurant, a service station, a school, and a church. The property had once been used for raising champion racehorses. Peoples Temple used a classroom building there, free of charge, for about two years.

The tenets of this utopian church were much to the liking of the Reverend Jones; the group believed that "economic equality is the only enduring foundation upon which to build industrial, business, political, national and international relationships; and that to insure such equality, the property and earnings of all individuals should be used to glorify God and to illustrate the teachings of Jesus Christ." He liked it. He saw people living together, primitive Christians, working without pay, working for the common good. He saw his own utopian dream in action, and he liked it. He liked it so much that he made it all too obvious he wanted it for himself. His ambition did not escape the notice of the officials of the Church of the Golden Rule.

"I think he would have liked to take over our membership," one church official said. One of the tenets of the church forbade the ascension of one person to a position of leadership. "We were not interested in personality leadership," the official continued. "It was almost idolatry, the way they conducted their meetings." A confrontation was inevitable.

The elders of Christ's Church of the Golden Rule called a special meeting. They invited Jim Jones and his flock. Temple members had no idea what the meeting was to be about; they were shocked and angered when the elders said that Peoples Temple was no longer welcome at Ridgewood Ranch. Jim Jones's followers defended their leader vociferously, but it was a losing battle. Peoples Temple was ordered off the property.

Cast out of two churches in as many years, Jim Jones's ministry was at a low ebb. He found shelter for his flock in an exhibition building at the Mendocino County fairgrounds in Ukiah. The building housed Four-H exhibits during the fair; it was finished in rough-hewn redwood planks and as stoically functional as a high school gymnasium, with folding chairs that would seat between a hundred and fifty and two hundred people. Jimmy's gift of prophecy had failed to foresee such an abrupt descent. The fairgrounds humbled him. He had not seen such a struggle for survival since the monkey business days. Things could not get much worse.

The cause of his misfortunes, Jim Jones told his people, was the evil in the community, the evil forces that hated him for having black brothers and sisters in his congregation, the racist attitudes that were threatened by his uncompromising fight for racial equality. He moved from the fairgrounds to his two-car garage in Redwood Valley, and there held services that were always packed to overflowing. People sat on benches. People squatted under benches, in aisles, on other people's feet. People squeezed against the walls of the garage and backed up into the corners. Offering baskets had to be passed overhead, and it was a tight squeeze to reach into pockets for change for the baskets.

Of course, it didn't take very many people to pack Jim's garage. Edith Parks's letter—dated April 26, 1968—to Virginia and Rodger Morningstar expresses concern for the growing attendance, and for a few other things:

> . . . All work at some thing. They have to; rent is $90–$125 for small houses and groceries are so high. Most of them pay 25 percent tithes. It will take care of them all later some way. Jim is turning them away from church. 85 for Easter. 35 last Sunday. People are awakening and are worried but he says it is too risky! He sends them back to their own churches and tells them to pray and work where they are. There isn't time to reeducate new ones, even those who have been taught far ahead of our "type" of religion. A few have even been allowed to come and they jump in with both feet. You don't have to teach them anything. They know & they know who he is & what he is here for. He knows every thought, act or deed. In the message Sunday he said everything that is to happen in the future has been seen & met for all who will meet conditions they must. He knows just what will happen to each one, even how they will die. . . .
>
> It will happen yet, right here, too. If only I could write it all but the American people have already been conditioned to go the way they

are going and acting, so they will think we need the laws that will be put thru Congress, each one taking away more of our rights! Just watch who is for them! Reagan is a full-fledged fascist.

At the top of Edith's letter is the admonition "Burn this." Edith's loyalty and conviction were typical. People flocked to the garage; the services went on. Loretta Cordell continued to pound out the hymns on whatever keyboard was available. The people continued to sing them. Jim Jones himself would often lead the hymns in a rich, if sour, baritone. When the singing was done, Jim would settle behind his pulpit, propped up on a makeshift platform, and begin his preaching—not from the Bible, but, in the dim light and the crowded quarters, like a fifties comic in a San Francisco nightclub, from newspapers, reading articles and offering commentary in the style of a Garner Ted Armstrong with a leftist slant, a Mort Sahl without wit.

He almost never used the Bible by the late sixties except to throw it down, pick it up, rip out its pages, stamp on it; once he set a Bible afire to dramatize his growing impatience with people who worshiped it as "a paper idol. It's just another goddamned book," he said. He knew because his Father in his recent incarnation had told him so; God was in touch with Jim Jones daily. How else could he know the secrets he knew? Even in that humble garage, revelations came to him as brightly and clearly as before, and it was there in that garage that Jim Jones had the first of what was to become one of his favorite revelations: that one of his men was guilty of child molesting. The first member to be so honored was Whitey Freestone. Jim told everyone in the garage that Whitey had molested his stepdaughters. Whitey denied it. Jones kept pressing it. Whitey held his ground. Jones scoffed. There was nothing for Whitey but to stand red-faced before the congregation and shake his head.

In September of that year, 1968, the Temple applied for a permit to build a youth center between the parsonage and East Road. It started simply as a roof over a newly built swimming pool; by October, the Temple submitted plans for a church building. Every able-bodied man in the church got to work swinging hammers, wielding saws, digging trenches, laying pipe. Denny Parks—he and his wife, Sandy, had started attending services at the fairgrounds, then went with the others to the packed meetings in the garage—helped with the foundations and the plumbing, some of the really heavy work, while others nailed up the siding, set the doors and windows, painted the interiors. When the building was finished, it was the pride of its builders: simultaneously rustic and modern, solid with redwood and a low-sloping roof, and perhaps the only church in America built on top of a swimming pool.

The coins that landed in the baskets during collections in Jim's double garage could not have paid for the new building; offerings and tithes together were hardly enough to keep pace with the bills. The Jones family alone had six mouths to feed: Jim, Marceline, and their son, Stephan Gandhi, and their adopted children, Suzanne, Lew Erick, and James Jones, Jr. Jim hadn't worked since he settled in Redwood Valley, and Marceline's salary wasn't enough to keep the larder packed and the kids in clothes. Jim told his followers he would have to go out and get a job.

He created a job for himself. He went to Anderson Valley School District in Boonville, a community about forty miles southwest of Ukiah along the winding, hilly Highway 253, and promised the school district sixteen additional students in exchange for a teaching position. Jim Jones got his job teaching sixth grade, and the school district got thousands more in state money for the additional students. He taught there through June of 1969, having been recommended for the position by district superintendent Robert Mathias.

Jones told Mathias that he wanted the Temple students at Anderson Valley High because he was "disenchanted with the Ukiah School District." He would pick up his sixteen "disenchanted" students in two cars—Steve Addison drove the other one—and pack them in for the forty-mile ride every day. There was some tension on the campus; many of the Boonville white students displayed open contempt for the "niggers" Jones brought with him, even though the new students were bright and well behaved. Fortunately, there were never any serious confrontations, never any violent episodes, even though Boonville was the kind of place that might have been ripe for such outbursts. Boonville was a low-income community, so isolated since its beginnings that at the turn of the century Boonville's young people had invented their own language, "Boontling," which survives today as a recognized dialect of American English.

Robert Mathias remembers Jim Jones as "kind, gentle, and quiet." Mathias's son was in Jones's social studies class; he seemed to be impressed by the way Jones "stimulated [the boy] in certain ways to become aware of the whole world's society." Jones would discuss world affairs, often playing the devil's advocate, and would encourage unstructured debates on a variety of topics, his favorite being capitalism versus communism. As the devil's advocate speaking for the communist side, Jim Jones seemed remarkably authentic.

Perhaps the racial tensions remained under control because Jim Jones advised his Temple students not to mingle with the other students at Anderson Valley High. If they mingled too freely, Mike Cartmell, unofficial spokesman for the Temple students, would make it known; he reported regularly to Jim. Close-knit and suspicious, the Temple students were told to watch one another at all times lest one of them stray too far from the flock.

Faith Worley observed all the instructions and still managed to get into trouble with Jim Jones. She didn't stray, but in her senior year, the boys in the school voted Faith—she was a pretty girl and seemed to have "been around"—their Homecoming Queen, despite her association with Peoples Temple. The night of the 1968 Big Game, during half time, she received a kiss from the captain of the football team. Jim didn't like it at all; there was nothing he could do about having a Homecoming Queen in the Temple, since, having been elected by secret ballot, Faith could not control her ascension to the honored position. What bothered Jim is that she permitted the boy to kiss her on the mouth. Jim saw the whole thing from the stands, and it really burned him. He showed Faith the picture in the local paper, with her demurely receiving the bouquet of flowers and the blushing kiss, and said that he didn't really mind the publicity, but the kiss was not acceptable to Peoples Temple.

Jim Jones didn't have to worry about Big Games, Homecoming Queens, and unacceptable kisses at his other teaching job. Despite his disenchantment with the Ukiah School District, he taught an adult class in American history and government evenings at Ukiah High after his daytime classes in Boonville. Adult school classes at that time were offered only if there was sufficient enrollment. Again, Jim created his own job. He sparked interest in the class during the Sunday services and asked his members to raise their hands and volunteer. Among those who signed up were Linda Dunn, Marvin Swinney, Faith Worley, and Opal Freestone. Jim's history lessons, Linda remembers, were not much more than rambling discussions of current events, with a lot of attention to Jones's pet concerns; he was especially alert to pending legislation that threatened the Bill of Rights and its guarantees of free speech, freedom of religion, the right to bear arms, and so on, and he took pains to provide the names and addresses of those in government who might be swayed by letters. He urged everyone in the class to get involved.

The principal of the adult school while Jones was teaching there, William Tatum, recalls that "eighty percent of [Jones's] classes were Temple people from Indiana who lacked high school diplomas." He describes Jones's teaching style as "very strange. . . . He would come off the wall and get really carried away with sex issues and Marxism. He was anticapitalistic." A few students outside the Temple complained about Mr. Jones's "preaching" in class, but Tatum didn't investigate further. Jones was "considered effective," according to the criteria for evaluating teacher performance; there was tremendous interest in his class—attendance grew from twenty-five to nearly ninety in less than two years; his students were punctual, polite, and eager to participate; the district left him alone. Jones's students added to the total number enough to earn a windfall in state aid funds for the adult program, which was just getting off the ground, and the additional funds paid Jimmy's hourly wages and then some.

One of Jim's students, Wanda Kice, knew nothing of Peoples Temple when she enrolled in his history class in 1967. She thought it a little strange that Mr. Jones closed the door and permitted no one to leave after he started his lectures, but all teachers, she figured, have their quirks. She liked what he had to say and she respected his concern for humanity even if he was a bit odd. He lectured a lot about Marxist-socialist theory after the door was closed, and what he said made sense to Wanda. "I had social feelings I did not know what to do with," she says. She was impressed. She was so impressed she decided to attend a service at Peoples Temple. She was screened for three weeks by Jones's staff, then finally allowed inside the church. She looked around and saw familiar faces. Almost everyone from her history class was there.

Jim Jones was quite a teacher with the history class at the adult school, the daytime classes in Boonville, and his regular church services. He told his followers he was sleeping only about five hours a day. The demands of the teaching jobs were interfering with his ministry, he said, and he needed more money if he was going to carry out his plan for mankind. Although he was collecting money with both hands day and night, he had no more than a few dollars cash to his name. He lived a humble life in the service of God. He was not interested in acquiring wealth. His life was so Christlike that, according to an early *Temple Newsletter*,

> Our Pastor wears clothing given to him *used* by people who no longer need it. His two pairs of shoes were both given to him second-hand.

This humble ascetic and his wife had, according to public records in Indianapolis, considerable real estate holdings, despite his public show of austerity. Among them was the Anthony Hall Nursing Home on North Alabama Street, which the couple bought in the early 1960s and transferred ownership to Jim-Lu-Mar in 1965. (Jim-Lu-Mar was an Indiana corporation, for profit, whose officers were Jim, Marceline, and Lynetta.) In 1968, the nursing home's ownership reverted to Jim and Marceline, and there remained until December 1977. They owned at least four other pieces of property, possibly more under their corporations, all in Indianapolis; they let one of the pieces go on the auction block for nonpayment of taxes—$1,098—as late as December 1971, but they held on to everything else. They did sell their property in Redwood Valley—their home and the surrounding acreage—for $27,500, an incredibly good price for the buyer. The buyer was Peoples Temple, and, as corporate president, Jim retained control.

As if Jim Jones weren't busy enough with his two teaching jobs, his church services, and his real estate, superior court judge Robert T. Winslow named him to serve on the county grand jury in 1967. Jones hadn't sought the appointment; it came as something of a surprise. Of thirty names submitted by judges, only nineteen were to be selected. The selection was accomplished by drawing lots, and Jim Jones had no guarantee that his name would be among those chosen; but it was, and Judge Winslow appointed him foreman. Winslow believed, he says, that a minister would provide "balance" to the grand jury. The juvenile justice commission, an advisory group to the courts, must also have needed "balance," because Winslow appointed Jones to that body in 1968. The grand jury got right to work examining the county's various agencies and departments, and its 1967 report is about as controversial as a cake-mix recipe:

> All of the departments of Mendocino County that we examined seemed to be operating smoothly. The county officials appeared to be competent and dedicated and cooperated with us fully in answering our questions and opening their departments for our inspection.

In the course of the grand jury's routine investigations, Jim Jones met several county officials. Among them was Timothy O. Stoen, who had been deputy district attorney since October 1965, a year after he graduated from Stanford University Law School. He had done his undergraduate work at Wheaton College in Wheaton, Illinois, and taken his degree in 1960. Stoen's boss, District Attorney Arthur J. Broaddus, remembers the baby-faced deputy as a "crackerjack prosecutor" who racked up thirteen consecutive convictions despite some inner conflicts "because he was always sympathetic to the underdog."

Stoen quit the DA's office in August 1967 and went to work a month later as the first directing attorney of the Legal Services Foundation of Mendocino County, an organization founded the previous May to assist people who couldn't afford a lawyer in noncriminal matters. One of the seats on the board of the nonprofit foundation had been occupied since July by Marceline Jones; she resigned in August so that her husband could be seated and elected vice-president.

It was also in August that the Legal Services Foundation acquired a rent-free office on West Perkins Street. The place had been used as a storeroom. It had to be completely renovated before it could open its doors. To the rescue came a work crew from Peoples Temple to paint the walls, wash the windows, and scrub the place until it was shining. Jim Jones shared the work with his fellow members; Tim Stoen was quite impressed to find the humble leader busied himself with the odious task of scrubbing the toilet.

If Tim Stoen was impressed with Jones's humility, his former boss, A. J. Broaddus, was not. He was not impressed with Jones's performance as foreman of the grand jury, and he did not trust Jim Jones. None of these feelings, however, were put to the test until the 1968 political campaign. Broaddus was challenging Judge Winslow for Winslow's seat on the bench; there was a third candidate, a Merle Orchard. Lined up on Winslow's side was the pastor from Redwood Valley and his Peoples Temple troops. Jones backed the liberal judge, of course, because of past favors. When Broaddus saw all those organized troops backing Winslow, he stepped up his campaign efforts to counter the deluge of phone calls to registered voters and letters to the *Ukiah Daily Journal* supporting Winslow. It was obvious where the letters were coming from; every one of them mentioned Jim Jones as well as Winslow, and every one of them heaped praise on the Temple's leader. Broaddus recognized the same pattern of self-aggrandizement he had observed when Jones was on the grand jury and the juvenile justice commission. The voters in Mendocino County apparently reached the same conclusion. Winslow came in a distant third, while Broaddus and Orchard faced a runoff in November.

The Reverend Jim Jones had a reputation as a liberal, although county records show he was registered as a Republican throughout his residency in Redwood Valley. He once sent what former county Republican chairman Marge Boynton describes as a "swarm" of Temple members to assist the party in compiling lists of newly registered eighteen-year-olds. Mrs. Boynton says Jones used to call her periodically to express his support of Republican candidates. He was certainly not a Republican in the tradition of conservatism, however; he disliked capitalism, he advocated Marxism, he had few kind words to say about the Republican leaders, and, unlike most of his fellow members of the Republican party, he took a firm stand against the war in Vietnam. He even demonstrated.

On Mother's Day, 1968, the activist pastor led a march against the Vietnam War down State Street in Ukiah, which ended in front of the courthouse. Like peace marches everywhere throughout the country, this one ruffled the feathers of the hawks and stirred patriotic indignation in the hearts of conservatives. Neither Jim Jones nor Peoples Temple sponsored the march and the silent prayer vigil that followed it. Jones said he had agreed to join the march after making a deal with one of the organizers. If the young man would cut his long hair, Jones would cancel his Sunday services and participate in the march. The young man agreed. Jones paid the price of the haircut and showed up as promised, along with several dozen of his two hundred and fifty followers.

Jones's participation in the peace rally earned him a reputation as a "commie" among some circles, namely the Ukiah chapter of the John Birch Society. His long-standing distaste for criticism had him trace the political invective to Walter Heady, a leader of the ultrarightist group, so Jones telephoned Heady to chastise him for the remark. Heady was flabbergasted at Jones's audacity; his phone call had interrupted a Bircher meeting. Heady maintained that raising a clenched fist and singing "We Shall Overcome" at the rally were "commie acts." As soon as the meeting was over, Heady, on his own initiative, grabbed an armful of films and headed for the parsonage in Redwood Valley. The two men debated on Jones's doorstep for about an hour, until Jones invited his adversary inside. They talked, first guardedly, then cordially, until half-past four in the morning. Jones asked Heady to screen his films at the Temple to "show both sides." He invited Heady back for repeat performances for the next nine years, in both Redwood Valley and San Francisco. And for the next nine years, Heady received periodic phone calls "at all hours of the day or night" from Jones requesting political advice.

Whatever the political advice, Jones responded to the community's backlash to his blunders by assuming his familiar posture as wronged martyr, as he had in Indianapolis. His first move—in May 1968—was to buy a half-page ad in the *Ukiah Daily Journal* to answer rumors about Peoples Temple, which even then were rampant throughout the community. The ad, placed by a "private citizen," reads like a political primer on candidate Jones, complete with a compendium of his philosophy and good works. Kathy Hunter of the *Daily Journal* also rose to Jones's defense in an article headlined "Local Group Suffers Terror in the Night" (June 3, 1968). The article recalls Jones's harassment in Indianapolis—with a few embellishments and a new story about his being shot at there—and reports on his recent persecution in Ukiah:

> A telephone rings in the middle of the night, but when it is answered the only sound is someone's breathing on the other end—then the click of a receiver.
>
> Or it rings and, in a measured voice—all the more chilling because of its utter lack of emotion—comes the threat: "Get out of town if you don't want to get blown out of your classroom window." Besides his duties to his parish and his many community services, Jones also teaches in Anderson Valley and Ukiah.

Mrs. Hunter blames the harassment on white supremacists. Jones, she writes, "first puzzled, then embittered and finally fighting mad, blames politics." Linda Dunn, who was in the church office when one threatening call came in, recalls that the voice on the other end of the line sounded "an awful lot like Jim."

Arthur Broaddus—Judge Broaddus now—dealt the final blow to Jones's political career in Mendocino County when he decided not to reappoint Jones to the juvenile justice commission in 1970. Jones realized that he hadn't as much political clout as he had hoped when Judge Winslow lost his seat to Broaddus two years earlier, and he retreated to his church in Redwood Valley and rarely ventured into enemy territory in Ukiah—not even to attend meetings of the juvenile justice commission. Judge Broaddus checked Jones's attendance record and found it wanting. Jones had nowhere to go but out.

When Jones got wind of Broaddus's decision, he phoned the judge in his chambers to suggest—politely, of course—"how disastrous it would be" if he were not reappointed to the commission. "It didn't take much reading between the lines to get the point," the soft-spoken judge recalls. His brother, William, was running for county superintendent of schools; but Jones's few hundred votes in Redwood Valley were hardly persuasive enough to sway the judge. He was not about to reappoint Jones. Jones's heart softened, however, and the

84

Temple gave its "lukewarm" support to William Broaddus's candidacy. William Broaddus lost.

Perhaps Jim Jones's dream of expanding his influence into the political sphere was premature. Perhaps the opportunities to make his first moves appeared before he was ready. He withdrew to Redwood Valley to assess his losses, lick his wounds, and let his strategy emerge, as it had in the past, piecemeal. He had long since sown the seeds for future glory in the hearts and minds of his loyal followers; perhaps all he needed was more time. He would play it by ear this time—literally. Patty Cartmell—his most unquestioningly loyal follower—and her husband, Walter, were hired to manage the Ukiah Answering Service shortly after they arrived in Mendocino County.

A home business located in Redwood Valley, the Ukiah Answering Service was one of the nerve centers of the community, a constant source of confidential information on community crises. Jones had ready information on who was in need of a physician and why, who requested an ambulance, who had urgent messages for whom, who was doing business with whom. Patty was superbly effective in the position; with her photographic memory, Patty had no need to take notes. When she wasn't on duty, others in the Temple took her place: Faith Worley worked there for a while; so did Wanda Kice, Patty Parks, Loretta Cordell, and Donna Cooper, who always suspected "the answering service was a front for gathering information." Both Faith and Wanda remember a police radio crackling away in the office twenty-four hours a day; they were to notify Jim immediately of any calls about the activities of the Temple or its members.

Given his humanitarian bent, though, Jim Jones used the answering service not to exploit confidential information or to thwart law-enforcement efforts, but to learn which families in the community were deserving of cakes on their doorsteps. When people made calls for physicians or ambulances, Jones had their names. He learned of others from accident stories and obituaries in the papers, or from Temple members who worked in local hospitals. Temple women would work into the early morning hours baking cakes in their homes. A committee would pick up the cakes and deliver them to the doorsteps of deserving families—always anonymously, except for the little note on the box that explained the cake was an expression of condolence from Peoples Temple, the Reverend James W. Jones, Pastor. Jones's information sometimes was not as complete and precise as it might have been, however; Supervisor Al Barbero, whose district includes Redwood Valley, received one when he was recuperating from surgery on his esophagus.

These sweet gestures were strictly for the community outside Peoples Temple; for those inside, the offering was growing increasingly bitter. After the disastrous 1968 election campaign Jones kept his members busy thinking not about Ukiah politics but about his old standby bogey, the nuclear holocaust, this time with a new twist: the deadly threat of nuclear fallout, even in Redwood Valley, which was safe from the blast. Southerly winds could carry the poisonous nuclear particles from the Bay Area bombing targets north to Ukiah, but there was hope. Jim Jones had a revelation about a cave near Redwood Valley that was large enough for every man, woman, and child in Peoples Temple. The entrance to the cave was protected from the winds, and after two weeks in the cold and dark, it would be safe to come out—except for the contaminants in the water and the food chain. They had better get ready. The holocaust was coming soon. The revelation of the cave was truly a godsend, for Jim Jones wanted fervently to save his people from the slow but certain death of radioactive poisoning. It mattered little what happened to outsiders, but his own people must have enough food and water in the cave to last until it was safe to emerge. Should anyone fall sick or get injured—as would be inevitable—his people must have adequate medical supplies as well.

There wasn't a moment to lose; the Temple people mobilized a massive drive to collect canned goods and plastic water containers. Other provisions, including medical supplies, were purchased with a special fund Jones established for the holocaust. Toward this fund, members were expected to contribute another 15 percent of their incomes, on top of the 10 percent they were already giving up in tithes. Those who couldn't pay the full amount were to earn their places in the cave by giving more time to the church. There were a few holdouts; Denny Parks, for one, flatly refused to surrender 25 percent of his hard-earned money to support Jim Jones's paranoid fantasy. There were even rumors that there was no cave, that Jim Jones had concocted the story not out of revelation, fear, or paranoia, but simply as another way to fleece his sheep.

If Jones couldn't nip these rumors, he could at least distract his followers, and he did so with periodic "survival drills" in the vineyard next to the church, along the Russian River. Sometimes he would lead the entire congregation on these drills—they had had a little practice while they were still at Christ's Church of the Golden Rule, where there was a lot of open land to run around in—and he would lecture them on how to survive without the benefits of civilization: what plants to eat and to avoid, which snakes are poisonous, how to find water, how to keep warm.

Whitey Freestone's daughter, Theresa, went along on a hiking trip in Oregon; so did Vicky Moore's son, Tom. Everybody was sitting around having dinner under the trees. Jim Jones was talking of the necessity for Peoples Temple members to be prepared to survive the holocaust. Wanda Kice's son, Tommy, about four years old, was sitting next to Jim at the table. Tommy balked at eating his dinner. Jim Jones spanked Tommy and demanded he eat. Tommy started crying; Jones made him eat, anyway, and Tommy stuffed himself until he vomited. That angered Jim. Jim Jones took a spoon and ladled Tommy's vomit back into his mouth; Tommy threw it up again, but Jim Jones was determined. He would make an example of Tommy. He spooned the vomit back into Tommy's mouth six times. Tommy never did succeed in holding it down. A few days later at the Sunday service, Jim Jones told the story in all its gruesome details. When the holocaust comes, he said, and there isn't enough food to go around, people will have to rely on whatever sustenance is available, even vomit.

Holocaust or no, this Spartan training was more than some members had bargained for in a church, and they left. Among those who remained, however, the rumors persisted: there was no cave, it was Jim's imagination, it was an excuse for collecting more money. Jim finally had to prove to his people that the cave was a reality. He took a group of people—Faith Worley was among them—up to the cave in 1969, and they could spread the word to the others that the cave did, in fact, exist. It was a good hike to the top of a hill visible from the highway, up along a dirt road between Redwood Valley and Willits near the Church of the Golden Rule, forty-five minutes of climbing over steep and rugged grazing land to a dome-shaped clay hill. At the summit were three trees—two oaks and a buckeye—and a rusting barbed-wire fence around an oblong sinkhole about the size of a small backyard swimming pool, a noticeable depression among jagged, moss-covered rocks, a pit that narrowed sharply to a passage large enough for one person to crawl into. Faith walked around the cave's narrow entrance and wondered how Jim Jones planned to get the old fat ladies in.

During one of the hikes, Jim Jones climbed down the hole with a rope around him, descended about fifty feet, and hollered to be pulled back up. Another member went down about a hundred and seventy-five feet before he asked to be returned to the surface. He saw, in his descent, one narrow shaft branching to one side, a few feet below the surface. It might accommodate about twenty people, he observed, but the walls around the shaft didn't look very stable. "You could fart in there and the thing would fall apart," he says. On the way down, he checked for other suitable shafts. He didn't see any landings or ledges. He tossed a few stones along the way, but he never heard them hit bottom.

Jim Jones told some tall tales about the cave, but he never mentioned the local lore about it. Back when there was a stage coach stop nearby, old-timers recount, a black man raped a white woman near the spot and vigilantes tossed the rapist down into the cave. It was known thereafter as "the Nigger Hole."

Jones must have thought the cave's capacity was limitless, for he wasn't satisfied with the size of his congregation. He started a campaign of "sheep-stealing" from black churches in San Francisco. His first foray occurred in 1968, shortly after the assassination of Martin Luther King, Jr. After King's death on April 4, there was a void in the leadership of the black community; Jim Jones was ready to step in. He responded to an ad in the San Francisco papers calling for the unity of black and white Christians in the wake of Dr.

King's death. The ad had been placed by the Reverend George L. Bedford, pastor of the Macedonia Missionary Baptist Church at 2135 Sutter Street in the heart of the Fillmore ghetto. Jones took about fifteen of his followers to the Reverend Bedford's service. The fellowship afterward was warm and friendly; Jim Jones asked to return in a couple of weeks.

On his return, Jones was only slightly bolder. He brought a hundred and fifty of his followers with him, and he preached from Bedford's pulpit. "He just came sort of as a lamb," says the Reverend Bedford, "and he preached in his own way. It was very enjoyable." When the Reverend Bedford suggested there be an offering, the Reverend Jones sanctimoniously declined. The two preachers became close in Christian fellowship, and the Reverend Bedford returned Jones's honor by sending eight busloads and several carloads of his own congregation, which numbered more than seven hundred, up to Redwood Valley.

By the time Jim Jones returned to Macedonia Missionary Baptist Church the third time, the black community throughout the nation had absorbed shock after shock. Black ghettoes in all the major cities had erupted in riots and flames in the rage and thirst for vengeance that followed Dr. King's murder. Chicago was so bad that Mayor Richard Daley ordered arsonists shot on sight. In Oakland, Black Panther leader Bobby Hutton was killed in a shoot-out with the Oakland police; Eldridge Cleaver was wounded. Then, in Los Angeles, in June, it all came down: Bobby Kennedy was shot after winning the Democratic primary. RFK had been the last Great White Hope for blacks. He had been revered, almost worshiped, as his brother John had been—and now he, too, was dead.

It was in the atmosphere of this gloom that Jones sent his members down for the third visit. At the services in his Macedonia Missionary Baptist Church, the Reverend Mr. Bedford began to suspect something was not as it appeared to be when he saw some of Jones's people circulating through the audience taking down the names, addresses, and phone numbers of Macedonia's members. Jim Jones preached as before about Dr. King and brotherhood, about his own interracial family in Redwood Valley where black and white lived together in peace, about his humility, his austerity, his dedication to a simple life free of attachments to things material. The "old brown suit" he wore, he said, was the only one he owned. He was just about to finish his sermon, or so Bedford thought, when he started having revelations. He called out members of the Macedonia Missionary Baptist Church and revealed intimate (but never embarrassing) details about their lives. The performance was astounding; the Reverend Dave Garrison, an assistant pastor who had been ordained by the Reverend Bedford, says Jim Jones "was doing things that we read about in the Bible but never saw in action."

The Reverend Bedford was somewhat less astounded. He didn't think much of this "fortune-telling," and he thought less of the so-called healings that followed. For one of them, Jones called out from the audience a woman who had been suffering with migraine headaches for eighteen years. Jim Jones simply snapped his fingers and pronounced the woman healed. The woman jumped up and down; she shook her head to test the cure. No headache. Yes, by God, there was no headache. Then Jim Jones called out the Reverend Garrison and told him some things about his life that he hadn't remembered in years. At that moment, Garrison knew that Jim Jones was a prophet. He listened with absolute credence when Jones told him that a cancer was about to spread from his bowels through his body. He followed with childlike faith when a Temple nurse led him to the bathroom. When the nurse returned a few minutes later with a bloody hunk of meat upon a platter, the rejoicing Reverend Garrison testified that the tumor had been removed from his rectum.

The Reverend Bedford had already agreed to attend one more service at People's Temple, and he was not a man to renege on his promises. He sent another fleet of buses up to Redwood Valley. He assumed the pulpit and began to preach. Jim Jones walked out in the middle of Bedford's sermon. Jim Jones returned and did another healing service. The Reverend Bedford rounded up his flock and shepherded them home.

Bedford paid a heavy price for his association with Jim Jones. He lost a hundred and fifty members from his congregation to the faith healer from Redwood Valley. He even lost his assistant, the Reverend Dave Garrison, because Garrison was convinced that Jim Jones offered the "promise of a long life." The Reverend Bedford heard nothing more of Jones—and just as well, too—until one day one of his followers returned with the story that Jim Jones had preached from his Redwood Valley pulpit that Bedford had tried to seduce two young Temple girls who had stayed at Bedford's home with their parents.

George and Estelle Bedford knew the story was a lie, and refused to dignify it with a response. Sometime after the first of the year, Jim Jones sent the Reverend Garrison with an offer to buy the Reverend Bedford's church and to retire the Reverend Bedford "on a good salary." The answer was no. Mrs. Bedford was discerning enough to observe, "If Jim Jones knows so much, he would know that Macedonia is not for sale." She also reminded the Reverend Garrison that Jim Jones was "not in a position to retire Reverend Bedford because the Holy Spirit is the one to retire a preacher."

Although the new black converts seemed to be impressed with Jones's healing and his belief in the philosophy of Dr. Martin Luther King, they had heard about the end of the world too many times, from too many ghetto preachers, to take the revelation of the holocaust seriously. No matter; Jim Jones had an Armageddon for everyone. If the holocaust didn't get you, the earthquake surely would. Jones claimed to have had a revelation that the coastline of California would plummet into the ocean after breaking off from the rest of the continent, the consequence of a tremendous earthquake, the worst in all history. Jones was not the first to have such a revelation; talk of the imminent catastrophe buzzed through California at the time, partly because of a book by Curt Gentry that expressed the fears of many immigrants to the state, partly because of a prediction by a doomsday geologist.

If the holocaust and the earthquake weren't enough—they would be, after all, gigantic tragedies and no respecters of persons, black or white—there was Title II of the Internal Security Act of 1950. The little-known law gave the president of the United States the authority to set up concentration camps in the event of insurrection; the facilities already existed, in mothballs—the relocation centers used to house the Japanese-Americans during World War II. With all the riots in the ghettoes, Jones said, the pervasive fascist forces at work in America were primed and ready to throw every black man, woman, and child back into slavery in these relocation centers. With Richard Nixon president and Spiro Agnew his vice-president, the black brothers and sisters knew that Jim spoke the truth. They knew what "law and order" meant; its leading evangelist, George Wallace, mounted an impressive campaign for the presidency, and people were taking him seriously.

Peoples Temple provided sanctuary from all the forces of evil that would subjugate the blacks, from the FBI to the Nazis, but to fend them off required constant vigilance. And vigilance required organization, strict and solid, so Jim Jones replaced the church board with a ruling body called the planning commission. Its members were the elite of Peoples Temple, the most trusted and tested, the most devoted and uncompromising, the most white. Its size over the years varied between sixty and a hundred members, all appointed with Jim Jones's approval. Its functions were something more than the name implies. The planning commission planned, all right—things like future needs, growth, costs, revenues, activities, publicity—and also discussed, at its Monday night meetings, power strategies and discipline problems. To be named to the planning commission was an honor unlike any the Temple could bestow.

Although the job of the planning commission was to represent all interests and points of view in the Temple, it was far from democratic. Jones sat in a reclining chair and presided over the meetings, reserving for himself the final word on every issue, large and small. The PC, as it came to be called, was made up of an inner core of Jones's closest aides, a group of counselors who organized on an ad hoc basis, the assistant and associate pastors, officers of the church corporation, and later, the security guards. Many individuals functioned in several of these capacities. Jack Beam, for example, was an assistant pastor, veteran of the Indiana campaigns; he was also, on occasion, a counselor; but most important he led the inner core, along with Carolyn Layton, Jim's most frequent mistress, queen of the harem, deeply in love with Jim Jones, willing to do for this all-too-human son of God anything at all, even procure for him other women to feed his voracious sexual appetites. Jim Jones

90

told the planning commission his "gift" so charged him with energy he had to masturbate thirty times a day.

Often five members of the planning commission formed a "council" when the need arose—thus becoming "counselors"—and went from home to home to give advice and to keep Jim Jones's followers within the fold. The counselors were strict believers in the tenets of apostolic equalitarianism. Head counselor Grace Stoen recalls that beginning in late 1973, Jim Jones ordered all counselors to wear red uniforms so that they could be readily identified in the audience. The counselors were but one of several groups that wore distinctive dress. The security guards had their uniforms. So did the nurses. Even the greeters at the door and the collectors of the offerings had their uniforms. Father could cast his eyes on the assembled multitudes and pick them out immediately—and so could the general members who came to worship. For all of them—the counselors, the security guards, the greeters, and the collectors—the distinctive dress was a badge of honor, a public sign that those so attired were trusted keepers of the faith, loyal to Father and obedient to his rules.

The counselors were extremely attentive to anyone who seemed not to understand the rules. Anyone in the Temple who drank alcoholic beverages or took drugs or expressed doubts or failed to pay tithes was subjected to a mobile Synanon game with the counselors—who usually wore street clothes rather than uniforms when they went to members' homes. Marriage and family problems became a real specialty; the counselors had plenty of experience because the demands of membership in Peoples Temple destroyed nearly every marriage it touched. Marriage, the councils decided, was a form of "ego"; and ego was anything that did not further the cause of apostolic equalitarianism. Romantic love was ego; how could anyone in that state keep Jim Jones first in his heart? Falling in love in Peoples Temple was possible, however, provided the couple first obtained "clearance" from a council. Some couples didn't. Danny Pietila and Robin Wages didn't, and they were disciplined repeatedly. Danny had to drop his pants and shorts in front of the counselors while they mocked him. Jim Jones told Danny he would never again have an erection.

The clearance of the counselors was necessary for nearly everything a Temple member did, and certainly for every major purchase a member hoped to make. Members could not buy a home, a car, furniture, carpeting, or appliances without prior approval of the counselors. Denny Parks once let it be known that he was looking for a good used car; Jack Beam was, at the time, working for a used-car dealer in Ukiah, so he gave Denny a call and invited him down to take a look. "Come down and I'll sell you a good car," Jack told him, and Denny hightailed it down to Jack's place of business. Damned if Jack Beam didn't try to sell him a clunking old four-door Ford with more miles on it than a map of the world.

91

"Jack, I don't want the damned thing," Denny told him, but Jack wouldn't take no for an answer. He insisted the old Ford was a good car. Denny refused again. He told Jack he already had his eye on a Pontiac at another car lot. Jack warned him that he could buy the Ford or he'd have to get approval from the counselors if he wanted to buy the Pontiac. When Denny pointed out that he, not the Temple, would be paying for the car, Jack warned him again: it could be done only if the counselors approved. Denny bought the Pontiac. The Temple left him alone. They left him alone right up to the time he dropped out in 1969.

Denny decided he would rather drink beer and listen to popular music than pay 25 percent of his income to hear Jim Jones's eight-hour sermons. He quit Peoples Temple completely, but his wife, Sandy, got more and more deeply involved, even though Jim Jones never gave her an explanation of why her eight-year-old daughter had to die of hepatitis in November of 1969. She had caught the disease from another Temple member. Jones, of course, blamed the death on everybody except himself and the Temple—it was Denny's fault, it was Denny's mother's fault, it was the fault of anyone on whom blame might be laid. Denny was damned fed up with Jim Jones. His daughter had died at the age of eight in the shadow of this great man of miracles, this Prophet of God who could cure cancer, and when some Temple members stopped by the house after Denny got the bad news from the hospital, he had only one question for them: "Where the shit is his 'power' at?"

Sandy retreated; her mind was "a blank" for two years following her daughter's death. "It was like part of me had died with her," she says. She immersed herself in Peoples Temple because "there was nowhere else to go at that point." When she first joined, she had been put in charge of the holiday parties, Christmas and Halloween. She oversaw the committees that brought the food, made the decorations, kept things running smoothly. She did her job well; everyone looked forward to the Halloween parties, especially Jim Jones. Each year, Jim went to great lengths to devise a costume that would disguise him completely. He even disguised his voice. For Halloween in 1970, he slithered among the crowd in a slippery red outfit with forked tail, moving and whispering like the devil himself. He would walk up to an unsuspecting group, tail in hand, and burst out in grotesque laughter, believing absolutely that not a soul recognized him.

For Christmas, Sandy planned the party weeks in advance. Within the limits of apostolic equalitarianism, Christmas was a festive time at Peoples Temple. There was always an enormous, old-fashioned Christmas tree adorned with decorations Temple children made by hand. Relatives who were not members of Peoples Temple were excluded from the festivities, for the Temple's edict against associating with outsiders was not in the least sentimental; it extended even to Christmas. The children lucky enough to have been born after 1965, the really young ones, of course, received toys for

Christmas, and older children received gifts of cash. The procedure was standardized: each child got twelve dollars from his parents and two dollars each from both sets of grandparents. On Christmas Day, a counselor would call the names of the children one at a time and have them step to the podium for an envelope of cash. As soon as all the children received their money, an offering would be taken while Jim Jones or one of his assistant ministers spoke of the Temple's many programs to help the world's unfortunates. Invariably, a few of the children would drop their envelopes into the collection buckets, and soon peer pressure had the others doing likewise. Older children in the Temple received and exchanged no gifts at Christmas, except possibly on the sly, at home. Even that was risky; any adult caught observing the "capitalist" tradition of gift giving faced certain discipline, and presents from unknowing relatives had to be turned in to the Temple for distribution to the needy.

Among Sandy's responsibilities was organizing the Christmas feast, which in later years fed a couple of thousand people. She was usually quite efficient, and everyone had plenty to eat. Danny Pietila and Robin Wages, however, recall one Christmas Eve when something seemed to go awry. As usual, they were breaking the rules by sitting in back of the church and looking into each other's eyes while they enjoyed the aromas of sauces and pies wafting pleasantly from the kitchen. From where they sat in the back, they could see Jack Beam hurry into the church, then into the office, carrying two big red-and-white cardboard buckets graced with the goateed caricature of Colonel Sanders.

Up at the pulpit, the Reverend Jones was finishing his five-hour Christmas message. "I'm told we don't have enough food," he rasped, then promised that he would "materialize some chicken through the telephone wires. Look toward the back of the church, and you'll see this miracle."

What Danny and Robin saw at the back of the church was Don Beck entering the hall with a large tray of fried chicken resting against his pot belly, then waddling up the aisle past hundreds of cheering believers, who couldn't wait to grab a piece of chicken from Don's tray. As Don passed Danny and Robin, the young lovers observed that the pieces were uniform in size and cooked to a uniform shade of amber, and that they looked finger-lickin' good. Later, they sneaked away from the Temple and had a good laugh about Jim Jones's special Christmas Eve performance. They called it "the Kentucky Fried Miracle."

Like all of Jim Jones's miracles, the Christmas special was more work than magic, and the work was done by people like Sandy Parks. She was exhausted most of the time from her kitchen duties, but her responsibilities did not end there. There was always plenty to do, and Sandy, retreating from the tragedy of her daughter's death, volunteered to do as much as she could in twenty-four hours every day. In 1971, she volunteered to be secretary to Tim Stoen, assistant district attorney for Mendocino County and chief lawyer for Jim

Jones. On Sundays after services, Tim ran a legal clinic whose services were absolutely free to any member of Peoples Temple. Tim kept an office in the church, and whenever he was there, so was his secretary, Sandy.

Shortly after she had volunteered for the secretarial position, Sandy was appointed to the planning commission. Jim Jones wanted her on the PC because she was privy to information known only to Tim, Jim, and a few members of the inner core. Her presence there was important because when Jim was absent from the PC meetings, Tim Stoen would preside, and Sandy was his secretary. Tim also missed an occasional meeting, but he was usually kept informed; there wasn't much going on in the Temple that Tim Stoen didn't know about.

Sandy kept her mouth shut at planning commission meetings and hoped she hadn't broken any rules. The more she saw and heard, the more she was convinced she would never be allowed to leave the group. She hated the disciplinary hearings, when the planning commission heard the unresolved problems referred by the counselors. Each case was scheduled precisely; most cases took about a half hour to settle, and there was always someone ready to help Jim Jones berate a wayward member. When the agenda of regular members was finished—usually about one or two in the morning—the PC would take a penetrating look at itself. PC members were expected to be living examples of apostolic equalitarianism; they always treated one another more harshly than they did the regular members. "You were liable to have anything hurled at you," Sandy recalls. The punishments got so brutal and bizarre that, in May of 1975, Sandy decided to leave the church forever.

Sandy was not the only planning commission member whose disgust overwhelmed fears of leaving. "When [Jim Jones] came into PC," says Wanda Kice, "he showed his true colors, and that's why there are so many defectors from PC who were threatened and beaten." Jim Jones did everything possible to keep planning commission members under his thumb. He employed a wide variety of means, from threats of beatings by Temple heavies to public humiliations that would challenge the imagination of a Marquis de Sade. He began compromising the women on the planning commission in the early 1970s. He and members of his inner core spread the word that to be impregnated by Jim's anointed penis was an honor without equal, a pleasure without peer, and the women who sampled it testified—at Jim's persuasive urging—that the sanctified schlong was all he claimed it was, and then some. There were a few holdouts, however, women who adamantly refused to put the devil into Hell. When Carolyn Layton, Jim's emissary for sexual affairs, approached Linda Dunn, Linda told her, "I'd rather screw a wino."

Equally unappreciative of Jim's holy hoagie were the majority of the men in the church, despite the fact that many of them testified they would feel "honored" and "blessed" if he were to bugger them. Wayne Pietila, Wanda Kice's oldest son, was one of the few men who had the moxie to stand up at a

PC meeting and tell Jim Jones he would never submit to Jones's anal baptism. Jones became angry and shaken at Wayne's defiance; he wanted Wayne under absolute control because of Wayne's substantial responsibilities in the church: Wayne was one of the apostolic guardians, the armed guards who protected Jim Jones from the swarm of attackers he feared; Wayne was one of the drivers of bus number seven, Jim's traveling pleasuredome; Wayne was one of Jim's look-alike decoys, made up to look exactly like Father to fool would-be assassins. (Rose Shelton, who cooked Jim's food and kept his clothes together, dyed Wayne's hair raven black and painted on sideburns so that he could have been mistaken for one of Jones's clones.) In short, Wayne was too close to Father—what with a weapon at his side or a steering wheel in his hands—for Wayne's behavior to be left to Wayne's whims. Father wanted absolute control. Wayne, although he was willing to be a sitting duck for Jim Jones, was not willing to be Jones's punk, even when Jones told him he had to be buggered for his own good. "That was going to be his way of setting me straight," Wayne says, but he chose to tell Jim to shove it elsewhere.

Duties of planning commission members outside the closed commission meetings were not all so distasteful as what went on inside. There were the visits to members' homes, which sometimes could be pleasant, and the routine organizational matters, which were a far cry from the discipline problems. Whatever they did, wherever they went, however, PC members had to be ever vigilant against infiltration. During services, several of them were assigned to the front door to watch for infiltrators. Jim Jones said that the Temple's enemies could walk in the front door, sit through a service, and spy on everybody there. Jim made sure there were always at least five counselors at the door to screen out anyone whose skepticism was too deep or whose politics were too far right. One of the questions asked all strangers was what they thought of socialism.

Jim Jones was paranoid about being secretly tape-recorded. He was paranoid about having his own tapes stolen—tapes of services and PC meetings—by infiltrators. He was paranoid about being found out by the FBI or CIA or Interpol or any one of a number of right-wing enemies, so when he spoke of his own political leanings, he never said directly that he was a Marxian socialist. Rather than utter the damning words, he would point to something red—a red shirt, or a book cover, or a choir robe—and the reference would never appear on a tape. His planning commission members, however, were expected to be more direct in their commitment to Marxism. On February 28, 1971, Jim had them sign a piece of paper with the sentence, "I am a Communist." Linda Sharon Amos was gleeful; to hers, she added, "Hooray! *Forever.*" Patty Cartmell was no less enthusiastic; to hers, she added: "& I am happy I'm a communist & I shall die, live & breath by the Communist motto & live."

Tim and Grace Stoen signed their disloyalty oaths only eight months after they were joined in holy matrimony, June 27, 1970, by Jim Jones in a joyous ceremony at the Temple in Redwood Valley. Tim had left his job with the Legal Services Foundation of Mendocino County in late 1968 to practice law in the Bay Area. In April 1969 he was hired as a staff attorney in the West Oakland office of the Legal Aid Society of Alameda County. He worked there until February of the following year. The office was in the heart of one of Oakland's black ghettos and Tim paid his dues to the poor and assuaged his liberal guilt by accepting a salary of only twelve thousand dollars a year. He even volunteered his services to the Black Panther Party. Clifford Sweet, deputy director when Stoen worked there, recalls that Tim was "an all-American, clean-cut boy." Sweet remembers Stoen "proselytizing" about the Temple, "not like the Hare Krishnas at San Francisco International Airport," but in more subtle ways.

Tim Stoen was a tasteful dresser whose subdued sartorial elegance did not upstage his flashy Porsche when he paid court to young Grace Grech, a San Francisco girl nineteen years old and twelve years Tim's junior. She was head over heels in love with the young attorney. She was impressed with what she saw of his church in Redwood Valley; she had some reservations, however, when Tim decided to commit his life to apostolic equalitarianism. Grace was not completely comfortable with Peoples Temple or with Jim Jones, but she certainly was with Tim. She believed in him implicitly. She followed him to Redwood Valley when he sold his Porsche and accepted what amounted to a promotion in the district attorney's office after a two-year absence from Mendocino County.

The Stoens were bright, articulate, and untiring. Jim Jones appointed them to the planning commission almost immediately. They were an ideal young couple, outside the Temple—charming, witty, easy to like, quick to befriend, truly caring of others—whose exemplary lives offered nothing embarrassing by which Jim Jones could extort loyalty if ever there should be a doubt as to the worth of his cause. Jim Jones summoned his inner core to find something, anything, that would serve as a lever of control, but the mission was fruitless.

On January 25, 1972, at Santa Rosa Memorial Hospital, Tim and Grace Stoen celebrated a blessed event: Grace gave birth to John Victor Stoen—and Jim Jones had his lever. Within ten days after the boy's birth, Jim Jones asked Tim to draft a strange document as a test of loyalty. The document, which Stoen signed "under penalty of perjury," declares:

> I, Timothy Oliver Stoen, hereby acknowledge that in April, 1971, I entreated my beloved pastor, James W. Jones, to sire a child by my wife, Grace Lucy (Grech) Stoen, who had previously, at my insistence, reluctantly but graciously consented thereto. James W. Jones agreed to do so, reluctantly, after I explained that I very much wished to raise a child, but was unable, after extensive attempts, to

sire one myself. My reason for requesting James W. Jones to do this is that I wanted my child to be fathered, if not by me, by the most compassionate, honest and courageous human being the world contains.

The child, John Victor Stoen, was born on January 25, 1972. I am privileged beyond words to have the responsibility for caring for him, and I undertake this task humbly with the steadfast hope that said child will become a devoted follower of Jesus Christ and be instrumental in bringing God's kingdom here on earth, as has been his wonderful natural father.

The statement bears the signature of Marceline Jones as a witness. Tim signed it in the same spirit he signed the "I am a Communist" paper. It was just another test.

If the "evidence" that he had sired Grace Stoen's child were not enough, Jones had another way of tightening his grip on the Stoens: he named Grace head counselor. She was the perfect candidate—sensitive, compassionate, dedicated to the cause of justice: all the other counselors reported to Grace the infractions committed by Temple members, and Grace passed on to Jim the list of those to be called on the carpet. Her role became one of the truly cruel jobs in People's Temple after Jones started the beatings. People feared her—not for who she was, but for what she was willing to do for Jim Jones.

Her position did not exempt Grace from being the object of the planning commission's abuse, as she discovered shortly after John-John—as her son came to be known—was born. She decided she wanted to leave the Temple, to abdicate her responsibilities, to be a loving mother, but the planning commission wouldn't hear of it. Her responsibilities, she was told, far transcended motherhood, and besides, John-John would best be raised collectively. Grace pressed the issue. The PC tore into her without mercy. The child did not belong to her, but to everyone in the church. She was selfish to take the child away from his natural father. "Ego! Ego!" someone shouted, and "Ego! Ego!" came the echo from around the room. They were offended that Grace Stoen would dare to hurt Jim in that way. Jim Jones said he would rather see John-John dead than living under capitalism, and his utterance carried heft because, among other reasons, he was—he claimed— John-John's natural father. Grace again tried to speak for herself; it was a lost cause. "Ego! Ego!" screamed the planning commission members once again. Grace was defeated. All she could do was cry and tremble. Jim Jones would stop at nothing to further his cause.

The cause—apostolic equalitarianism—was synonymous, as the loyal followers all learned by 1972, with Marxian socialism. As early as 1971, it was clear to Gwen Johnson that Peoples Temple was only pretending to be a church. She came out to California with her mother, Georgia, from

Indianapolis that year, when she was fifteen years old, because she felt she needed a change in her life, a warmer feeling toward others, and Peoples Temple, from all she remembered from home, seemed to offer an answer.

"I didn't have very good grades," Gwen recalls. "I was at that age where I was interested in boys and I was never asked out. All through high school I was never asked out, and I couldn't figure out why."

Her introduction to Peoples Temple gave her the warmth she craved. "The kids were real nice," she says. "They'd walk up and talk to me. It didn't bother them what kind of clothes I had on, who I was, or anything." Georgia was opposed to Gwen's joining up with the Reverend Jones in Redwood Valley, but Gwen joined anyway.

Jones's "church" offered not Bible studies but socialist indoctrination. Jim Jones's new "Bible" was Huberman and Sweezy's *Introduction to Socialism*. The authors, Leo Huberman and Paul M. Sweezy, were the editors of the *Monthly Review*, an established and respected socialist journal, and they had persuaded Albert Einstein to write a foreword to the slim volume. The book has been required reading in college-level political science courses; it is neither a hysterical tribute to socialism nor a scholarly Marxist polemic, but a simple, straightforward presentation of socialist principles, with clear explanations, to be sure, but hardly a source of Christian inspiration.

Everyone in the socialism studies group was assigned a section of the book to read each week, Gwen recalls. The group would discuss the passage for a while with the group leader, then move on to chanting. An abbreviated version of the church's Sunday band would warm things up with a spirited beat and soon everyone would be dancing around and chanting, "Socialism! Socialism! Socialism!" After about an hour and a half, the chant would change to "Communism! Communism! Communism!" until the group leader decided it was time to stop.

The evolution of Peoples Temple from church to political movement gave Jim Jones ever greater justifications for vigilance. The fascists, he said, were threatening his life almost daily; unless the Temple set up twenty-four-hour security, the life of everyone in the apostolic brotherhood was in serious danger. Jim Jones had a close brush with death shortly after the church was built in Redwood Valley, according to Denny Parks. A jilted lover blamed Jim Jones for his misfortunes and went after Jim Jones with a knife; there was no doubt in anyone's mind that the assailant meant business.

The assailant—one Bill Bush, a professional hairdresser who had started a business in Ukiah with his partner, Jim Barnes— had had by that time about as much as he could take of Jim Jones and Peoples Temple upsetting his life. He and his common-law wife, Beverly, had moved to Ukiah in 1968 with their son, Billy, Junior. They and Jim Barnes shared a house; Jim and his kids lived upstairs, along with Jim's new friend, Jerry Livingston, a reformed burglar who had joined the Temple; and Bill, Beverly, and Billy lived downstairs. Bill was a man with a social conscience; he devoted much of his free time to cutting and setting hair, even giving free lessons, for the inmates at Mendocino State Hospital in Talmadge. When his busy schedule had him commuting half the week to the Bay Area, he wasn't around to keep track of things around the house. He was the last to know about Beverly and her Temple-member boyfriend, Jerry, a man nine years her junior who was evidently willing to forsake his close friendship with the man upstairs in order to take up with her. Bill moved out and had to be content to see his son on weekends.

It wasn't easy, Bill recalls, because often when he went to pick Billy up, he was told that Billy was at the church. Bill would hop back in his car and drive the few miles from the house in Ukiah to the church in Redwood Valley. On one such occasion, he went to the front door and asked to see his son. Jim Jones emerged from the hall with, according to Bill, "fifty to a hundred people around him, threatening me, menacing guys. . . . They were coming on. I was an intruder."

The mood was ugly. The men exchanged harsh words. "Where is my child?" Bill asked, but Jones didn't answer him. Bill threatened him. Some say Bill flashed a knife that he kept inside his coat; some say he actually pulled the knife and went after Jones. In any case, Don Sly stepped between the two men and prevented mayhem while Jim Jones regained his composure. He was pale and shaking after the incident. Bill went back to the house in Ukiah.

The next morning, Bill was arrested and brought down to police headquarters. There were, according to Bill, "a stack of depositions, of maybe fifty depositions, that they had seen me hurt him, kick him to the ground, maul him, kill him—anything that they could make up. Every deposition was different." The incident was played up as a front-page story in the *Ukiah Daily Journal,* apparently one of the town's more serious crime stories. Jones never pressed charges, and Bill got off with a misdemeanor fine.

After the incident, Jim Jones organized a small security force. Members of the Temple, both men and women, were asked to volunteer their time for around-the-clock guard duty. Guards were posted at the church. Guards were posted at Valley Enterprises, the church publishing company in downtown Ukiah. Vicky Moore was one of the volunteer guards; she patrolled the church properties until dawn with a flashlight. Despite all the paranoia, nothing ever happened while she was on duty, and she was on duty much of the time; as relief security supervisor, she was always the one to fill in whenever one of the others missed a shift. The work was boring. It was lonely. But it was also an opportunity for Vicky to show Jim Jones how humble she had become.

Guard duty gave Vicky a chance to think continually about her growing humility. Had she been left to her own thoughts, not the teachings of Jim Jones, she would have hated every minute standing out in the middle of the cold nowhere of Redwood Valley. She wasn't even interested enough—the duty was so boring—to be scared. She never carried a gun, although other guards did. Denny Parks was not influenced much by the paranoia, either, although he did volunteer for guard duty. The first time he showed up for his shift, he was given the keys to the church and a .38 caliber revolver. He kept the keys; he gave the revolver back.

Along with the new wave of fear, the by-now concrete evidence of persecution, and the presence of guns, came a startling realization among those who knew what was going on. Some members were willing to kill for Jim Jones. Whitey Freestone found out; he figures he came pretty close. One day he let slip a forbidden word during a conversation with a Temple member. He had been discussing a traffic accident a friend had. Bob Gillespie, the Temple member on the other end of the discussion, asked Whitey how it happened.

"Oh, some big nigger hit him," said Whitey. "Smashed him up at the truck stop on North State Street."

Whitey forgot all about his conversation with Bob Gillespie.

Monday at 1:00 A.M. the phone rang at Whitey's place. He and Opal were alseep, and Whitey was only half-conscious when he picked up the receiver. The message was a summons from Jim Jones. Whitey was to come to the Temple immediately, and from the tone of the voice on the phone, it must have been an urgent matter. Whitey was "afraid to go. I'll tell you the truth. I was afraid of what they might do. They beat you up, you see. Crazy. That place is full of 'em—black and white." Whitey decided it was better to show up and see what Jim Jones wanted than to gamble and see what he'd do. He and Opal arrived at the church at about 2:00 A.M. The Sunday service was still in progress. Most of the congregation were hanging on in a stupor of fatigue and boredom, but a few were still alert. Jim Jones was still alert. Whitey was damned sure alert.

"Whitey," said Jim Jones from the pulpit, "I guess you know why you're here."

"No."

"Whitey," said Jim Jones, "Bob said that you called a man a nigger."

"Yeah," said Whitey, "I called a man a nigger."

Whitey saw Jones's forehead, above the sunglasses, wrinkle into a frown. "Whitey," he said, "don't you know that when you called that man a nigger, you called us all niggers? I'm gonna ship you off for Indiana in the morning. You get on that seven o'clock bus."

They would kill for Jim Jones. Whitey bolted down the aisle.

"I'll have the sheriff after you, Whitey," Jones bellowed. Whitey ran out the door.

Whitey ran for miles, all the way to North State Street, turned, headed toward Calpella, running like a frightened deer. Whenever a car's headlights lighted the road, he threw himself to the side of the road and slid down into the ditch, maybe five or six feet deep, and got up and ran again until he saw another set of headlights. Again and again he threw himself into the ditch, through the brambles and the dirt and the gravel, until his clothes were tatters and the skin on his shins and forearms was a mass of scratches and dirt. His breathing hurt. His legs were soft rubber, there was cotton in his mouth, and he wasn't even sure of what he was running from—the Temple guards, the sheriff, the FBI—but he kept running, and he kept turning his head to look for headlights. They would kill for Jim Jones.

When he returned home, Opal told him the Temple people had taken his guns, his kitchen knives—even the scissors. They were afraid Whitey would use them to harm Opal. Bullshit. Opal kept on baking cakes and showing up for Sunday services. Whitey never set foot in Peoples Temple again.

Whitey's fears found sympathetic harmonies in the hearts of other Temple members; by 1972, no one dared speak lightly of conspiracies against Jim Jones. Dozens of people had witnessed the alleged attack at the hands of the maniacal hairdresser; dozens of people had witnessed the attempt to assassinate Jim Jones in the parking lot of the church in Redwood Valley. It was a hot, sticky night, and Jim had stepped outside to get some air during the break between the afternoon and evening services. Suddenly, from the rear of the church property, from down by the Russian River, there came a gunshot. Jim Jones collapsed. He held his stomach; blood gushed from between his fingers. Women and children screamed. Jack Beam rushed to his side and kept the curious crowd away. The fallen prophet lay there lifeless in his bloodstained shirt. A group formed—spontaneously, it seemed—and ran off toward the river to find the assassin.

The voice of reason prevailed; it called to the milling crowd to gather inside the church for silent meditation. The helplessly faithful gathered inside to pray while the few who remained outside witnessed a historical first: Jim Jones healed himself of the gunshot wound. For a few moments, he lay lifeless on the pavement; then, suddenly, he sat upright, as if nothing had happened. "I'm not ready," he said, "I'm not ready." Jim Jones dusted himself off and walked—on his own steam—back to the parsonage, with Jack beside him. A few minutes later, he strode triumphantly into the church, awash in tumultuous welcome. The shirt he wore was clean; the one held up before the congregation was stained with his martyr's blood. "Take this shirt and analyze it," Jim Jones challenged, "and see if it's my blood." No one took it for analysis. The next day, the shirt was placed in a wood-framed glass case—which Archie Ijames built—before the altar so that everyone might see the bullet hole and the blood.

On June 22, 1973, sheriff's deputies responded to a call from the Temple. Four shots had been fired from a passing car. The target was the church building. Deputies scanned the area and found not a single bullet hole in the building or in the trees nearby. They did find paper fragments of a firecracker, and, nearby, a firecracker that had apparently fizzled.

Many of the numerous gunshots heard at the Temple were never reported to the police. Marvin Swinney remembers one; he saw Steve Addison fire a shot into the air out near the parking lot, then quickly put the pistol back in his pocket. There were others. Jim Jones could predict them with amazing accuracy. Denny Parks remembers lending Eva Pugh his .25 caliber automatic. Eva asked to borrow it because, as church treasurer, she often had to carry large amounts of cash. She reassured Denny that she could get a permit for it; all she had to do was "go down and pick it up." The next night, during services, Jim Jones had a revelation that someone would fire a pistol at the Temple. "Here it comes," thought Denny, and within a few minutes, a shot rang through the air, just as predicted. Denny looked around the church; Eva was nowhere in sight. Later, she came up to to Denny to ask him how to unload the pistol.

With all of that gunplay, Jim Jones had no choice but to protect himself and his people by turning the Temple into an armed camp. A neighbor, Mrs. Vera Rupe, who lived two doors down East Road from the Temple, recalls seeing guards at the gate armed with rifles and pistols, only a year or so after the church was built. The glare from the spotlights on the guard tower was so intense that she had to put thick curtains over her bedroom window in order to sleep at night. Then there was the loudspeaker; Jim Jones's voice would come booming out in the middle of the night, proclaiming, "I am God! I am God!" Mrs. Rupe and her husband, Alvin, didn't really give a damn about Jones's theology as long as it didn't disturb their sleep. Alvin went to Jim Jones and complained about the noise, and Jones was effusive and apologetic—of course, he'd turn it down. Alvin neglected to mention the electric gospel band, which amplified its music to ear-shattering levels, and he had to complain again. Again, Jim Jones was conciliatory, and turned the volume way down.

One morning Mrs. Rupe was walking out to get her mail when she noticed guards with rifles and binoculars standing on the roof of the church. The guards watched every move she made. She told Alvin. Again, Alvin was on the phone to Pastor Jones. Again, Jones apologized profusely. Then one day Mrs. Rupe was out in her front yard and she saw a man mowing the lawn in front of the Temple; he had a submachine gun strapped to his back. Alvin Rupe marched immediately over to the parsonage, knocked on the door, and advised Jim Jones he was breaking the law by having such a weapon on his property. Alvin's complaints about the weapons were frequent and unrelenting, until finally the guards started carrying their weapons in tackle boxes.

The Rupes were not the only people in Redwood Valley who were upset by this new church that looked like a border checkpoint in East Berlin. Al Barbero, who was a county supervisor then, remembers getting several calls from his constituents expressing their concerns about Peoples Temple. They wanted to know why the Temple was arming itself. They wanted to know what might happen if some unknowing person wandered on to the church property. To someone driving past the Temple on East Road and seeing nearly two thousand people of all races bristling with paranoia, the spectacle was eerie and formidable.

The police could do nothing about the armed camp because the weapons were not concealed. As long as the guns were visible and were not pointed at anyone, as long as they were confined to private property, the Temple had every right to arm itself; Jim Jones was entitled to the same freedoms under the Bill of Rights that other citizens enjoy, under that same Bill of Rights that guarantees freedom of religion and the right to assemble. Perhaps there was not too much to fear as long as the weapons were visible; but the people of Redwood Valley had no way of knowing that Sheriff Bartolomei had, between September 1972 and May 1974, issued concealed-weapon permits to Jack Beam, Tim Stoen, Marvin Swinney, Wayne Pietila, Harold Cordell, and Sandy Bradshaw—all ranking members of the Temple hierarchy.

Naturally, this Christian church's unorthodox style engendered rumors. One rumor was that Jim Jones was going to buy up everything in Redwood Valley.

Another rumor—more sinister than the first—was that the Temple was holding mock suicide drills. Mrs. Rupe heard that rumor. A California Highway Patrol officer, Mitchell Gibberson, heard that Jim Jones had everyone in the Temple drink a sweet liquid that he told them later was deadly poison; after several minutes had passed, and the "poison" had no effect, Jones admitted that it was only a test. Temple members confirm, though, that as early as 1972 there was talk of dying for the cause of socialism. There were mock drills limited to members of the planning commission. Each PC member was asked to write a statement that began, "I committed suicide because . . ." Vicky Moore signed her suicide note when Jim Jones appointed her to the planning commission in 1973. She didn't take it seriously because she couldn't imagine how it might be used against her; it was probably just another test.

Jack Beam had said many times that he would die for Jim Jones. So had Patty Cartmell. By the summer of 1973, Jim Jones wanted everyone to be willing to die for him. He even set into motion a plan for such an event that very summer. It was a warm, starry night—actually, a Tuesday morning at about four o'clock—and the planning commission had just broken up their meeting at Cleave Swinney's ranch outside Redwood Valley. The people were walking in small groups down the long dirt road from the house to the parking area. Jim Jones was followed by Faith Worley, close by as usual with her oxygen tank and first-aid kit for the master, and by the usual crowd of loyal followers of the PC and the inner core. He was holding forth on the glory of committing suicide for the cause of socialism. Who among his most trusted followers, he wondered, would die for him?

Jim Jones asked Faith—she was the nurse in the group—what drugs could be used successfully in a mass suicide. Faith told him an overdose of almost anything—perhaps tranquilizers—would work. Jim was not satisfied; he wanted something else. Faith knew only of chemicals that had a medical use, but another member suggested chemicals from a pesticide company. Good, thought Jim. "How about cyanide?" he asked. "That's what the Germans used."

After that, Jim Jones talked of mass suicide for several months. Grace Stoen remembers being at a planning commission meeting sometime in September of 1973 and hearing Jim say, "We aren't getting anywhere and the best thing we can do is to commit mass suicide, but I will have to stay alive to explain to everybody why we did it." Jack Beam objected to the idea, but Jim persisted. A few weeks later, Jim was able to announce to the planning commission that one of his most loyal followers—Patricia Cartmell, the high-school-age daughter of Patty Cartmell—had set the example. She was ready to die for the cause of socialism. She demonstrated her conviction by carrying with her, at all times, a cyanide capsule.

Life is a gamble and I'd damn well rather gamble on the side of communism. . . . I don't see that capitalism is the way to live. I look at what Castro has done, and I think that he has done tremendous things. I wish I'd had his circumstances, being on an island, fighting a real battle, and winning a revolution, and had the challenge of building a society, a nice society. But some of us are not born with that opportunity.

—from the transcript of an interview
with Jim Jones, found in Jonestown
and published in the *Guyana Chronicle*
December 6, 1978.

IV

Father's Dominion

"There is but one sun in the sky," declares an ancient Buddhist scripture. The followers of Father Divine knew there is but one God on this planet manifest in the flesh, yet Jim Jones tried several times to inherit the paunchy deity's diadem. George Baker became Father Divine (God) in 1919, and thereafter was known affectionately as Father throughout his long incarnation on Earth. His followers marked his every deed with magnificats and hosannas that might have embarrassed a lesser man—"Praise Father!" and "Thank you, Father!"—and the adulation was sweet, so sweet that Jim Jones wanted some for himself. Although young Jimmy made efforts to taste that sweetness as early as 1958, he had a long wait—thirteen years—before he dared promote himself, in 1971, from the Prophet of God to Father.

Jim Jones spoke before Father Divine and the Elders in 1958, beseeching them to name him heir apparent. He tried again in 1959. Each time, his humble pleading was met with equally humble answers: No, no, never. Jones thought he may have had a better chance after Father Divine had cast off his mortal coil in 1965, much to the surprise of his followers, and Jim Jones made his plea directly to Mother Divine, Father Divine's blond, blue-eyed widow, who was then in her late thirties. According to Dorothy Darling, Father Divine's longtime secretary, Jim Jones offered Mother Divine his home in Redwood Valley as a refuge from the holocaust. Jones's offer was, again, humbly declined.

Never daunted, Jim Jones showed up in July of 1971—this time with two hundred and sixty Peoples Temple members in buses—at the Divine organization's Woodmont Estate in Philadelphia. Jones treated the Divinites to a spirited sermon replete with criticisms of government policies. His followers moved among the Divine believers to spread the gospel that Jim Jones had inherited their deceased leader's mantle as God on Earth, documenting their claims with tales of healings and miracles to surpass human understanding, while the Divinites listened politely. Then, without warning, Mother Divine and the Elders rustled out of the room like a covey of startled quail. Jones was flabbergasted. Moments later he was asked to leave.

One does not blaspheme the Prophet of God. Jones declared war on the Father Divine Peace Mission only four months after the expulsion. Armed with pens and typewriters and reams of paper, Peoples Temple members sat down to their tables and fired off a salvo of letters, each a personal invitation to a follower of Father Divine to join Peoples Temple and to share in the blessings and the glory that only followers of the Reverend Jones enjoyed. Furthermore, each letter noted, there would be Peoples Temple buses in Harlem and Philadelphia, on designated days that month, to provide free transportation to California for all who wished to recognize their new Father. The invitations were followed with leaflets bearing a message like that of the letters, handed out in the ghetto streets, while Peoples Temple buses cruised the neighborhoods with loudspeakers blaring. Grace Stoen was one of those whose voice was heard around the Divine Mission,

> . . . I was really good, too. . . . We went around to the Divine Mission from one of their churches or their hotels and gave a speech saying, "If you want to go, the buses will be leaving at such-and-such a time," and talking about Jim Jones's work and stuff like that.

The assault was effective; when Peoples Temple left Philadelphia, there were fifteen former Divinites on the Temple's diesel-powered Glory Train to Redwood Valley.

Mother Divine would not be moved. Jim Jones would not be denied. On the next summer trip, in July of 1972, he tried once more to win her over in a visit that was all too brief. Jones had his buses park in front of Heaven in Philadelphia while he went inside to enjoy a private audience with the renowned Mother. Minutes later, he emerged pale and shaking, ordered his drivers to get the fleet rolling, and admitted to his followers that Mother Divine had succumbed to the weakness of the flesh and made amorous advances on him. He, being pure of heart, felt compelled to leave without a further word.

Mother Divine immediately issued an edict that begins with a prayer to her late husband, who "with or without a Body . . . remains the same and is at all times present":

> I thank YOU that YOU have taught us how to entertain strangers lest we entertain angels unawares. We have entertained Pastor Jones and the Peoples Temple. We were entertaining angels of the "other fellow"! We no longer extend to them any hospitality whatsoever! Not a one of them is welcome in any Church under the Jurisdiction of the Peace Mission Movement, here, or in any other country! They are not welcome in any of our public Hotels, they are not welcome in any of our public Dining Rooms. They are not welcome!

Although the gates of Heaven were forever closed to Jim Jones, he did manage to make off with a few of the pearls. He had made enough visits to

Father Divine's institutions to have learned a few lessons about empire building. Like Father Divine, Jim Jones aimed his message toward black people in the inner city; Father Divine did it in Harlem and Philadelphia, Pastor Jim did it in San Francisco and Los Angeles. Like Father Divine, Jim Jones fed the hungry multitudes; Father Divine did it at the banquets that accompanied his services, Pastor Jim did it in his various free restaurants. Like Father Divine, Jim Jones had his followers live communally; Father Divine had his Heavens and Extension Heavens, Pastor Jim had his communes.

There were other similarities. Both Jones and his guru denounced capitalism and proceeded to build financial empires that grossed millions of dollars. Both demanded of their followers a "one-hundred-percent commitment," which translated as surrendering to their respective churches all savings, cash, property, valuable jewelry, automobiles, quality suits, shoes, and whatever else could be turned to a profit. For neither of them, though, was the wealth acquired for personal gain—at least not in any way that could be traced. Father Divine's enterprises were many and varied: from apartment houses to restaurants, from armies of men bearing shoeshine boxes (all bearing the word *Peace!*) to chains of grocery stores, barbershops, laundries, huckster wagons and coal trucks, all owned and operated not by Father Divine himself but by his Angels and his Children, to whom he entrusted every enterprise in his remarkably successful empire. On paper, Father Divine was penniless. Once, one of Father Divine's Peace Mission buses was involved in an accident. An attorney tried to collect, on a civil judgment. Father Divine claimed he owned no buses or anything else. The attorney inquired. Father Divine (God) didn't even have a bank account.

Father Divine's example was not lost on Jim Jones. The bulk of Jones's empire was in the name of Peoples Temple of the Disciples of Christ, a California nonprofit corporation with James Warren Jones as president. As president, James Warren Jones had twice as many votes as the others on the nine-member board. Although for tax purposes and legal matters a corporation is an entity distinct from any individual, under the circumstances it would have been hard to distinguish Peoples Temple of the Disciples of Christ from one of Jim Jones's grasping appendages. Like his pauper mentor, Jim Jones was nearly penniless, and, like his pauper mentor, his authority was absolute.

Despite the numerous similarities with Father Divine's operation, Jim Jones's Peoples Temple was no carbon copy. There were significant differences. Father Divine's empire was a well-diversified conglomerate; Jim Jones's main business was care homes whose main source of revenue was public money—social security, disability, or foster-care payments. Jim and Marceline Jones were well versed in the business, having owned and operated two twenty-one-bed nursing homes in Indianapolis until they moved to Redwood Valley. Jim and Marceline had helped Archie and Rosabell Ijames set up one of the first Temple-affiliated rest homes in Mendocino County in August of 1966. It was among more than a dozen such homes owned and operated by Temple members in the Ukiah area between 1966 and 1977. Most of the homes were the next-to-last resting places for elderly persons, but a few housed emotionally disturbed children and adults, and the disabled.

On paper, Peoples Temple owned only two of the homes. The others were tied into Jones's empire, however, by hidden cords. Nathaniel and Maxine Swaney, for example, leased a rest home on East Road for five hundred dollars a month in August of 1972 and agreed to assume all responsibility for business expenses, maintenance, and repairs. Above the Swaneys' signatures on the ten-year lease is that of the lessor: one Timothy O. Stoen, identified as the Temple's "chairman of the board." Those care homes that were not owned directly by the Temple were tied in by unrecorded deeds, usually left unfiled for years after they were executed; of course, if the member whose name was on the deed left the fold—no easy task—the deed was filed posthaste.

In addition to the deeds, Jones's grip on his people was tightened through other documents, documents giving the Temple power of attorney and documents stating that the signer was a Communist or a child molester or a party to an assassination plot. No "owner" of a piece of property dared abscond with what was rightfully Father's. Property owned by Temple members was property owned by the Temple itself. Asserting rights of ownership was too risky. There were not many—if any—members of Peoples Temple who could withstand the unrelenting barrage of guilt associated with owning something.

Jim Jones used guilt to persuade people to volunteer their time in service to the elderly by working in Temple-affiliated rest homes. The free help kept overhead costs to a minimum, and low overhead meant high profits for the operators of the homes, and operators contributed to the Temple—at the very least—25 percent of their incomes. Some of the operators turned over every dime.

Elderly residents of Temple care homes had three sources of funding for their room, board, and care: social security, railroad pension, or Old Age Assistance, a state-funded program subsidized by the federal government. Under Old Age Assistance, each recipient receives a grant that covers the cost of care and allows for a margin of profit for the operator. The system was perfectly suited to Jones's empire, which flourished on the tithes of taxpayers. It flourished even further after April 21, 1969, when the Supreme Court of the United States ruled that residency could no longer be required to determine eligibility for welfare payments. The case was *Shapiro* v. *Thompson;* it involved a nineteen-year-old unwed mother who had been denied welfare benefits, and the Court's ruling was a landmark decision based in part on the constitutional guarantee of the right of travel without restriction. The ruling also opened a new scam for Jim Jones: government-supported "sheep-stealing."

Father Divine's flock were not the only sheep Jim Jones baited. Beginning in

1971, Jones initiated long bus trips to spread his gospel. On each of the trips, the Temple would gather converts along the way, many of them old black women who were living on Social Security. Two Temple bus drivers, Marvin Swinney and Harold Cordell, remember loading the feeble old women on the buses to take them to Redwood Valley, where, Jones promised them, they would lead a long and happy life. They suffered the illnesses of old age, most often heart disease, and they required constant medication, but they had become believers: they had seen cancers passed; they had seen the lame made to walk; they had seen cataracts wiped away. They were absolutely convinced Jim Jones had a gift—especially the believers who themselves had passed cancers through their rectums or had spit them up—and they knew that if they had been healed once, they could be healed again. Once the elderly arrived in Mendocino County, they were housed in Temple care homes, taken down to the welfare office in Ukiah and signed up, and placed on government assistance usually by the first working day after the buses arrived.

The bus trips could have been a hint of the arduous life in the Temple, for not all the old ladies survived. One old woman died on a bus trip coming back from the East Coast, recalls Marvin Swinney. The story was that the woman died in the hospital, but Marvin knows she died on the bus. Her death was never discussed. Deaths were not discussed in Peoples Temple. There were no funerals. People just disappeared.

Father Divine held no funerals, either. Undertakers, doctors, pharmacists—all were unnecessary, he said, because none of his followers ever became seriously ill, none of them ever died in Heaven or in any of its Extensions. Whenever it appeared that death was imminent, the sick Divinite would be carted away to a nearby flat that had no connection with the Divine Peace Mission, then to a hospital where he or she became a ward of the county, listing the address of the flat as the last residence. The county paid burial expenses.

Peoples Temple had a similar approach for dealing with its senile and terminally ill members. They were taken, one at a time, to Fair Oaks Convalescent Hospital in Pasadena, a Temple-affiliated ninety-nine-bed facility licensed to Willie D. and Clevyee Sneed. According to state officials, Fair Oaks was cited repeatedly for "poor care of elderly patients," and its Medicare and Medi-Cal certifications were revoked for a while. The state department of health started proceedings to revoke the Sneeds' license in late 1976, but the Sneeds decided to retire in Jonestown, Guyana.

Birdie nearly lost one of her charges to Fair Oaks. She had in her rest home an elderly gentleman named Harvey Lawson. Harvey was in his mid-eighties and was beginning to show signs of senility; he liked to take walks around town and talk to anyone who would listen about space ships, flying saucers, and Jim Jones. Word of these strange conversations got back to Jim Jones and he ordered Harvey transferred to Fair Oaks immediately. Jim sent two members over to pick up Harvey, but Harvey wasn't sure where the Temple wanted to take him, so he refused to cooperate. The two members left Birdie's rest home empty-handed. Once Harvey had a chance to think about it for a little while, he changed his mind; he figured anywhere Jim Jones wanted him to go was all right with him, so he told Birdie he wanted to go. She passed the word back to Jim. Jim would send some people over to pick Harvey up at a designated time and take him to Pasadena, he said.

Harvey waited for hours. No one showed up. The old man went to bed for the night. Then, around eleven o'clock, Birdie's phone rang. It was Tim Carter saying he'd be by right away, and Birdie told him that Harvey was already asleep. "Well, wake him up," said Carter, "because Jim wants us to bring him. Jim wants us to bring him dead or alive."

Within a few minutes Tim Carter and Lew Jones were at the front door. They went straight to Harvey's room, Birdie recalls, and tied up the old man's hands and feet while he caused a terrible commotion, kicking and shouting and carrying on until Carter said he would have to give Harvey some medication. Harvey had just taken some and Birdie was afraid that more might kill him, so she called Marceline. "They gonna kill him," Birdie pleaded. "He's already had his medicine." Marceline just repeated what Carter said: that Jim Jones wanted Harvey picked up "dead or alive." Tim Carter stuffed Harvey's mouth with cotton, Birdie claims, and he and Lew Jones carried the old man out to the car.

Birdie went down to the welfare department and told the social worker who had licensed her home about the incident. The social worker notified the county welfare director, Dennis Denny, who traced Harvey to Fair Oaks. Denny got on the phone and talked to someone at Fair Oaks who said abductions "happen all the time." Denny called Jim Jones on Friday and demanded that Harvey be returned to Mendocino County by eight o'clock Monday morning. Peoples Temple flew Harvey up from Pasadena to a rest home in Willits well before the deadline, and because Jones complied, the welfare department filed no kidnapping charges. The following week, Denny's desk was covered with a pile of letters from the Temple chiding him for his "inhumanity" and his "lack of understanding of the aged." Some of the letters suggested he resign.

As welfare director in Mendocino County, Dennis Denny had a sizable job just licensing care homes. Thanks to Peoples Temple, Mendocino County had more care-home beds per capita than any other county in California. As welfare director, Dennis Denny was aware that a large number of the county's care homes were affiliated with Peoples Temple, just as he was aware that Temple members were working in his office. Carrie Minkler, now retired, was a social worker in the Mendocino County Welfare Department. She was not one of the Temple people, however. She remembers the climate of fear in the office while the Temple members were working there. "You didn't open your mouth," she says. "You didn't mention the Peoples Temple in our department. Even the walls had ears. There wasn't anything that went on in our office that Jim Jones didn't know the next day. . . . Peoples Temple workers went through other workers' case files. The CIA could have used them. The atmosphere was really tense."

Among Mrs. Minkler's duties was overseeing the inspection and licensing of foster homes in the county. According to her, Dennis Denny licensed "no more than eight or ten" Temple-affiliated foster homes. The rest—more than twenty—were classified as "illegal." The Temple needed several more foster homes than it could have licensed, for, beginning in 1971, Jim Jones started breaking up families and the children from those families had to have some place to live. Vicky Moore recalls that Jim Jones "encouraged you to have your children live at other homes" as a way of helping them achieve "maturity." Vicky placed her son, Tommy, in Temple hands, and he lived in various homes over the years—Jack Beam's and Joyce Touchette's, among others. Each child was given eight dollars a month for spending money; Tommy says the money had to be spent at the Temple.

Those foster homes that were not licensed just came into existence on an ad hoc basis; they appeared as they were needed. Under California law, any home that houses children other than siblings must be licensed as a foster home. Any home that houses children not of the family and is not licensed is illegal. The Temple got away with this illegality because, for the most part, the children living in its unlicensed homes were not on the welfare rolls. Mrs. Minkler pieced together the pattern of unlicensed homes from various sources—a tip from a neighbor, from a school nurse, or from a teacher who had called to inquire about a certain student who was showing up at school with insufficient sleep or without warm clothing for the winter. Typically, a teacher would assume that the unfortunate child was on AFDC—Aid to Families with Dependent Children—and have a social worker check the files. When nothing turned up, the worker would check the child's address in the school's records. When social workers turned up unexpectedly at a child's home, they would find up to a dozen children living in a Temple commune. The welfare department would send two warnings before threatening court action through the district attorney's office, and the Temple attorneys would respond with a threat to file suit against the welfare department for "harassment." While the matter languished in the bureaucratic limbo, the Temple would move the children to another illegal home.

Mrs. Minkler referred the illegal homes time and time again to Dennis Denny, who sent the two warning letters and the third letter threatening court action. Although Denny never once filed a complaint with District Attorney Duncan James, his threats of legal action caused enough consternation for Temple attorneys Eugene Chaikin and Tim Stoen to devise a legal way of circumventing the foster-home laws. Instead of playing the game of musical homes, the Temple filed guardianships for its itinerant wards. Guardianships normally are approved as a matter of course—all that's needed are a parent's signature and the approval of a superior court judge—and, for the Temple's purposes, there are several advantages: homes that house children under guardianships do not have to be licensed as foster homes, and the guardians are eligible for welfare and Social Security payments to cover the children's living expenses.

There was a flurry of Temple guardianships filed between late 1970 and August 1977; the guardianship of Julie Ann Runnels follows a tragic pattern. Court records in Mendocino County show that Julie Ann Runnels, born September 13, 1966, was placed under guardianship on March 23, 1973, to a Diane Patricia Fischer of Redwood Valley. The papers were filed by Eugene Chaikin. The reason for the guardianship, the records show, was that the child's natural mother was ill. Julie Ann Runnels received a hundred and ten dollars per month from Mendocino County's welfare funds between May of 1973 and April of 1974. Julie doesn't show up again on court records until August 22, 1977, when she was placed in the guardianship of Paulett Jackson. Shortly thereafter, Paulett and Julie moved to Jonestown, Guyana, where they lived for nearly fifteen months, until November 18, 1978.

The Temple's foster-care hustle resulted in noticeable demographic changes in Ukiah and Redwood Valley: there was a huge influx of children to the two small towns, mostly from San Francisco and Los Angeles. Some of them came from Contra Costa County, where Guy B. Young did double duty as a probation officer and an assistant minister of Peoples Temple. Earlier, Young had worked as a probation officer in Mendocino County. He was one of several Temple contacts in government who placed children in Temple homes. Once the children were placed, they became immediately eligible for welfare payments. Like the old-age care homes, the foster homes surrendered most of their money directly to People's Temple after expenses were met.

According to Ruby Bogner, who taught fifth grade at Redwood Valley School from 1965 to 1975, most of the Temple's charges were "hard-core ghetto kids." The tiny school, she says, was "not equipped to handle" these street-wise urchins. They spoke an urban dialect the locals didn't understand; they kept to themselves probably as much by choice as by fear of the trouble they might suffer if they displeased the Prophet of God by mingling. Mrs. Bogner complained repeatedly to school officials that children from the Temple kept falling asleep in class, and she got results—surprising results.

"Parents came by committee," Mrs. Bogner recalls, all wearing sunglasses. The dark-glasses ploy didn't work; Mrs. Bogner was not about to be intimidated by a motley bunch of inscrutable faces hiding behind tinted glass, and she told them so. She told them her only concern was the welfare of the children in her class. She told them children shouldn't be kept up so late they can't function the next day. She never backed down from her admonitions to the parents, and she continued to complain about the treatment of Temple children, and all the while she taught at Redwood Valley School, Mrs. Bogner received telephone threats on her property, her job, and her life.

By 1972, Peoples Temple was reaping a sizable harvest of dollars from payments for the homeless, the mentally ill, the retarded, and the elderly. Jim Jones knew instinctively how to build an empire. From his Mother Church in Redwood Valley he launched two successful satellites: one in San Francisco at Fillmore and Geary, the other in Los Angeles at Hoover and South Alvarado. The San Francisco building had been built as a Scottish Rite temple in 1902. In 1964, the Henry Marshall Foundation purchased the building and used it, until 1972, as a center for the WAY (Western Addition Youth) Club. Peoples Temple acquired the building at 1859 Geary, in the core of the black ghetto, for $122,500.

The brick structure in Los Angeles was truly majestic, a blending of Middle Eastern and Roman styles. For this palace, the Temple paid the Christian Science Church $124,700, which included the palm trees lining the sidewalk. The building sat in a predominantly Chicano neighborhood, but for a faith-healing, socialist, hard-times evangelist, it was definitely a move uptown.

Jim Jones discovered the edifice on one of the many trips to Los Angeles when he went down to preach at the Embassy Auditorium on Ninth and Grand. Sally Stapleton was on one of the trips to the Embassy Auditorium; she rode Jones's bus, number seven. She overheard him boasting to his staff about how well he was going to do in Los Angeles. "Those suckers in LA," he said. "All you have to do is tell them, 'This is a ten-dollar blessing,' 'This is a twenty-dollar blessing,' or 'This is a hundred-dollar blessing,' and they will fall in line and give it to me. We gonna clean those suckers out!"

Los Angeles had strange effects on Father. On December 13, 1973, he sneaked away from the Los Angeles Temple and walked six blocks up South Alvarado Street to a matinee showing of *Jesus Christ Superstar* at the Westlake Theater, across from MacArthur Park. Father left his clerical garb at the Temple; it would not have been appropriate during an upbeat musical extravaganza on the life of Christ. He walked up to the ticket booth nattily dressed in a green coat, black pants, and a red-and-blue striped shirt.

Father sat in the balcony to watch the movie. Shortly before 4:00 P.M., Father walked down to the rest room to relieve himself. He had to pee fairly often owing to an inflammation of the prostate gland. His urologist, Dr. Alex L. Finkle of San Francisco, described Father's prostate condition as chronic, necessitating the consumption of large quantities of water to avoid prostatic surgery. While Father was emptying his bladder, an undercover vice officer with the Los Angeles Police Department, A. L. Kagele, was at the sink washing his hands. Kagele had been summoned to the movie house to investigate a lewd conduct charge (not involving Jones; the theater was a busy place) and the bathroom was the logical place to start.

114

Officer Kagele left the bathroom and went up to the balcony to check for lewd activity. Kagele was standing at the top of the stairs when he caught Jones's attention.

> . . . Officer observed the defendant sitting near the back of the balcony and [he] appeared to wave to officer to come up. Officer sat down for a few minutes, then got up to check the activity in the rest room. Officer entered the rest room, and within a minute officer heard the rest room door open and observed the defendant . . . go to the same toilet. Officer observed the defendant's right arm moving, and at this time the defendant turned to officer. Officer observed the defendant's penis to be erect and the defendant, with his right hand, was masturbating and showing his penis to officer. The defendant then walked toward officer with his erect penis in his hand. Officer exited the rest room and signaled his partner of the violation.

Officer Kagele and his partner, Officer Lloyd Frost, placed Father under arrest at 4:00 P.M. and took him to the Rampart police station, where he was booked—as James Warren Jones, age forty-two, of Indian descent—on lewd conduct charges. He was later released on five hundred dollars' bail and ordered to appear in court on December 20.

If the Prophet of God had gone to trial for his alleged indiscretions during the rock-opera on the life of Jesus, he would have faced the prospect, if convicted, of having to register as a sex offender. Sandy Parks, Tim Stoen's secretary when he was doing legal work for the Temple, was in on the discussions after Father was busted. "Tim Stoen got him off of that," recalls Sandy, "Tim Stoen went to bat for him."

Stoen went to work immediately. He contacted officials in the state attorney general's office and the LAPD. The officials listened to Stoen's arguments for quashing the criminal complaint because he introduced himself as the assistant district attorney of Mendocino County. The day after Jones was arrested, his urologist, Dr. Finkle, sent a letter to Jones's attorney, David W. Kwan, objecting to "the preposterous allegations against Reverend Jones!" Although Finkle didn't say so directly, he implies that what Jones was actually doing in the bathroom was trying to pee: "Even prior to seeing me, Reverend Jones had learned that jogging or jumping in place afforded improved initiation of urination." Officer Kagele disputes Dr. Finkle's inference, claiming that Jones was "nowhere near a urinal," and was definitely masturbating.

On December 20, 1973, Municipal Court Judge Clarence A. Stromwall granted a motion by the city attorney's office to dismiss, "in the furtherance of justice," the case of the *People of the State of California* v. *James Warren Jones.* Along with the dismissal, the judge rubber-stamped the docket: "Defendant stipulates as to probable cause"—that is, Jones agreed through his attorney that there was reason to presume that he did commit a lewd act in public. Six weeks later, Judge Stromwall amended the court record to read, "No evidence of violation based on documents provided to city attorney. No stipulation to probable cause. Record ordered sealed and destroyed." Jones's record was wiped clean.

Los Angeles had a lasting effect on Jim Jones's style. He still wore his old brown suit, but now it was usually hidden under one of the choir robes he had asked members to bring from their former churches. He added other suits to his wardrobe and upgraded his dark glasses to a more fashionable style. When his hair started showing signs of gray, Rheaviana Beam dyed it for him so it was always a uniform black, in keeping with his prophecy that when Jesus returned, his hair would be black as a raven. Jim Jones changed not only his wardrobe and his dark glasses and the color of his hair; he took pains also to assure that it was styled properly. Before 1972, an unruly forelock dangled over his brow, but as he swung into the 1970s he had his hair shaped and styled, and by the latter part of the decade Jim Jones was always well tailored, well coordinated, and slick. He looked the part of the salesman par excellence, and indeed he was.

He traveled with an entourage of bodyguards, attorneys, secret aides, nurses, road managers, singers, dancers, mistresses, money counters, and cosmetic doubles. Harold Cordell was one of the cosmetic doubles. He had put in years of duty as one of Jones's road managers, bus drivers, and aides-de-camp, and he became one of several loyal men who were tapped, at a moment's notice, to be made up to look like Father. The masquerade was calculated to thwart any would-be assassins, for Jim Jones was convinced it was only a matter of time before his enemies—the Nazis, the Klan, the FBI, the CIA, some obscure right-wing terrorist group—would make their move to kill him. Father's doubles considered it an honor to die in his place.

Harold Cordell worked also as the sound man for the traveling road show. He set up the mikes for the choir, the band, and for the Prophet of God himself, who liked to roam through the audience, guards in tow, and never be hindered for lack of enough microphone cord. The seemingly endless cord was in itself a miracle to the unsophisticated hordes. As he moved through his audiences like the host of a television game show, down the aisles and into the balconies, Jim often made reference to "stretching" the cord, and many folks believed him. "The cord kept getting longer and longer and longer," Gwen Johnson recalls. "He went all over that Temple, and there was no end to that cord." In truth, Cordell had provided about a hundred and fifty feet of cord and would draft a couple of boys before the service to reel the cord in and out as Father moved. Harold Cordell supervised all the sound equipment for Father, including the tape recorder that had to be going at all times during services. Even though Jones was a long way from Nixon's Oval Office, he, like his bête noire in Washington, insisted that his every word be recorded.

116

In many ways, Jim Jones was a caricature, a preacher with Las Vegas show-biz savvy, a hip comic versed in Scripture, a straight-talking, straight-shooting son of a gun, a Lenny Bruce poking fun at rich faith healers, a born-again Lord Buckley who put down religion, the Bible, other preachers, money, politicians, superstition, reality, everything and anything that could be grist for his cynical, manipulative mill. Like Billy Sunday, he exploited sex with frequent lurid references to various acts of intimacy, enticing women in the audience like a rooster strutting through a hatchery. Holding the mike close to his lips Elvis Presley style, he would whisper repeatedly, "I love you I love you I love you I love you I love you I love you I love you," until the dry desperation in his voice had women writhing in their seats and groaning, prostrate, on the floor. And they would moan back at him, "Oh, Father, Father, Father!" He answered, invariably, that they could not have him. Whether the ritual was substance or show, no one knew or cared; it was effective, it was fun, and it seemed, at the time, well worth the price of admission.

The show varied from service to service, week to week. There was no telling what the man would do next, what outrage he would perpetrate, what ideas he would expound from his pulpit. During one service, he started talking about snakes as if they were man's best friend. People shouldn't fear snakes, he said; they are not aggressive creatures. He proved his point by grasping a three-foot rattlesnake behind its jaws and carrying it through the audience; it didn't move much, according to George McCown, who assumed the snake was drugged, but there was no doubt it was alive, because it coiled and rattled feebly while Jim carried it all over the church. "He put that snake almost in my face," recalls Lena McCown, "and I'm scared of a snake, anyway. If I could have got through the wall, I would have got away, but there was no way I could have got away."

The snake-charming prophet had other surprises. At one marathon service, he chided those who had complained about not being able to use the bathrooms. They may have thought they knew suffering, he said, but they knew not the suffering of Father, who endured constant pain from inflammation in his urinary tract. The crowd agreed that Father suffered enough for everyone; he should not have to suffer himself. Father thanked the crowd and reached under the pulpit. He pulled back his choir robe, unzipped his pants, and leaned forward into the pulpit. There was a sound of liquid trickling into a metal can while he kept on preaching. He called for Jack Beam, and Jack took away the can and returned moments later to replace it under the pulpit.

He was witty, brash, lucid, sanctimonious, and zany. He was a surreal version of Carl Sandburg's "Bunkshooter" and Sinclair Lewis's Elmer Gantry, a Daliesque carnival barker every Sunday morning whose sideshow attracted everyone from those who wished to see a healer and a prophet to those who loved a wise and bizarre freak who could put on a hell of a show and was nonetheless politically effective. Instead of Kewpie Dolls and "Oh, You Kid" buttons, he had Birdie circulating through the crowd with her box of trinkets, photographs, lockets, keychains, egg timers (all bearing his picture), and the tiny plastic bottles of "annointed" oil squeezed from olives (purchased at some supermarket) and blessed personally by Father. That was the pitch—every item was blessed personally, was touched by Father's holy hands, and was available for five dollars and up. Birdie knew exactly what the trinkets were, but she was good at what she did, talking to her fellow members and explaining each of the trinkets, from the cheap plastic key chains to the eight-by-ten portraits "suitable for framing," which she got from Deanna Mertle, who dreamed up the entire line.

Money, money, money, was the keystone of Father's conversations with his inner core. Money came from everywhere. It was generated and administered by Valley Enterprises in Redwood Valley, the Temple's money factory. There at Valley Enterprises were the trinkets and the photographs put together; there was the "annointed" oil anointed; there were the newsletters and the mass mailings penned; there were published *The Living Word,* the Temple's monthly magazine, and *The Temple Reporter,* the first Temple newspaper. Valley Enterprises was a partnership of Archie Ijames, attorneys Eugene Chaikin and Timothy O. Stoen, Carolyn Layton, Carol Stahl, Marceline Jones, and Suzanne O. Cartmell, formerly Suzanne Jones, one of Jim and Marceline's adopted children. Jim Jones was not listed as one of the partners.

Valley Enterprises' primary responsibility was to market Jim Jones. The presses ran until the early morning hours day after day, cranking out "personal" letters from Pastor Jim to the faithful. Some of the envelopes contained two-inch-square strips of purple ribbon—"annointed" prayer cloths—and letters testifying to "more than a thousand" miracles. Some Temple members kept the prayer cloths in their wallets; others sewed them in their clothing where they would not be readily seen. The attractively printed brochures said of the prayer cloths:

> The cloth is purple, a rich and royal color considered in ancient days fit only for kings. To Pastor Jones, though, you are just as important and deserving as the richest of kings. And he wants you to have all the health, abundance, and prosperity that you desire.

Valley Enterprises handled the Temple's mail-order business, which sent out to believers the lockets, the protection pictures, the "Love Picture," the "annointed" oil, even locks of Father's hair. These blessed amulets were free for the asking; however, a "love offering" was not inappropriate with the request:

> Dear Pastor Jones,
> I understand that these blessed gifts work only by faith as it was in the days of Scripture. I also understand that there is no charge for the

gift and since there is a limited supply I must order soon. Please send me GIFT NO. ——— for my blessing. Here is my love offering: $———.

Sometimes the "love offering" was specified as a "magic number"—$27.33 was used more than once—that Jim Jones had in a revelation. The numbers were seldom the same, but they were always more than ten dollars.

Besides the trinkets, Valley Enterprises sold Jim Jones through its publication, *The Living Word*, a pamphlet-size magazine with cheap paper covers and amateurish typographical design—free use of boldface type, narrow margins, coarsely screened halftone reproductions, two colors of ink. It touted Jim Jones on every page, and his photograph graced both the cover and the title page, as well as many pages inside. The folksy rag spoke also of a utopia in Redwood Valley:

> Take a moment, if you will, and consider in your heart and mind what the Garden of Eden might look like if it could be translated into our day. It would be a place where people of all races and all walks of life could live and work together in appreciation and understanding; where all children could look forward to the full development of their abilities; where all adults would contribute according to their talents and receive as they had need.
>
> When the members of Peoples Temple speak in glowing terms of our Redwood Valley Mother Church, we are giving thanks that here, indeed, we have discovered this very Garden of Eden. In this apostolic community of Christian sharing, our fondest expectations are being met. Senior citizens are living productive, healthy lives in several church-sponsored homes. Children benefit from special tutoring and enrichment courses throughout their school days, and they are guaranteed college education in the field of their choice through the Temple college program. Free legal assistance is provided by members who have careers in law. Hundreds have found help in our drug rehabilitation program. Even countless animals have found their way to this Eden of protection and abundance.
>
> At the center of this great work is the character and example of Pastor Jim Jones. It is his devotion to these Christian principles of brotherly love and sharing that has inspired thousands to visualize and materialize the Kingdom "in Earth as it is in Heaven." Pastor Jim is our teacher in word and in example. Surely we are blessed to have this God-sent man in our midst.

Spreading the message of a Garden of Eden in Redwood Valley required long hours, and the lights at Valley Enterprises burned all night. Butcher paper on the windows made it impossible for passersby to tell what was going on inside, but everyone who walked by could hear the rumble of printing presses and the clatter of folding machines. Had anyone been curious about the business inside, he'd have had to get by the lookout who was always stationed out front, presumably to warn of any imminent attack by the Fascists.

The guard outside attracted the attention of Officer Mitchell L. Gibberson of the California Highway Patrol. Gibberson was patrolling Redwood Valley with Officer Bob Kingsley. "You want to have some fun?" Gibberson asked. Kingsley couldn't imagine why his partner wanted to park at the stop sign on School Way until he noticed the guard in front of Valley Enterprises. It was three o'clock in the morning. In just a few minutes, a charade Gibberson had witnessed previously was repeated. The guard on duty stuck his head in the door; two other guards limped out with rifles down their pants legs. The guards and the cops eyed one another for a few minutes. The guards grew increasingly nervous. A car pulled up from the direction of the Temple on East Road and six more Temple members got out. Soon all nine of them were pacing back and forth, keeping their eyes on the CHP car. Gibberson and Kingsley sat in their black-and-white until they tired of the game, then drove on.

The well-guarded Valley Enterprises building was but one of several in a shopping center that Peoples Temple acquired in a real-estate shopping spree that, over the years, had much of Redwood Valley property in the hands of Jim Jones. Among other businesses in the small center—which represented about a third of downtown Redwood Valley—were a laundromat and some apartments. Located there also was the Temple's bus garage for its fleet of thirteen used Greyhounds, a huge steel building that gave the rural landscape a touch of industrial Oakland. The Temple, incidentally, paid cash for the little shopping center; the transaction could have been seen as one indicator of the church's inordinate influence in the small community.

The Temple had ears everywhere in the valley. Joseph Allen, Mendocino County district attorney from January 1, 1979, says that, over the years, the county employed between forty and fifty members of Peoples Temple in various agencies. One of Jim Jones's staff and a member of the Temple's inner core, Sandy Bradshaw, was hired as a juvenile hall counselor in 1970 and by 1972 was sworn in as deputy probation officer, a job she held until March of 1977, when she was granted maternity leave. Mike Cartmell, the Temple's corporate vice-president, worked with Tim Stoen in the district attorney's office. Bonnie Beck, a member of the planning commission, started as counselor at juvenile hall three years before Sandy did, in June of 1967; she continued working for the county until February, 1977. Member Paul Flowers ran a high school work-experience program for the sheriff's office, where member Phyllis Houston worked during 1975 as dispatcher. Former members of the planning commission say that Mrs. Houston gave Jim Jones weekly reports on the activities of the sheriff's office.

120

Phyllis Houston was one of several Temple members in the employ of the county's law-enforcement agency. Former sheriff Reno Bartolomei estimates there were five to seven part-time reserve deputies working for him who were also members of Peoples Temple. Among them were Harold Cordell and Timothy O. Stoen. Bartolomei initially expressed some concern that for Tim Stoen—who was assistant DA—to put in eight hours a week as a reserve officer could be seen as conflict of interest, but Stoen laid his worries to rest by telling Bartolomei he had "talked it over with [District Attorney Duncan] James and Duncan didn't feel there would be any conflict." Bartolomei wasn't totally convinced, but he went along with the decision since James was also his legal adviser.

Money to pay for uniforms and side arms for up to seventy-five reservists came from state and federal grants, Bartolomei recalls, and there was no reason to ask questions as long as the applicants came up clean, without criminal convictions; Bartolome welcomed his volunteers into the training program. All went well until one of Bartolomei's lieutenants informed him that "too many" of the applicants were members of Peoples Temple. Bartolomei called Tim Stoen and told him "that Peoples Temple was getting too many reserve deputies in my organization and I told him that I wanted it stopped." He stressed to Stoen that his request "was not to be construed as discrimination in any way." Stoen agreed to put a lid on the applications, says the former sheriff, but he was never sure which of his reservists were Temple members, which were not.

Law-enforcement agencies in Mendocino County were one link in the chain of infiltration. The Office of Economic Opportunity funded an agency called North Coast Opportunities, which employed James McElvane, the Temple's chief of security, as a low-cost housing coordinator. He is remembered by his fellow workers as a big man, aloof, with cold, piercing eyes, who used to drive around in a retired California Highway Patrol car bristling with antennas. His secretary at NCO was Edith Roller; she moonlighted as an associate editor of the Temple's Living Word. In various other capacities North Coast Opportunities also employed Temple members Cleveland Jackson, Ron Talley, and Theresa Cobb—and, for about three months, the coordinator of senior citizens' activities was Lynetta Jones.

The Temple's real specialty in finding jobs for its members was in the area of social services. Between 1966 and 1977, the welfare department employed eight Temple members and one of the Temple's team of nurses, Sharon Cobb, who worked as a county public health nurse-practitioner. The county's mental health department employed, from 1973 to 1977, member Jerry Gardner as a psychiatric social worker. Jerry moonlighted, too; during his off hours he picked up some extra work as an accredited counselor at Temple-affiliated homes for the emotionally disturbed.

The Temple's assault on the community's mental health did not stop at the county level. Dozens of Temple members, including Marceline, worked at Mendocino State Hospital until it closed its doors in 1972—despite a flood of protesting letters from the Temple—and turned out entire wards of geriatric patients. The phaseout began in 1966, when the patients were gradually returned to the community and placed in licensed care homes. A half dozen of those homes were licensed and operated by Temple members. The hospital closed its doors, and its former employees who were also Temple members found health-related jobs in the community.

Marceline Jones landed a real plum. She went to work for the licensing section office of the state department of public health in Santa Rosa in August 1972. In 1974, she was transferred to the Berkeley office. Her primary responsibility during her five years with the state was to inspect convalescent hospitals; consequently, she was on the road much of the time, she didn't return to Redwood Valley for days at a time, and, because of the demands of her job, she had to forgo the spiritual blessings of the Temple's Spartan life-style and drive around in a shiny new car, with her hair freshly done and her clothes befitting her professional status.

The Temple's assault on government-funded jobs was waged on yet another front: education. A few members, good disciples all, followed Father's example and got jobs as teachers. Don Beck and Carol Stahl worked with the kindergarten classes in the Ukiah Unified School District. Carolyn Layton, Jones's confidante and mistress, taught French, and Jean Brown taught English at Ukiah High School. Jean Brown also kept herself busy as the Temple's corporate assistant secretary and as an editor of *The Living Word*.

With Temple forces successfully entrenched in law enforcement, health, education, and welfare, Jones's people invaded the private sector. Many of them got jobs in the lumber industry. Some of them, like Jack Beam, worked as custodians and maintenance men; Jack pushed a broom for four years at Ukiah General Hospital. Some of them worked downtown as retail clerks. Wanda Johnson worked for Wards, and she brought Jim Jones the personnel files he requested. Temple members waited tables in downtown cafés. Temple members pumped gas and repaired cars. Temple members punched typewriters and answered phones. Jim Jones required all able-bodied adults to find jobs; the cause needed their wages. About the only places of business Temple members did not work were the bars; and the bars were the only places in Ukiah where one could talk about Peoples Temple without word getting back to Jim Jones, because any conversations Temple members overheard on their jobs, any conversations critical of the Temple or its worthy founder, any negative statements or suspicious questions, were reported immediately to a counselor.

Temple members themselves had little opportunity to complain or criticize the Temple. If they bitched to one another, they would surely be reported. They were not to associate with other workers at their jobs, not even during lunch hour, and their instructions were to decline invitations to meet after work. "I wish we could get together," they would say, "but I'm terribly busy with my church right now. My church takes up all of my time."

Tired, red eyes were so commonplace that they became a reliable mark of Temple membership. Father himself, he said, now got only three hours of sleep a night. Tim Stoen had no more. Passersby late at night would see the lights still burning in Tim Stoen's office in Ukiah and would assume their assistant DA was a workaholic serving the public trust. As Jim Jones's empire grew, so grew his demands on Stoen for time and effort in legal work. Often some Temple crisis late at night kept Stoen's lights burning because the crisis demanded immediate resolution; Tim would leave the courthouse doors unlocked until the Temple's trusted few had filed into his office, where they met until the early morning hours.

Tim Stoen's dual responsibility sometimes had him hard put to decide where his loyalties lay. When put to the test, Stoen made it clear which of his duties came first. There was an incident on March 5, 1971, when two employees of North Coast Opportunities observed a couple of pickup trucks in Redwood Valley with somewhere between fifty and eighty cases of surplus dry milk, part of the United States Department of Agriculture's commodities program. The cases were clearly stamped "USDA." Mrs. Eunice Mock—she'd spotted the USDA stamp—followed the trucks for about a mile. She was supervisor of the commodities program for Lake County and Mendocino County, and she wanted to find out where the trucks were headed; they were loaded with food that was distributed usually only by her agency.

When the trucks pulled over on the shoulder of the road, Mrs. Mock pulled up behind them. The two trucks eased back on to the road. Mrs. Mock followed them for another mile and a half. They stopped again. One of the drivers—James Bogue, a member of Peoples Temple—emerged from his truck and approached Mrs. Mock's car. She asked Bogue about the USDA stamps; he replied that the dry milk was "for the poor." The other driver refused to identify himself, but he told her the commodities were from outside Mendocino County and were, therefore, none of her business. Mrs. Mock jotted down the license number of Bogue's pickup. She informed Bogue that she'd be reporting the incident to authorities.

Mrs. Mock called Dennis Denny, the county welfare director, and Denny referred the incident to Donald Scotto, his welfare fraud investigator. Scotto ran a check on the license number; the pickup truck was registered to Peoples Temple. He and Denny went straight to the Temple in Redwood Valley, confronted Jim Jones, and Jones denied the truck was still registered to Peoples Temple, denied any knowledge of the commodities, grasped his chest as if in pain, went inside the Temple to take a pill, and left Denny and Scotto waiting outside.

At Tim Stoen's office, the phone rang. Stoen was at a meeting of the board

123

of supervisors—one of his jobs was legal counsel for the board—when his secretary handed him the message: he was to call Jim Jones immediately. Stoen left the meeting abruptly. He got into his car and sped to Redwood Valley. When he got to the Temple, the pickup trucks were already on their way to San Francisco, but Bogue had stayed behind. Bogue was waiting there. So were Denny and Scotto. Jim Jones poked his head out the door. "Don't say anything! Don't say anything!" Stoen shouted to Bogue.

Denny was furious. "You're going to have to decide," he said to Stoen. "Are you going to be my attorney or his attorney?"

"It's quite obvious where my loyalties are," was Stoen's reply.

Subsequent investigation by the United States Inspector General's office (a division of USDA) revealed that the commodities had been taken from a warehouse on Sutter Street in San Francisco that had been leased by Community Health Alliance, Inc., a nonprofit corporation that distributed commodities to the city's poor people. The president of Community Health Alliance was Peter M. Holmes, a member of Peoples Temple. He denied any knowledge of the dry-milk theft. His statement ran counter to Bogue's assertion that Holmes, who had a lengthy criminal record, had brought the commodities to Bogue's home. He didn't even know Bogue, Holmes said. Bogue said he had returned the boxes to the warehouse.

When Stoen showed up at the next meeting of the county board of supervisors, Supervisor Al Barbero confronted him about his speedy departure from the previous meeting. Stoen explained that he had received an urgent call from the church. Barbero pointed out that Stoen's boss, District Attorney Duncan James—who was not prepared to advise the board on legal matters— had to fill in for Stoen. Stoen's response was that he had told James when he accepted the job of assistant DA that the "church came first, the county, second."

Two days later, Stoen asked Barbero to do him a favor. The church was being falsely accused in the commodities theft, Stoen said, and he wanted Barbero to contact some of his political connections in San Francisco to determine whether there were any charges pending against the Temple. Barbero always thought it strange that a man with Stoen's intelligence and education believed that the Second Coming of Christ was living in Redwood Valley, but he liked Stoen and he trusted his honesty. Barbero called State Assemblyman Willie Brown, then-Supervisor Dianne Feinstein, and Thomas Mellon, the city's chief administrative officer. They promised Barbero they'd find out what they could. The investigation proceeded for several weeks, until the San Francisco Department of Health stole the thunder when it "seized control of the warehouse," and Holmes resigned. No charges were ever filed. District Attorney Duncan James was aware of the entire incident. When he had the full story, he confronted Stoen and reminded him of his duties as an assistant district attorney.

According to Duncan James, not a single complaint against Peoples Temple ever reached his office; perhaps that explains why James's successor, Joe Allen, could find no file on Peoples Temple or Jim Jones. Duncan James, who is now in private practice, says, "People did not come forward to me. These people, if they knew anything, chose not to be involved." With Tim Stoen on board as first mate, it's no wonder the citizens kept their complaints about Temple activities to themselves. People outside the Temple were beginning to wonder just who was running the ship of state. Stoen's influence in Mendocino County was impressive. His recommendations got two Temple members—Archie Ijames in 1972 and Linda Dunn in 1973—appointed to the county grand jury. Job applications all over town, if they were made by Temple members, showed Stoen's name as a character reference.

Jim Jones hid behind Stoen's respectable aura while he continued, with Stoen's help, to build the empire. By 1972, the flow of money into the Temple coffers was unceasing. One trip to Los Angeles could mean twenty thousand dollars in offerings alone. The daily take at Valley Enterprises for all the trinkets of faith was averaging between eight hundred and a thousand dollars. Offerings were pouring in in response to Jim Jones's radio program, "The Voice of Peoples Temple," which was heard on stations in San Francisco, Los Angeles, Seattle, Philadelphia, Middletown, Ohio, and across the border in Mexico. The money was coming in so fast that Eva Pugh, church secretary, told several trusted members that she was burying it in coffee cans in her backyard. Thousands of dollars were tucked away in two Ukiah banks. The two Ukiah banks weren't enough for the Temple, however; thousands more went into a tiny bank in Lake County. To avoid overloading the banks, the Temple stashed a few thousands in savings and loan institutions as well.

Sandy Parks was in charge of counting the offerings and keeping the books on tithes in Redwood Valley until she left the church in 1975. During an average week, she recalls, the Temple would take in about ten thousand dollars. That figure did not include the life insurance policies and properties that were signed over to Peoples Temple. That figure did not include the big bucks pouring in from Los Angeles and San Francisco, or the gifts of personal belongings the Temple converted to cash.

Vicky Moore was one of the money counters in San Francisco. After she finished counting the money, she—and the other money counters, too—had to submit to complete body searches before they left the room. "You had to take down everything," says Vicky. "You had to spill out your bra. You had to take down your socks. You had to drop your drawers and everything."

Jim Jones trusted no one, not even the people in his inner core, not even the people who trusted him so much that they had already given him everything. Tom and Wanda Kice were among those people; they demonstrated their complete dedication to the apostolic life as early as May of 1968, when they donated all of their property—two homes and eight acres of land—to Peoples

Temple. Both homes were turned into communes that housed about eight persons each. According to Wanda, Jim Jones appointed Helen Swinney, Cleave Swinney's wife, overseer of all the communes; she would decide who lived with whom. Each commune had a leader, in the early days; the leader collected all payroll checks (endorsed to Peoples Temple) and turned them over, assigned work duties, and purchased the food and whatever else the commune needed. There were about a dozen communes. Within each, meals were shared—all meals with all residents—and it was a cheap way to live, cheaper, easier, and more secure than whatever alternatives were available to them. Communal residents shared their meals that way until 1973, after the expansion, when they were bused to the Temple three times a day for meals.

Apostolic living took various forms. There were children's communes, teen communes, adult communes. Husbands and wives, parents and children, lived separately. They would see one another at church or at special meetings arranged through the counselors. Vicky Moore made the decision to go communal in 1974. For a while, she was able to live with her son, Tommy, at a teen commune in a mobile home, although she had to spend most of her time in the adult communal quarters, where she and seventeen other adults—six men and eleven women—shared a large home on West Road in Redwood Valley, near the railroad tracks. There were three bedrooms; in one slept the six men, in each of the others, six women. All were committed believers. "I didn't want to be halfway committed," says Vicky of her decision. "I wanted to be totally committed." The situation could have been a bachelor's paradise, with the women outnumbering the men two to one, but Vicky recalls not a single sexual indiscretion. Temple rules forbade sex, of course; beyond that, the tripled-decked single beds rendered amorous behavior a matter of fantasy or futility, or both.

The decision to go communal was not, at first, a forced issue. Although Father exerted—along with the others who had made the decision—tremendous pressure, not everyone in the church was willing to take the giant step. Some members—like the Reverend Dave Garrison from the Macedonia Missionary Baptist Church—gave the Temple nearly all their property, but drew the line at giving up their homes and their hard-earned paychecks. Father did his best to convince them otherwise, but the American dream of having a piece of the land and a decent income was so deeply ingrained that it withstood Jim Jones's unrelenting affronts.

Yet there were those—in abundance—whose dream of private property crumbled under his assaults. Public records show twenty-four outright gifts of property in Mendocino County and eleven in Los Angeles County. Curiously, there is record of only three gifts in the Bay Area, including San Francisco County, despite the fact former members claim the Temple was in the real-estate business there in a big way.

The Reverend Dave Garrison tells of one gift of property in the Bay Area—

126

in Richmond, Contra Costa County—that illustrates one of the devious ways the Temple was able to conceal its real-estate dealings. Garrison recalls a black couple in Richmond who wanted to give their property to the church but didn't know how to go about it. The church advised the couple to sell their property and give the proceeds to Peoples Temple. Garrison—who spent most of his time in Peoples Temple appraising and remodeling properties—asked a friend who was a real-estate broker to appraise the property. The broker estimated the worth of the lot at between three thousand and four thousand dollars, and remodeling on the house at about five thousand. Garrison was part of the work crew that spent days cleaning, repairing, painting, and upgrading until the house was ready for the market at thirty thousand dollars. "I understand we made good money on that house," says Garrison. People were turning over property right and left in the same roundabout way all over the Bay Area and Los Angeles. "So many people turned over property," Garrison says, "until we had people that was busy every day working with the property, bringing it up to date, and evaluating and selling it." By asking for cash on the line, the Temple avoided the headache and possible embarrassment of deeds, which are on public view in county offices, and the burden of property taxes. All Father wanted was the cash anyway.

The full extent of the Temple's real-estate dealings may never be known. Public records show total property sales of $2.9 million, but a November 1978 raid on a Los Angeles real-estate office sheds further light on the methods the Temple used for acquiring properties and reveals sales amounting to another $1.8 million. The tiny, second-story office on South Crenshaw Boulevard—Enola M. Nelson Realty—was connected with Peoples Temple. Enola M. Nelson was an active member of the Temple, and sister to Temple Chief of Security James Nelson McElvane. The raid originated with a complaint filed May 25, 1978, with Steve Ramirez of the Los Angeles District Attorney's Office. Ramirez is a fraud investigator. The complaint was filed by Wade and Mabel Medlock, an elderly black couple who were members of the Temple. They charged that "Reverend Jim Jones and James Nelson McElvane and other members of Peoples Temple Church had extorted from them the proceeds from the sale of two parcels of real property amounting to $135,000." The Medlocks further claimed they were forced to list the property through Enola Nelson's realty office.

The Medlocks provided sufficient documentation for Ramirez to obtain a search warrant, and on November 24, 1978, he and other investigators swooped down on Enola Nelson Realty. The office appeared to have been abandoned for some time. On the walls were pictures of Jim Jones and the Jonestown Agricultural Mission. In the chaos of files and papers in the office, Ramirez and his team found two hundred rounds of ammunition and what looked like a time bomb, its clock and battery not yet connected. A bomb squad investigation later revealed the "bomb" was a phony. The investigators also found ledgers showing fifty pieces of property were handled by that office after the owners had agreed to turn the proceeds over to Peoples Temple. The properties in question were located in the San Francisco Bay Area, Mendocino County, and Los Angeles. They were sold between July 1975 and July 1978. Records in the realty office also showed unsold properties that were expected to net the Temple $1.7 million. Based on what he found in the real-estate office, Ramirez concluded "that a statewide conspiracy existed between Jim Jones and others to acquire real property from the members of Peoples Temple and convert that property to cash for their benefit, and that the methods used were fraud and extortion."

If fraud and extortion had worked to pry loose gold and silver fillings, Jim Jones would have used them. Father wanted his people to donate everything. Those who owned cars and couldn't demonstrate a need for them were asked to sign over the pink slips. Counselors visited the homes of members and pointed out what they could and could not keep. Sally Stapleton listened to the counselors' demands and flatly refused to go along with them. They wanted her to sell her bed and her expensive clothes. "They asked me," she says, "but I refused. I told them I would pickle my clothes, and I wasn't gonna sleep on nothin' secondhand, 'cause I wasn't raised that way." Sally is still proud that she can show people her diamond wedding ring. "He stripped people of their diamonds. I gave him a small one, but I didn't give him this one 'cause it's been on there too many years." The counselors told Sally they would "kick her ass" if she didn't hand over that ring. She's still wearing it. She feels most sorry for the elderly black people. "The old people," she says, "worked all their lives for a dollar and a half a day, some in the fields before I was born, and he'd come along and take what they had. He had them selling their furniture, selling their clothes, everything out of their house."

The tokens of total commitment were sold at Temple rummage sales, in at least three Temple-operated used-merchandise stores, and on the streets in San Francisco. Some of the more valuable items were fenced, according to former members, by a reformed drug addict named Chris Lewis. Lewis had a long criminal record, and apparently a long list of connections to whom he could take members' rings and watches and return to Father with a handful of cash. According to Lewis's testimony in the July 1972 issue of *The Living Word*, Lewis was "healed" of heroin addiction by Jim Jones in 1969.

Chris Lewis was big and mean-looking, and wise in the ways of the ghetto. He had served time in prison for grand theft and second-degree burglary following his conviction in 1964. In 1971, Lewis acquired further notoriety at a public meeting of the San Francisco Redevelopment Agency; he jumped over a table and choked the agency's director, M. Justin Herman. Police managed to restrain Lewis and no charges were filed. Two years later, at another public meeting, he was charged with the murder of an official of the Western Addition Project Area Committee. Lewis claimed he wrested the gun away from the WAPAC official and it went off, killing the official, Rory Hithe, and wounding Hithe's sister; Lewis faced charges both of murder and of assault.

Sandy Parks was in Tim Stoen's office at the church when the call came in about the charges against Lewis. She says Stoen became immediately involved in planning Lewis's defense. "I know he handled all this stuff," she says. "He stayed in the background and advised. He advised what to do. I was at his office working when the call came in about that." The Temple raised bail money and assisted him in hiring one of San Francisco's top criminal lawyers, James Martin MacInnis. Lewis was acquitted on both charges.

According to those who knew him, Chris Lewis never shook the monkey off his back for more than a few months at a time. Some of the same connections that fenced the rings from the Temple could score just about any drug imaginable; in that milieu, Lewis didn't take much time getting strung out again. Throughout his difficulties, he was fiercely loyal to Pastor Jones, and Jones, in turn, warned those who dared cross him that Chris Lewis would "take care" of them. Someone took care of Chris Lewis on December 10, 1977. He'd gone out to the store in Hunter's Point, one of San Francisco's black ghettoes, when two gunmen walked up behind him and plugged four fatal shots into his back. The gunmen left the thousand dollars Lewis had in his wallet. The murder remains unsolved.

In addition to Lewis's fences, there were several legitimate outlets for the donated items, in both Ukiah and San Francisco. George McCown recalls that many of the items—the furniture, television sets, appliances, and mattresses—were stacked at the rear of the bus garage in Redwood Valley—where he worked—as they were donated. From the garage, the items were distributed to two Temple-operated secondhand stores in Ukiah and to two in San Francisco. At first, the clothing, furniture, appliances, and other large items were sold along with rings and other baubles either at the Temple's thrift store on North State Street in Ukiah or at two shops along Divisadero Street in San Francisco. The Ukiah thrift store—More Things—operated for only about two years, when the fever to go communal was at its peak. Later, many of the smaller items—wedding rings, watches, other pieces of jewelry— were sold at Relics 'N' Things, a tiny secondhand store at the corner of School and Henry streets in Ukiah. The store opened in June 1975, when the Temple was moving its base of operations to San Francisco, and stayed in business for about a year, until most of the smaller items were sold.

The shops, like every Temple enterprise, made money because there was no way not to make money. The only overhead was rent and utilities; the merchandise and labor were free. With money coming in from donations, government checks, and the fruits of slave labor, there was no way the Emperor Jones could lose; his empire stretched from Redwood Valley to Los Angeles, with outposts in Seattle and back home in the Midwest. Jim Jones missed out on two counties immediately north of San Francisco, however:

Marin and Sonoma. Marin was far and away too hip for the socialism-preaching faith healer; he'd have looked ridiculous at a Grateful Dead concert on Mount Tamalpais, and besides, Werner Erhard and his est movement and the psychobabble–hot-tub contingent already had the populace there charmed. As for Sonoma County, Jones would have faced some stiff competition in Santa Rosa, the county seat, not from the occasional faith healers who passed through but from Santa Rosa's own minor-league Billy Graham, a fundamentalist preacher who was busy building an empire of his own.

Jim Jones did make some inroads into Santa Rosa, however. A few people from that city took the trouble to drive the nearly seventy miles up to Redwood Valley to attend his services. More significantly, there were several Peoples Temple students enrolled at Santa Rosa Junior College. According to Temple literature, all the young people in the church were given scholarships to attend college, and most of those who received scholarships went to Santa Rosa JC. They lived in homes in town that had been converted to dormitories. There were male dorms on Frazier Street, a predominantly black neighborhood, and on Dutton Avenue, a semirural area west of town, a mix of poor and middle-class residents. The dormitories were close replicas of the communes in Redwood Valley and San Francisco.

Because of these living accommodations and the Temple's scholarships there were in 1972, according to *The Living Word,* sixty-one Temple students "training for careers of human service" at Santa Rosa Junior College, and at the University of California (Berkeley, Davis, and San Francisco campuses), at Hastings School of Law (San Francisco), at the University of San Francisco, at San Francisco State University, and at Sonoma State University in Rohnert Park, a suburban community just south of Santa Rosa.

The November 1973 issue of *The Living Word* reports one of the success stories of the Temple's college program. The subject of the report is a reformed drug freak named Larry Schact:

> Study time is here again! The college students who have been helped by Peoples Temple are returning to the church-maintained dormitories for another nine months of study and fellowship together. Many of these young people have come from lives of drugs, crime and hopelessness. . . .
>
> . . . Larry heard about Jim Jones three years ago when he was living in Berkeley; aimlessly wandering around, his mind ruined because of the drugs he had been using for several years. He met one of the members of the San Francisco Temple. She talked with him about Jim Jones, a man who cared about him, even though Larry did not know him in person. Larry wanted to know more about Jim Jones and Peoples Temple, so he arranged to visit one of the services. . . .

Larry became a new man; his craving for drugs was completely gone. He found a job and began to think about his future. Previous school years had been so marred by social problems that he had been an "F" student; now he was making "A's." He continued in college and graduated with honors.

Now Larry, along with another young man, Steve Buckmaster (who also had a background of drugs), is attending medical college in Mexico, sponsored by Peoples Temple. He and Steve have dedicated their lives to helping others. They plan to be doctors in a Peoples Temple Free Clinic as soon as they graduate.

Not all of the students in the Peoples Temple dorms were drug catastrophes, but there were among the fifty or so attending Santa Rosa JC enough burnouts to justify constant pleas for donations. Despite their apparent neediness, the Temple students made their presence on campus felt.

David Harrigan, an English instructor at the college, was adviser for the Current Affairs Club, an organization founded by Peoples Temple students to bring leftist speakers to the campus. "They were active," Harrigan recalls. "They were obviously people who didn't state their ideals in terms of liberal principles, but tried to state them in terms of action." Politically, Harrigan agreed with the students' left-leaning views; he really caught hell from the school administration when he permitted the club to invite Black Panthers to speak on campus. Harrigan developed a fondness for many of the Temple students. He became concerned about their "paranoia" and their pessimism about the fate of the world. Temple students feared, Harrigan recalls, "there was a definite . . . conspiracy, not against the Temple, but against the left. . . . There was almost a feeling of Armageddon."

Another faculty member who looked after the Temple students at Santa Rosa Junior College was a member of Peoples Temple. Richard Tropp was a teacher of English. He was a quiet, studious man, prematurely bald, who sported horn-rimmed glasses and narrow, dark sideburns that extended well below his earlobes. Tropp didn't talk much about himself, although he did tell several Temple members that his parents had died in a Nazi concentration camp. Tweedy and rational, Tropp joined the Temple in the early 1970s while he was working as education coordinator of a Redwood Valley boarding school for troubled youths. He had graduated cum laude in English, 1964, from the University of Rochester in New York. He was Phi Beta Kappa when he received his master's degree from UC Berkeley in 1967. He had other feathers in his academic cap before Berkeley: he was a School of Letters scholar at Indiana University and he saw Europe as a Woodrow Wilson Fellow. Tropp was not the scholar given to strolling the halls of ivy and mumbling to himself in Middle English, although one might expect him to, given his field—

medieval and Renaissance literature; rather, he was committed to social change, a white scholar who completed his teaching internship at black Fisk University in Nashville.

By July of 1972, when Dick Tropp was hired by Santa Rosa Junior College, he and his wife, Elisabeth, had followed Jim Jones's example and had taken in three foster children, two of them black, one white. Tropp's dedication to his church was all too apparent. When Charles Miller, chairman of the English department, interviewed Tropp, he asked Tropp about his dedication to Peoples Temple, whether his "dogma" might not interfere with his approach to teaching. "I'm a Christian," Tropp replied, "but I'm not into converting you." There were never any conflicts between Tropp's religion and his job; he seemed able to serve two masters, and serve them well. "There wasn't any issue there," Miller recalls. From the moment Dick Tropp arrived on campus in his battered Rambler station wagon of uncertain vintage, he was in all ways the professional. In class, Miller recalls, Tropp "conducted a good discussion. The students were alive and interested."

The students may have been fully alive, but Tropp himself was operating on about half power. Like other professionals in the Temple, he had at least two full-time jobs; his other life as head of the Temple letter-writing campaigns, intellectual spokesman for the cause, and evening tutor for the Temple children in San Francisco consumed all his time away from the college. Harrigan remembers seeing Tropp asleep on his desk whenever he had a spare hour. Tropp worked himself so hard, Harrigan says, that he developed an ulcer and became "pale" and "withdrawn." Despite earning twenty thousand dollars a year salary, Tropp looked as if he hadn't a dime; he bought his wardrobe at Salvation Army Thrift Stores. "It was pretty obvious he was not putting money into himself," says Harrigan. "He was putting it elsewhere." Harrigan found out just where the elsewhere was. One day he broached the question with Tropp. Tropp replied, quite matter-of-factly, that in Peoples Temple "money was held in common" for the "good of the society."

On campus, Dick Tropp was a ghost, a man apart; not even in his own department did anyone know anything about him. He stayed by himself. He didn't drink beer with other faculty members at the end of the day. He didn't participate in on-campus activities. He did attend the obligatory meetings of the English department, and he was rumored to have been one of the bodies counted at meetings of the American Federation of Teachers, the faculty union, but he was quiet, almost invisible. Temple students there were more outgoing, but only within the limits of classroom decorum. They raised their hands in class when they wished to speak, and they spoke for what they believed. Of those outspoken Temple students, Dick Tropp's sister, Harriet, was probably the most vocal. She spoke with a discernible New York accent, Harrington recalls, and "she seemed to know exactly what she was doing, why she was doing it in terms of school. She was excited by ideas. Read widely.

Absorbed ideas quickly, applied them well. . . . She wrote well: passionately, yet factually, so that her work was delightful to read." Her talents eventually qualified her to become spokesperson for Jim Jones. During the summer of 1977, her brother, Dick, took a one-year leave of absence to go to The Promised Land in Guyana; Harriet joined Dick there. They stayed there for the rest of their lives.

His kind face, his unassuming demeanor, his quiet dedication had everyone he met liking Dick Tropp; even the committees of Temple members that stayed up till all hours writing letters under his guidance liked him, working tirelessly, uncomplainingly, under his wing. The letter-writing committees were an important part of the Temple's political posture. Depending on the issue—always one that deserved special attention from congressmen and senators—each committee member wrote fifty to one hundred letters every week. Dick Tropp's efforts were responsible for a blitz of letters opposing Senate Bill One, the Nixon administration's infamous legislation that threatened civil liberties unlike anything since the McCarthy era. Each committee member was given two sheets of paper. One sheet listed the names of all the members of the Senate Judiciary Committee; the other offered sample letters. The first sheet had the following instructions: "You write your letter, have it cleared, and then write one of the fifteen senators above (unless otherwise instructed). Please put stamps on your envelopes—do not seal envelopes." Most of the sample statements are innocuous, but one in particular must have caused some consternation after dozens of repetitions:

> When the American people get the full story on Senate Bill One, they will be mad, indeed. It looks like the Senate is either ignorant or deliberately trying to precipitate a new wave of radical dissent. We have had enough in recent years. So stop provoking it with this kind of foolish legislation.

The letter blitzes cascaded mail on Washington and Sacramento. Most of the letters were handwritten, from the Temple's "concerned citizens." Most of them were either verbatim copies of Tropp's ideas or close variations. When the letters were not geared to influencing legislation, they championed in other ways the causes Jim Jones espoused. Tropp was widely read on propaganda techniques, and the letter campaigns were a substantial backup for the Temple's humanitarian causes; whenever Tropp thought it appropriate, the letters made direct reference to Jim Jones and Peoples Temple and the wondrous works in which they were engaged.

The propaganda was far from empty. Real action, good works, greased the gears of the propaganda machinery in ways that could be recorded and demonstrated. Most of what came off the presses at Valley Enterprises made reference to the "thousands of dollars" the Temple donated to worthy causes:

the Big Brother program, the Heart Fund, the American Cancer Society, the Redwood Valley Fire Department, the National Association for the Advancement of Colored People, Ukiah teen and community centers, various police funds, scholarship programs for deserving students in the community, even the treasuries of other churches. Donations of money were often backed up with community action. When Redwood Valley was in an uproar about the huge influx of street-tough kids, the Temple brought in a work crew and donated $2,800 worth of labor to painting Redwood Valley elementary and junior high schools. They even repainted the yellow stripes in the parking lot.

The schools were not the only beneficiaries of Temple civic-mindedness. It was the thought that counted. It was the Temple's interest in the cause that counted, not the money, and for the small amounts of money the Temple dispensed, it received uncalculable goodwill. Peoples Temple allocated $4,400 in January of 1973 for distribution to the media in support of freedom of the press. The gift was not large, considering that it was shared by twelve newspapers, a news magazine, and a television station, but it was the best public relations gesture Peoples Temple could possibly have made at the time. The top "commendation" awards—$500 each—went to the newspapers that happened to have the largest circulation in Jones's domain, the *San Francisco Chronicle* and the *Los Angeles Times*. Receiving awards of $300 were the *Los Angeles Herald-Examiner,* the *San Francisco Examiner* (which later returned the money), the *Oakland Tribune,* the *Indianapolis Star, The* (Santa Rosa) *Press-Democrat,* and the *Ukiah Daily Journal,* all of them brightly shining stars in the firmament of responsible journalism. The *New York Times* received something less—only $250—as did the *Christian Science Monitor,* the *Cincinnati Enquirer, Newsweek* magazine, and KGO-TV, San Francisco. There was even a stipend of $250 left over for the Inter-American Press Association, a bastion of the free press in the Americas.

Of course Peoples Temple requested no acknowledgment of its largesse; nonetheless, each of the recipients responded with expressions of gratitude. It was a trying time for the press; Richard Nixon was president; reporters were being jailed for refusing to disclose their sources; newspapers throughout the country were decrying the erosion of First Amendment rights. Accompanying the awards was the Temple's statement of belief, couched in terms that brought lumps to the throats of editors from coast to coast:

> We believe that the American way of life is being threatened by the recent jailings of news reporters for refusal to reveal their sources. As a church, we feel a responsibility to defend the free speech clause of the First Amendment, for without it America will have lost freedom of conscience and the climate will become ripe for totalitarianism. . . .
>
> We wish simply to demonstrate . . . that there are churches and

other groups in society which are not connected with the institutional press who do indeed care about this threat to freedom of speech, press and conscience.

Officials of the Inter-American Press Association said the contribution "moved us deeply." Editors and publishers stammered their statements of gratitude: "No one before has been so thoughtful as to make such a contribution," said Evert Person, publisher of *The* (Santa Rosa) *Press-Democrat.* Charles de Young Thieriot, editor and publisher of the *San Francisco Chronicle,* thanked the Temple and turned the money over to Sigma Delta Chi, a professional organization of journalists.

The articles on Peoples Temple's good works caught the eye of John Longbrille, press secretary for California congressman George E. Brown, Jr. (Democrat—Colton). Longbrille was so impressed to see a church defending the First Amendment that he decided to credit the Temple's good works in the "Extensions of Remarks" section of the *Congressional Record* for May 29, 1973. This section of that publication was, in 1973, primarily a repository of small favors. Technically, only congressmen were allowed to contribute to the section, but often legislative aides wrote puff pieces and dropped them into the copy box for inclusion in the *Record.*

The little piece on Peoples Temple was sufficiently innocuous, Longbrille thought, to include in the *Record* without bothering Congressman Brown for approval. The item reads like actual House dialogue to the uninformed, though in fact it is no more than facsimile for print purposes; no dialogue ever occurred on the subject of Peoples Temple. When the *Record* item was reprinted in *The Temple Reporter* and *The Living Word,* however, no effort was made to educate the readers that the paper dialogue was all fluff. The editors of the Temple publications went so far as to delete the name of the congressman, except to say that he was a "prominent Caucasian Congressman." Congressman Brown was at that time, in the eyes of many observers, a flamboyant liberal and a staunch opponent of the war in Vietnam; perhaps the Reverend Jones thought it unwise to ally himself in print with such a prominent Caucasian, although he hesitated not at all to use the logo of the *Congressional Record* as a seal of approval for Temple activities.

Jim Jones collected plaudits from the press and from public officials the way some people collect autographs. Temple publications inflated even the slightest hint of praise beyond any resemblance to the original intent. Jones used every opportunity to his advantage, even misfortune and catastrophe. One such catastrophe Jones exploited so masterfully that it seemed hardly unexpected. A fire—very obviously the result of arson—gutted the San Francisco Temple on Geary Street less than a year after Jones acquired the building, on August 23, 1973. Shortly after 4:00 A.M. on that date, someone used gasoline to start fires in the first-floor bathroom, the base of the stairway to the second floor, and the base of the stairway to the third floor, according to the fire department's report. The flames spread quickly to all three floors. While the fire was still blazing, Jim Jones arrived on the scene and told arson investigators that he "had an intuition that something was wrong," so he bused a group of forty students up to Redwood Valley for 6:00 P.M. services the evening before. The only person left in the building was a custodian, who was taking a nap and was awakened in the nick of time by two Temple women who, luckily, had come down from Redwood Valley to get some membership files.

Predicting that the arsonist would "reap the whirlwind for touching God's annointed," *The Living Word* for November 1973 notes that "Pastor Jones made several references to the church being burned, but he told the congregation of 1,000 members that it would not hinder our work." Father's revelation about the fire was not the only miracle to occur that fateful August morning. According to *The Living Word*,

> . . . The custodian was not in her room—which was burned up—but in another room from which she was able to escape unharmed. This was only due to Pastor Jones leading her out through a window which had a grill over it—although he was in a bus travelling at the time! MIRACULOUSLY, not one person, animal or plant was injured.
>
> In several of the rooms there were Anointed Pictures, and although the frames were burnt and the plastic around the small pictures was completely melted, the ANOINTED PICTURES WERE NOT DESTROYED nor were they hurt in any way.
>
> The musical instruments were literally melted by the heat. The microphone and public address systems, along with the chairs and other equipment were also melted. The whole interior of the building was destroyed. Nothing is left with which to begin to rebuild. We need to replace everything. . . .
>
> The robes which Pastor Jim wears were hanging in one of the rooms that was destroyed by the fire. Although everything else in the room was demolished by the blaze, these robes were left totally intact. Pastor Jim has had a Revelation that these robes should be used to make Prayer Cloths which would be a special blessing to those who care enough to help.

The arsonist was never apprehended, even though he made his crime apparent: he left behind a gasoline can attached to a rope, leaving no doubt as to the origin of the conflagration. There were never even any suspects. No one who did not know the layout of the doors and windows could have slipped inside very easily, for the buildings was under twenty-four-hour security. It was even more unlikely that an outsider could have known about the ventilation hole in the concrete wall, which the fire department's investigators

136

identified as the arsonist's route of access to the building. It was truly puzzling; a stranger could not have known the building well enough, and all the insiders were attending services more than a hundred miles away.

Faith Worley recalls a few odd coincidences. The weekend before the fire, all of the Temple's privileged files were taken from the San Francisco Temple to Redwood Valley. They had never been moved before, since they contained information only on San Francisco members and there was little need for them—for all of them, anyway—up north. The night of the fire, while everyone was at the meeting in Redwood Valley, Faith recalls thinking it was odd that one member of the inner circle was not at his usual place on the stage beside Jim Jones, nor out in the audience to help with the healings. She didn't see Jack Beam anywhere that night.

After the fire, Jim Jones told his flock there was no insurance on the building. He had said many times that he did not believe in insurance of any kind—a ploy that persuaded his members to cash in their insurance policies—so everyone believed he was telling the truth. Numerous "emergency" collections followed this disclosure. According to the Temple's insurance agent in Ukiah, there was actually a $90,000 insurance policy on the church, which the Temple had purchased for $122,500. Immediately after the fire, Temple officials approached the insurance agent for increased coverage on the Temple's real estate holdings, but the insurance carrier decided instead—at the agent's recommendation—to cancel all policies with Peoples Temple.

While the inside of the building was being renovated, the Temple held meetings two blocks away at Benjamin Franklin Junior High School, at the corner of Scott and Geary streets. They had held meetings there before the purchase of the big church, and, being on Geary Street, the school auditorium was convenient and familiar to most Temple members. Geary Street is one of the main thoroughfares through the Fillmore ghetto; it starts downtown where it joins Market and Kearney streets and stretches west all the way to the beach. The street is also familiar to the city's Black Muslims, for on the corner of Geary and Fillmore, next door to Peoples Temple, is Muhammad's Mosque Number 26, one of the largest Black Muslim congregations in California. Often families in the neighborhood split their church attendance between the two buildings, with the clean-shaven, neatly dressed young men of a family worshiping with the Nation of Islam while their mothers walked a few steps farther to worship with Jim Jones.

Diagonally across the street is the Japan Center, the corner of San Francisco's *Nihon-Machi* (Japan Town), a monument to the city's pride in its mixed ethnic heritage. A few steps to the south and around the corner on Turk Street is the office of Dr. Carleton B. Goodlett—physician, newspaper publisher, and articulate spokesman for the black community. From his complex on Turk Street, Dr. Goodlett conducts a successful medical practice and publishes the largest-circulation weekly newspaper in northern California, the *Sun-Reporter*. This weekly owes its huge circulation to wide distribution in Bay Area black neighborhoods, where its words are considered more credible than those of the establishment press.

Dr. Goodlett was Jim Jones's personal physician for seven years. His support of Jim Jones, perhaps more than any other single person's, was responsible for a great deal of Jones's success in San Francisco. Goodlett doesn't talk much about Jones's miracle cancer cures, but he has talked and written profusely about Jim Jones's humanitarian deeds. In April 1972 Dr. Goodlett presented Jim Jones with the *Sun-Reporter* Special Merit Award. During the presentation, Dr. Goodlett said of Jim Jones:

> In the implementation of his life he has lifted his hand to reach the oppressed, the distraught, the lost at every opportunity. Every minute of the day, he searches for new opportunities to reach out and touch somebody. . . .
>
> No man can do any more than open up his heart or place under his roof the children of God of all colors, all creeds, all races. He has found an opportunity to snatch from the living hell of narcotics, hundreds . . . of young people, and he has made their life meaningful. I can spend a lot of time talking about this God-serving man . . . but when you look at the social gospel of Jim Jones, not only is he concerned with the beginning of life, the Alpha, but he also has a profound concern for the ending of life, the Omega. This is a man for all seasons.

Jones appealed to the more left-leaning segments of the black community with the support of the hip-talking, street-wise pastor of Glide Memorial Methodist Church, the Reverend Cecil Williams. The Reverend Williams attracted a truly colorful and unorthodox mix of characters to his Glide Church on the edge of San Francisco's Tenderloin District. His free-flowing services were populated by the neighborhood's flower children, pimps, whores, junkies, gays, and radical leftists not only from the immediate neighborhood but from all over the Bay Area; his success in bringing the gospel to the misfits, the jobless, the lawless, the aged poor who lived in the decaying hotels was unprecedented. When Cecil Williams was not at the pulpit, he was demonstrating at peace rallies, counseling the poor and despairing, walking the rough streets around his church. He was the conscience of the Tenderloin and of the larger community of the disfranchised hip of the city.

The Reverend Williams recalls first meeting Jim Jones in 1970 or 1971. "I got a call," Williams says. "He wanted to meet me and said he admired the work I was doing." Williams says he was unaware of the faith healings Jones was performing, although he heard "rumblings" that such things were going on. Jones, he says, used to call him late at night—sometimes at midnight or

138

1:00 A.M.—and talk about one recurring theme: criticism. "He didn't like for people to criticize him," Williams says, "and that's what he talked to me about, the fact that he was getting criticism." Williams advised Jones that "all of us have to be open to criticism . . . especially if you're a public figure."

Williams's support of Jim Jones was literally visible; he had Jones as guest on his television show, aired on alternating Sundays on a local station, more than once. Through his connection with Cecil Williams, Jones gained entree to the left's idealistic fringe, the people who were no longer satisfied with talking about the way the world should be and wanted, instead, to live their ideals, live them every day, and see them realized in the community. They wanted action; they found it at Peoples Temple.

Jones's exposure on Cecil Williams's television show aroused the curiosity of another television personality, not well known, certainly no celebrity, but a hardworking reporter and cameraman for KXTV, Channel 10, Sacramento. Michael Prokes was a deeply religious young man, a Christian Scientist with a strong sense of social commitment, when he decided in late 1972 to do some film footage on People's Temple. Prokes's assignment was to string for KXTV in Stockton and Modesto; he covered the two San Joaquin Valley cities all alone. He toted around a movie camera, a minicam for sound, and a tripod. He filmed his own stand-up interviews and on-the-scene reports without help by setting the camera's self-timer, then standing in front of it, microphone in hand, to interview his subject of the day. His news director, Jim Drennan, recalls that Prokes was "competent" as a one-man news crew, but was "a little too unflashy for television."

Drennan recalls that Prokes described his Peoples Temple project as an exposé, even though San Francisco was not Prokes's turf; he was supposed to cover Stockton and Modesto. Nevertheless, Prokes was determined to do his exposé at the Temple in San Francisco, and he set his camera up on a tripod in the Temple's balcony after first receiving permission from Jim Jones and his aides to shoot some footage there. Jones was initially leery of Prokes, Faith Worley recalls; he didn't trust him. Jones's staff kept their eyes on Prokes while he sat in the balcony and watched the service. Prokes was so impressed by what he saw—the music, the testimonials, the interracial brotherhood, the commitment to social action—that he told Pastor Jones he would like to join Peoples Temple. Within a week, Prokes gave notice to Drennan: he would not be returning to KXTV. "He gave all of his worldly possessions," Drennan recalls, and Grace Stoen's memory confirms that Prokes emptied his savings account and gave Peoples Temple a check for ten thousand dollars.

Prokes rose quickly in the Temple ranks. His background in television and news writing became an important weapon in the Temple's public relations arsenal, arriving just in time to bolster the campaign that lay ahead—winning San Francisco. Within weeks, Prokes was named to the planning commission; soon after, he enjoyed much of Father's authority in Father's absence. Prokes was called upon frequently to speak for Father with the press and the outside world. With Prokes speaking for him, with Dr. Goodlett praising him, with the Reverend Cecil Williams offering exposure, Jim Jones was ready to move.

Jim Jones made his first political moves in San Francisco during a period of leftist euphoria: Richard Nixon was sinking fast and the left was growing stronger with every lie that was uncovered, until, in August 1974, Nixon's resignation gave the left one of its few victories in American history. Jim Jones, the faith-healing Prophet of God, grabbed the chance to move among the triumph-intoxicated Democrats and liberals and spread the news of his good works. He had his letter-writing committees slinging ink toward every politician and community leader with any clout at all in San Francisco. Terry Francois, a prominent black attorney, liberal supervisor, and president three years running of the San Francisco Chapter of the NAACP, suddenly received "an inordinate amount of mail from people who were singing my praises and telling me what an outstanding job I was doing and that Pastor Jones had spoken very highly of me." The letters invited Francois to visit the newly renovated Temple on Geary Street, but he was "wary from the outset" and never responded to the invitations.

Pastor Jones's reputation as a faith healer spread like a melanoma throughout the Fillmore. Supervisor Francois "began to hear disturbing reports, particularly about the faith healing and people turning over their properties." Francois says he "knew some of the people" involved with Jim Jones; he decided not to involve himself, one way or the other. There was no point in risking incurring the wrath of Dr. Goodlett, whose *Sun-Reporter* could make or break a black politician in San Francisco.

The renovated Peoples Temple on Geary Street reopened in spring of 1974, before the SF supervisor received his fan mail, and soon after the reopening, word spread among the people that Jim Jones was doing wonderful things for the poor. Every Sunday before the miracle healing services he served—as did his mentor, Father Divine—a free banquet that fed more than a thousand people. Sandy Parks supervised the banquets. She remembers seeing scores of old black folks, mostly women, lining up for the chow. "This is how he got a lot of the people. . . . He served a big meal on Sunday and some of them would come just for that meal because they were hungry. Then they would give every penny they had in their pocketbook, give him their watches, their earrings, anything they had on them they would give to him because he fed them once a week and nobody else would feed them." For some of the old ladies, it was "the only meal they ever got," Sandy says.

He fed the hungry; he nursed the sick. Jones turned Peoples Temple into a drug-rehab center where Fillmore junkies could shake one "Jones" (street slang for "habit") and get hooked on another. The Temple literature maintains that there were scores of hopelessly strung-out addicts who quit cold turkey after they found Jim Jones. Counselors would sit with the addict in shifts, watching the unfortunate twenty-four hours a day while he suffered the pangs of withdrawal. Sometimes the addicts were taken up to Redwood Valley, where they were given a dose of clean country air and a chance to exercise in the indoor swimming pool, and a responsible job if they chose to stay.

Peoples Temple also offered a free legal clinic manned by Tim Stoen and Eugene Chaikin. Each month the clinic counseled more than a hundred people with civil and criminal problems. There was also a medical facility at the church. Staffed by Temple nurses, it offered general checkups, pap smears, and sickle-cell anemia tests. Physical therapy equipment was available for members who suffered from arthritis and other crippling conditions.

For all the junkies, the misfits, the down-and-outers, and other lost souls, the Temple offered vocational rehabilitation in the form of training in its printing plants and its garages, along with experience in construction, electronics, woodworking, and counseling. By 1973, the Temple's list of vocational activities included agriculture: there was now a farm, the Peoples Temple Agricultural Project in Guyana. At first, Jim Jones was coy about the location of the place he called The Promised Land. In 1974, he revealed only that it was "south of the United States." Some members of the church assumed he meant The Promised Land was in Cuba. In August of that year, Jones leased 3,824 acres of land in a remote jungle region of Guyana near the Venezuelan border. Two months later, eleven Temple members cleared thirty acres and were living in a "bark cottage," according to a progress report the Temple published in 1977. One of the brochures says of this agricultural mission:

> Jones persuaded the Guyana government to let him start a model farm to show the advantages of multi-crop agriculture in the tropics. He also wanted to use the farm as a haven where San Francisco misfits could get away from their pressures. Guyanese officials were dubious at first, but Pastor Jones is a persuasive man.

Now he had an international base of power. Now he had a long list of good works to his credit. Now he had the endorsements and support of key community leaders in San Francisco. And now, by the mid-seventies, Jim Jones and his Peoples Temple were becoming a potent force in San Francisco politics. What other preacher—or any leftist leader—in the Bay Area was capable of delivering a thousand demonstrators or a thousand dollars on a moment's notice? Peoples Temple came up with nineteen thousand dollars for Ka-Mook, the wife of American Indian Movement leader Dennis Banks, for her bail when she was arrested by federal authorities after the battle at Wounded Knee, South Dakota, in 1973. On February 14, 1974, two days after the first communiqué from the Symbionese Liberation Army following the abduction of Patty Hearst, Jones and four other Temple members—Tim

Stoen, Karen Layton, Michael Prokes, and Annie Moore—offered themselves, in *The Press Democrat*, as hostages in exchange for the newspaper heiress. The Temple even offered to contribute one of the first checks—in the amount of two thousand dollars—to the Hearst family for the People in Need program that the SLA demanded as ransom for Patty. The check was reportedly returned, but not before the Temple's generosity was widely reported in the local media.

Peoples Temple also came up with a series of smaller checks—no more than several hundreds of dollars each—for other causes dear to the left: the American Civil Liberties Union, Cesar Chavez's United Farm Workers, the Ecumenical Peace Institute, the Freedom of Information Center, and various neighborhood medical clinics and defense funds, including the one for American Communist party leader Angela Davis.

Jim Jones was a godsend to leftist organizers who had spent most of their lives trying to get people to contribute money or time, to show up at demonstrations, to pass out leaflets, to make phone calls; the sight of several busloads of people—all races, ages, shapes, and sizes, all responding to a single phone call—showing up with placards in hand was a joy to behold. All organizers of such demonstrations share the same nightmare: after weeks of planning, nobody shows up for the rally, or the crowd is so small that passersby on the street react with the indifference they accord to Jews for Jesus picketing a porno house. If Jim Jones was going to make a public appearance at a rally or a demonstration, the organizers' fears were quelled. His presence guaranteed the appearance of a thousand troops on the line.

After the glory days of the 1960s, when demonstrations were so common that motorists were continually having to find new detours for their commutes, the 1970s were an exercise in futility. The thunder of activism had been stolen by the drizzle of the "Me Decade," a time when people of conscience and chronic malcontents alike began toying with the notion that the source of their misery was not in the society around them but within themselves. Activists of the sixties flocked to gurus, nirvana hucksters, and cradles of the born again. Rennie Davis, one of the Chicago Seven, cast his lot with a chubby, pubescent teenager from India who called himself the Guru Maharaj Ji. Black Panther leader Eldridge Cleaver, fearless dues-paying author of *Soul on Ice,* returned from exile in Algeria "born again" with Jesus, supporting without hesitation the "I Found It" advertising blitz that packaged and sold the Lord like so many potato chips. Sackcloth and ashes became the uniform of the day for many of the sixties' most vocal activists.

But there were those who remained committed to social action. They were accustomed to speaking before thousands of people, but in the seventies they found themselves lucky to be looking at a few hundreds of movement groupies—unless, of course, Peoples Temple made an appearance. Hard-line activists wouldn't—*couldn't*—buy what was being peddled in the name of religion, but they showed up at the Reverend Cecil Williams's church, down on the corner of Taylor and Ellis between the Hilton Hotel and a gay bookstore, because Cecil at least reminded them, street-talk preaching with a boogie beat, he at least made them feel good, dancing in the aisles and clapping hands, made them feel good, white and black alike, about living in the past.

If Cecil made them feel good, Jim Jones showed them that it was still possible to get things done. His people were on the picket lines. His people were out carrying posters, passing out leaflets. His people were out there collecting money for Huey Newton, for Dennis Banks, for Angela Davis. And the Temple sent the money to these worthies, and the Temple sent out piles of letters laden with accolades, inevitably they would mention the activist pastor Jim Jones, and inevitably the worthies would be invited to visit the Temple on Geary Street—Huey Newton, Dennis Banks, Angela Davis.

Vicky Moore was on the committee that prepared the Temple for Angela Davis's visit. A couple of days before Ms. Davis's visit was scheduled, a religious group had taken a tour of all three floors of the old Scottish Rite building, and the bedroom doors still sported the signs that showed those rooms were used for Bible classes and exercises in Christian stewardship. The doors were locked; none of the visitors was so presumptuous as to ask to see inside. On the walls in the hallways and the landings of the stairs smiled the face of the Lord Jesus and his good buddy, Jim Jones.

Before Angela arrived, Vicky and her committee took down the pictures of Jesus and replaced them with leftist posters and examples of art by black people. She took down the sign that said "Bible Class" and replaced it with a sign that said "Culture Studies." (The bedroom doors remained locked.) When Angela arrived, she was ushered through the front door to a friendly congregation. The choir sang "Joe Hill," an old labor movement song about the I.W.W.'s revolutionary troubadour whose 1915 death sentence before a Utah firing squad made him a *cause célèbre*. Well rehearsed, the choir and the audience sang chorus upon chorus of "We Shall Overcome" and raised clenched fists at appropriate intervals. Then came Jim Jones's sermon; it was a call to action, whose words dwelt sweetly on Angela's ears.

Now, Jim Jones varied the show at Peoples Temple to suit the tastes and persuasions of the minor celebrities in the audience. If the visitors were fundamentalist ministers, he'd have members practice talking in tongues for days in advance. Members were told to "act churchy" and to wear their Sunday best. For leftist political figures, the faith healing was minimized, the members wore T-shirts and jeans, dashikis and sandals, anything casual, and the songs and musical skits were heavy with social messages. When, in 1975, Jim Jones announced that the guest of the day would be state senator George Moscone, candidate for mayor of San Francisco, the Temple took great pains to simulate the appropriate atmosphere for a white liberal politician. A few hours before Moscone arrived, Vicky Moore and another woman were busy in a back room applying whiteface to black people, making them up to look Caucasian, according to Father's orders.

"There weren't enough white members," Vicky says. "We made them up with makeup and put white wigs on them and put them in the balcony so . . . you could not detect who they were." Neither Vicky nor the black people in whiteface questioned Father's motives. Vicky says she "was caught up in the concept that he must have known what he was doing because I didn't know enough about what Moscone represented and why it was important to do that." For Moscone, the roles assigned to members were the same as for any other visiting dignitary: only a few persons were to ask questions of him, and only a designated few were to answer his questions.

Like a traveling carnival hootchie-kootchie show, the Peoples Temple entertainment extravaganza made the rounds of other sympathetic churches in the city and, even without Jim Jones, wowed the crowd with its smiling soul vitality. Ted and Selma Vincent saw the Temple dance troupe perform at Glide Memorial Methodist Church in late 1975. The Vincents were so impressed by the black teenage dancers that they decided to look into Peoples Temple. "We were looking for some sort of religious experience," says Ted. He and Selma had, throughout the sixties, participated in every demonstration of any consequence in Berkeley. Gradually, though, in the early seventies, the black power movement polarized the civil rights front, and white leftists like Ted and Selma were squeezed out of the movement, even though Ted had been the only white man to write a regular column in *Muhammad Speaks,* the Black Muslim newspaper. Gone forever were the glorious days of brotherhood, solidarity, and marching together arm in arm down the boulevards of offended towns. Ted and Selma missed those days of passionate commitment and were searching for something to fill the void.

Behind Ted and Selma's decision to join Peoples Temple was something more than nostalgia for activism. Ted had three children with black skins from a previous marriage, and he was concerned about their ethnic deprivation as a result of living with two white parents. Ted wanted his kids to learn the black experience firsthand, from people who grew up black. Ted's oldest son wanted nothing to do with Peoples Temple, but his youngest son went a few times, until the time the guards confiscated his cake-slicer Afro comb and he told his father he couldn't take the discipline. Ted's daughter, however, attended most of the services and seemed to have no trouble fitting in with the other children in the Temple.

Ted and Selma's first exposure to the Temple style came on the first Sunday they showed up for a service and had to submit to a one-hour interview in the downstairs lobby with Dick Tropp and four other counselors. They were mildly surprised at the depth of the counselors' probing into their motivations for joining Peoples Temple. After the interview, there were further surprises: Ted and Selma had to submit to a pat search and to sign their names to blank papers, or papers on which was typed "Everything on this page is true and correct to my knowledge." Selma didn't care much for the pat search, but Ted didn't mind after he was told the reason for the security. Forces working against the Temple, he was told, set fire to the building in 1973, and their harassment since had been unrelenting. Because Ted had been associated with some pretty heavy leftist movements, he understood perfectly the need to be cautious with new faces.

The Vincents were finally escorted upstairs to the meeting, confident they had satisfied the requirements for membership. They were immediately impressed with the interracial congregation—about three-quarters black—and the spirited music and good vibes. They were impressed with the buildup of emotional fervor, which peaked when Father approached the pulpit wearing a polyester leisure suit; the welcome for him was tumultuous. Ted and Selma listened to the preacher talk; they were impressed by Jim Jones's understanding of the problems of poor people. "He'd spend hours putting down phony ministers, and putting down corruptions of the church . . . and neighborhood pimps and other exploiters," Ted recalls. Jones spoke in street language, without the jargon characteristic of most white leftist leaders. "Sometimes he'd speak rather resentfully of the fact that all those eggheads . . . can't do anything." Jim Jones would point with pride at the Temple's accomplishments in San Francisco. Peoples Temple was out on the streets demonstrating, bailing people out of jail, providing safe housing for the elderly. While most leftists were sitting around yakking and trying to understand the 1970s, Peoples Temple was "out doing something." Ted was not faking it when he got up to dance in the aisles to the music of the Temple band, and Selma was not faking it, and they were not faking their desire to become a part of the activist church. They both tried to apply for membership, but they were told they'd have to attend more services before they could even be considered. They hoped the time would come when they wouldn't have to submit to the pat searches, but they saw members in good standing for five years going through the same rigmarole. After several months, they finally received their membership cards. Selma was disappointed. The card bore her photograph and name, but no indication that she belonged to Peoples Temple. Instead, the bearer of the card was identified as a member of "Redwood Valley Christian Church." Selma had wished the card said something like "Peoples Temple Marxist Faith-Healing Church." One consolation was that being identified as a Christian made it easier to cash checks when she flashed the church card along with her driver's license.

In some ways, Peoples Temple was a Christian church in the best tradition. The Vincents were deeply moved to see all the old black matrons, some over ninety years old, lined up in front of the pulpit to be hugged and kissed by every member of the church. This touching scene, repeated at nearly every service, was one of the positive experiences the Vincents accentuated when

145

they described the Temple to their leftist friends. Accentuating the positive, however, became more difficult after a particular piece of Wednesday night business. Ted and Selma both saw a five-year-old boy get a beating with a board in front of the whole congregation. One of Jones's aides held a microphone near the boy's mouth so everyone would be sure to hear his screams. It was one of the things, Ted recalls, "that led us to getting out."

Ted and Selma were convinced when they first joined People's Temple that Jim Jones was using his powers to good ends. He had most of the people in his church meditating for a few minutes before they started their cars. The ritual, Jones claimed, would assure his protection of those traveling on the highway. Members would whisper, "Thank you, Father," before turning the key in the ignition. Ted did it, too; he likes to think that it was Father who guaranteed his safe passage all the way to Philadelphia and back in a dilapidated 1963 Dodge sedan that had survived a roll of several hundred feet down Topanga Canyon before Ted bought it for seventy-five dollars.

Initially, Ted saw Father's protection as a positive manifestation of what the Temple was fond of calling his "suprahuman powers," but eventually Ted began to see another side. Ted remembers Jim Jones saying, "Bad things happen to people who leave Peoples Temple." Ted says, "He referred to your need for his power, and when that power was withdrawn, you were in bad trouble." Ted freaked out at one meeting when Father was hammering away at everyone about a man who had left the Temple and died shortly thereafter. Jim Jones said the man died because he no longer had Father's protection. Ted stood up and made a scene, accused Jim Jones of using the black arts against people, and stormed out of the meeting. He was afraid Father would put a hex on him, too, but he was enough of an anarchist to summon up the courage to stand up even to Jim Jones.

Ted and Selma began to see Peoples Temple as a dead end. They were attracted to the communal life but not so much attracted that they were willing to pay the price of sexual abstinence and relinquishing their daughter to the Temple. They withstood enormous pressure to give up their daughter so she could be raised by a black family. Just before they left, they had a talk with Father for about an hour. He tried to persuade them to stay. When they were finished Selma was exhausted by the energy that burned in Father's eyes.

The demonstrations of "black magic," the beatings, and Father's bizarre behavior were confined to closed meetings at the Temple. With guards posted at all entrances, it was impossible to saunter into the brick building on Geary and attend a service. Politicians who wished to visit announced their plans far enough in advance for the Temple to stage the proceedings down to the smallest detail. There were no searches at the door, and the guards were careful not to let their weapons show. The politicians and the other influential outsiders who visited occasionally always left the services convinced they had seen the "real" Peoples Temple. The show was so impressive that no one on

146

the outside wanted to believe otherwise. Ugly rumors about Jim Jones were dismissed as right-wing smears or sour-grapes utterances of jealous rival preachers who had lost to him the sheep they had fleeced for years.

Some of California's most influential black leaders courted Jones because they recognized that he and his followers (reputedly twenty thousand, but actually something less than half that number) carried enormous political clout in the black community. State Assemblyman Willie Brown, former Lieutenant Governor Mervyn Dymally, and Los Angeles Mayor Tom Bradley all shared the pulpit with Jim Jones. "I am really pleased and inspired by what I have seen," Bradley told the cheering throng. "Here truly is a man—Pastor Jim Jones—who is touched by God." Dymally was so impressed with the Temple's agricultural mission in Guyana that he visited it twice. By the mid-seventies, San Francisco's liberal pecking order was top-heavy with politicians who viewed an invitation to visit Peoples Temple as an opportunity to be ignored only at peril to their careers. Among his allies Jim Jones counted United States representatives John and Philip Burton, District Attorney Joseph Freitas, Sheriff Richard Hongisto, and Police Chief Charles Gain. There were others who courted Jones, or at least appeared to be courting him, either by attending services themselves or by sending emissaries.

While Jim Jones held court at the Temple, his troops established beachheads in black community groups. According to Grandvel A. Jackson, a leader in the NAACP, Peoples Temple infiltrated the organization sometime in 1975. There were, Jackson recalls, "large numbers" of Temple members in the NAACP when Jones was elected to the board the following year. Elected along with Jones to the office of board secretary was Vera Young, a black Temple member. The board later hired Laurie Efrein, a young white Temple member who had once worked for the Mendocino County Welfare Department, as the paid office secretary.

Jones tried the same ploy with the San Francisco Black Leadership Forum, a black political endorsing group, according to board member H. Welton Flynn. At about the same time Jones was moving into the NAACP, Flynn recalls, he sent between thirty and forty troops into a Black Leadership Forum meeting "just before the annual election." If that election had been allowed, Flynn claims, there would have been more Temple members voting than Forum members. Flynn, a San Francisco accountant, had heard about Jim Jones when he first came to the city with his miracle healing services. One of Flynn's clients wanted to deduct sixty-six hundred dollars from her federal income taxes because she had paid Jones that amount for "curing" her of cancer at a meeting in Redwood Valley. "We knew this was a dangerous man," says Flynn, "so we rewrote the bylaws" to exclude Temple members from the voting.

Jim Jones and his Temple troops took San Francisco by surprise. They may not have won all their battles for control of city politics, but they always managed to leave behind a reputation for solidarity. The Temple was committed to the same issues as the ragtag leftist coalition that was girding itself for the November 1975 election. In the race for mayor, the two front-runners from the beginning were Supervisor John Barbagelata, a realtor who spoke for the city's business interests, and former state senator George Moscone, who spoke for the same liberal and leftist coalition that Jones was courting.

The stage was set in April 1975 for a series of events that catapulted Jim Jones to one of the most powerful positions in city politics. On April 14, 1975, in San Francisco's city hall, there was a meeting whose purpose was to discuss the proposed relaxation of voter registration requirements. The meeting was called ostensibly because more than 118,000 registered voters—almost a third of the city's electorate—had failed to show up at the polls during the 1974 election and had been summarily stricken from the rolls for the 1975 election. The participants in the meeting were Lawrence Leguennac, registrar of voters; Thomas J. Mellon, the city's chief administrative officer; Agar Jaicks, chairman of the city's Democratic Central Committee; William Thomas, an aide to U.S. congressman Philip Burton; and a contingent of labor leaders. To make up for the loss of a third of the city's electorate, the group wanted the city to fund a voter registration drive, to relax the training of deputy registrars, and to issue large numbers of books of voter registration forms to deputized registrars. Each of the forms was to have a numbered yellow duplicate, which was to be all that had to be presented at the polls by the citizen who wished to vote. Each receipt would be compared with its original in the registration books as a safeguard against stuffing the ballot box. Everyone at the meeting in Mellon's office agreed to the plan, and it was quietly set into motion.

The plan called for the Democratic Central Committee to pay thirty-five cents per registered voter to the Coalition to Register 100,000 New Voters, which coalition comprised more than thirty community groups. Although Peoples Temple was not on the coalition roster, there is evidence that the Temple participated in the registration drive, which resulted in voter fraud on a massive scale. With its fleet of thirteen buses, the Temple could move its members to where the voting action was. In 1974, Wanda Kice recalls, the action was in Mendocino County, where there was a hotly contested race for the office of sheriff. Jim Jones ordered Wanda to register busloads of Temple members from San Francisco, even though they were not residents of Mendocino County. "They'll be moving up here eventually," said Jones. Wanda was instructed to list Redwood Valley and Ukiah addresses for the San Francisco members. Jones asked members of the congregation, row by row, whether they were registered to vote. Those who were not he ordered to register with Wanda at the back of the church.

According to former Temple members, it was "common knowledge" that Jones used the same ploy during the 1975 voter registration drive in San

Francisco. Busloads of members from Redwood Valley and Los Angeles were asked during services at the San Francisco Temple whether they had registered to vote. Hands went up all over the crowd of those who were not, and the Reverend Dave Garrison compiled a complete list just in case someone forgot Father's admonition to appear before a deputy registrar as soon as possible. Although the Reverend Garrison does not recall seeing a voter registration table at the service, he remembers Jones directing people to the nearest deputy registrars at supermarkets, businesses, and Temple communes.

While the citywide registration drive was winding down, Democrat George Moscone's forces were gearing up for a tough election battle against Republican Supervisor John Barbagelata, and they needed all the help they could get. Moscone was worried, and so was his campaign manager, Don Bradley, who had successfully managed the California election campaigns of Presidents Kennedy and Johnson. After Moscone visited the Temple, Bradley recalls, "there was a meeting here in my office with Jim Jones, [Michael] Prokes, Moscone, and myself. We requested help in securing volunteers and they said they could."

Moscone was sold on the idea of Peoples Temple providing volunteers, but Bradley was more cautious. "I was a little leery we were getting into something like the Moonies," says Bradley; he had already asked around about Peoples Temple and Pastor Jones. One of the people Bradley called was Al Barbero, who attributed his loss in the 1972 Mendocino County supervisorial election to the Jones vote. "Well, I think . . . if they say they're gonna work for ya," Barbero recalls telling Bradley, "they'll work for ya." Everyone Bradley talked to had nothing but praise for Jim Jones; the responses confirmed Bradley's initial feelings that Jones was "a very impressive guy" who "talked a very liberal line" and got things done.

Bradley took Jones and Prokes up on their offer of volunteers, and one hundred and seventy-five Peoples Temple members showed up at Moscone's campaign headquarters. "They did the work," Bradley recalls, "in tough areas, fairly rough areas [like] the Tenderloin and south of Market." Jim Jones's troops, without a doubt, made the difference for Moscone. The election results placed Moscone in a runoff election to be held the following month. His opponent now was Supervisor Barbagelata, not a field of five candidates, because neither Moscone nor Barbagelata, although they beat out the others, had received a clear majority.

The Temple went all out for Moscone in December, importing campaign workers from the Temples in Redwood Valley and Los Angeles. "We got out [of the buses] and went door to door, passing out leaflets, telling people where to vote," says Vicky Moore, who admits she was unaware of the issues in the campaign. "I woke up," she says, "when I started doing things like that, because I didn't know enough about Moscone to tell you which side of the

149

street he lived on. All I was doing was mimicking what Jim said about him. I did it because . . . Jones said Moscone represented the cause, whatever the cause was."

The night before the election, the Temple staff manned the phones and called all of the communes and the homes of Temple members. Hundreds of times the same message went over the wires: "Father loves you very much and there's a danger out tonight. Get a pencil and paper and take down these names. . . ." What followed was a complete list of the candidates and the ballot propositions that received Father's blessing.

With Father's voting instructions and yellow voter registration slips in hand, the Peoples Temple army swarmed to the polls in the Temple's buses. The entire liberal slate won, if only by a slim margin. Moscone squeaked in by a mere four thousand votes. His campaign manager, Don Bradley, thanked former Mendocino County supervisor Al Barbero for his candid and accurate assessment of Jim Jones's troops. "I saw Don again," Barbero says, "and he said, 'Boy, those people really worked. They really delivered; they put out door to door; they worked the precincts for me.'" It was obvious both to Jim Jones and to George Moscone that Peoples Temple made the difference. Five days after the election, Jones made a bold move; for the first time since he arrived in California in 1965, he changed his party registration from Republican to Democrat.

Neither the loser, John Barbagelata, nor his campaign workers suspected that a new political force was at work in their fair city until months after the election. They knew nothing of the meeting in Bradley's office that put the Peoples Temple troops into action, and they certainly didn't connect Moscone's volunteer legions to an obscure faith healer in the Fillmore named Jones. Barbagelata and his people suspected something was amiss with the election, but they were not sure what it was. The closer they looked into the election, the more they suspected voter fraud. Those yellow receipts—the pieces of paper that entitled the bearers to vote—were never compared to the originals because in most precincts there were no originals. Many of the registration books were not, as required by law, returned to city hall six weeks before the election. In March 1976, three months after the election, there were more than four hundred voter registration books still in circulation. To make matters worse, election officials neglected to require that the duplicate registration forms—the yellow receipts—be turned in at the polling place. "You could have run around to twelve hundred precincts and voted twelve hundred times," says Barbagelata, who later chaired a special committee of the board of supervisors to investigate voter fraud in the 1975 election.

During four days of testimony, Barbagelata's committee heard from every group that had anything possibly to do with the suspected voter fraud except one: Peoples Temple. Neither the existence nor the impact of Jim Jones's mobile congregation had become apparent to the committee, which did find evidence of nonexistent addresses and forged signatures on those registration forms that were returned to city hall. Names were printed when they should have been signed. Signatures didn't match. Then there was the clincher: more ballots were cast than the total number of voters on the rosters at the polling places. Two areas of the city that showed widespread voter fraud were the Tenderloin and the south of Market area, where Peoples Temple campaigned heavily for Moscone. There were also widespread "irregularities" in the Fillmore and Western Addition areas, where the Temple was an influential neighbor.

Several of the voter fraud allegations were turned over to District Attorney Joe Freitas for further investigation even before the committee's public hearings began in June 1976. Freitas had been elected along with Moscone and was in no position to drag his feet. He created a special election crimes unit and hired a supervising attorney to oversee it. Freitas chose the attorney he thought best qualified for the responsibility: Timothy O. Stoen, assistant district attorney of Mendocino County and legal counsel to Peoples Temple.

A week or so before Freitas announced Stoen's appointment, a letter went out on Freitas's stationery requesting letters of recommendation from Stoen's associates and cronies in Mendocino County. The letter reads in part:

> A number of very prominent people have written or otherwise suggested that I hire Timothy O. Stoen, who is presently the Assistant District Attorney of Mendocino County. They feel he has exceptional trial ability and administrative ability. Most important, they feel he has great integrity and is not afraid to stand up for his convictions.
>
> The results of my investigation convince me he is the best person for this job. Mr. Stoen has indicated to me he is happy with his job and life in Mendocino County, but would, as a matter of public service, accept the above-mentioned position for a two-year period upon one condition. The condition is that I first obtain letters of recommendation from persons in a position to know his performance as a lawyer so as to substantiate the basis for my selecting him.

Although the letter went out with Freitas's signature, the original draft was written in Stoen's distinctive pen.

According to Freitas, Stoen was hired "through normal personnel procedures." Freitas denies that the hiring of Stoen was in any way connected to Peoples Temple having worked the precincts for the liberal slate. Freitas claims further that he was unaware Stoen was a member of Jim Jones's church until after he was hired. "I didn't know Jim Jones, nor that there was such a thing as Peoples Temple, until after I was elected district attorney," says Freitas, "in fact [not until] after I took office, which was January 1976."

Stoen's immediate superior during the probe was not Freitas, but Daniel H. Weinstein (now a municipal court judge), who served at the time on the board of directors of the Delancey Street Foundation, one of the organizations in the Coalition to Register 100,000 New Voters that was under investigation. The probe resulted in a few insignificant convictions for violations of the elections laws. Delancey Street was cleared of all charges. Peoples Temple was not even part of the probe.

After that investigation was concluded in December 1977, someone made sure there would never be a conclusive probe of 1975 voter fraud. Jay Patterson, the city's deputy registrar of voters, says that all the rosters showing who voted, which were kept in three locked vaults, have disappeared. The last time Patterson recalls anyone looking at the files was in the spring of 1977. He discovered that the records were missing when state and federal agencies, who began to take a second look at Stoen's investigation in December 1978, requested them. The voting rosters are only part of a lengthy list of records—all of them having some connection with Peoples Temple—missing from government offices in Indianapolis, Ukiah, and San Francisco.

Despite the voter fraud controversy, the newly elected city officials went about the business of molding San Francisco government to fit their purposes and fulfill their obligations to those who helped them get elected. Moscone's first offer of spoils to Jim Jones was a seat on the city's human rights commission. Jones declined the offer; he was much too busy with church business. He was much to busy to accept such a minor post. Privately, he was furious that Moscone thought such an offer was adequate reward for the man who delivered the votes that made the difference. Jones wanted a much juicier plum: a seat on the housing authority commission, overseer of the $14 million-a-year bureaucracy that acts as landlord to the city's poor.

The board of supervisors got wind of Moscone's intentions even before he submitted the list of names (including Jones's) he was considering for the prestigious post. The board wrote a letter to Moscone in August 1976 asking, as diplomatically as possible under the circumstances, for assurance that all of the nominees to city commissions receive background checks before their names were submitted to the supervisors for approval. Moscone ignored the letter and left the decision up to a nominating committee he appointed from among his campaign workers. Black leader Dr. Carleton Goodlett was on the nominating committee, and so was Jones's chief aide Michael Prokes. No one in San Francisco politics was at all surprised when Moscone submitted for approval, in October of 1976, the name of Jim Jones.

Three members of the board of supervisors—Francois, Barbagelata, and Quentin Kopp—initially balked at the thought of naming a faith healer to one of the most important posts in city government, although the board minutes of September 7, 1976, show that Francois and Kopp were among the six supervisors (Barbagelata was absent) who voted to award a certificate of honor to Jones. When it looked as though Jones's confirmation might have to face some vocal opposition, Moscone's people worked quietly, behind the scenes, to assure Jones's appointment. First, state assemblyman Willie Brown, whose district includes the Fillmore, sponsored legislation in Sacramento to change the rules for appointments to the housing authority commission. The legislation passed handily. It removes from the supervisors the authority to approve commission nominees and places the decision squarely in the hands of the mayor. Even if the board voted against the appointment of Jones before the first of the year, Moscone could get him a seat on the housing authority commission any time after January 1. Stripped of its powers, its voice now a matter of formality, the board of supervisors unanimously confirmed Jones's appointment. Peoples Temple was further rewarded with additional spoils; three Temple members—Jean Brown, of the church's board of directors, Carolyn Layton, of the inner core, and Vera Young—were given key jobs on the housing authority staff.

The appearance of the Prophet of God at a meeting of the housing authority commission was a sight to behold. Surrounded by his apostolic guardians— sometimes a dozen or more—flanked by his attorney, Eugene Chaikin, and by his chief aide, Michael Prokes, the Reverend Jim Jones came down like a wolf on the fold, or like the exiled dictator of a banana republic maintaining the trappings of power. Even for San Francisco, the spectacle was outrageous, bizarre. Jones would take his seat, with Chaikin at his side like a ringside coach and his rooting section of black grandmothers in the audience ready to mark his every word with unquestioning applause, and ostentatiously assume command, well groomed with every hair sprayed into place, inscrutable behind his ordinary sunglasses, dapper as a Los Angeles Jaycee in his polyester leisure suit.

Despite the sideshow atmosphere Jones brought to meetings of the housing authority commission, Mayor Moscone intervened in February 1977 to assure that Jones was named chairman. The mayor sent his chief aide, Bernard Teitelbaum, to spread the word to each of the other commissioners. Commissioner Cleo Wallace, however, had seen Jones in action; she balked and insisted on discussing the matter with Moscone. Moscone told her "things would get heavy" on the commission soon, and Jones was the man to handle the situation. Although she was still wary, Cleo joined the other commissioners in approving Jim Jones as chairman

Cleo Wallace sat next to Chairman Jones at the dais during his half year in the post. She recalls that he used to get a complete script of the meeting, from the call to order to the adjournment, in addition to the agenda. Jones kept the meeting running smoothly as long as everything on the agenda was routine. He'd read off the script in a monotone, pausing occasionally to sip a frothy white beverage from a paper cup brought to him either by Michael Prokes or by one of the apostolic guardians. He would sip and read, with no ad-libbing and no deviating from the text except when he had a statement to read into the record or when there was an element of controversy. Whenever something controversial came up, Jones would turn immediately to Chaikin—especially when Jones himself was under fire—and Chaikin, studious and mid-fortyish, "would always write notes to Jim," Mrs. Wallace recalls, "and Jim would state very clearly, 'Oh, wait a minute, my attorney is saying something.' If he got mixed up from what was on his paper, then he would be totally lost. I'd . . . have to guide him back to where we were on the agenda."

Jones's career as a public servant was singularly undistinguished; but for his "ordinary" sunglasses, his entourage of guards and aides, his flock of cheering grandmas, he would have been quickly forgotten by all who saw him in action at housing authority commission meetings. To the thousands of poor people who rented from the agency, however, Jim Jones was The Man. Many of those tenants lived in the low-cost housing projects in the Western Addition, not far from Fillmore Street, and to them Jones was also a neighbor; he presided over his dominion only a few blocks away from them in his Temple at 1859 Geary Street.

The Geary Street Temple became the headquarters of Jim Jones's empire in early 1976—he'd been working out of Redwood Valley until then—after he had established a strong foothold in San Francisco through Mayor Moscone. The Temple still held occasional meetings at the Mother Church in Redwood Valley and kept a skeleton crew on hand there to oversee its substantial holdings, but the action after 1976 was in the city. The decision to move the church's operations to San Francisco was abrupt; the move took only a few days, and Redwood Valley, once touted as Paradise on Earth, became an ancillary mission in the boondocks. After most of the members had cleared out, there were some minor cleanup missions to perform: Jim McElvane and Jack Beam shot all of the dogs in the animal shelter and buried them in a large grave on Temple land.

With the move to San Francisco came tremendous pressure on the holdout members to go communal. Tim and Grace Stoen were among the last of the holdouts, but they succumbed and made the total commitment in April 1976. They lived in separate communes and took their meals, with scores of others, at the Temple on Geary Street. Peoples Temple boasted that its dining room daily fed more people than St. Anthony's dining hall, a venerable haven for the city's derelicts. That may have been true, but with few exceptions, the people who ate at Peoples Temple were Temple members who had given up all their worldly possessions.

People outside the Temple were no more aware of the living arrangements of Temple members than they were of the strict discipline members suffered. The politicians and march organizers who called on Jim Jones never bothered to ask how Jones could load a thousand or more people into his buses and show up at a demonstration on a few hours' notice. "You could get them together in about an hour or so," recalls one Temple member. "You really didn't know for what. All you knew was Jim wants it done, so you do it." The communal people were on standby during the day, like the U.S. Marines, and they were ready to march to whatever battlefields Jones chose.

The battlefield in September of 1976 was the Fresno County Courthouse, where four newsmen were being held in jail on contempt charges for refusing to reveal their sources of information. Newsmen throughout California tried to organize car pools to the demonstration and were frankly worried that only a small crowd would show; they knew their fraternity well—newsmen are probably, outside of stray dogs and dandelions, the most difficult to organize of all God's creatures. The march organizers sweated it out with the worry and the heat—it was still summer in the San Joaquin Valley—until they saw the buses arriving from Peoples Temple. The newsmen were grateful as the Jews in the Sinai, for Temple members by the hundreds poured out of the buses like manna from Heaven, carrying placards and ready to march. The press fell all over itself to praise Peoples Temple and Jim Jones, proving once again that the way to every newsman's heart is a strong defense of freedom of the press. Among the plaudits the Temple received were praise on national television from muckraking columnist Jack Anderson and the first Freedom of the Press Award ever given by the National Newspaper Publishers Association. Presenting the award on behalf of the black publishers group was its president, Dr. Carleton B. Goodlett.

Dr. Goodlett's newspaper, the *Sun-Reporter*, began printing the Temple's own semimonthly newspaper, *Peoples Forum*, in April of 1976. *Peoples Forum* was available free just about everywhere in San Francisco and boasted a circulation of six hundred thousand, larger than any other newspaper in the Bay Area. The circulation figure was undoubtedly inflated, considering the fact the largest circulation daily, the *San Francisco Chronicle*, averaged about a half million morning readers. There never was an independent circulation audit of *Peoples Forum*, so no one will ever know just how many copies were really on the streets, but Temple members worked hard to get the papers out there. The troops left *Peoples Forum* under doormats, tucked behind doorknobs, in laundromats, in restaurants, anywhere the public passed. Temple children hawked the *Forum* on the streets as soon as school let out, or they'd go from door to door, leaving copies where they'd be sure to be found. Most of the teenagers of the door-to-door battalion attended Opportunity II High School, where one-third of the student body were Peoples Temple kids. The school principal, Yvonne Golden, a leader in the Black Teachers Caucus, was a great admirer of Pastor Jones and was mentioned frequently in the pages of *Peoples Forum*. "To see the positive effects that we got out of these teenagers out of reform schools and jails was just amazing," recalls Ted Vincent. "To deliver papers with these kids and see them running up and down the steps trying to outdo each other—girls trying to impress the boys, and vice versa—

showing how effective they could be in doing something productive, was just wondrous."

Peoples Forum was designed initially to appeal to the reading tastes of poor working-class people, the same people who buy copies of tabloids like the *National Enquirer* and the *Star* every week. There were socko headlines announcing major breakthroughs in the treatment of cancer, predicting mass starvation, warning of coming invasions of killer bees. Some of the items were clipped directly from the tabloids; others were rewritten. These sensational articles were to suck the reader in to the point where he would look further and learn of the wondrous works of Peoples Temple. Many of the articles reported on the rallies and demonstrations where the Reverend Jim Jones, pastor of Peoples Temple Christian Church, was a featured speaker. The issue for April 2, 1976, tells of a rally in San Francisco's Civic Center that attracted "five thousand enthusiastic supporters" of American Indian Movement leader Dennis Banks, who was fighting extradition to South Dakota. Sharing the podium with Banks and Jim Jones were William Kunstler, the Chicago Seven attorney, Lehman Brightman, president of the United Native Americans, District Attorney Joe Freitas, Assemblyman Willie Brown, gay leader Harvey Milk, the Reverend Cecil Williams, and several Black Muslim leaders. After the rally, the article reports, Banks and Kunstler went to worship with Jim Jones at services in Peoples Temple.

A month after the Dennis Banks rally, Jim Jones bused his flock to the southland for an enormous unity gathering with the Black Muslims in the Los Angeles Convention Center, where Pastor Jim shared the stage with Wallace D. Muhammad, chief minister of the Nation of Islam. Only the year before had the Muslim leader ended the forty-five-year practice of his sect's labeling whites as "the Devil" and excluding them from Muslim services. Muslim leaders had heard glowing reports on the Reverend Jim Jones from their brethren at Muhammad's Mosque Number 26 at the corner of Geary and Fillmore in San Francisco, next door to Peoples Temple. As a gesture of goodwill, the two congregations attended each other's services. "Every few weeks," recalls Ted Vincent, "the Muslims would come to his service, or we'd go down to their service. Jim would cut it short, and we'd all go down to the end of the block."

The unity meeting in Los Angeles was the culmination of years of artful courting by the Prophet of God. Sharing the stage with Jim Jones and Muhammad were Angela Davis, Lieutenant Governor Mervyn Dymally, Los Angeles County supervisor Kenneth Hahn, Los Angeles mayor Tom Bradley, Dr. Carleton Goodlett, and the Reverend Priscilla Chaplin, director of the Southern California Council of Churches. Ted and Selma Vincent wondered on the way down to the meeting whether Jim would be his outrageous self in front of the Muslims, whether he would pepper his sermon with the obscenities and profanities he habitually used during his services at the

Temple. They knew the Muslims did not like naughty words. When Ted and Selma arrived at the convention center, they were escorted to seats next to straitlaced Muslims, who teach black capitalism and a strict Islamic code of behavior. The Muslims are taught not to stand for their leader, not to applaud. Temple members were taught to show enthusiasm. With Muslims on either side, Temple members were too self-conscious to give Father his usual rousing welcome. "We didn't want to make the Muslims feel ill at ease by acting out in ways that were, like, against their religion," says Selma, "so we were being considerate of them and Jim was furious."

Jim Jones was not so considerate. "Everyone thought Jim was going to talk straight and nice in front of the Muslims," Selma recalls, "and he didn't. It was a real surprise, because nobody thought he would say 'Shit' or anything, but he did. Everyone went 'aaaahh' [because] he really did say 'Shit' in front of the Muslims." After a few of Jim Jones's colorful anecdotes, a few of the Muslims lost their composure, too. "The Muslims were laughing, too," Ted recalls, "and I'm sure when they got back to their temple, they were read the riot act for laughing." On the bus trip back from Los Angeles, Father gave his flock a tongue-lashing over the radio intercom for their lack of enthusiasm at the rally. Although in Jim Jones's eyes the rally was marred by the dearth of praise, *Peoples Forum* treated the event as another triumph.

Peoples Forum recorded in words and in photographs every contact Pastor Jones made with the influential and the powerful. During the 1976 presidential campaign, Rosalynn Carter visited San Francisco—Jimmy Carter was running behind in the California polls—a couple of months before the election. She shared the podium with Jim Jones, who brought with him to the Democratic campaign headquarters some six hundred of his own troops. Jones received a thunderous ovation from the crowd (which numbered about seven hundred and fifty) while Rosalynn was greeted with a trickle of polite applause. That evening, reports *Peoples Forum,* Rosalynn invited Jones to a "private dinner engagement" where they discussed "the free press issue, including the plight of the Fresno Four, and he found a receptive ear." When Senator Walter Mondale made a brief campaign stopover on behalf of the Carter-Mondale ticket, Jim Jones was one of the privileged few invited to a private reception aboard the aspiring vice-president's chartered jet.

Jones always made certain there were members of his staff at hand during these meetings to record every accolade for future use. He liked to be photographed with celebrities whenever possible, and he pulled off a great public relations coup in the fall of 1976 when Bob Wallach, a prominent SF attorney, introduced him to Ralph Nader. Jones shook hands with America's favorite advocate, and the photograph of the event ran on the first page of the first November issue of *Peoples Forum,* right below a gushing letter from Mayor Moscone. The impression was unmistakable: Jim Jones had not only the key to the city but the Ralph Nader seal of approval as well.

Peoples Forum was published sporadically—first semimonthly, then monthly—for almost two years, without advertising or paid circulation. Although its primary purpose was to promote Jim Jones and Peoples Temple, *Peoples Forum* gradually evolved into a leftist-socialist community newspaper. Every page plugged worthy causes, many of them struggling to survive—health clinics, counseling services, community centers, legal defense funds. With Jim Jones's direction, *Peoples Forum* took strong editorial stands on community, national, and international issues. After a while, every article was an editorial, a call for solidarity and action. *Peoples Forum* editorialized against racism, child abuse, the Chilean junta, discrimination against gays, nuclear proliferation, Pentagon boondoggles, militarism, terrorism, the death penalty, and the bludgeoning of baby seals. In many of the paper's tirades, there was a morbid fascination with atrocities and grotesque tortures, occasionally illustrated with drawings and photographs of southern lynch mobs, Jews in Nazi concentration camps, and Chilean soldiers cutting off the hands of Victor Jara, a popular folksinger. With each issue, the rhetoric became increasingly hysterical:

> . . . From this day forward, we want the Nazis to know that we would *like* them to come by our church—any time—and try to start something. We will not be bullied. We are quite able to defend ourselves. This is not the Third Reich; there is no Adolf Hitler running things; everyone is not goose-stepping yet. *And no matter if they were:* WE WOULD RESIST WITH OUR LIVES! WE WILL RESIST DOWN TO THE LAST MAN, WOMAN AND CHILD! The Nazi response has only made us that much more determined to expose their insidiousness and cowardice.

While *Peoples Forum* taunted the Nazis, Jim Jones moved about the community as a peacemaker. One of the great San Francisco battlegrounds of the seventies was the International Hotel, the dilapidated Kearney Street home of a group of tenants determined not to be evicted. The first eviction attempt occurred in 1974, when the building's owner, Four Seas Investment Corporation, was cited by the city for building code violations. Through legal maneuvers and demonstrations, the tenants postponed the inevitable for two years. The issue surfaced again in October of 1976, when Mayor Moscone announced plans to buy the building for $850,000. Although the plan had widespread support, including the endorsement of the housing authority commission, Four Seas wasn't satisfied with the price and filed suit to block the forced sale to the city. Four Seas won its lawsuit, and the tenants were again served with eviction notices. More than three thousand demonstrators—nearly two-thirds of them from Peoples Temple—formed a human chain in front of the building to prevent the evictions. When the situation began to get nasty, *Peoples Forum* reported in a February 1977 article headlined "Catastrophe Averted," Pastor Jones conducted his own peacekeeping mission:

> Although [the] Rev. Jones does not doubt that law enforcement did receive reports of weapons, he and his delegation made an unannounced and thorough tour of the building, scrutinizing from roof to basement. He conducted separate interviews with the tenants, found them to the last person committed to the principles of nonviolent resistance, and found no weapons of any kind.

While he was on the battlefront, Pastor Jones reviewed his cheering troops, who had earned the respect of the seasoned veterans of the antiwar protests, civil rights marches, and other demonstrations of the preceding decade. Jim Jones waved to his crowd of admirers and flashed his triumphant half smile.

While the International Hotel controversy was still raging, Peoples Temple hosted on January 15 one of the largest interracial celebrations in San Francisco's history. The occasion was the forty-eighth anniversary of the birth of Dr. Martin Luther King, Jr. A crowd of more than nine thousand people packed the Temple on Geary Street and overflowed into the street. Sponsored by the San Francisco Council of Churches—of which Peoples Temple was a member in good standing—the gathering featured speeches by Governor Jerry Brown, whom Jim Jones had invited to speak; by Ben Brown, a Georgia legislator who was a member of President Jimmy Carter's transition team; by several prominent black ministers; and, of course, by the Reverend Jones himself. Mayor Moscone was there with a host of civic leaders. The same day, during a separate celebration at Glide Memorial Church, Jim Jones received the coveted Martin Luther King, Jr., Humanitarian Award "in recognition of his outstanding efforts to further the ideals of civil rights and civil liberties championed by Dr. King."

As a leader in the black community, the pastor of the largest Protestant congregation in California, the chairman of the housing authority commission, political power broker, noted humanitarian, and international goodwill ambassador, Jim Jones was at the peak of his power. Forbes Burnham, the prime minister of Guyana, hosted a dinner in his honor. Exiled Black Panther leader Huey Newton met with him in Havana. In the city, in the state, and in other nations, Jim Jones's star was rising; nothing on the horizon was any brighter, at least not in San Francisco. In *Peoples Forum* for February 1977, second issue, Jones made his declaration of noncandidacy, apparently compelled by forces that seemed to be elevating him to deny ambition:

> There is a rumor circulating that Jim Jones would consider running

for Mayor in the next election. Some people have suggested and even encouraged him to become a candidate. His unqualified response was: "It is ludicrous. Some need to be on the outside of political institutions so they can form non-partisan judgments. I appreciate those who feel they can render service in the political arena, but it is clear where my own duties lie."

The buses were way overloaded . . . and he'd have eighty people on there. It would just be crowded, clam-packed, like slavery ships. I'm going to tell you how it is.

—Tommy Ijames, age eighteen

V

Glory Train

What the *Ukiah Daily Journal* once described—or praised—as a fleet of beautiful "gleaming silver buses" was the affluent realization of a lesson Jim Jones learned back when he made his forays from Indiana into central Ohio: that a congregation both experienced and portable could guarantee a successful service. Cripples were healed time and again of the same afflictions in different cities. The style was set early when a few carloads of people would drive a hundred and fifty miles or so to cheer young Jimmy in small Ohio towns on the Bible circuit and respond to his miraculous healing touch. In California those few carloads grew to a dozen busloads of close to a hundred each, so that Jim Jones brought with him wherever he performed upward of a thousand true believers, all well rehearsed in pleasing their master and providing examples for the new, the hopeful, and the untested seekers who jammed auditoriums from Seattle to LA.

Once a year Jim Jones took his followers on a tour across the United States, a thousand strong, and played one-nighters in most of the major cities. The well-oiled responses of his audience were impossible to question; strangers in these cities coughed up their dollars as readily as the faithful coughed up cancers, and Jim Jones always returned to California with legions of marveling yokels in his wake, his coffers made fat by their bucks.

From 1972 the buses traveled every weekend to San Francisco and Los Angeles, usually on alternate weekends, occasionally descending on both cities in the same weekend. Jim Jones used his buses to transport hundreds of bodies to demonstrations—to picket the *San Francisco Examiner* for printing unfavorable stories at one time, to march in Fresno in support of four jailed reporters at another. Those few members who had legitimate excuses for missing the bus trips stayed at home in Redwood Valley and attended services with tape-recorded sermons to keep them loyal in Jim Jones's absence, but by far the greater number spent as much time—or more—crammed into crowded buses as they spent sitting in church listening to Jones's interminable lectures. In transit from capitalist barbarism to socialist utopia, they quietly endured some discomfort.

*   *   *

162

Richmond, Indiana, knows Jim Jones because its high school spawned him in 1949 without a hint or a dream of the glory his future achievements would reflect. Today, June 29, 1976, that town's newspaper, the *Palladium-Item*, runs an article by Florence Lawson, telling of a visit to Jim's hometown, Lynn:

> Each summer the pastor takes persons who belong to his 10,500 active-member congregations to an educational and cultural tour of the United States. This year the tour visited Washington, D.C., Philadelphia, Pa., Cleveland, Ohio, Detroit, Mich., and Chicago, Ill. They are now on their way home.
>
> They visit historical sites, museums and other points of interest. Each member pays what he can toward his trip. The rest is subsidized by the church. They stop at churches of the Disciples of Christ to stay overnight whenever possible. One tour member said most of the persons would never have the chance to learn of the nation's history and culture, first-hand, if it was not for this opportunity.

Everyone has heard of Niagara Falls. It's the best-known honeymoon spot in the United States. More water tumbles over Niagara Falls than over any other falls in the world. The water provides electricity for the western world's largest power project—$737 million worth of materials, labor, and engineering built it. On the Peoples Temple buses, Niagara Falls is the hottest topic of conversation after Martin Luther King's grave in Atlanta. The members are tired—most of the trip is behind them—but they're not about to doze off and miss one of the most highly touted stops on their tour. Some of the members were hoping they'd stop and see the falls at night when word got around that the colored lights that played on them lent the falling waters, the foam, and the constant mist a majesty and splendor that rival the aurora borealis.

Sandy Parks lost the food truck in an accident just outside Syracuse, and now she rides a bus just like all the other members; and, like all the other members, she is squeezed in three to a seat. Tired and uncomfortable as she is, she shares the thrill of anticipation as the caravan pulls into the parking lot overlooking the falls. "Look, everybody!" someone shouts from across the aisle, and everyone turns toward the window and leans to the side, straining and squinting to get an early glimpse of nature's spectacle.

Sandy moves too slowly. Before she can get near the window to see, the buses are already leaving the parking lot. They didn't even pause. Next stop: Detroit.

The last time the Peoples Temple buses stopped in Detroit, Odell Rhodes's old friend went to a meeting. He joined the Temple then and there. Maybe religion was going to be better than the constant boozing with shortnecks of cheap tokay and the aches and shakes every morning. Odell hadn't seen his old friend for a year or so; he'd gone to California.

Odell's condition wasn't any better than his alky friend's. He was tired of the heroin treadmill that had him holding still for things a healthy man would have found grotesque and humiliating, tired of learning and accepting the limitless grip of recurring need for overpriced junk, tired of facing the streets every day prepared for violence. He had tried twice—and failed twice—to kick his habit.

This trip, Odell's old alky buddy looks him up and invites him to a meeting. The friend is clean and sharp, dried out from the booze, and happy. He looks like a successful businessman, Odell observes, and goes with his buddy to the meeting. In a short time, Odell will have a job in California, some respect in the community, the love of children, and the ability to walk the ghetto streets with money in his pocket—and hold on to it.

Jay Lund is a regional field officer for the Office of Emergency Preparedness in Santa Rosa, California. Vacation this year finds him driving through southern California. Interstate 5 is the new highway; you can take it from the Bay Area down to Los Angeles almost on automatic pilot, there are so few turns in the road, except where you turn off to stop at the rest stops along the way. Button Willow is usually a pretty busy rest stop. Not far from Bakersfield, it is the logical last stop before Los Angeles.

Jay watches a fleet of Greyhounds pull up. People pour out of them and crowd around the doors to the luggage compartment while others make a beeline to the rest rooms. When the crowd by the side of the bus walk away, there are a few more kids in the group. In the dash for the rest rooms, one woman trips on a water spigot sticking out of the ground. She hits the ground hard; Jay imagines he hears her splatter, but of course the sound is exaggerated. No one falls that hard. Jay rushes over to help the woman. Two men from the bus intercept him. "She's all right," they tell him. "She's fine." They pick her up from the pavement, and Jay feels a little useless.

Jay wonders who these people are, where they come from, where they are going. Odd group. When he asks, no one answers his questions. No one introduces himself. Even the kids won't tell him their names; they run off when he talks to them.

Jay leans against the side of his RV and scratches his head. Odd group.

Joyce Touchette looks after Mr. Muggs, chimpanzee-in-residence at Peoples Temple, Redwood Valley, California. Mr. Muggs enjoys equal treatment with the other members, even though he is only eighteen months old. He loves children. He loves animals. He seems to have adopted Joyce Touchette as his surrogate mother; she knows what to feed him. He has become something of a gourmet under Joyce's tutelage; among his favorite things to eat are salad with

164

garlic dressing, whipped cream, and rocks from the roof of the Touchette house in preference to rocks from the ground. Mr. Muggs often converses with Jim Jones in their common language. "Wahoo?" the Reverend Jones will ask; "Wahoo!" will Mr. Muggs reply. Often these conversations go on for several minutes, although Mr. Muggs does not like the company of adults. In fact, Jim claimed, Mr. Muggs had been trained to attack.

Joyce holds Mr. Muggs on her lap in one of the seats near the front of the bus. He is a treasure. The Reverend Jim Jones found him a grossly mistreated object of voyeurs and carefully nursed him back to health. Now he trusts both Jim Jones and Joyce. Periodically Joyce has to get up, lay Mr. Muggs on his back across the bus seat, and change his diapers.

George McCown keeps those buses in tip-top shape so they will pass the California Highway Patrol inspection. He makes sure the buses are safe; he's a mechanic, glad he can use his occupation in service of Peoples Temple. Rick Cordell and Marvin Swinney are glad to have George's help. They're bigwigs in the Temple, much closer to Jim Jones than George is, and sometimes George just can't understand some of the things they do. They are really good mechanics, both of them, good drivers, too, boy; but sometimes they'd stop along the highway and get phony receipts from people and then spend the money on booze or something—you could use up the money because you had receipts for it, see?—when everyone knows you ain't supposed to drink. Hell, Lena even got whipped for it. But they're good mechanics. Down in the garage is some of the best times. Of course, George always takes his own tools back home with him; too smart to leave them there. Might never see them again.

George checks the mirror on his left and sees a California Highway Patrol cruiser signaling the buses to pull over. Father's voice crackles over the intercom with the order. George pulls over to the shoulder and stops. He listens for the hiss of the braking system, then pops the door open in a hurry so Jack Beam can jump down and talk to the cop before the cop can get on the bus. George doesn't know what the hell Jack Beam says to the cop, but never, not once, has the CHP got on a Peoples Temple bus. George is relieved. He knows the CHP would not be pleased. There are more than seventy persons on George's forty-three passenger bus—not counting the kids in the luggage compartment.

The press accounts . . . talk about how uncomfortable it is, yet you can go find all these hippies lined up to cram into the Grey Rabbit and take a trip across the country on a bus and they don't even get to sit up for four days; they're crammed in like slaves on a sardine ship.

Ted Vincent and his wife, Selma, enjoyed their trip to Los Angeles; the price of a ticket was whatever you could afford to give. For nine dollars, Ted and Selma were able to attend the unity meeting with the Black Muslims.

They recall with pleasure their experience on that trip. The Grey Rabbit was a hippie alternative to Greyhound, perhaps not as efficient and reliable, but at least the no-smoking rules were not enforced. The Vincents maintain that Peoples Temple bus trips were no more difficult than those in the Grey Rabbit, and considerably less expensive.

And the glory is you get a big mattress to sleep on. But you also have to sleep in the rafters, it's a double-deck. For the Grey Rabbit, the glory of going hippie-style, you pay the same fare as Greyhound and half of you have got to sleep in the luggage rack; it's an expanded luggage rack.

And yet they talk about Jim Jones's buses as this terrible treatment of the people driving these long hours on these buses and the esprit de corps there is the same fun esprit de corps as on the Grey Rabbit. You cram them in and the kids don't mind sleeping on the bus for the weekend. . . .

"What bus did you ride on? Was it number seven?"

No. Number two. But the radio was going. All the drivers are hooked into a radio. And the lawyers were sitting in the front of various buses, talking back to different people, had different things to do, various different things to do—and all night long here's Jim Jones talking over the damn radio.

". . . Dick, Dick? You got some papers for the movie that's coming up?"

"Yeah."

"Did you get the legal appeals?"

"Yeah, got 'em."

"Good." Ted's attempt at reproducing Jim Jones's voice is not convincing. Selma adds:

And you took turns talking to the driver to keep him awake, and you had to stay awake, too; you didn't know when your shift was going to be.

Their daughter wanted to go along, too, and begged to be able to sleep up in the luggage rack with the other kids.

The air conditioning works beautifully on bus number seven. There are even two or three empty seats, and there is room to walk up and down the aisle. Diana Mertle prefers this even to the luggage compartment on another bus. Here there is space. This bus is cool and comfortable. This bus carries Diana's friend, Cindy Cordell, and maybe two dozen others. Diana and Cindy occupy two seats. No one else sits with them. Cindy's father, Harold Cordell, is the driver, and this bus is the best bus because this bus is Father's bus.

Diana looks over her shoulder when she hears the door to Jim Jones's special compartment open. Grace Stoen backs out and closes the door behind her. She is head counselor, so she can go to Father's compartment. Back there, besides the bed that replaces the last row of seats, Father has a desk, a refrigerator, and even his own bathroom.

Diana hopes she'll be as pretty as Grace when she grows up. Jim Jones has convinced Diana that she is ugly, but maybe she'll outgrow it; she's only twelve. Grace must be the prettiest woman in Peoples Temple. She is tall and delicate, more than a half foot over five feet tall, with big warm round brown eyes so moist they seem always on the verge of tears, with hair cropped close and neat around a classic face. She is efficient. She has just gone over, with Jim Jones, a stack of papers various members have turned in to her. On each of the papers is a complaint. Each of the complaints reports one member's mistreatment of another, or an infraction of Temple rules, or a lapse in faith or dedication. Members "write up" one another, even their relatives, for such sins; Diana hopes she has not been written up for eating an apple all by herself. Head counselor Grace Stoen, tall and delicate, backs out of Father's compartment and closes the door carefully behind her. She has just helped Jim Jones decide who should be beaten.

Services in Los Angeles this weekend were so successful—thirty thousand dollars in donations from two services—that the weekend's Sunday night service is held back home in Redwood Valley. Faith Worley, Temple nurse, young and pretty, dispenses aspirin right and left to the members who have developed headaches on the six-hundred-mile return trip. Danny Pietila and Robin Wages have headaches. They thank Faith for the pills with genuine gratitude.

During the service in Redwood Valley, Jim Jones stops midsentence and points to Danny and Robin. "You two were kissing on the bus. Don't you know how selfish that is? Don't you know what can happen to you? I feel—I feel— your fingers and toes, Danny and Robin, your fingers and toes are tingling, going numb, tingling, and you're confused now, aren't you? And you know why, don't you?"

Faith knows why. When Danny and Robin asked for aspirin, Faith gave them Quaalude—two 300-milligram tablets each. Jim Jones's revelation coincides with the waves of sensation that mark the drug's taking hold.

This is not the first time Faith has given Quaalude to members at Jim Jones's behest, nor will it be the last. She has access to Jim Jones's traveling pharmacy; the drugs are kept in Father's room on bus number seven— Quaalude, Sinequan, Percodan, liquid caffeine, uppers, downers, pain-killers, sleepers, leapers, soapers, and tranks, oxygen to refresh Jim Jones and vodka to slow him down, and nitroglycerine for his heart condition. In the doctor's bag the pill jars are uncapped and their contents spill randomly across the bag's bottom, pink, yellow, white, orange, blue, green, and black, tablets and capsules, like an assortment of penny candies in a dope fiend's dream.

Like the other nurses—Joyce Beam and Janet Phillips—Faith rides bus number seven on every trip. She has been a part of Peoples Temple since she was a little girl in Indiana. She came along to California in the early days with her parents, Whitey and Opal Freestone. Whitey and Opal left the church a few years ago, before the 1972 expansion, before the weekly bus trips to San

Francisco and Los Angeles, before the annual cross-country pilgrimages. But Faith stayed in. She grew up in Peoples Temple, studied and became a nurse, worked in hospitals and stole drugs for Jim Jones.

Faith is glad she's done her bit tonight by giving Danny and Robin the Quaalude. Like everyone else, she's tired, so tired after the weekend—Friday night services in San Francisco, load up the buses, get off the buses, Saturday morning and evening in Los Angeles, load up the buses, get off the buses, Sunday morning in San Francisco, load up the buses, get off the buses, on the buses again, and finally, six hundred miles from LA, Sunday night in Redwood Valley—so tired that she doesn't know what time it is or how long Jim Jones is going to speak or how many times everyone has to force a smile or get hit for falling asleep. Her eyes stay open only because she is too spaced to remember to blink.

The door to the luggage compartment is held ajar about four inches to admit air and light, and the first light of morning awakens Diana Mertle. One of the advantages of riding down below is that you never get disturbed for the collections. One of the disadvantages is that there's no place to pee. Early morning is especially difficult, but Diana has ridden down there in the luggage compartment, where you can't sit up and you can't stretch out, often enough to figure out how to relieve her bladder without sitting in her own urine. Smart kids like Diana save their pop-top cans and learn to aim.

On Birdie's bus, the toilet worked at the beginning of the trip, but, she says, "Most of the time it didn't."

It were terrible. You had to ask could you use the bathroom, and you had to time yourself. It was just horrible, you had to time yourself going to the bathroom, especially for the old peoples.

They wouldn't let you use the bathroom on the bus. You had to go to the bathroom . . . like, they'd stop at this park, and you'd have to go to the bathroom. You can imagine, about a thousand, a thousand peoples lineded up at one, at some café. And the peoples wondering, "What in the worlds are all these peoples here? All these black, and white, and my God, where is all of 'em going?" I mean, it wasn't fair to the customers, you know. Jim—Damn buying anything, you better not even buy any thing—but you understand, we wanted to go in and use the people's bathroom, see? This was taking advantage of peoples.

By the time the buses reach Detroit, Birdie can't stand it any longer. She has headaches and her stomach is so painful she can't stand up and she can't sit down. When she threatens to go to the people next door to the church in Detroit, she tells the counselors, "I'll tell you one thing—they ain't goin' to treat me no worser than I been treated here." One of the Temple nurses gives Birdie an enema, and the Christians in Motown are none the wiser. Maybe it's Motown; after two weeks or more on those buses, it's hard to know for sure.

168

One thing Birdie does know for sure: she'll never ever take another trip on a Peoples Temple bus. "The way they treat the old peoples, it's a shame."

The *Washington Post* for Tuesday, August 14, 1973, reports on a "California Church Group" in an article headlined "Tourists Pick Up and Go":

> A 13-bus caravan of Californians arrived with thousands of other tourists at the U.S. Capitol yesterday, but instead of staring up at the dome they spread out over the Capitol grounds and began picking up litter.
> The group of 660 members of the Peoples Temple Christian Church was doing what it has done in . . . dozens of other cities it has visited since it left Redwood Valley, Calif., last Wednesday.
> "We like to leave everyone, everywhere we go, thinking we left the place a little bit better than when we came," said one 82-year-old woman. . . .
> The church group now plans a "leisurely" trip back to Redwood Valley, cleaning up along the way, Mr. Jones said.

Tommy Ijames rides in the same stinking bus that the other kids ride, and breathes—or tries to avoid breathing—the same stinking air. Sometimes the five-gallon can that serves as the toilet is kept in the stairwell by the front door, and sometimes it's hidden in the back, by the last row of seats. Whatever you have to do, you do it in that five-gallon can when you can find a friend to hold up the towel for a little privacy. Some poor kid can't wait, so he perches unsteadily, loses his footing, and kicks the can over. The kids on the floor jump up, anywhere, up into the luggage racks and on to the laps of the people in the seats, anywhere to get away from the fetid slop that covers the floor from the back of the bus clear up to the driver and drips thickly down the stairs to the door.

For a young teenager, Diana Mertle has a lot of responsibility. She helps Liz Forman on the housing committee. She talks to all the people on the bus to find out whether they have accommodations for the weekend in Los Angeles. She wakes up two hours earlier than everyone else because it takes that long to get all the information. Nobody wakes up smiling. Nobody tells her thank you.

On the paper on her clipboard, she writes the name, age, sex, and race of every person she talks with, and she writes whether that person has a place to stay for the weekend, and she writes the name, address, and phone number of the host. She writes all the information for one person, then for the person sitting behind the first person, and for the person above in the rack and below on the floor, before she is finished with the first row. Diana steps cautiously and unsteadily back, placing her feet wherever there's a spot of floor showing, and shakes the shoulder of the lady in the next seat. By the time she's finished filling out her sheets, two hours have elapsed. It's time for a collection.

Diana is hostess on her bus, too. Besides making out the attendance sheets for the housing committee, she must report illness, keep the driver awake, fetch soda pop for those who request it because there's no room for others to move, and take the collections.

Diana hates the collections more than any of her other duties. They're always taken for a good reason; this morning, Father has learned that a new member of Peoples Temple has lost his job, and he and his family are about to be evicted from their home unless they can pay the rent. In the spirit of apostolic equalitarian sharing, fellow members must share the burden so that this family will not be homeless. Diana's job is to go to each rider on the bus and ask for money. She has to tell her fellow passengers to empty their purses for stray coins, turn their pockets inside out, extract a pledge for a portion of next week's check or allowance—she herself has pledged her allowances for the next ninety years—until the goal is reached. The goal for this collection is one thousand dollars.

Diana counts the money she has collected. For her bus, the total is less than four dollars. The buses pull over to stop and the counselors come in to beg. "What do you mean, you have no money? You were seen buying a hot dog back there, and you got change. Hand it over."

Elmer Mertle is falling asleep at the wheel. The buses have to keep rolling. "Diana. Diana. DIANA." Elmer's voice penetrates the warm fog in Diana's sleepy mind. She's hostess, and she's supposed to keep the driver awake.

"Huh?"

"Diana, throw some water on me. All of it."

Diana stands up, takes the lid off the water bucket she's been sitting on, and empties the bucket of water over her father's head.

"Thank you, honey."

Elmer's bus keeps rolling.

Robin Wages is eleven years old. She has never been across the United States of America before. From her perch up in the rack above the seats, she can look out the window opposite and see the power poles that line the highway pass in endless succession against a background of amber waves of grain, and every time she opens her eyes she knows it's true, it's true, America is beautiful, she is so tired and hungry, no food now for eighteen hours, rolling under spacious skies nonstop, get back over purple mountains' majesty and try not to look at the fruited plain, it's too much like food, over the purple mountains and back home and crown thy good and get back home and hide.

For I was an hungred, and ye gave me meat

170

O beautiful for pilgrim's feet rolling nonstop from St. Louis come a long way over amber waves of grain and amber waves of grain, mile after mile. The luggage rack

I was thirsty, and ye gave me drink

above the seats on the old Greyhound is two feet wide, stretches the entire length of the bus, and is made of inch-thick metal tubes spaced about three inches apart and running parallel longitudinally along your chest and stomach and thighs and feet whose stern impassioned stress, O beautiful, hang your head and cry over the rack; there's Diana keeping the driver awake. The metal tubes impress the flesh

I was a stranger, and ye took me in: Naked, and ye clothed me

so that you have to move every few minutes or wake up with bruises striping your flesh and the motion of the bus swaying on the turns

I was sick, and ye visited me: I was in prison, and ye came unto me

makes you fight back the dry heaves while God sheds his grace on thee but nothing else, nothing else, nothing to eat or drink; the water was rationed and is long gone, one bucket per bus. Robin sees Diana sitting on the water bucket talking to her father, Elmer the driver, keeping him awake, daughter to father, but aren't they all in the same family? And crown they good with brotherhood.

Then shall the righteous answer him, saying, Lord, when saw we thee an hungred, and fed thee? or thirsty, and gave thee drink?

Robin watches the highway and the endless farms slip past the green glass of the window across the aisle. The kids on the floor are sound asleep now, every one of them. It's good that no one wants to walk back down the aisle because it would be impossible to avoid stepping on the children with heavy feet a thoroughfare for freedom beat across the wilderness, America, America,

When saw we thee a stranger, and took thee in? or naked, and clothed thee? Or when saw we thee sick, or in prison, and came unto thee?

God mend thine every flaw; confirm thy soul in self-control, and Robin (nothing to eat) opens her bag, thy liberty in law, and she takes out (*When saw we thee an hungred?*) her tube of toothpaste and twists off the cap all caked with white and eats.

And the King shall answer and say unto them, Verily I say unto you, Inasmuch as ye have done it unto the least of these my brethren, ye have done it unto me.

The women—Linda, Sharon, and Faith—lift Jim Jones and lay his twitching body on the bed in the back of bus number seven. Seattle is hours away and Jim's son Steve sits on the floor quietly, shielded from the crisis by a deep sleep. Faith sits on the edge of the bed. Father is fallen victim to a rare kind of seizure that has no name: his body jerks, but his eyes are not rolled back, his lips are not blue, he does not swallow his tongue, his hands are not cold, his pulse seems normal. Faith wonders at the origin of this seizure. Jim Jones supposedly has a heart problem, but seizures do not normally accompany heart problems.

Jim Jones opens his eyes and sees Faith sitting beside him. "Faith," he says, "sometimes when I have these heart problems the best thing for me is sexual arousement." Jim Jones takes Faith's hand and puts it on his penis. Her fingers curl; she can tell, under the trousers, that it is erect. Jim chuckles a little.

"What are you laughing about?"

"Well, you know, to tell the truth, I've been having these fantasies about you—and Linda and Sharon, you know. . . ."

Linda and Sharon leave the room and shut the door carefully behind them. Faith and Jim are alone on the bed, protected by the armor plate that forms the back wall and by the conspiracy of silence. Steve Jones is asleep. Linda and Sharon are up front. Faith has no idea what to expect. She sits there with her hand over his penis—he has boasted during services of having ten inches—and she is baffled.

"Faith, remember when I told you about some sexual fantasies I had about you and Linda and Sharon? I just said that because they were there, but I was really referring to you. I'd like to have intercourse with you." He pulls Faith's head down close to his face and grinds his mouth against hers. His fingers squeeze at her breasts. He unzips his pants and whips out his penis, keeping Faith's hand on it while he raises her dress and puts his hand up there and kneads the warm flesh through her panties.

"I'd like to put a bambino on your titties."

"Look," says Faith, "I don't want to get pregnant."

This is one side of him I'd never seen and it sort of scared me. It was like—before, I'd always had this idea of him. I'd never related to him as sexual, in my mind— then when this thing happened to me, he had me touch his penis, it was like that image I had of him as the leader, whatever, was gone. . . . He told me to go the next day and get fitted for a diaphragm, and he wanted to see me Monday night.

Sandy Parks drives the food truck. The food truck is one vehicle in a caravan of eleven buses, two automobiles, two small trucks, and one semi towing a van full of equipment and supplies for services in cities across the country: Houston, New Orleans, Atlanta, Washington, New York, Philadelphia. The goddamned truck flipped in Syracuse and right behind Father's bus, too. Sandy loads the truck all by herself: huge cartons of cereal and dried milk and canned goods, boxes of white bread and margarine, cases of Dr. Pepper and Pepsi-Cola, paper plates and plastic spoons.

That's one of the reasons Jim didn't want me to leave. He said, "You're one of the hardest workers I got." I said, "Yeah . . ."

Whenever there's a stop, Sandy doles out the food to the representative from each bus. Everybody eats at least three times a day. Sandy plans the menus. This morning's breakfast is cereal. So was yesterday morning's, and so will tomorrow's be—homemade granola from a great big box lined with plastic, dried skim milk solids mixed up and doled out, bread and margarine, juice when there's time to mix juice, all served up on paper plates with plastic spoons, and the people are good, so good, about cleaning up after themselves.

Halfway through the turnaround to come back west—the South is behind, and so is Washington—the food gets a little short. Whenever the food runs out, Sandy can always go to Mike Prokes for the money to feed those hundreds of people. He goes to Jim and gets the money—seventy-five dollars.

Sandy does what she can. She buys big solid tubes of bologna, slices it and slaps it on white bread until it runs out, then substitutes peanut butter. The diners can wash down their sandwiches with cold Dr. Pepper; there's always plenty of ice to keep it cold. Sandy does the best she can. She's even had her helpers scrounging on the streets for food, or for money for food, to feed her brothers and sisters.

This trip, the line is drawn at Philadelphia, twenty-nine hundred miles from home. Out of food and out of money, Sandy approaches Mike Prokes again. Mike Prokes goes to Jim Jones. Jim Jones says no.

The death certificate says that Truth Hart, age sixty-five, died at the Marabelle Rest Home in Ukiah, California; but Birdie was gone on the bus trip when Truth died. Birdie was the "getting-happy one." "Birdie, you're a drawing card to me," Jim Jones told her when he begged her to go on the trip.

> One tour member said most of the persons would never have the chance to learn of the nation's history and culture, firsthand, if it was not for this opportunity.

They did not sing on the buses, they did not even talk. They would sleep or try to sleep but were awakened every hour or two for collections, for announcements, for standing up and jogging in place, for passing cans of cold beans to the po' old peoples in the seat behind, it were terrible, it were terrible. "Birdie," says Jim Jones, standing on the steps of the Temple, "Birdie, don't you tell anyone what happened.".

173

Birdie keeps her mouth shut. She keeps her mouth shut and never goes back to Peoples Temple.

Diana, tell me, do you remember anything that made you feel good, made you happy, any kind of happy feeling at all? Maybe not just for yourself, but for anyone else?
I don't remember anything happy about the whole thing.

July, 1976: Three weeks on the buses were enough to push Grace Stoen to make her decision, and now she sits on the beach at Lake Tahoe. She can't stop thinking about her four-year-old son, John-John. She dare not forget that, as head counselor, she knows everything about Jim Jones. She dared not take her baby when she decided to leave the Temple. She dared not even tell her husband, Tim. "I couldn't trust him," she says. "He'd tell Jim."

She spends the July Fourth weekend trying to relax at the California resort, trying to enjoy the warm sand, pleased with the Tahoe sun. She stretches her arms and fakes a yawn and turns over. Every now and then she glances over her shoulder or scans the bright sand to see if any Temple members have tracked her down.

I was completely healed of a fatal malignant growth soon after I made my commitment to Apostolic life. But I did not join People's Temple because I hoped for a healing. The real reason I joined is that Jim Jones is the most principled, compassionate, and dynamic human being I have ever encountered.

—Eugene B. Chaikin, Attorney-at-Law

VI

Backstage with the Special Effects Department

They called themselves "the girls." There were eight of them. They gathered material for Jim Jones's revelations and assisted him with his miracle cancer cures. Although few people recognized them, they were there at every meeting, stomping into the office with their suitcases jammed with files, frantically collating "obs"—observations—of Temple members and new prospects, sitting quietly in the congregation waiting for their cues with bits of beef brains packed in plastic bags hidden in tissues palmed in their hands. Disguised as wizened spinsters and black matrons, they would rise on cue out of wheelchairs or throw away their canes. They would lurk in the ghettoes of San Francisco and Los Angeles, faces blacked with theatrical makeup, waiting for the chance to break into a prospective member's home or rummage through the garbage can in search of anything at all. They would appear at a door as ingenuous dolls having car trouble and ask to use the phone and make mental notes of the number of house plants and the color of the phone and the condition of the furniture. They would ask to use the bathroom, then search the medicine cabinet and copy the labels from prescription bottles and the brand of razor blades and the number of tubes of Preparation H. Only a handful of people in the Temple knew anything about them. They knew everything about everybody.

They were Patty Cartmell, Linda Sharon Amos, Carolyn Layton, Sandy Bradshaw, Janet Phillips, Joyce Beam, Faith Worley, and Linda Dunn. A ninth member of the girls was Joyce Beam's father, Jack Beam; he and Patty Cartmell were the old troupers from the Indianapolis days, and so was Marceline Jones, until she got a job. She went to work as inspector of nursing homes for the California Department of Public Health and could no longer take the risk to her reputation nor the time for her Temple specialty: rectal healings. Marceline set the style for getting the afflicted to pass their cancers. She would take the patient into the bathroom for a quickie enema and, with her hands beneath the patient's anus, pop open a plastic bag containing a rotting chicken gizzard and some clotted human blood in time to catch a swoosh of liquid and mix it with the blood and chicken guts. The patient would emerge from the bathroom a true believer, blessed with a miracle no less spectacular than Jesus' turning water into wine. Jim Jones turned chicken guts into cancerous tumors.

The girls, as a group, didn't have a name. Temple members knew only that these eight women and one man were Jim Jones's personal staff. When they were preparing for a meeting, the guards at the door to their office had strict orders to let no one in; even the guards didn't know what was going on. All of the girls worked without pay and supported themselves with jobs on the outside—all except Jack Beam and Patty Cartmell.

Patty Cartmell, five feet five inches tall, one hundred and ninety-five pounds, was the workhorse of the group. It was she who perfected the sophisticated intelligence-gathering techniques and began the intricate filing system that permitted the girls to match names from obs cards with information sheets in seconds. Patty had a knack for getting information and a photographic memory for the physical details of a home. She was gifted with a tongue and manner that would elicit conversation with even the most hostile or suspicious souls. Despite her impressive talent for organizing data and systems, she was personally the epitome of chaos; she kept her hair short so she wouldn't have to bother with it, and she hid her obesity under generous bright muumuus.

Jack Beam was the most direct link to Jim Jones; the gruff, balding assistant minister kept the pressure on by constantly demanding material for Father's revelations. Carolyn Layton, first in command, issued the assignments with frequent reminders that "Jim Jones really has a gift, but he can't do it all by himself; Father needs our help." She was also resident makeup artist and drama coach.

Linda Sharon Amos was an early innovator in Redwood Valley; her fertile imagination was responsible for combining chicken guts and limburger cheese to simulate rectal tumors, and for those grandiose stories of Jim Jones's powers: how he walked through walls, how he healed himself of bullet wounds. Sandy Bradshaw, a probation officer in Mendocino County, was an expert at the shakedown. When a disgruntled member would leave the church or start talking to people on the outside, Sandy and Linda would show up and threaten dire consequences and personal calamities for those who strayed from the umbrella of Father's guidance. Linda Dunn, Jim Jones's private secretary, kept up the filing system in a shack near Redwood Valley when she wasn't gathering information in Los Angeles. In her spare time she worked forty hours a week, Monday through Friday, as a secretary in the local lumber industry.

Faith Worley, Joyce Beam, and Janet Phillips were the Temple nurses. They were always with Jim Jones during the healings, performing their sleight-of-hand miracles either at his side or off in the bathroom. When Faith Worley joined the staff in 1968, she added her own innovative talents to those of Linda Sharon Amos and Marceline and improved the healings with the benefit of her experience with terminal cancer patients. She knew well the odor of death from cancer, and she replaced the chicken guts with meat that smelled more like the real thing: beef brains aged a couple of days without refrigeration. She implemented another innovation, too: to the vials of blood the girls—and Jim Jones—would draw from their own veins she added Heparin, an anticoagulant, before packing the blood with the brains in the little plastic bags. The "cancers" were stored in a locked refrigerator at Faith's house. They could be kept indefinitely.

These were the girls. The eight of them, and Jack Beam, were the muses in Jim Jones's pantheon. Three of them eventually descended from Jones's Olympian heights and returned to the world of ordinary mortals.

Faith Worley first met Jim Jones in 1958, when she was eight. From about age sixteen, Faith was kept busy in the Temple writing letters—more than fifty a week, each in a slightly different hand, slightly different language, signed with names culled randomly from the telephone book—to senators and congressmen, urging them to vote the way Jim Jones wanted. Faith did her work earnestly, and by the time she started nursing school, she was in charge of the meticulous medical records Jim Jones insisted be kept on each Temple member. Father had to know who had diabetes or hypertension, insomnia or narcolepsy, anxiety, depression, heart trouble, or arthritis, the better to minister to the needs of his flock. He wanted blood types, medical histories, dietary information. When the holocaust came, Jim Jones wanted to be sure everyone who needed medication had an adequate supply.

When Faith got a job in a local hospital, Jim Jones had her get all the medical supplies she could lay her hands on. She bought the supplies at first, but the increasing demands from Jim Jones and Jack Beam were soon more than she could afford. She figured the hospital wouldn't miss a few items each week from its storeroom. Faith would hardly make a dent in the supply of sterile syringes and needles, bandages, and I.V. bottles; and the hospital checked the supplies of adrenaline, liquid caffeine, and nitroglycerine only to replenish them. But the controlled substances—tranquilizers like Dalmane, Haldol, Quaalude; narcotics like Percodan, Demerol, and codeine; stimulants—these presented a greater challenge. Strict record-keeping requirements make such drugs difficult to steal. Faith had to use her wits; she'd wait until a patient was discharged and steal whatever dope was left in the bottle, then destroy the inventory sheets. Faith did her best, and the store of drugs that was intended to maintain the members through the nuclear holocaust grew to mountainous proportions.

One day Jim Jones approached Faith with a new mission. He wanted her to work on the healings and revelations. "Father has this gift," he said, "but it is so heavy on Father that he needs help. He needs help to impress the people and bring about socialism."

Jim Jones needn't have bothered to offer an explanation for the request; a word or a suggestion would have been motive enough for Faith to jump into any task, no matter how deceitful, no matter how distasteful, as long as it served to further Jones's apostolic equalitarianism. After a few years in the Temple, even the rationale of apostolic equalitarianism became redundant; it was enough to serve Father. Any early training in values and ethics was ultimately wrung from Temple members' hearts and minds by the constant activity, the sleeplessness, the unrelenting criticism of selfish pursuits like love and new clothes, the dizzying efforts to follow Jim Jones's circular rhetoric with minds too fatigued to do more than hold one's eyes open, the burden of guilt mounting increment by daily increment, the knowledge that some Temple member somewhere may write you up to the council, the fear that anyone might be beaten anytime for anything because the rules kept changing, you could sin and not know it, you could do right and be mistaken, you could speak up or keep silent and be damned or praised for either, by the walls implanted in the mind by the fear of talking to outsiders, but mostly by the fatigue, until to get any assignment at all was an honor and a delight because if Jim Jones didn't tell you what to do you would sit motionless, watching the hands go around on the clock and feeling, rather simply, like a bubble gone burst in an indifferent air.

Faith went to work immediately. After a brief training session with Linda Sharon Amos, Patty Cartmell, and Jack Beam, she got her first assignment. She and Linda Sharon Amos drove to San Francisco one Friday evening to gather information. They worked all night, slept a couple of hours in Linda's rented car, and resumed work early Saturday morning. Linda Sharon Amos taught Faith how to disguise herself with a wig, heavy makeup, and loose clothing. She taught her how to get into someone's house by feigning car trouble. She taught her how to blend into the ghetto with an Afro wig, blackface, and nostrils flared with cotton. With Faith's deep brown eyes, the disguise was perfect; she looked born black.

They gathered information until late Saturday night, then went to the San Francisco Temple on Geary near Fillmore to put it all together for the Sunday services. Faith learned how to type the revelations according to form. The name of the subject—the person observed—and the location she typed in the upper-left-hand corner, and below these, the words *Revelation to* followed by her initials, then the date and whether the visit was "direct" or "indirect." Direct visits occurred in the presence of the subject or in the subject's home. Indirect visits were more varied. They included outside surveillance, calls to distant relatives, chats with neighbors, and detailed lists of the contents of the subject's garbage can: *Envelope from NOW Women's Center, 1736 I St., N.W., Washington, D.C., postmarked 2/10/73; bag "Busy Baker" fig bars (whole wheat fig bars); 1 dozen La Reina Corn Tortillas, San Jose, Calif.; canned vegetarian beans in tomato sauce Heinz (2 cans 16 ozs each); Vita-Crunch Granola (no preservatives);* and so on.

For their inventory, they would take the contents of a garbage can to the

179

Temple or to a motel and spread it out on a long table. The girls listed each item under *Garb* in the revelations file. Linda Sharon Amos was painstakingly accurate and thorough; her inventory of the garbage of Tim and Grace Stoen, the Temple's assistant minister and head counselor, for May 16, 1972, is four pages long. The inventory she did on the garbage of the Temple's other attorney, Eugene Chaikin, and his wife, Phyllis, was almost touching. A little more than halfway down the page—dated February 14, 1973—is the notation *white paper cut out in shape of heart.*

Faith worked often with Linda Dunn, usually in Los Angeles. Faith liked to do revelations with Linda because Linda was the only member of the staff who insisted on staying in comfortable motels. They would drive down from Ukiah on Friday night and catch a plane at San Francisco International Airport. They would rent a car in Los Angeles, get a motel room, and gather information until dawn. At some prospective member's house, they would appear at the door, two innocent girls fresh out of high school, with their car fresh out of gas, and could they please use the telephone? They were sweet and friendly, irresistible, certainly not quite helpless, and people succumbed to their charm without hesitation. People would talk to them—about their families, their jobs, their hopes and their fears. Mind if I use the bathroom? Straight down the hall and first door to the left. Open the medicine cabinet. Copy prescription labels verbatim: the name of the drug and the dosage, the doctor who prescribed it, the date, how many times a day. Move fast. Flush the toilet. Run water in the sink. Go through all the drawers. Write down everything that could possibly be used in a revelation.

When no one was home, Faith and Linda would raid the garbage can. It was always easier when the can was lined with a trash bag because they could just take the bag with them and replace it with a new one. Patty Cartmell taught them how to break into a house without leaving a trace, how to pry open windows and pick locks. She taught them to be thorough when going through drawers and cabinets, and careful; anything they moved had to be returned to its proper place. Under no circumstances were they ever to return without information. They were under strict orders from Jim Jones to gather material on everyone who walked into the Temples in Los Angeles, San Francisco, and Redwood Valley. Faith Worley and Linda Dunn followed those strict orders to the letter.

The two women had worked together before, writing letters every week to congressmen. Linda Dunn was in charge of the letter-writing campaigns, a responsible position since letter writing involved nearly everyone in the church. She had joined the church in 1967 just after she and Larry, her husband, and their three children moved to California from their home in Ohio. They had hoped to save their teetering marriage by making a new start, left family and friends behind in Ohio, and settled into a two-bedroom apartment in Ukiah because Larry's parents had moved there with the Temple group from Indianapolis. Linda had no idea what this group was about, except that it was headed by a minister named Jim Jones who had "big revival meetings in Cincinnati."

Larry was just out of the service and looking for a job. He didn't bother to ask his parents where they were spending their Sundays. Linda got hired right away as a secretary in the lumber industry, but the job didn't pay enough to support a family of five comfortably. There was barely enough money for groceries, let alone furniture for their unfurnished apartment.

A few days after they arrived in Ukiah, Linda and Larry were visited by callers bearing gifts: groceries and enough furniture to fill the void in their tiny apartment. The callers were from Jim Jones's Peoples Temple Christian Church, and although Linda and Larry "weren't into religion or anything like that," they felt obligated to go to a Sunday service. They drove up to the Church of the Golden Rule, where Jones held services before the Temple was built, and attended Sunday services for a year, bored and doubting, before dropping out.

One night about three months after Larry and Linda dropped out, Larry's father, Nathaniel, stopped by and told Linda that Jim Jones had just had a revelation about Larry and Linda. Jim Jones foresaw that, if they didn't get back into the church, they "were going to have some serious problems." Jim Jones was right: Larry and Linda's marriage was in trouble again. They showed up at services the following Sunday.

While Larry and Linda had been sitting at home resting on the Sabbath for three months, Jim Jones had been gearing up in a big way for the holocaust. He'd had his revelation about a cave nearby that was large enough for all his people. The end would come on the sixteenth, he said, but he never told the month or the year. That number was revealed to him during meditation, as clearly as the sun on a summer's day, but he never told a soul the exact date because it was better simply to be prepared.

Larry was making good money at the time driving a beer truck, so he and Linda and their three kids could afford to move to a two-story house on Oak Street. An entire room upstairs was devoted to Temple activities. Stacked in one corner of that room were the provisions members were collecting for the holocaust: canned goods, old Clorox bottles filled with water, bandages and other medical supplies. The room was constantly buzzing. Besides the letters—fifty to a hundred each week from each member—there was the newsletter, *The Temple Reporter.* Linda also taught Sunday school. She drove Temple buses. She directed the children's choir. There were marathon services all day Saturday and Sunday in three cities. There were meetings Monday and Friday nights.

What had started as a Sunday obligation became the defining fact of Linda's and Larry's lives, and their marriage once again began to crumble. Larry took care of the children while Linda worked for the church until dawn and then somehow dragged herself to work. Theirs wasn't the only marriage in the Temple that was faltering. Linda and Larry joined a group of Temple young couples who were having encounter sessions on Friday nights on Temple property along the Russian River. The meetings ended with bitter bickering among the couples about their sex lives.

The group met separately from the church until Jim Jones found out and denounced it as a "clique." The following Wednesday, he started his own catharsis sessions. During one of these sessions—after hours of screaming and yelling about impotence and frigidity—Jim Jones issued his marriage decree: no more sex among couples. Linda was among those who pledged celibacy, and Larry left for Ohio a few days later.

As soon as Jim Jones heard of Linda's decision, he started lavishing praise on her. One day a few weeks after Larry left, Jim Jones took Linda aside and told her he had appointed her to his personal staff. Linda was honored. She saw Jim Jones as the only hope for turning the United States away from war, poverty, and oppression. Vietnam had divided the people of this country as nothing had since the Civil War—there were antiwar protests, ghetto riots, bombings, arson, wiretaps, agents provocateurs on every campus, National Guardsmen marching into campuses and busting heads and teargassing students, even shooting four students in Ohio, Bobby Seale chained and gagged in an American courtroom—and the world as it was was not a world Linda wanted for her children. The signs were clear: the Fascist dictatorship Jim Jones predicted was moving in high gear. Linda would do what she could to help; it was an honor.

Soon after she joined the elite staff, Linda realized her schedule was not conducive to raising a family. Truly dedicated members, she was told, "were not supposed to hold on to their children." She placed them in the care of the Temple and moved into the shack in Redwood Valley where the files were kept.

To prove their loyalty, each of the girls had to do at least one dramatic healing. Linda's debut was as an elderly white woman in a wheelchair who hadn't wanted to walk for years, ever since she saw her husband and children die in an auto accident. The staff chose to do the healing in Seattle because Jim Jones told them he wanted "something very effective" there. Seattle was a weak spot, and he wanted to build his following. Linda flew there from San Francisco and arrived early Saturday morning. She met Carolyn Layton, Sandy Bradshaw, and Linda Sharon Amos in a motel room and they started rehearsing immediately. First they worked on the woman's tragic story; they went over it again and again until Linda got it down pat. They worked on teaching Linda how to stand as if she hadn't been on her feet in years—slowly, shaking, hesitating at first while she got used to her leg muscles working, and then gradually to step with increasing confidence until she was walking as if nothing had ever happened. Carolyn Layton worked on Linda's makeup most of the day. She applied egg whites to Linda's face to make it appear wrinkled. She highlighted crow's-feet lines and covered them expertly with powder. She fitted a gray wig on Linda's head and topped it off with a matronly pillbox hat. She draped Linda in an old lady's dress that concealed her youthful figure.

After a few dress rehearsals in the wheelchair, Linda was ready for her debut. The cab picked her up in front of the motel and took her directly to the meeting, where she was helped inside by aides. She sat helplessly in the wheelchair for about an hour, until she heard her cue from Jim Jones. She recited her lines without a flaw, without a hint she was anything other than what she appeared. Nobody recognized Linda Dunn, not even the people she had known most of her adult life. Jim Jones met her in front of the pulpit with a hand-held microphone. He placed his healing hands on her shoulders and commanded her to rise out of the wheelchair. She tried but nothing happened. She struggled against her crippling thoughts, but her mind was still winning. He commanded her again and she pushed against the wheelchair arms with all her strength and faith and courage and—Praise Father—rose up and stood on her own two feet, victorious for a moment, but she began to falter and Father, praise him, held her steady and told her to walk. And walk she did. It began as a slow shuffle until she remembered how to lift her feet off the floor and put them back down, ever so carefully, one right after the other. She walked. The tense silence of the crowd broke to wild cheers and shouts of Praise Father and Linda walked right out of that hall as fast as she could and caught a cab. She didn't wait around for curtain calls.

Faith Worley did only one dramatic healing; she was afraid she'd be recognized. She preferred, instead, the dual role of nurse and spy. She was always front and center for the cancer healings, but she was little more than a shadow of Jim Jones. Even when she carried the cancers through the crowd, people weren't looking at her; they were looking at the gruesome thing in the tissue. Faith remembers a time when Jim Jones was trying to convince his flock that he was Jesus Christ incarnate. He would walk through the crowd with blood dripping from his hands. He would touch the members of the congregation with this blood, and they would know they had been blessed by the Holy Spirit, Praise Father. They would see Jim Jones, they would see the divine blood issuing from the stigmata; they never bothered to look at Faith walking directly behind him. If they had, they might have seen Faith reaching under the wide sleeves of Jim Jones's choir robe to pass him little plastic bags of blood.

Faith was usually at Jim Jones's side during the miracle cataract healings. Jim Jones would call old women up to the pulpit, look into their eyes, and tell them they were about to go blind. He would meditate for a few moments and order the cataracts removed. Faith would rub tissues over the women's eyes to wipe them clean. Miraculously, there would be traces of a viscous yellow liquid on the tissues that looked just like cataracts. Faith circulated the tissues through the crowd the same way she did the cancerous tumors, and the money would flow from the people's pocketbooks as fast as the tears of joy would flow from their eyes. Faith was always careful not to leave the cataracts lying around. Someone might recognize the tapioca pudding.

Faith replaced Marceline as nurse in charge of the rectal cancer healings after Marceline went to work for the California Department of Public Health. For these healings, it took some research to select the mark—it had to be a person, a man or a woman, who would really believe Jim Jones had the power to command tumors to pass from the bowels. Most of the marks were uneducated blacks with the capacity to be true believers in this Prophet of God. The staff already knew from the revelations files what medications people were taking. They were especially alert for empty antacid or laxative bottles, or complaints to Temple nurses of irregular bowel habits. Linda Dunn would type this bowel-habit information on three-by-five cards that Jack Beam would pass to Jim Jones in the pile of newspapers, songbooks, and notes he kept in front of him at the pulpit. He would glance down at one of the cards and amaze the mark with a few revelations during the service. After he'd wowed the mark with these tidbits of personal information that only God could know, Jim Jones would slide into deep meditation and knit his brows with heartfelt concern.

"You've been having trouble with your bowels," he would say. "You've been taking laxatives, haven't you?" Oh, it was true, the mark knew, but how did Jim Jones know?

Faith stood at the back of the church with a wad of Kleenex in her hand. Inside the Kleenex was the plastic bag with the rotten beef brains and somebody's blood—maybe her own—sealed up tight and odor-free. Every once in a while, she'd wipe her nose with that wad of Kleenex to show there was a reason for her to be holding it. When Jim Jones informed the mark that the irregularity and the stomach pains were caused by cancer, and that he would use his divine powers to make that cancer pass, Faith would step forward and lead the mark to the bathroom. Some of the older women—and some of the men, as well—would cry as they took those fateful steps, afraid for their lives, afraid it may be already too late to pass the cancer that ate away at their bowels, hoping against hope that Father could do it.

Inside the bathroom, Faith would have the old lady sit on the toilet and bend forward. She would lean over her, talking the whole time about Father's miracles, soothing, comforting, then stick her finger into the lady's rectum.

"Bear down, now," she'd say, "like you're having a bowel movement." With her left hand, she'd pop the plastic bag into the Kleenex beneath the anus. She'd move her right forefinger around in the rectum as if she were digging out the tumor. Actually, she'd be scraping out feces to mix with the blood and the brains. She always left a little blood near the anus so it would show on the toilet paper when the lady wiped. A look at the toilet paper striped with blood would be almost convincing; but when Faith held up the Kleenex and showed the mark her tumor, all red and rank with fetid waves emanating toward her face, covered with blood and shit, the mark would cry for joy. "Praise Father!" she would sob as Faith led her out of the bathroom. "Praise the Prophet of God!"

The guards at the door would form a phalanx around Faith as she carried the tumor through the frenzied, foot-stomping crowd. "Don't get too close!" Jim Jones would warn. "Don't breathe it!"

The oral healings were a challenge, too. They could not be done behind closed doors. Faith was the first to do an oral healing in California. She had heard about someone vomiting up some chicken guts with the help of Jack Beam and Marceline Jones back in Indianapolis, but no one had yet performed that stunt on the West Coast. Jim Jones approached Faith before a Sunday meeting in San Francisco and said he wanted her to do an oral healing. The mark this time was to be a black woman with thyroid problems; Jim Jones was sure she would attend. He wanted Faith to be ready when he called the woman's name.

Faith was nervous all morning. The trick was basically the same as the rectal healings—plastic bag, beef brains, blood, Kleenex—but it had to be done at the pulpit, in front of the entire crowd, not in the bathroom where no one could see. She worked out the routine in her mind and waited at the back of the hall. The palms of her hands were sweaty, especially her left hand. That was the hand that held the Kleenex and the cancer.

"There is a soul here today," Jim Jones said, "a woman who lives right here in San Francisco. She has pain when she swallows." He groped for the woman's name and asked her to step forward. The woman stood up. Faith moved toward the pulpit with the cancer concealed in her left hand and a box of Kleenex in her right.

Jim Jones meditated over the woman and told her the problem in her throat was cancer. The woman's lip quivered and a tear spilled from her eye as Faith pulled several tissues from the box and grabbed a wad in each hand. She cupped her hands around the woman's mouth, making of the tissues a nest for what was about to pass. "Open wide," Faith instructed her, while she positioned the cancer in her left hand, reached into the woman's mouth with her right hand, and thrust her middle and index fingers down the woman's throat. When the woman started to gag, Faith broke the plastic bag and spewed the brains and blood into the woman's mouth. The woman's body rebelled from deep inside her stomach. Up came her last meal; she retched and gagged until she was sweaty and weak. But there in the Kleenex, soaked in the vomit and the blood, was the offending cancer. Praise Father!

The woman complained about the bad taste in her mouth, and Jim Jones offered her water from his own glass standing on the shelf in the pulpit. Her tears mixed with the water and the vomit on her chin as Faith wiped the mess away before parading through the congregation with the cancer held high. The healing was a smash; Faith couldn't believe her own success as she watched the collection buckets fill with bills. She did about seventy-five more throat cancer cures and perhaps two hundred and fifty rectal healings during her career as one of the girls.

Jim Jones put the girls to work on a way to knock people out without their knowing what happened. People in the Temple were always tired from the endless meetings, so the nurses figured it would take only a tranquilizer to do the job. They decided on liquid Haldol—colorless, odorless, flavorless—because it could be slipped to some unsuspecting member without his knowing it. Jim Jones would set the stage with the revelation that someone in the congregation would die that evening. At the dinner break, the chosen member would eat a piece of cake or drink a glass of Kool-Aid laced with the drug, and shortly after services resumed, he'd keel over in a heap on the floor. The nurses would try to revive him without success, consume enough time to let the drug wear off, then ask for Father's help. Just as the member was regaining consciousness, Jim Jones would take over, work his magic, and call the soul back from the nether regions.

Sometimes he would call souls who had departed years, even generations, earlier. Faith recalls a time in 1971 when he was trying to convince his flock that he was a reincarnation of Lenin. The revelation came to him while he was preaching the Christian virtues of socialism and communism. He was the Marxist messiah, the only man alive who could save the world from the evils of capitalism. As Christ, Buddha, Bahaullah, God, and Lenin all in one body, he alone had the power to lead his people to glory. Although no one in the church dared question these lofty claims, Jim Jones sensed some of the people in his flock had strong doubts. He took the problem to his staff and together they worked out a scenario that would prove Lenin's spirit had found a host in Jim Jones's body. The scheme involved placing Patricia Cartmell, Patty Cartmell's daughter, in the attic of the Redwood Valley church. Carrying a day's supply of food, a jug of water, and a script, she climbed a long ladder up to the attic early one morning when no one was around and waited all day.

During the evening service, Jim Jones went into a trance. He was in touch, he said, with "the ethereal waves." He could hear the voice of a woman who was in limbo because she had betrayed Lenin. As he meditated, the people in the congregation began to hear, with increasing clarity, a ghostly female voice. The voice spoke in Russian. Jim Jones had no trouble translating; he had been Russian in a previous life. The woman wanted Jones to help her find peace in the spirit world. She needed his divine powers to help her out of limbo. He forgave the woman for her betrayal, and she thanked him profusely. The voice faded back to the spirit world until it was no longer audible. Jim Jones came out of his trance, and Patricia Cartmell stretched out in the attic and went to sleep.

Such miracles were entertaining and, at the worst, deceitful. At least no one got hurt. Healing broken bones, though, could be risky. Whenever Jim Jones decided it was time for a cast removal miracle, the girls would go through the files and find an elderly uneducated woman with poor eyesight. Faith, or one of the other staff members, would wait for the woman to walk by on her way to a service, run up behind her, and knock her off her feet. Faith pushed one black woman down some stairs and threw her glasses down, then ran away down the street while the woman screamed. She was still crying when Faith showed up a few seconds later, bright and helpful, and introduced herself as a Temple nurse. The woman asked for her glasses and Faith told her they had broken when she fell. The woman had a terrible pain in her ankle; she was grateful Faith showed up when she did. Jim Jones sent her. He must have seen it in a revelation, seen those hoodlums knock that woman down and run away. Faith checked the woman's ankle. It was probably a minor sprain, but Faith didn't tell the woman that; when the other "girls" arrived, they advised the woman to get X-rays, loaded her into a car, and drove to the hospital.

The woman couldn't see much, but she recognized the building by its shape. Once inside, the woman knew where she was by the sounds: the calls for doctors over the intercom, the rush of feet scurrying over slick linoleum, and the carts and gurneys rolling on rubber wheels. The girls walked the old woman down the hall and took her not to the X-ray room but to the women's bathroom. Carolyn Layton came in wearing a clean white smock and her best bedside manner and examined the ankle. She was supposed to be the doctor. "It looks broken to me," she said in professional tones. "We'd better take an X-ray."

They laid the old woman down on the cot that is standard furniture in ladies' rooms and went through the motions of taking X-ray photographs. The myopic old lady saw nothing but blurred figures huddled near her feet and waited patiently for the diagnosis. Carolyn examined some imaginary film and pronounced her verdict: "It's broken." The afflicted ankle would have to be placed in a cast immediately, and the girls got right to work with the materials a Ukiah orthopedic surgeon unwittingly provided. Before the cast was dry, they had the old woman on crutches, hurrying toward the car and back to the Temple, so fast that not a single knock was heard on the bathroom door.

They gave the old woman her glasses, which they said had been repaired, and when they returned to the Temple, the service was still in progress. Jim Jones called the woman's name. She hobbled up to the pulpit and Jim Jones ordered the nurses to remove the cast. He told the woman to stand on her broken foot. He told her she could stand on that foot because he had healed it. The woman took a cautious step forward and Jim Jones told her to throw away the crutches. Praise Father, she could walk again. The woman cried with joy.

"Thank you, Father," she said through her sobs. "Thank you, thank you, Father."

Some of the healings were real, but they had nothing to do with Jim Jones's powers. The meetings would go on and on for fifteen or sixteen hours and the old people would often forget to take their medication.

People who were terminally ill, who saw Jim Jones as their last hope, would forget what the doctor said and pray for a miracle. They would sit through the meetings, clapping their hands and praising Jim Jones, then collapse on the floor. The nurses would rush to their side and perform CPR and heart massage right there in the meeting. They saved several lives, but as soon as the person started to come around, Jim Jones would take all the credit.

Nobody in Peoples Temple was supposed to die. Faith recalls an incident in front of the Los Angeles Temple involving an elderly black woman who collapsed on the sidewalk. Jim Jones stood by and watched the nurses do everything possible to bring the woman back. It was soon obvious that the woman was past hope. Jim Jones walked up to Faith and whispered a sharp order. "Get her out of here," he said, and the nurses carted the woman off to the hospital in the back of a station wagon. She was dead on arrival. Not a word was ever said.

For a man who could heal his own bullet wounds, Jim Jones had more than his share of health problems. He was seeing a urologist in San Francisco for a recurring prostate problem. Privately, he was often irritable before and after meetings. He'd stomp around with a mean look and explode with anger at the slightest provocation. He would hear sounds no one else heard. He blamed his condition on hyperinsulin, but Faith knew better. Behind the scenes with his staff, he rarely wore his sunglasses, and Faith noticed several times that his pupils were unusually dilated. He would get so wound up during the day that he couldn't sleep at night. He called Faith into his private quarters once and asked for five Quaaludes, which he promptly downed with a generous slug of the wine he kept around for "medicinal purposes." He tossed and turned for a while, then finally went to sleep. At other times, Jim Jones downed his Quaaludes with vodka, which he also kept around for medicinal purposes.

Jim Jones also had a heart problem, or so he said. He frequently had attacks or seizures. During one of them, Faith examined him and could find no evidence of either a heart condition or epilepsy. His head jerked, his arms and legs twitched, he even passed out, or seemed to, after each attack; but his eyes did not roll back, his tongue did not stick in his throat, his lips did not turn blue, his pulse did not speed up. Faith decided to take a look at Jim Jones's medical file, at the office of a local physician. Loretta Cordell, the Temple organist, worked for the physician and had a key to the file cabinet. She and Faith went to the office late one night, and while Faith was looking for the EKG strips, she stumbled upon a San Francisco psychiatrist's report. Faith

188

was so appalled by what she read that she forgot the EKGs. The report described Jim Jones as a sociopath.

Loretta told Jim Jones that Faith had looked at the file. Jim called Faith into his room and told her not to tell anyone, under any circumstances, about that file. The only reason the psychiatrist wrote such a critical report, he told her, was that it was the only medical explanation for his supernatural powers.

That after-hours search yielded nothing to explain Jones's seizures, nor anything to explain why, as he came out of those seizures, he wanted to be sexually aroused. If he was having problems with his heart, he'd be too exhausted for sex; even if he wasn't exhausted, the increase in pulse rate would surely be dangerous. Her preliminary diagnosis was angina, an inflammation of the throat that causes suffocating spasms.

The explanation for Father's seizures may have been less esoteric than Faith suspected. The syndrome was one that is all too familiar to street hypes and amphetamine derelicts. His irritability, his hypersensitive hearing, his dilated pupils, his twitching movements all are symptoms of amphetamine abuse. Faith was one of the connections for Dexedrine. Not only Jones himself but everyone in the inner circle was permitted to use the drug. With it, they were capable of superhuman feats—of working for two or three days without sleep, even longer in a pinch, then coming down with spaces in the synapses that Jim Jones would fill with his constant paranoid bitching or his unrelenting indoctrination to his ideas.

Jim Jones did, in fact, occasionally overdo his pills and suffered a condition speed freaks call being "overamped." Sounds would be exaggerated; a car's horn was enough to drive him up the walls. He would get wild-eyed and threaten to attack people who annoyed him, but guards always held him back before he did any harm. He told Faith sometimes that he felt "like a locomotive engine," and, when he was really strung out, like ten locomotive engines. Jim Jones blamed his gifts—of prophecy, healing, divination—for getting him all "keyed up inside."

One time at the Temple in Los Angeles, Jim Jones had taken a bunch of pills—he selected them by color—and the locomotive inside had built up such a head of steam, the boiler was about ready to explode. Jim Jones had to take a walk. He had to work off all that energy. He quickly summoned his guards— all nine of them—and Faith to accompany him. Father would go nowhere without a nurse close at hand with a first-aid kit, oxygen, and pills.

The entourage—Jim Jones, the nine guards, and Faith—walked out a side door on to South Alvarado Street. Father was rushing—in more ways than one—and everyone in his group had to walk faster than normal, with larger steps, to keep up with him. Suddenly he stopped. He turned around and pushed the guards away. His eyebrows nearly met in a frown, and beneath them, his dark eyes were wide open and intense.

189

"Are you all right, Father?" asked one of the guards.

"Did you hear that?"

"Hear what, Father?"

"Did you hear the baby frog croaking?"

He paused a moment. He said nothing, but he continued to listen intently. He asked Faith to come toward him. He put his arm around her, and they and the nine guards walked back to the Temple.

When Jim Jones came out of his seizures, there was nothing for his loyal staff to do but relieve his tension. The problem could not have been his heart, and how could it have been angina? He was not suffocating. It didn't matter whether Faith believed that Jim really had a heart problem. When he asked for nitroglycerine tablets, he got them. When he wanted oxygen, all he had to do was turn a valve. Whatever Father wanted, Father got. When he wanted Faith on Monday nights at midnight, Faith was always there. She got fitted for a diaphragm the day after her first sexual encounter with Jim Jones on bus number seven. She drove from her house in Ukiah to the parsonage in Redwood Valley. Jim Jones was already in bed when she arrived. He was wearing only a T-shirt, presumably to conceal the lack of scars from his nonexistent bullet wound. He told her to take her clothes off. She lay down next to him on the bed. He climbed on top of her. No foreplay. He stuck his penis into her vagina. Tight and dry. It hurt. As soon as he got it all the way in, he started growling, making strange, animal sounds as he fucked on her, at her, every way but with her, fast and furious, lunging and thrusting, biting at her neck and shoulders, digging his fingers into her back. She was out of the room in less than fifteen minutes.

Faith saw Jim Jones every Monday night for three months, and every time his performance was the same. Faith could not call what they did together making love; there was no love to it. She'd grown up with the idea that Jim Jones was the ultimate lover. He'd said so himself. The women he'd slept with agreed with him in front of the entire congregation. Making love to Father was like making love to God. Faith doubted her own sexuality. If Jim Jones was such a great lover, why didn't he turn her on?

Marceline Jones found out about the arrangement. Jim explained his adultery as an act of mercy. Faith was suicidal, he said, and if he didn't screw her every Monday night, she'd kill herself. As for Faith's husband, Bob Kice, he wouldn't find out; he worked the graveyard shift and wouldn't miss her. Not that it would have mattered. They rarely saw each other. Their marriage, too, was on the skids.

Faith's Monday night arrangement with Jim Jones waned as he took on other women in the church. By the time she left in September of 1973, Faith knew of thirteen women who had gone to bed with Father, or were going to bed with him regularly. She talked with some of these women, and they described the same hissing, growling, unfeeling scene. She was happy to see the relationship end; she realized the only reason she was seeing him was fear. He became impatient with her because she did not respond. He wanted her to bite him, to sink her teeth into his flesh and growl the way he did. Father would still call for her occasionally when he had one of his attacks. She always complied. She was afraid of what would happen if she didn't.

Faith was afraid for her life. She had become too deeply involved. She knew too much. Jim Jones called her to the pulpit after a meeting, just before she left, and asked her if she knew of a way "to have somebody killed" without leaving a noticeable trace. Faith wasn't sure whether Jim Jones meant what he said or was simply testing her loyalty; would she kill for Jim Jones? She said she knew of a drug that induces blood clots, especially in persons with a history of heart problems. She gave him the name of the drug and he wrote it on a slip of paper. Under the name of the drug, he wrote the name of a woman who had refused to deed her property to the church. Faith recalled how, back in the early days in Redwood Valley, Jim Jones would call her aside and tell her things he didn't want repeated. Once he confessed to her that he had killed a man in Brazil by smothering him with a pillow. Faith never heard the story again, so she assumed it was just a test of loyalty. This blood-clotting drug business, to murder a helpless old lady just for her property, was probably another test. Faith didn't really believe it until she heard that two of the other girls started putting the drug in the woman's food.

Jim Jones was dying to sleep with Linda Dunn, although he never approached her himself. He sent Carolyn Layton instead. Carolyn told Linda that "Father felt badly" because Linda was "working so hard." He wanted Linda "to have some release," but Linda declined. Jones had to resort to his heart attack ploy. Linda never did believe that Jim Jones had a heart problem. She saw that attack he had on the bus trip when he approached Faith, and it looked to Linda like nothing more than an excuse to get laid. "It must have been midnight, one o'clock in the morning. He was not in the building yet and Carolyn came and got me. . . . She said he was having an attack and he was going to die if he didn't have his sexual stimulation. I said, 'Carolyn, you do it,' and she said, 'I've already done it.' . . . I said, 'Well, do it again,' and she started crying. 'No, Linda, I can't. You don't understand how sick he is. He's got to have this,' and I just walked out and said, 'No, I can't.'"

Privately, there were a lot of things Linda couldn't do. She and Faith played with the forbidden whenever they could get away with it, like the episode at Linda's house in Redwood Valley when they dared to drink chocolate mint liqueur while they packed the beef brains and the blood in the little plastic bags. In the summer of 1973, when Jim Jones and hundreds of others were away on a bus trip to Philadelphia, Faith and Linda were in Los Angeles to gather information. They were walking down Sunset Boulevard when they passed a bar. "I've never been in a bar before," Faith remarked. The two women laughed—outwardly—about Faith's cloistered life. They didn't go into the bar; but they didn't gather any information either. Breaking the rules together, acting without Jim's clearance, they gradually learned to trust each other.

A few weeks later, the two nurses, Faith and Janet Phillips, were in the ladies' room at the Temple in San Francisco, discussing the cancer healings like the good and loyal followers they were. Somehow they were soon admitting the extent of their misery in the church. Such talk was dangerous; either or both of them might snitch. But they talked anyway.

Then Linda walked in. Janet clammed up, but Faith encouraged Linda to join the conversation. After the initial caution, a few tests and feelers, they were spilling out their deepest resentments and fears. They had reached the point at which, no matter the consequences, they had to talk. After that first encounter, they sneaked away as often as they could, cherishing their meetings as a lover cherishes his assignations. They met at a restaurant a few blocks away from the Temple. They talked together for about three months, and ultimately learned to trust one another enough to plan their escape.

Janet's mother, Claire, had a sister in another state who was director of nurses at a hospital there. Linda and Faith were nervous about involving anyone else in their scheme, but they finally agreed. Claire called Betty—her sister—and briefly explained the situation. Betty agreed to hire the two nurses immediately, and no questions asked. From an old vacuum cleaner that Claire kept stashed in a closet, she withdrew ten thousand dollars in cash. She had managed to save it over the years, despite the church's extortions. That should be enough, Claire reasoned, for the seven of them—Janet and her younger sister, Linda and her three children, and Faith—to make a new start.

Two or three days before the three women decided to leave, Faith and Janet were hunkered down on the floor in the back seat of Faith's car outside a meeting while Jim Jones's voice slithered over the public address system and armed guards patrolled the parking lot. The women whispered. When they finally joined the meeting, they learned that there had been a calamity: a group of eight young people—Jim Jones said they were armed counterrevolutionaries—had escaped into the hills near Redwood Valley. Guards had been sent to look for them.

Linda was at work the next morning when Danny Kutulas came into her office to tell her of a meeting—a special planning commission meeting—to be held that night to discuss "treason in high places." Linda was sure that she and her friends had been discovered, that the cover for the escape plan had been blown. She called Faith and Janet right away. They had to decide what to do next, so they met in a nearby barn. Their decision was that they might as well go to the meeting and face the music.

"Treason in high places," it turned out, was actually the defection of the eight young people who wandered off into the hills. Faith and Linda spoke out, as they would at any planning commission meeting, against the defectors, and Linda, as usual, took notes.

The following day, Linda grabbed her luggage, the files on Los Angeles, and some tapes and other files, and packed them all into the trunk of her car. She picked up her children. She picked up Janet and her sister. She picked up Faith. With the car bulging with people, files, and suitcases, they headed for San Francisco International Airport. They stopped at the A&W drive-in in Cloverdale for hamburgers and watched Temple buses rolling south on U.S. 101, headed for a meeting in San Francisco. Some of the members waved from the bus windows. The women smiled and waved back.

Linda did not get on the plane. The others did. Linda decided it would be best for her to keep her job in Ukiah; that way she could continue to support her children once it was safe for them to return to California. In San Francisco, at the Peoples Temple church, Jim Jones observed that his nurses were not there to help him with the miracle cancer cures. He soon learned that Linda had walked away with the files on the Los Angeles members. The cancers were locked up in the refrigerator and Faith had the only key. Father panicked. When a woman of the inner circle called, Claire stalled her with the story that the girls had left at seven o'clock, heading for the meeting.

When Linda returned home at midnight, the phone was ringing. "They're on the plane," Linda said to the caller from the Temple. "We're leaving. This is it. The girls are gone—and you'll never know where they're at."

Linda's phone rang several times during the next few days. Jim Jones was heartbroken and full of praise for the work of the three women; he bubbled with promises of the "great things" they would be doing if they returned to the fold. Jim's last phone call reached Linda at a laundromat in Ukiah. What could he do to help the three women? He didn't even mention the missing files and tapes. Because the primary problem was to finance a new start, because the three women had for years devoted all of their time, all of their energy, all of their hopes and ideals—not to mention their paychecks—to Peoples Temple, Linda answered that the only way he could help was to come up with some money. For seven people, Linda asked only ten thousand dollars.

Jones balked. "The Temple doesn't have that kind of money," he claimed. "Come to my place tomorrow night and I'll see what I can do."

Linda showed up at the appointed hour. There to meet her were Jim Jones, Carolyn Layton, Linda Sharon Amos, and Sandy Bradshaw. They handed her a document stating that she had agreed to accept a sum of money "for services rendered," but she refused to sign it. Jim Jones had nothing but praise for his lost sheep, but he couldn't reach her. Linda was not to be persuaded; when Jones finally accepted that, he gave in, and Carolyn Layton handed Linda a brown paper bag stuffed with cash. Linda went to Claire's house and opened the bag. There were 300 one-dollar bills in it.

10   He hath destroyed me on every side, and I am gone: and mine hope hath he removed like a tree.

11   He hath also kindled his wrath against me, and he counteth me as one of his enemies.

12   His troops come together, and raise up their way against me.

—Job 19

VII

Father's Wrath

Francis of Assisi whispered to the birds. Pastor Jim of Redwood Valley loved all God's creatures with a love as warm as an Indiana summer's sun, and no less bright was his countenance when he was with them, beaming with the glow of protective affection. A photograph of Jim Jones in *The Living Word* lovingly hugging a goat bears a caption remarkable for its understatement: "Pastor Jones's concern for every living thing is manifested by the number of stray and abandoned animals he has taken into the animal shelter." Elsewhere in the same publication, Temple attorney Eugene Chaikin attests to the truth of the claim: "He loves people, FEARS NOTHING, and stands publicly for everything he believes privately. . . . His respect for little insects and all other life in the eco-system is immense." But perhaps nothing so effectively illustrates Father's concern for animals as Deborah Layton Blakey's testimony at a meeting in August of 1973:

> . . . If anybody's been back towards the back of the property, you notice we have over a hundred chickens. When Father comes home, he takes time from all his duties—even if it means not getting anything or eating—he'll go back there and he'll individually pick up each and every chicken and kiss it and love it. He does it every time. And I thought about this, and it's, it's—so wonderful!

The vastness of Pastor Jim's love for animals was merely a hint of his love for his fellow human beings. Children were special, according to the summer 1973 issue of *The Temple Reporter:* "Pastor Jim Jones is very busy with the many duties of Peoples Temple's vast human service ministry, yet he always finds time to extend his love to the many hundreds of children in our churches. The smallest child is never turned away, and he always takes time to respond to their questions and needs."

Setting the example of loving for an entire apostolic brotherhood was a heavy burden for Pastor Jim, and often his moods were about as predictable as Vesuvius. The man who could kiss a hundred chickens was also capable of suddenly leaping from the pulpit in anger at some member of the congregation.

Usually the inner core was apprised well ahead of time that Father was going to make a scene.

There were times, too, when his anger was not planned. He would strut and fret and shout, "Stop me! You better stop me!" and the guards' efforts at restraining him were real and unrehearsed. Father was quite capable of explaining this behavior as a perfectly rational reaction to a member who was being downright annoying. When, during one of the Redwood Valley services, Jim Jones pulled from behind the pulpit a .22 caliber pistol and waved it around while speaking of the Temple's need to protect itself, his impulsive behavior caused mild consternation even among his most devoted lieutenants.

From that day on, no one dared publicly dispute, deny, or insult the man at the pulpit with the pistol in his hand. The man with the pistol, however, felt no inhibition about insulting everyone in the church and outside it, with the exception of his corpulent epitome of apostolic equalitarianism, Patty Cartmell. Patty was privileged as none of the apostles were; during services, even, she was permitted to stretch out on a chaise longue and nod off, cool and comfortable in her muumuu and zoris. Only when Jim felt he was saying something important for Patty to hear would he awaken her. Anyone else who fell asleep was "brought on the carpet"—an experience humiliating at best, painful at worst.

The usual punishment for nodding off was a public tongue-lashing administered by Father himself. By late 1971, however, those who incurred Father's wrath by breaking the rules were made to suffer worse than verbal abuse. Minor infractions like talking about fellow members behind their backs, falling asleep on guard duty, or refusing to follow the guidance of superiors were punished with a public strip—usually down to underwear, occasionally down to skin—in church, in front of the congregation. Each penitent would strip down, say, "Thank you, Father," run down the aisle, and plunge into the unheated water of the indoor pool.

There were more serious offenses than falling asleep or talking about fellow members, and they required more serious penance. Offenses like drinking liquor, smoking cigarettes, and associating with outsiders were punishable by five or more swats with a thick belt. Planning commissioners on the stage behind Jim Jones usually decided how many swats, and how hard, were appropriate for the infraction. Sometimes Jim decided, but usually he stepped in only to call a halt to the proceedings, as an act of mercy. While the people in the church would shout, "Harder! Harder! More! More!" Father would raise one arm and fan out his fingers in a gesture of absolution. The beating would stop; the believers would utter, "Thank you, Father!"; and anyone who neglected to shout when the others were shouting left himself open for a challenge and a call to the carpet with the other offenders.

During closed meetings and Wednesday night catharsis sessions, it was not uncommon for fifty or more people to line up for a half dozen swats apiece, like an inoculation line at a public health clinic—with one significant difference: everyone was certain he would be hurt. For the guilty to receive their catharsis, it took—depending on the speed and energy of the person wielding the belt—between twenty and thirty minutes.

Not even the Prophet of God was exempt from punishment, in keeping with the tenets of apostolic equalitarianism. "Jim even took whippings sometimes," recalls Sandy Parks. "I've seen him get up to twenty at one time." He would summon Jim McElvane, chief of security, or one of the other big guys, and take his whacks without flinching. At services the following night, Father would complain about how sore he was and members of the congregation would volunteer to take his place under the belt. "He would make everybody feel so sorry for him," says Sandy, "that they would take a whipping for him the next time, whether they did anything wrong or not."

Sometime in 1972, the whippings with the belt were stopped. The belt was replaced with the "Board of Education," a big paddle that can be bought in novelty shops by folks who think spanking is funny, about three feet long, three inches wide, a half inch thick. The design was perfect for causing a sting without serious injury—not for the first few whacks, anyway. Initially, the paddle was used with some discretion, used with limits, used to give no more than a half dozen swats per offender—initially.

The number escalated. Vicky Moore could not keep up with her duties in the Temple. In the course of a week, she slept only about twelve hours and still had too little time to keep up. For several days, Vicky dared to sit down only very gingerly, and it took two weeks for the bruises to heal. Vicky got fifty whacks.

Linda Mertle hugged a lesbian. The counselors prescribed a punishment, and Father concurred. He ordered Linda to pull down her pants and bend over while her parents, Elmer and Deanna, sat and watched their sixteen-year-old daughter take blow after blow until "her butt looked like hamburger." Only a meat grinder might have been more effective than the oaken board swung seventy-five times.

Father smiled. No one uttered a word of protest.

Tommy Ijames dropped some papers on the floor in school one day and bent down to pick them up. His teacher walked by and tripped, accused Tommy of tripping him intentionally and sent Tommy to the principal's office. The Temple counselors found out. They told Jim. Jim Jones asked Tommy to step forward at the meeting. He handed Tommy the Board of Education. "I want you to beat me first," he told Tommy, and the congregation protested loudly while Jim Jones bent over and waited for the whacks. Although Father asked Tommy to hit him hard, Tommy couldn't very well inflict pain on the Prophet of God without incurring the wrath of a thousand people and God knows what painful consequences from the mystic and the supernatural. But what a chance it was! Tommy hated the sonofabitch, wanted to let go and swing like

Reggie Jackson waiting for a fastball strike, to sock it to him, the punk, the brutal, money-hungry, nigger-hating pimp, break the paddle on his ass—but no. Tommy gave Jim Jones a couple of light strokes and the congregation rallied to Father's defense and came down heavy on the boy for subjecting Father to such pain. Then Jim Jones told Tommy to bend over. Tommy knew what he could expect.

Jack Beam struck first. Bone-rattling, the first few whacks from Jack. He was another nasty brutal sonofabitch and Tommy hated him nearly as much as he hated Jim Jones. Tommy stayed cool.

Jack Beam handed the paddle to Ruby Carroll. Now, Ruby was no lady; she was big and black and bad as a hungry bear, and she grasped the paddle with both hands and swung it full. Ruby had a talent; sometimes the people she hit would fall to the floor and vomit from the pain. Tommy stayed cool.

Jim Jones kept grinning at the boy as the count approached one hundred, and after taking one hundred whacks with the wooden paddle, Tommy Ijames stood up, said, "Thank you, Father," and walked away, feeling like a piece of road under an eighteen-wheeler truck.

By the mid-seventies a two-foot length of rubber hose found its way into the arsenal of implements for discipline. The rubber hose was considerably more efficient than the board; only a few swats were needed to persuade even the most recalcitrant offender to toe the line. The dull thud of the length of rubber squashing flesh was also more effective a deterrent for the witnesses to the beatings than was the smacking slap of a flat piece of wood. The hose was, however, used only for the more serious infractions or for repeated violations of Temple rules. Vicky Moore got the hose for being lax, supposedly, with Lynetta Jones's medication.

Vicky worked as a licensed vocational nurse in a Temple care home, where Lynetta was recuperating from a stroke. Vicky shared the responsibility for Lynetta's care with Joyce Beam, a registered nurse. Vicky always followed Joyce's instructions to the letter. She left Lynetta's pills on the table beside Lynetta's bed—both the morning pills and the noontime pills. The staff of the care home became concerned when, apparently, Lynetta gulped down all the pills at one time with her breakfast.

When the planning commission called Vicky on the carpet, she explained she had followed Joyce Beam's instructions and it was not her fault that Lynetta decided to take all the pills at once. Jim Jones became furious. He had always indulged and protected his mother; even more than Patty Cartmell, she was privileged and sheltered from the rules of the Temple. Father decided Vicky needed another lesson in humility. Vicky's son, Tommy, was permitted to watch the punishment, along with two hundred of the Temple's communal members, and his aunt Anita—Vicky's sister—had the honor of being the first to wield the rubber hose against her sister before handing it over to other Temple women to finish the job.

Punishment wasn't enough; Father wanted answers. "Would you tell me why you're so RESISTANT TO DISCIPLINE?" he shouted at the top of his lungs, his jaws clenched tightly and his face beet-red. He waited.

Vicky hesitated a moment to catch her breath and to find her equilibrium after the repeated shocks of pain. "I . . . I don't know," she whispered.

"IT'S ABOUT TIME YOU FOUND OUT!" Father yelled, and the counselors led Vicky to her room to recover. She surveyed the damage to her body; as a nurse, she could evaluate its extent. On her back, buttocks, and legs she found welts the size of her fingers, painful enough to prevent sleep, and when she did manage to doze off, the pain would awaken her again, she would open her eyes, and see lying next to her Ruby Carroll, the same Ruby Carroll who had beaten Tommy with the board, lying there watching her in case she tried to escape.

Vicky always tried to leave before the beatings got started. She would wait in the back for an opportunity and slip out the door, and when guards would stop her she would tell them she had to give medication to a patient. She slipped away the night Peter Wotherspoon—a gentle young medical student who might have had a future and a happy life with his wife, Mary—was beaten. Peter told Vicky later that the beating was done with the rubber hose, just like hers, but in different places. Vicky didn't see the beating; she saw only the results.

At a planning commission meeting in San Francisco, Jim Jones summoned the apostolic guardians and had them fetch Peter Wotherspoon from the room upstairs where he had been hidden to recuperate. Peter was clad only in a pair of loose-fitting shorts when the guards brought him in. His legs and back were a mass of welts and the pain was such that he could barely stand before Father, who reclined comfortably in a lounge chair. "Let this be an example," Father declaimed, "for anyone who hurts the Temple in any way—and more!" Father told Peter to drop his shorts.

Peter was able to pull his shorts down only part way. Father called on one of the nurses to help. Peter's penis was bruised to a dark purple, thoroughly, and swollen to at least twice its normal size, distorted and grotesque, with a catheter through the urethra to enable him to empty his bladder. Peter said not a word to the planning commission—not even "Thank you, Father." Peter was kept in the upstairs room under twenty-four-hour observation. He had to be watched; they were afraid he would commit suicide. He threatened to, but they wouldn't let him—not until November 18, 1978.

It was about the same time the rubber hose came into use that Jim Jones added boxing matches to the repertory of his disciplinary theater. The Temple never had a real boxing ring. Father just ordered a few chairs pushed back out of the way so there would be room to move around, up front where everyone in the congregation could watch and cheer.

Vicky Moore's defiant spirit landed her a bout with Shirley Smith, the

Temple choir's husky-voiced gospel singer. Vicky had it coming. Instead of taking a group of children to the Peoples Temple booth at the Mendocino County Fair, she decided on her own to take them to a bowling alley in Ukiah, without first getting clearance from the planning commission. Again, Vicky's arrogance infuriated Father. "That's a honky place!" he shouted, and he railed at her for several minutes before ordering a space cleared for the fight.

Vicky had never boxed before in her life, but it was probably just as well; the object was not to win, because winning meant facing another opponent, then another and another, until there was neither strength nor will to fight back. Father, in his mercy, always kept the matches from becoming too drawn out by pitting the sinner against an opponent who was clearly bigger and stronger.

Shirley Smith was poised and ready. Her size, strength, and experience gave her not only the physical advantage but the edge that comes from confidence, and she was ready to kick ass. Ironically, the ass she was ready to kick belonged to the first black woman to stand up and complain about the absence of blacks on the planning commission, the first black woman appointed to that body, the first to get Jim Jones to grant, in at least a token gesture, that black women should have a voice; and, yes, Shirley was primed and ready to kick Vicky's black ass.

Vicky slid her hands already slippery with sweat into the Everlast gloves. Vicky knew what she was up against. She had already treated black eyes and bloody noses and swollen cheeks countless times, she had applied ice packs to ease swelling and she had wrapped bandages to stop bleeding. She had daubed Merthiolate on the cuts on a five-year-old's face, cuts that resulted from a boxing match Jim Jones ordered. She knew what to expect.

Shirley came out swinging as soon as Father gave the order to begin. Vicky ducked; Vicky bobbed and weaved. With her forearms Vicky blocked the blows intended for her face until her arms became so sore and tired she couldn't hold them up. Shirley threw some haymakers, connected, and stunned Vicky silly, but she kept her feet. Shirley kept pounding until Vicky lost track of where she was being hit, until in Vicky's eyes the congregation, the counselors on the stage, and Jones were all spinning. The crowd cheered, they cheered Shirley, not Vicky, all of them except Tommy cheered his mother's beating, until Father in his mercy stopped the bout just before Shirley cocked her arm for the knockout.

Anger that could prompt such punishments was usually reserved for people like Vicky, who served on the planning commission. Planning commission members felt the belt, the board, the rubber hose, and the boxing gloves considerably more frequently and more intensely than did the general members. General members—especially those who lived in their own homes—were allowed a little slack, unless they were caught in the act of an infraction by one of the counselors. But they were by no means exempt from the same kinds of punishments the PC members suffered—except perhaps for some of the more kinky and grotesque forms.

Steve Addison was part of the original exodus from Indianapolis in 1965. He came out to California with his mother, Virginia, and Faith Worley. He had been afflicted from an early age with cerebral palsy and had a slightly clumsy gait. At times, he was forgetful of his responsibilities; his roommates in the Temple dorm at Santa Rosa Junior College complained frequently of his slovenly habits. As a member of the planning commission, Steve had been called on the carpet several times for the same offense. Jim Jones noted that fact at a meeting at Valley Enterprises in April of 1975, when Steve was once more brought before the counselors. On top of the sin of slovenliness, Father noted also, Steve Addison had the temerity to conduct an affair of the heart without clearance. Father prescribed a punishment he felt appropriate for both offenses.

Father called Patty Cartmell to the front of the room and had her sit on a stool facing the seventy-five people at the meeting. Patty confirmed, when Father asked her, that she was that day in the midst of her menstrual period; she was not at all shy. Father ordered Steve Addison to come forward, in front of Patty, and go down—perform cunnilingus—on her. He approached the chubby matron humbly, with his shambling gait, and dropped to his knees as Patty raised her skirt and revealed the black patch of hair beneath the roll of fat on her belly. She wore no underwear. Steve dropped to his knees and somehow worked up the nerve to stick his face between the gelatinous thighs of the one-hundred-and-ninety-five-pound Temple goddess, who obviously enjoyed being in the spotlight.

Steve lapped his penance for a few seconds, then suddenly backed away coughing and gasping for air; Patty's hot piss in his face had caused him to choke. She sat laughing on the stool over the puddle on the floor, making funny faces while Father joined her in the chuckles. A few of the other planning commissioners laughed, too. Everyone else was silent.

"Throw up, Patty," said Father in a stage whisper. "Throw up."

Her body still quivering with laughter, Patty shoved two fingers down her throat until she gagged and vomited on Steve's head still clamped between her thighs. Steve Addison learned his lesson in humility, and he ever after kept his surroundings clean.

Sandy Parks witnessed the scene. She quit the church a few days after. "I walked away feeling like I was worth two cents," she recalls. "I felt so sorry for Steve when I left that meeting, and I knew if I said anything that they would make me do something like that, so you kept your mouth shut and you never voiced your opinion, not even off to the side to someone else about what went on that night. You kept your mouth shut." Although she never said anything about the incident to anyone in the Temple, Sandy was so deeply troubled by what she had seen that she decided it was time to break away. "I came home Sunday night and I told Denny I was pulling out of the church. He says, 'Are you really serious?' . . . I went back to work on Monday morning, typed up a note, gave it to Denny. . . . He took it down to the [church] office, dropped it off, and I pulled out."

After seven years with the church, breaking away was, for Sandy, as painful an experience as a divorce or the death of a spouse. The church had so consumed her time that she became terribly restless; it took her months to get over the guilt of being a traitor to the cause. Her divorce from Peoples Temple was trying, it was painful, it was wrenching, but at least she had a home to go to and a husband who understood what she had been through. Those who lived communally, who had surrendered to the church worldly possessions, all of their money, and their family ties, more often than not had nowhere to go and no loving family to welcome their return.

Vicky Moore was one of them. Vicky had witnessed Steve Addison's humiliation; she had tended the wounds on the faces of five-year-old children; she had been beaten and badgered, humiliated, and almost destroyed in her soul, and she had, many times, thought about leaving. But where could she go? She had no money to live on and no place outside the church to go home to. Her parents, both father and mother, were leaders in Peoples Temple; and her son was a prisoner there. She couldn't ask her parents for help. Her whole family—except for one sister—were involved with Peoples Temple.

Lack of family ties outside the Temple and lack of the necessities for starting a new life were fearsome enough, but Vicky was also afraid of what Father might do to her if she left the apostolic family. Father had spoken many times of the "terrible things" that happen to those who stray from "Father's protection." The church's files were filled with personal embarrassments severe enough to dissuade even the most determined potential defector: confessions of child molesting, revolutionary activities, Communist leanings; statements taken during the Indianapolis days of each member's worst fears; and all the sexual compromises with Father that involved men and women both. Vicky never had a sexual experience with Jim Jones, although she felt for a time the same longing for him that other women in the church felt. Father let it be known in no uncertain terms that he was the most desirable hunk of male on the face of the earth, and Vicky, like the others, naturally was curious; but Father's tastes were limited to young, slender white women (and an occasional man). At planning commission meetings, Father would discuss each new conquest and would call upon his latest liaison to testify of his amazing sexual powers: how he could come and come and come, how he could remain erect for hours at a time.

Father, of course, allowed himself as many affairs as his omnipotent whims dictated, but that privilege was not extended to the common folk. Vicky, for example, caught a lot of flak for being close friends with one of the white men in the church, and all they ever did together was talk. "I felt like I was being a traitor in a way," Vicky recalls of her platonic relationship. Because even such a friendship was impossible in the Temple, Vicky began looking critically at her life, and she wrote down her thoughts in a journal she kept hidden in her room. What Jim Jones was asking of her, she wrote, "is not keeping with the laws of nature." She questioned again the "predominantly white" leadership of the church, as she had before Jim Jones named her to the planning commission. One question suggested another until a Vicky Moore who had been subdued and hidden for years began to emerge:

> I was beginning to draw these questions out of myself that were there all along, but I didn't dare let them out before. [I was] to the point where I was beginning to have severe migraine headaches. Finally I went to UC Med Center and I said I know I'm having conflict with myself. I'm having conflict with the fact that Jim is white. I had this big picture of Jim and I went home and made an Afro, a big old Afro. I was darkening his skin, and I thought, "Oh, that's not gonna do it. . . ." It wasn't right for him. I thought, "How can he justify his relationship with men . . . his relationship with all these women . . . you know, how can it all be right?" Then, as I began to pull the questions out of my mind . . . I went to a yard sale and picked up the book, The Life Story of Hitler, which I still have on my bookshelf.

The book changed Vicky's life. She read through it furiously, underlining passages and writing comments in the margins, noting the parallels in the ways both Hitler and Jim Jones used songs, photographs of themselves, group pressure, slogans, "and all the things that indoctrinate the people. . . . After reading that book, I knew I had to get away." Vicky was working two jobs at the time and she had two paychecks in her purse that she was not, not this time, going to turn over to the church. She needed that money to start her new life.

> They were going to call me on the floor that night. I knew that if I didn't turn them in, I was due to come up that night, but that was my key to freedom. They had already sensed my hesitation. They had already put a twenty-four-hour watch on me. This young lady in the commune had been assigned to watch me.

Vicky pretended she was unaware the guard was watching her and went about her business. While the guard was in another room, Vicky went through her personal papers and took out anything that could be used against her at a later time. She took the pile of potentially incriminating papers and placed them in a trash bag. She sneaked out the door with the trash bag when the guard wasn't looking, tiptoed down the stairs, walked briskly to the bus stop on the corner, and took the bus to a nearby park, where she dumped the contents of the bag into a trash receptacle and burned them.

Vicky decided not to make her escape directly from the park; she may have been followed. She returned to the commune on Fillmore Street to allay the suspicion that she was about to break the ties that bind.

> When I came back, [the guard] was furious. "Where did you go?" she said, and I pretended like I didn't even know the watch was there. I knew I had to pretend that or else I was cooked. I said, "I just went for a walk. What's your problem?"

The guard started to make a phone call to report Vicky's behavior, but Vicky interrupted her. Vicky confessed that she was going through inner turmoil. She broke down in tears. She tried to follow Jim Jones's teachings, she said, but she admitted she had "a lot of livin' to do to really come up to them." Vicky continued with her compelling story:

> I said, "You know, I've supported him but I've not actually thrown myself in there. I've had a lot of questions. . . . I feel that I don't deserve to be here."

Dinnertime was approaching. After Vicky had talked with her guard for a while, they both changed into their Temple uniforms. Vicky dressed quickly; she wanted to leave with the first group when they headed for the communal dining hall at the Geary Street Temple. Her timing was perfect; Vicky was able to grab her purse and announce she was leaving for dinner before her guard was finished dressing.

Vicky walked one block down Fillmore Street to the bus stop; the bus was still taking on passengers as she approached. She rode the bus to the nearest BART (Bay Area Rapid Transit) station under Market Street and telephoned her oldest sister, Arlene, to tell her she was leaving the Temple for good and would she pick her up? "I cannot be seen from this point on," she whispered into the phone. Arlene came and picked her up at the BART station. Vicky's ex-husband, Ollie, drove her to Sacramento. From Sacramento, she caught a plane to Texas. There, she lived incognito with some friends of her sister's until she decided it was safe to return to California.

Father freaked out when he learned Vicky was missing. He sent troops to cover every bus station and airport terminal in the area. They checked the house where her son, Tom, was staying, thinking she'd be by to pick him up. They guessed wrong; Vicky left her son in a Temple commune and she suffered agonies of guilt about it, but she knew too much and she knew Jim Jones too well even to hope he would let her leave peaceably with Tom. Father's troops showed up at Vicky's ex-husband's house and hassled him, demanding to know where Vicky was staying, but he could say truthfully that he didn't know. They asked Tom, back at the commune, the same questions, over and over: "Where is your mother? Who is she staying with? Why did she leave?" Tom had no answers. All he knew was that, wherever his mother was, he'd rather be with her than stuck in one of the communes of Peoples Temple.

Tom Ijames knew he was in for a rough time. His mother was gone; he was certain the counselors would zero in on him to make sure he didn't try to leave, too. He knew they believed his attitude was all wrong. If he didn't start behaving, he was told, he'd get it: the ultimate punishment for the children in Peoples Temple, a strange device called the Blue-eyed Monster.

> He would threaten little children with it. . . . There was this . . . silver chair, and there was this sort of square thing, it was about this big and . . . they'd place your arm [in it] and they'd just turn it on. . . . [T]hey'd always do it behind the door so if you passed out the nurse could do something about it.
>
> It looked like some kind of electrical generator. . . . It had this wheel, a rolling wheel, and it had these little pieces on it, and there was two points that came across like this that had metal pieces on both sides. They would spin, create electricity, and, you know, shoot it over into the box, and they'd have your arms strapped to this thing on to this thing on the table. It was like a clamp vise, you know, it came here and clamped on and your arm was strapped right here. And then they'd give you whatever Jim—uh, he would tell Grace Stoen, and Grace Stoen would go back and tell them how many and how long. And he did it to a lot of children, though not too many grownups. . . .
>
> It was painful enough because it was so painful, my hand, right here, I still got a scar right here. See these scars right here? That's where I got these scars at. See, you place your hand up on this thing, right here, and they would shock you, and it was so bad my hand was swollen up and I couldn't move it.
>
> Why? Oh, I called Jim Jones a son of a bitch.

Vicky knew nothing of her son's experience with the Blue-eyed Monster until he spoke of it, two years later, in the presence of a stranger, reliving the experience, to be sure, tense but emotionless. Vicky had no trouble at all believing Tom's tale of the torture Father reserved just for the children.

The reunion of Vicky and Tom would never have happened had Vicky not been fortunate enough to have two cousins in Los Angeles who happened to be attorneys. Vicky flew up from Texas to sign custody papers and begin a legal battle with Peoples Temple that lasted several weeks. The Temple capitulated only when Vicky's attorneys threatened action against them for holding Tommy against his will.

People like Vicky, who had the guts to stand up to Peoples Temple, usually got away and were left alone; the last thing Jim Jones wanted was the adverse publicity of a court battle. People who left in fear, however, were susceptible to harassment. Telephones would ring in the middle of the night with messages of dire threats from muffled voices. Often there would be, on the other end of the line, nothing but a chilling silence, then the click of the receiver hanging up; it made no sense at all—except to remind the defector that Father, too, was capable of making no sense at all, and so were his troops, blindly loyal, unquestioningly obedient, fiercely cruel. If a former member knew enough to cause Jim Jones some embarrassment, he'd send the Temple heavies out, inspired with vindictiveness and numb with mindlessness, to instill the fear of God into what he imagined was a quaking heart. A few days after Linda Dunn left the church, she was visited at her home by two members of Father's inner core, who informed her that she "would not have Father's protection anymore." Linda knew enough about the behind-the-scenes truth of the Temple to destroy Jim Jones, and he wanted her to get the message that she'd better keep her mouth shut.

> When I left, Linda Amos and Sandy Bradshaw came to my house and told me that I was going to lose my job, that I wouldn't be able to get a job anywhere in the United States. I was going to become an alcoholic. I was going to lose all of my children, and they were all going to end up in juvenile hall. I was just going to lose everything. When I finally got tired of them telling me all this crap, I slapped the one woman. We were standing out in my front yard and Sandy Bradshaw kept pointing her finger at me, telling me what was going to happen if I did anything to harm them, or if I told anything that I knew. . . . I just slapped her hand and I said, "Get out of my yard." She pulled a piece of paper out of her pocket and held it up for me to read, and it said: "We already have someone assigned to take care of you if you do anything to harm us." She ripped it up real quick and she mouthed the name, "Chris Lewis."

Two years later, Chris Lewis did show up at Linda's house, one of a group of eight Temple loyalists who appeared one morning while Linda was getting ready for work. There were two cars. Lewis was driving one of them, the one that blocked Linda's driveway, and none of the Temple men—not Lewis himself, nor Jack Beam, nor Elmer Mertle, nor any of the others—said a word to Linda. They just sat in the cars and glared. "I hadn't talked to anybody," she says. "I hadn't heard from anybody. I had no idea what brought it on."

After a few intense moments, Chris Lewis started his car. He leaned his head out the window and spat at Linda as he drove away. "I don't recall being scared," Linda says. "I just thought it was ridiculous."

Linda may not have taken the threat seriously; perhaps she should have been more concerned. At planning commission meetings, several members had pledged that they would kill for Jim Jones. Even if he called upon them to take their own lives, they would be happy, they pledged, to die for the glory of socialism. Linda may not have realized how serious they were, because it was about the time she left in 1973 that expressions of willingness to die and to kill for the cause became Temple rituals. Father became preoccupied with what he saw as the ultimate ritual of apostolic faith: a mass suicide by poisoning with either arsenic or cyanide. Along with the talk of poisons were questions Father asked among members of the inner core about certain other drugs and chemicals—substances that might be used to murder uncooperative members without leaving any traces or signs of death by anything other than natural causes.

One such drug—allegedly used on at least one elderly member who had a history of heart problems—was phytonadione, the generic name for vitamin K_1. Phytonadione is commonly known by its Merck, Sharpe, and Dohme trade name, Mephyton. It is dispensed in five-milligram yellow tablets. According to pharmaceutical manuals, K_1 is used primarily to stimulate the body's production of prothombin, a chemical that occurs naturally in blood to make clotting possible. Low levels of prothombin can result in a form of anemia called hypoprothombinemia, one of the symptoms of which is a tendency to hemorrhage. The drug is also used to treat deficiencies in vitamin K, a close chemical cousin.

Father's plot involved breaking up the tablets and mixing them with food. Sometime after dinner—theoretically, at least—the victim would suffer a sudden heart attack brought on by the formation of clots in the blood. The coroner's autopsy would conclude death was due to natural causes. In theory, such an abuse of K_1 would have made for a perfect murder. In fact, pathologists claim there is little chance that even excessive doses of K_1, even massive doses, would actually cause fatal clotting. Not only is it nontoxic but it does not accumulate in the tissues as some poisons do; even large daily doses would probably have no effect. Although one pharmaceutical manual warns that excessive doses can cause "a tendency toward thrombosis," most pathologists maintain that K_1 is about as harmful as vitamin C.

Although a couple of women in the inner core mixed K_1 with the intended victim's food, the woman survived for more than a year afterward and succumbed, finally, to the primary cause of death among the elderly: heart disease. Her family had taken her out of the Temple's care months before and had placed her in a convalescent hospital, where she died without Father's protection.

Truth Hart probably never tasted Mephyton at all, but she also died without Father's protection. Truth Hart was one of the fifteen converts from the Father Divine Peace Mission in Philadelphia who, in 1971, boarded the fleet of Temple buses destined for Redwood Valley. A middle-aged black woman, Truth lived for a while with Grace and Tim Stoen, until she was placed in a Temple care home. Grace remembers Truth as a "little weird woman" who seemed to live, much of the time, on an ethereal plane only Truth could understand. She used to get especially excited, Grace recalls, about certain foods. "Food was very precious to her," Grace says. Truth had a wide smile frozen on her face and a warm but vacuous look in her eyes.

This childlike devotee of Father Divine was convinced when she met Jim Jones in Philadelphia that he had inherited Father Divine's mantle; but when she saw Jim Jones in action in Redwood Valley, she soon became disillusioned. She was deeply disturbed by Jones's behavior at the pulpit. He'd throw the Bible down and spit on it and utter profanities and obscenities, and Truth was one of the few people in the Temple who had the courage to speak out against the blasphemy. "I don't see how you can bring such terrible things out of your mouth," she told him. After hearing such criticism, Jim Jones showed the lady some consideration by warning her whenever some devilish blasphemy was imminent: "Close your ears, Truth," he would say, "here comes another one."

Truth could stand it only so long. She wanted out of Peoples Temple, and she found an opportunity in July of 1973 when Birdie Marable introduced her to the Reverend Ross Case. Truth told the Reverend Case what she knew about the Temple, and, being a minister, he responded with some kind of help for her. He started conducting weekly Bible study meetings with Truth, Birdie, and two other black women who had left the church. On Sundays, he took Truth to the Ukiah Assembly of God church with him.

Jim Jones got word of Ross's sheep-stealing, and he didn't like it. He had one of the early members from Indianapolis, Leo Wade, give Ross a telephone call on August 24, 1973, while Ross was staying with friends in southern California, attending a conference of charismatic Christians at Melodyland. As soon as his friends told him that a man named Leo Wade had called several times, Ross knew something was up. He expected to hear some threats from Jones via Wade, so—after first consulting the local police chief—Ross taped the call.

The thirteen-minute conversation began innocently enough; Wade started by telling Case how much he missed him. Gradually, though, Wade started bending the expressions of friendship toward implications of a homosexual relationship with Case. "I *really* miss you," said Wade over and over. "When can we get *together?*"

Case replied in the kindest tones—Ross's voice is always kind—that he was a busy man. He would, he said, try to meet with Wade in the near future. In the meantime, Case advised Wade to seek guidance from another, to seek also the love of Jesus. Case tried several times to end the conversation as gently as possible, but Wade kept pressing for Case to say something in his response that might be construed as evidence of intimacy between the two men. "I feel so hot," Wade said. "I *really* want to see you." Case asked Wade what he meant by "hot." Wade started talking about wanting to feel Case's lips. Case hung up the phone.

A few days later, the Reverend Case received an unusual piece of mail—the results of a polygraph test on Leo Wade. The stationery bore the letterhead of a lie-detection service in San Francisco, George W. Harman Associates, and its contents showed that Leo Wade did not lie about homosexual acts with Ross Case, ten years earlier, when, Leo claimed, Ross initiated an act of anal intercourse. Jim Jones used this piece of paper—the polygraph test—and Leo Wade's confession to threaten Ross Case's teaching job, but Case suspected what was coming, knowing Jim Jones as he did, and fortunately had the sense to warn school officials before the Temple approached them. He knew when it was coming when he received a telephone call delivering the ultimatum that he show up at the church or risk something terrible. Case ignored the threat and went on about his business.

Temple attorney Eugene Chaikin, member Penny Dupont—who worked for a time selling ads for the *Ukiah Daily Journal*—and Leo Wade really did their best. They went to Bill Murphy, superintendent of the Redwood Valley Union School District, and told him that Wade had had a homosexual rendezvous with Ross Case on Penny Dupont's front porch, and furthermore that Penny had witnessed it. Chaikin, in righteous indignation, demanded that Case be fired. Case thwarted any further Temple pressure on school officials by appealing directly to the California Teachers Association, the state's largest union of educators, and Jones backed off, apologized on behalf of the Temple and his too-hasty followers, and claimed he had no knowledge of the scandalous charges until they were brought to his attention. Ross Case went on about his business.

While he fought off the Temple's attempts to frame him, he went on about the business of the weekly Bible study sessions with Birdie Marable, Truth Hart, and the other two black women who had left Peoples Temple. Ross Case continued to take Truth Hart to the Assembly of God meeting every Sunday. He continued to go on about his business with such steadfastness that Jim Jones became infuriated and got word to Truth that she'd better stop talking to Ross. The last time Ross Case took Truth to church with him was October 21, 1973, when Truth told him she would thereafter be attending services only at Peoples Temple. Case tried to talk her out of her decision, but to no avail; she was afraid of losing Father's protection.

Truth went along with Jim Jones for as long as she could stand it, for almost a year, until she became convinced again that Jim Jones was the Other Fellow

(Father Divine's euphemism for the devil). Truth was recovering at the time from an intestinal cancer operation at Birdie Marable's Ukiah rest home, suffering also from valvular heart disease for which she had to take medication, and living under the care of Mary Love while Birdie went off on the Peoples Temple cross-country bus trip. Like Truth, Mary had once been a follower of Father Divine; they knew each other from Philadelphia. Unlike Truth, Mary—who later went by the name of Mary Black—was regarded as a loyal and devoted follower of Jim Jones. If Truth, under Mary's care, had confided in her old friend her thoughts about leaving the church, word almost certainly would have reached Jim Jones's ears.

Jim Jones predicted Truth's death only days before it actually happened, according to Sally Stapleton, which indicates that Jones truly did have a divine gift, or a pipeline to Truth's physician's files, or perhaps a plan. Just before Birdie left on the bus trip, Truth had asked her to call Ross Case. In the hustle and pressure of preparing to leave, Birdie forgot to make the call and Case never got the message. Truth's condition deteriorated until she could no longer get out of bed without feeling immediately tired and weak, and finally, one day—July 16, 1974—Truth Hart, age sixty-six, died in bed of "congestive heart failure due to rheumatic heart disease." The death was reported at 11:00 A.M. by Temple nurse Judith Ijames.

Based on the statement of Mary Love and the results of an autopsy, Truth Hart's death was treated as a routine heart failure. Mary Love told a coroner's investigator that she last checked on Truth just before 11:00 A.M. and noticed "she wasn't doing very well." Mary Love said she was phoning a physician in Ukiah when Truth called out to her from her room. She rushed immediately to Truth's bedside only to discover that her old friend from Philadelphia had died. The coroner's investigation turned up no living relatives, and Truth was buried in the county potter's field.

A year and a half later, new evidence surfaced that caused Ross Case and others who knew Case to conclude she had been murdered. Ross had a conversation with Ella Mae Hoskins, an eighty-year-old resident of Birdie's rest home. Ella Mae claimed she had witnessed some strange activity just before Truth died, and Case notified an investigator for the Mendocino County Sheriff's Office on October 14, 1975. More than a month later—on November 21, 1975—the sheriff's office followed up the lead, a day after Case arrived with a delegation demanding action be taken immediately. A sheriff's investigator, Jan Kespohl, took a statement from Ella Mae Hoskins claiming that Mary Black (formerly Mary Love)

> . . . was pinching Truth and hurting her. She made Truth get up and take a bath and Truth was awful sick. Then Mary Black gave Truth a pill, and I was standing at the doorway watching. She then

211

gave Truth some water to drink and went back into the kitchen, and Truth was dead before Mary got back into the kitchen.

Ella Mae Hoskins marked her signature on the document with an X.

Ella Mae's statement was given more than a year after Truth was dead and buried, so the autopsy was limited to finding evidence of heart failure, the suspected cause of death. There is no indication on the autopsy report that the pathologist ran any tests for toxic substances or even examined the contents of Truth's stomach. Despite the insistence of Ross Case and the others, the investigation was never pursued beyond taking the statement of Ella Mae Hoskins.

Truth Hart's death was not the only one about which Jim Jones was prescient. Although there is no conclusive proof that Jim Jones or Peoples Temple committed any murders, most former members detect the hand of Jim Jones in several suspicious deaths. Father would have revelations about those whose death was imminent, and, sure enough, within a few days the individuals he named would turn up dead. Some of these revelations occurred, apparently, after the fact, when Jones would utter his I-told-you-so and then call people in the audience to verify that they remember his prediction, first one member, then another and another, until the peer pressure so rearranged the memories that the claimed revelation became historical fact.

There is no doubt in Vicky Moore's mind that Jim Jones said, "That bitch is going to die" a few days before Maxine Harpe was found hanging from the rafters of her garage on March 28, 1970. Others, too, heard Father's revelation about Maxine; they are equally convinced that Jim Jones knew in advance that Maxine Harpe was soon to die.

Maxine Bernice Harpe was a divorcée with three children. She became involved in Peoples Temple when she met and fell in love with James Randolph, the Temple's man in the Mendocino County Welfare Department. Although her welfare records are missing, the coroner's report indicates that she was receiving welfare funds "for medical help," and that her social worker was Linda Sharon Amos.

Maxine had married her high school sweetheart, her one and only love at Willits High, Daniel Harpe, and she bore him three children. She found herself at the age of thirty on her own for the first time in her life, responsible not only for herself but for the well-being of the three children. The burden was more than she could bear, and although she was outwardly cheerful, she was tormented with self-doubt and despair. According to the county mental health department, Maxine received counseling during most of 1969 and was "classified as a mental depressant, but not neurotic or psychotic."

Maxine had a couple of jobs. For a while, she was a dental technician at Mendocino State Hospital in Talmage, a small town immediately south of Ukiah—the welfare department got her the job—and for a while she worked

212

as a nurse's aide in a Ukiah hospital. She made her home in Talmage with her three children and a Temple member named Mary Candoo in a dilapidated rental house with asbestos shingles and peeling white paint on the window frames.

Maxine was trim and attractive. Her dark brown hair cascaded gracefully down to her waist, and she dressed in a hip—not hippie—style, as did many of the Temple members, occasionally using an Indian headband to hold back her hair. As soon as she joined Peoples Temple, Maxine cut nearly all ties with her family, excusing her distance from them with the story that she was "too busy with church work." She and Mary lived communally; they shared all their belongings except their clothes. Both Maxine Harpe and Mary Candoo believed that Jim Jones was truly a modern-day prophet who offered sanctuary in an indifferent world. Maxine had a special reason for believing that Jim Jones was everything he said he was, and more. She had been told she'd not be alive had it not been for Jim's mystic intervention, which kept her from carrying out her half dozen suicide threats.

The last day anyone in Peoples Temple saw Maxine alive was March 27, 1970. She had attended an early evening picnic and a dance at the Temple afterward. The Friday night Temple dances usually drew a sizable crowd, being one of few social outlets available in Ukiah, but they ended in 1972 when, supposedly, Jim Jones was shot and advised his followers to forsake their frivolity in the interest of security. Maxine left the dance with Jim Randolph at 10:30 P.M., according to Randolph's statement to the coroner's investigators. She went with Jim to his Volkswagen and packed in as well Mary Candoo, Maxine's three children, Tommy Ijames—who was going along to stay all night with Maxine's son Daniel—and Ron Crawford, a Temple member enrolled at Santa Rosa Junior College. Jim Randolph drove the car, dropped Crawford off first at his home in Ukiah, then drove to Talmage to take Mary and the kids home. Maxine stayed in the car; she said she wanted to talk to Randolph.

Then Maxine and Jim drove back to Crawford's house, for some reason that neither Randolph nor Crawford explains in his statement, picked up Ron, and the three of them went to Randolph's house to talk. But they didn't go inside. All three sat in the car until one o'clock in the morning. Randolph's account of their conversation tells little of Maxine's state of mind before she died:

> . . . Generally she wasn't distraught, but she did get upset when she talked about her divorced husband. She always used to ramble when she talked, so it is hard to remember the line that conversation followed. She had a way of coming back to things that hurt her, and I guess that is what she was doing Friday night.
>
> She was dear to me and we had talked a little of marriage, but nothing too definite. That night I think she must have been

trepidatious over the prospect of marrying me because she said she was afraid she wouldn't be able to fulfill the role of wife. . . . I remember thinking she needed a lot of reassurance, and it was reassuring that Ron was there because we both liked him. I said some little things like, "you know we're with you," and "you've got friends," and "you can talk to us." I think Ron just listened mostly. Really nothing too much seemed wrong and I remember she was cheerful when she left. The last thing she said to me was simply, "good-bye, Jim."

Jim Randolph left the car and went into his house. Maxine drove Ron Crawford home, a ride during which, according to Crawford, "no conversation took place." Maxine proceeded to her home in Talmage.

In Maxine's house was one eyewitness the coroner's investigators neglected to question, perhaps because he was only nine years old—Tommy Ijames. Tommy was spending the night with Maxine's son Daniel, the same age, and the boys were in Daniel's bedroom, still awake, talking in whispers so they wouldn't be found out and told to go to sleep, when Maxine came in the house and turned on the TV. Tommy and Daniel talked for a few minutes before they both nodded off to sleep.

Early the next morning, Tommy was awakened by the sounds of footsteps and voices. There were several people in the house, among them, Tom recalls, Jack Beam and Patty Cartmell; he doesn't remember the others. "In the morning," he says, "they so-called said she had hung herself and we went out to the garage." Maxine was hanging from a rafter, suspended by an electrical cord wrapped around her neck. Her face was purple and her eyes closed as if in a deep sleep. Tom was told that Maxine's seven-year-old daughter, Debbie, had discovered her mother hanging and had found a suicide note written on a piece of paper torn from a grocery bag:

> Call Jim, its *very* important if he not there try Edith. Tell her or him I'm not home and they should get here right away. Then stay in the house until they come.

Tom's recollection of the events of March 28, 1970, lends credence to the rumor that Jim Jones took immediate steps to remove any evidence linking Maxine Harpe with Peoples Temple:

> The children called the church before they called the police, and they came very early in the morning. They came in there and took all the pictures of Jim Jones out . . . [prayer] cloths they took from her, because like you'd have cloths you'd place around your waist, and they pulled her down off the [rafter] and took them off her waist, anything

214

that had to do with the church. . . . Jim [Jones], he stayed in the car and didn't come out. . . . They pulled her down and they took the cloths off of her. . . . They were taking all the . . . little pamphlets of Jim Jones, and then [after the coroner arrived] they acted like they didn't know her. . . .

According to Tom Ijames, Jim Jones and his elite troubleshooters left the scene of the crime about twenty minutes before the deputies arrived. Tom never did see what happened to Maxine's body; when he was shooed out of the garage and told to go back into the house, the body was still on the garage floor. The Temple members, including Jim Randolph, returned to the Talmage home about twenty minutes after Deputy Sheriff-Coroner Bruce Cochran drove up at 8:57 A.M. Jim Jones stayed behind at the parsonage in Redwood Valley.

The image of his friend's mother hanging dead from the rafters of the garage rather beclouds Tom's memory about some of the details. Tom is sure, however, that he saw a tall white man take Maxine down and set her on the floor. The coroner's report indicates that Maxine's corpse was hanging from the rafter when Cochran arrived.

[Reporting officer] opened the sliding door and saw a female body, hanging from a rafter suspended by an electrical cord. The electric cord was tied with three wraps around the neck and tied with a slip knot. The knot tied at the back of the head. . . . The body was fully clothed: blue Levi's, blouse, brown suede hip length coat, brown suede shoes. Beneath the body, a small travel trunk, approximately 18 inches by 12 inches by 30 inches, the trunk turned on its side. The deceased's right foot was on top of the trunk, leg bent at the knee and ankle, the left foot hanging to the side of the trunk.

Photographs in the coroner's file match Cochran's description, down to the detail of the odd positioning of the trunk and Maxine's feet, which Cochran seems not to have questioned. The trunk was directly below her when Cochran found her body, and had Maxine wished to change her mind, had her body, through its natural reflexes, made the decision for her, she'd simply have to stand on one or both legs to support her weight. Considering the cause of death was anoxia (lack of oxygen), she'd have to have been swinging freely; it seems unlikely that she could control her reflexes sufficiently not to have foiled her attempt when her body started feeling the need for oxygen. Tom Ijames's account offers a possible explanation of the strange positioning of the trunk: either the trunk or Maxine was put back in the wrong place when the Temple finished removing evidence.

Tom was told after the discovery of Maxine's body that she killed herself because Jim Jones ordered Jim Randolph to stop seeing Maxine. Randolph—like most Temple members—was always obedient to Father. Vicky Moore heard the same explanation, and so did others.

Less than a month before Maxine Harpe died, according to Cochran's subsequent investigation, she signed over a check for $2,493.81—her portion of a property settlement agreement with her ex-husband—to Randolph, who placed $2,000 of the money in his checking account and $493.81 in his savings account. Cochran contacted Randolph's boss, welfare director Dennis Denny, who indicated "he was very interested in this case as it may indicate a lack of proper conduct on the part of James Randolph." Randolph told Cochran that "within a couple of weeks after the deposit," he wrote a check for $2,000 to Peoples Temple. The check, he said, was turned over to church treasurer Eva Pugh, who supposedly placed it in a special fund for Maxine's children. "Maxine didn't want any of the money for herself," Randolph said, "and she wanted the children to have it." On March 31, Randolph withdrew $465 of Maxine's money from his savings account and turned it, too, over to the church. All the money, Randolph said in a written statement to Cochran, was to go to Maxine's children. Although Randolph indicated the statement was "true, correct, and freely given," he said he would sign it only after Assistant District Attorney Tim Stoen read it. The records show that Randolph never did sign his own account of the money transactions.

Randolph also volunteered during his interview with Cochran that Tim Stoen knew of the existence of a trust fund for the Harpe children, and when Cochran contacted Stoen the next morning, Stoen said he was a custodian of the fund, along with Sheriff Reno Bartolomei and a now deceased Ukiah civic leader. Each child received, according to Stoen, $988.33 in trust. When Cochran contacted Bartolomei, the sheriff confirmed the existence of the fund and noted that Peoples Temple had kicked in just over $470. Bartolomei claims he insisted the money be kept in trust after he learned it had already been given to the Temple. "I knew no one could touch that damn money until the kids were able to have it," he said of the trust fund, which met the approval of Maxine's father.

Whether the Temple intended to use the Harpe money to establish a trust fund for the Harpe children before their mother's suicide is a matter of speculation; the fact that such a fund existed after the suicide was reason enough for the sheriff's office to quit investigating. Whether welfare director Dennis Denny's expressed interest in possible improprieties by Randolph was genuine—Randolph did deposit a welfare recipient's money in his own bank accounts—is also a matter of speculation, since no action was ever taken and Jim Randolph remained on the county payroll for seven more years, until the summer of 1977.

Peoples Temple naturally felt that Jim Jones should officiate at Maxine Harpe's funeral, but her family would have none of it. Instead, a local Baptist minister, the Reverend Richard Taylor, conducted the services; he seemed to have an accurate picture and a good understanding of some of the questions, if not the answers, surrounding Maxine's death. Nevertheless, despite the family's rejection of Pastor Jim, some fifty Temple members showed up at the funeral. There was a strange irony in such a turnout; two and a half years later, the Temple had officially forgotten Maxine Harpe. The Temple was under fire in a series of articles by the Reverend Lester Kinsolving in the *San Francisco Examiner*. One of Kinsolving's charges was that Tim Stoen had counseled Maxine Harpe just before she died. Stoen's reply in the *Ukiah Daily Journal* for September 21, 1972:

> The woman referred to (who was not, incidentally, a member of my church) was somebody I did not know, had never talked with, and certainly had never counseled.

This position on the doubtful existence of a Maxine Harpe represented, to some degree, a reversal of Jim Jones's customary posture. He usually took credit, by implication or innuendo, for the death of every Temple member who strayed. Sometimes he would claim directly that the death was his fault; he had a premonition, he would say, but it was either too vague or too late, or he decided there was no way to prevent the inevitable. Whenever there were suspicious circumstances surrounding a death, Jim Jones would seize the opportunity to remind his flock that "bad things happen" to those who stray from Father's protection.

"Bad things" happened to John William Head, a twenty-two-year-old Temple member with a history of emotional problems. "Jim took some credit for that," recalls Vicky Moore. "Now, I don't know how. . . . He bragged about that and I was really perturbed. He did some bragging about that and I don't know whether he was bragging because he's psychic or because he actually did it." John Head died on October 19, 1975, from multiple head injuries he sustained when he either jumped or fell sixty-five feet from the roof of a three-story warehouse on North Vignes Street in Los Angeles. He landed on his head with such force that, apparently, he bounced twenty-five feet when he hit. He died instantly.

The coroner's office determined that John Head's death was a suicide after his footprints were found on the roof of the warehouse, leading to the edge. His glasses were up there, too. A thorough autopsy confirmed that his death resulted from the fall. Further investigation revealed he "had been mentally ill for the past four to five years" and had been hospitalized at Mendocino State Hospital for "depression." He was, by all appearances, what the coroner's office classifies a "jumper"—a routine suicide case. He left no suicide note. Apparently, he didn't tell a soul of his intentions before he made his fatal leap Sunday morning at 11:15.

John Head was involved with Peoples Temple for only a short time before he died. He had been living with his parents, John and Ruth Head—neither of whom were members—in Redwood Valley when he became increasingly active in the church to the point that he decided to make the total commitment in September of 1975. He handed over to the church ten thousand dollars' worth of silver bullion he had purchased from the Shamaz Trading Company in Ukiah. He kept the bullion in safe deposit boxes at that town's branch of Bank of America. His mother recalls that he bought the silver with money he received from an insurance settlement following a motorcycle accident. Harold Cordell and another Temple member—Harold doesn't recall who—accompanied John to the bank after John insisted he wanted the Temple to have his silver. John was, Harold remembers, "just another young guy who was looking for some direction. He seemed to find what he wanted there [in the Temple] and he kept saying he had to get rid of that money. It was getting to him. He wanted to give it to the church. . . . He just asked me to go with him, so I went, and I was present when he picked it up."

It was just after John turned over his silver that he joined Peoples Temple officially, his mother recalls. John had quit his job at a particle-board plant in Ukiah. He had been unemployed for "a couple of months." He turned over the silver on September 27, 1975. Two days later, the Temple sent him down to Los Angeles. "We tried to talk him out of this," says his mother. "He said he was going to go down there and live with the people at Peoples Temple."

Three weeks later he was dead. The day before he plunged from the warehouse roof, John Head made a collect call to a former neighbor in Redwood Valley. "He called over here," recalls the neighbor, "and I guess he had just gotten in the church. . . . He wasn't happy there. He said that he wanted to be in the church, but he didn't want to be in Los Angeles. He wanted to be over here in Redwood Valley. And they had made it a point that they wanted him over there, instead of over here." John said he was calling from a phone booth across the street from the church. The former neighbor offered John a place to stay; John said the church would not let him leave. Besides, he said, he had no money. "He was very anxious to come over here, and he was disturbed that he couldn't come. He didn't have no way of coming, no money. . . . He was in desperation, you know, and he talked to me very briefly."

John and Ruth Head will never be totally convinced their son committed suicide. "We do not think he did this on his own," says Mrs. Head, "and nobody that knew him thinks that." What shook Mrs. Head's confidence in the investigation of her son's death was the coroner's file; it is fraught with errors. The initial report indicates that John William Head was a "jumper from [a] bridge" on the "west side of the [Los Angeles] River between First and Temple." The case report says he jumped off the warehouse roof. The warehouse is two blocks away from the nearest bridge over the Los Angeles

River. The description of the victim in the autopsy report—brown hair, blue eyes, just over six feet tall, weighing a hundred and sixty-five pounds—fits John William Head, but the report has a curious omission: John Head had two prominent scars, one on his leg bearing the marks of three hundred stitches, the result of the motorcycle accident, and one on his hip five inches long. The report tells of the presence of alcohol in his blood—Mrs. Head claims her son did not drink—and traces of phenobarbitol. The only medication John was taking, Mrs. Head recalls, was Haldol, a tranquilizer. Despite the errors, omissions, and possible discrepancies in the autopsy report, however, Mrs. Head is certain that the body she identified was her son's. A coroner's inquest two years later simply reaffirmed the conclusion that John William Head's death was a suicide, but John and Ruth Head are convinced they have not yet heard the "whole story."

Other deaths of Temple members fueled suspicions and rumors. Anthony Buckley—his friends knew him as Curtis Buckley—died in San Francisco on March 21, 1975, of what the autopsy report described as a "spontaneous" cerebral hemorrhage. Curtis, a sixteen-year-old black, the picture of health, died in bed at a Temple commune on Sutter Street at 8:30 in the morning. A friend who found Curtis lifeless in bed took him to Mount Zion Hospital, where he was pronounced dead on arrival forty-five minutes later.

According to former Temple members, Jim Jones predicted Curtis Buckley's death at a Wednesday night meeting in San Francisco, about thirty-six hours before he died. Jim Jones predicted that Curtis Buckley would die from "rat poison in a Coke." The autopsy shows negative results for tests for common poisons like arsenic and strychnine, which are frequently used in some rat poisons; but there is one variety of rat poison that is all but impossible to detect in routine toxicology tests. The drug, sodium warfarin, kills rats by causing massive hemorrhaging. It has a medical use as an anticoagulant, and its presence can be detected by testing the clotting speed of the blood. Once the heart stops and the blood stagnates, clotting is irreversible; it cannot be measured. Detecting the drug requires testing more sophisticated than is normally used in autopsies. Although the autopsy on Curtis Buckley was fairly thorough, there is no indication a test for warfarin was performed.

According to pathologists, it would take about 125 milligrams of sodium warfarin to kill a human being. In such a dose, the drug would take about three or four days to be fatal. The usual symptoms are headaches and profuse bleeding from the nose, and eventually the victim would die from a brain hemorrhage. The coroner's report on Curtis Buckley says, "The deceased has complained of severe headaches and not feeling well for the past two days."

Curtis Buckley may have been murdered; but why? One of Curtis's close friends in the Temple—who declines to be identified—remembers that Curtis was kind of "gay-ish." Others in the Temple recall hearing that Curtis was in trouble with Jim Jones because he kept talking to his friends about wanting to leave, and the rumor is that Curtis Buckley was a sacrificial lamb, killed as an example.

A similar rumor persists over the death of Robert Houston, Jr., who joined the church in 1969 and later served as a photographer, leader of the band and chorus, and assistant pastor. Father was constantly down on Houston for his habit of questioning Temple rules and engaging in "intellectual" discussions. Father punished Houston severely for these sins; often making him submit to brutal boxing matches. He divorced his wife, Phyllis, in 1974. Two years later, on October 5, 1976, at the age of thirty-three, Bob Houston suffered mutilating fatal injuries at a Southern Pacific freight yard in San Francisco. He fell off a flatcar, apparently, and was crushed under the wheels. He was moonlighting at the yard as a switchman, working days as a counselor at the San Francisco Youth Guidance Center, and reportedly turning over two thousand dollars a month to the Temple. Houston might have been so exhausted from working two jobs and attending all-night meetings at the Temple that he fell asleep and just toppled on to the tracks. The rumor is that he was pushed into the path of the train by one of Jones's goons.

Undoubtedly the source of the rumors connecting suspicious deaths with Jim Jones was Jim Jones himself. Fear of death was the most potent weapon in his arsenal. When Chris Lewis—Jones's chief enforcer—was murdered in December of 1977 in San Francisco, where unknown assailants shot him in the back, Jones blamed the incident on critics of Peoples Temple. Jones milked Lewis's death even further: he put out the word that the Temple had barely managed to restrain Lewis's friends from taking revenge on the "conspirators" against the Temple who had had him murdered. According to Steve Zalkind of San Francisco, Chris Lewis's last attorney, his client was facing an almost certain prison term for having been caught with a pistol on the floor of his car while he was a convicted felon. While he was out on bail, Lewis and his wife, Dorothy, traveled to Jonestown, presumably to raise money for his defense; Lewis had told Zalkind he was counting on Jim Jones for money for legal fees. When Lewis received no answer from Jones, he radioed his message twice to Jonestown. Father never replied. Lewis was murdered within a few days of the last radio call, Zalkind recalls.

Any number of Lewis's enemies could have had him killed. Ex-junkies who get involved in ghetto politics and boast about how bad they are tend to have short life spans. Although no suspects have ever been apprehended in the Lewis murder, there is evidence the Temple may have been involved. The complaint filed May 25, 1978, by Wade and Mabel Medlock with the Los Angeles County District Attorney's office charged the Temple with extorting $135,000 worth of properties from them the year before. The Medlocks said the alleged extortion took place at the Temple in Los Angeles, and that they signed the papers "under duress" with Jim McElvane and Jim Jones present. Jones told the Medlocks—an elderly black couple—prior to the signing of the escrow papers that they would be moving to Guyana, where the Temple would "take care of their lives." The Medlocks refused repeatedly to make the move. In December of 1977, the same month Lewis was killed in San Francisco, the Medlocks were approached by Marceline Jones, who allegedly told them, "Jim told me to tell you to come to Guyana." Wade Medlock refused again. Marceline allegedly replied, "What happened to Chris Lewis will happen to you." The Medlocks told investigators they had heard Lewis was murdered by McElvane and another Temple member, a "Jim Crokes." The Temple repeated the threat, the Medlocks said, in a telephone call two days later from Hugh Fortsyn, an associate pastor at the church in San Francisco. "You know what happened to Chris Lewis," Fortsyn reportedly said. "You better watch it."

Death threats were taken seriously in Peoples Temple. Father had boasted many times that no one who left the Temple would be safe within five hundred miles of California. Anyone who hurt the Temple in any way, he said, would be tracked down by his avenging angels, a small group of Temple loyalists—no one seems to know exactly who they were—who would carry out Father's orders to kill. Jim Jones also boasted at several planning commission meetings that he had "Mafia connections" through a physician in San Francisco; the mob, he said, would "take care of" anyone who was a threat. All he had to do was make a phone call.

Perhaps these were idle threats, calculated to reinforce the fears already instilled in his followers by the beatings, the humiliations, the rumors of mysterious deaths, but the people in the Temple had seen enough of Father's wrath to believe anything. At one planning commission meeting, however, Father achieved an unprecedented level of absurdity; some of the former members still laugh about it, despite the tragedy in Guyana. Jim Jones passed around a note that read:

We now have the last part we need for the bomb.

After the note had made its rounds, Father burned it, but the message remained in the minds of his flock. There were some who pretended to believe him but didn't; there were others who believed that once Peoples Temple became a superpower, the world would finally listen to Jim Jones.

221

I've taken the position of moderation and I've received threats from both sides.

—Jim Jones, *Ukiah Daily Journal,*
September 26, 1972

VIII

Enemies of the Cause

Child molesters, sex perverts, Nazis, Trotskyites, radical revolutionaries eager to bomb bridges, right-wing extremists rabid with the desire to put the blacks in concentration camps, arsonists, racists, sexists, ageists, spies and agents provocateurs, the FBI, the CIA, INTERPOL, kickers of small animals and robbers of church poor boxes—who else would criticize Jim Jones? Who else but the dwarfed souls in the service of the devil would dare attempt to expose and destroy the good works and lofty idealism of Peoples Temple?

These critics of apostolic equalitarianism, former members who spoke out against Jones in the press, are described in a Temple news release of July 17, 1977:

> We note that those who have made their charges against our ministry include persons who constantly pressed *us* to take extremist postures and actions totally incompatible with our faith and organizational goals and principles. Some were even involved in manufacturing weapons and advocating that the church use them to advance its program of social change. When this was brought to his attention, Rev. Jones opposed these ideas vehemently. We saw that the individuals who put forward extremist ideologies were indulgent in their living style, hypocritical, and vainglorious. Some other members tended to share their views, but the testimony of their own lives did not square with their alleged ideals, and the extremist positions were rejected. We saw no principled living expressed by them. In certain extreme cases, persons were asked to leave our fellowship. Others left when their efforts met with no success.

Critics? Jim Jones had no critics. Jim Jones had enemies.

Jim Jones had enemies even from the Indianapolis days, and among the worst were those who knew him best. Cecil and Georgia Johnson were two of Jim Jones's earliest followers; Cecil was charmed for the first time when he heard young Jimmy's voice over the loudspeakers outside the Methodist

224

church on the South Side back in the early 1950s, and he and Georgia joined up with Jimmy Jones even before there was a Peoples Temple. They were convinced that Jimmy was a messenger of God, so convinced that Cecil once saw Jesus up there beside the pulpit, standing next to Jimmy. The Johnsons lost interest in the church when Jimmy left for Brazil in 1963. Even before Jimmy's departure, however, Georgia skipped a few services. "I made up every excuse under the sun to keep from going to church," says Georgia, "till I run out of excuses for him."

The Johnsons' next contact with Jim Jones's church was during the summer of 1971. Jim Jones and a dozen busloads of people came out from California for a rally at the old Temple at Tenth and Delaware streets in Indianapolis. The Johnsons' daughter Mickie—once, years earlier, the young preacher's "mascot" at his first church on South Keystone—read about the miracle healing rally in the *Indianapolis Star* and showed the newspaper to her mother. Georgia talked Cecil into attending for old time's sake. "We almost had to whip our kids to make them go," Georgia recalls. "I says church couldn't hurt nobody." Mickie and Gwen finally agreed to go along, and Mickie brought her twelve-week-old son, Joseph, too.

The family arrived early and found a seat in the front row, where they could get a close look at the Prophet of God. Georgia sat with the baby in her lap and kept him quiet while the Peoples Temple band and choir started cooking up the spirit. Georgia and Cecil tolerated the amplified music; fifteen-year-old Gwen felt like getting up and dancing with the other kids her age, and so did her sister, Mickie, six years her senior.

Cecil and Georgia could not believe their eyes and ears. The Jimmy they remembered sang traditional hymns in a sacrosanct, if somewhat sour, baritone while Loretta Cordell accompanied him with simple chords on the organ—the way church songs were supposed to be. Now they saw before them, twenty years later, a pretentious honky equivalent of Ray Charles, complete with shades and some kind of imitation of the Raylettes backing him up, offering up music that had people dancing like the devil's own, faking the funk like the Genius hiding in whiteface. "I am a prophet of God," said the white soul brother, "and I can cure both the illness of your body as well as the illnesses of your mind."

Somehow in the frenzy of inspiration, Cecil and Georgia lost sight of Mickie. They thought she was still sitting somewhere near them. "She disappeared and we went and looked in the rest rooms," Georgia recalls. "We looked everywhere except his office. He seen me fightin' with the deacons, or goons, or whatever you want to call them. I call them his goons, his Gestapo. I kept fightin' 'em and I kept tellin' 'em—I said—I said I knew that boy way back when. I knowed him before you ever heard tell of him, and I'm a-goin' up there to talk to him. So finally Jim seen me fightin' with 'em and he motioned for them to leave me alone."

225

With little Joseph still in her arms, Georgia approached Jim Jones and explained her predicament.

"Have you looked in the rest room?" the prophet asked.

"I've looked everywhere," Georgia answered.

"Have you looked around the grounds?"

"I've looked around the grounds."

"Have you looked in my office?"

"No, I didn't, because I didn't feel that was any of my business."

Jim Jones walked over to the office door and opened it. There stood her daughter. Before Georgia could say a word, Mickie announced she was going west with her baby to settle in Redwood Valley. Georgia voiced a mild protest: a trip like that in the summer's heat could be risky for the health of a twelve-week-old infant. Mickie had made up her mind. She was going to dedicate her life to apostolic equalitarianism.

"She's liable to get homesick," said Georgia, turning to Jim Jones. He promised her the Temple would be returning for another rally in October or November, and surely Mickie and Joseph would come along. There seemed to be no way Cecil and Georgia could talk Mickie out of her commitment to Jim Jones, and Mickie, little Joseph, and Mickie's thirteen-year-old nephew, Donald Moore, were on the bus when it pulled out of Indianapolis at 11:30 P.M.

Georgia was worried sick. This man of God—the same Jim Jones who borrowed Georgia's Bible back in 1952 because he was too poor to buy his own—didn't even listen to the plea about little Joseph's health and the risks of such a long trip. Georgia was so fired up that she decided to follow the Temple buses all the way to California. Cecil had to work; he stayed behind. Gwen, however, talked her mother into taking her along because, like most teenagers in her time and in her place, Gwen wanted to see California. Georgia feared that if she didn't take Gwen with her, Gwen would grab the next Greyhound or head straight for the Interstate 70 on-ramp with her thumb stuck out. Georgia feared that Gwen would travel by herself, run out of money, and end up turning tricks in Rock Springs, Wyoming, or in some mobile home park in Nevada, just another body in the army of teenage girls who head for California and land in some twenty-dollar bed. Or worse; Gwen might get sweet-talked into joining Peoples Temple.

So mother and daughter left Indianapolis at three o'clock in the morning, less than four hours behind the Temple buses, in the family's 1965 Chevy station wagon with its weak transmission, and ground out the asphalt nonstop, three and a half days without sleeping, over the Rockies and across the Great Basin until they hit the Sierra Nevada and the transmission went out. Georgia might have beat the buses but for that transmission. The wagon clunked and grunted at five miles per hour up the steep grades, running on nothing but fatigued steel gears and a mother's determination, but Georgia kept pushing.

The wagon limped into Ukiah, without Father's protection now, only one day after the Temple buses unloaded in Redwood Valley.

Georgia left the wagon at a repair shop in Ukiah, and she and Gwen moved in, temporarily, with Jack and Rheaviana Beam. In something more than half a day, Georgia and Gwen found Mickie, little Joseph, and nephew Donald. Then Georgia agreed to attend a couple of additional services at Peoples Temple.

The first service was uneventful, highlighted by Jim Jones's impromptu sermon on sex around his observation—stated clearly with an abundance of four-letter words that no one could misunderstand—that men who wear boots are not hung as well as men who wear ordinary shoes. The second service was more memorable; Georgia had to go to the bathroom. She got into some trouble with one of the guards because she stood up to approach the facilities while Father was preaching. The guard politely informed her that she would have to wait. "You want me to do it right on your foot?" she asked. The guard let her pass. Later during the same service, Georgia felt herself becoming faint from the stuffy air and the heat of a thousand bodies in the building. She headed for the front door to get some air. The guard at the door—a big man with a pistol in a hip holster—told her she could not go out. Georgia suggested to the guard, "You just try and stop me," and the man withdrew the pistol from the holster about an inch, then let it slide back. Georgia went outside and breathed some fresh air.

Georgia enjoyed the fresh air, and when she recovered from the staleness inside and tried to get back in, the guards wouldn't let her. Georgia sat outside the Temple waiting for Gwen. She sat outside waiting until four o'clock in the morning, and she told Gwen what had happened, and after a couple of weeks Gwen made her full commitment to Jim Jones.

Repairing the car took a month, during which Georgia was alone as she had never been before. Jim Jones tried to talk her into joining the church, but she resisted. He told her Cecil would die of a heart attack if he didn't move to Redwood Valley. Jim Jones would, he told Georgia, "take care of everything." All Cecil had to do was turn over all of his money and sign power-of-attorney papers. Georgia was scared. She was afraid Cecil would die if he didn't go along with Jim Jones's wishes. She called Cecil and pleaded with him to join the rest of the family, but Cecil wouldn't buy it. He'd already heard too many unfulfilled predictions of doom to go for this one. Georgia tried several times to persuade Gwen and Mickie to return to Indianapolis with her, but they were already programmed for loyalty to the Temple. Both of them promised their mother they would be on the next Temple trip to Indianapolis in October or November. Georgia returned alone.

Weeks passed with little word from the girls. Cecil called the Temple in early October to learn the date of the Temple's Indianapolis rally and he was. told October 12 and 13. The Temple called Cecil the next day to tell him that

227

Mickie, Gwen, and Joseph would not be on the buses unless each of them could pay fifty dollars, and Cecil wired the money the following day. After the money arrived, Mickie called Cecil collect and said the Temple still wouldn't let her, or Joseph or Gwen either, go on the bus trip because the Temple had a "policy" against returning converts to their hometowns. Cecil told Georgia about this "policy." She got on the phone, called Redwood Valley, and threatened Temple leaders with "Governor Ronald Reagan and everybody else." She might as well have been calling from Zanzibar for all the good her threats did.

The Johnsons didn't see their daughters again until the following June, when, during Cecil's vacation, they drove out together to Redwood Valley. They found Gwen right away; they knew she worked during the day at Hodge's Cafeteria in downtown Ukiah. It was more difficult to find Mickie. Georgia suspected the people at the church were not telling the truth about where Mickie was living, and Gwen's initial answer sounded ominous: "Mommy, you won't know her. It's better off that you don't see her." Georgia pressed her until Gwen agreed to help find Mickie. Gwen took Georgia to a house across from the post office. She knocked on the door and went inside and left her mother pacing back and forth on the sidewalk for what seemed an interminable time until, finally, Mickie emerged with two men, a white man and a black man, beside her. Georgia was a little puzzled; she had no trouble recognizing Mickie at all, and she ran up to her daughter without hesitation and embraced her warmly.

"Mom," said Mickie, somewhat shyly, "I want you to meet my husband."

Georgia extended her hand to the white man standing beside Mickie.

"No, Mommy," said Mickie, turning toward the black man, "I mean him."

Georgia screamed. She screamed so loudly she rivaled the noon whistle downtown. "I bet you heard me all over Ukiah," she says, "all over that whole town." Georgia ranted and raved in a hysterical shriek for several minutes, waving her arms about while Mickie and the two men tried to calm her. The white man—from the Temple—told Georgia he was concerned that the people in the post office across the street would hear what she was saying, but Georgia could not have cared less. "Let 'em hear me!" she shouted, and steamed down the block toward the offices of the *Ukiah Daily Journal*, moving like a locomotive, and pushed open the glass door and marched straight to the office of the managing editor, George Hunter. "I told that man everything about what Peoples Temple had done to my kids and me," she recalls. In Hunter's office, Georgia rambled on and on with her story, but not a word of it ever appeared in the paper. Georgia learned a few days later—from Gwen—that Jim Jones himself had arranged Mickie's marriage and that Assistant Pastor Tim Stoen had performed the ceremony. "That girl would never have gotten married," Georgia says. "I wouldn't give a darn if she was married to a green man, if he was good to her. Mickie was afraid of marriage."

With the assistant DA performing marriages for Peoples Temple and the managing editor of the local daily refusing to heed her story, Georgia was beginning to get the impression that Jim Jones controlled Mendocino County. Although she was furious, there seemed to be nothing she could do. She and Cecil headed back to Indianapolis with nephew Donald, but without Mickie, Gwen, or little Joseph. The lack of victory was a bitter pill to swallow for twenty-five hundred miles, but Georgia and Cecil kept their hope alive.

As soon as Georgia got back to Indianapolis, she sat down and wrote her story for the *National Enquirer*. She wrote everything she could remember about Jim Jones and Peoples Temple and sent the manuscript off to New York in a thick envelope. She waited for several weeks, when the manuscript came back with a note explaining that it was not suitable for publication. Georgia, undaunted, mailed her story again, this time to Byron C. Wells, a reporter for the *Indianapolis Star*. Wells had written the first exposé of Peoples Temple on October 14, 1971 after attending one of Jones's miracle healing services. The piece is eighteen paragraphs long and headlined "Church Filled to See 'Cures' by Self-Proclaimed 'Prophet of God.'" In it Wells reported how Jones had "cured" a "multititude of ills" and "even claimed to have resurrected the dead." Wells hinted, too, that there may have been shills present:

> In both services those called upon were told to place a white face tissue near their hearts, backs and other parts of the body to prevent "certain death."
>
> The people who were called upon in the evening had a striking resemblance to some who were called upon earlier in the day.

Wells's article did not go unnoticed. The *Star* received a flurry of protesting phone calls and letters from Temple members, but the editors stood their ground. When the *Star* editors learned that Jim Jones would be returning for another healing service December 10, planning to answer the allegations in the Wells article, they decided to send to cover Jim's defiant return not Wells—he'd be too easily recognized—but a black woman, Shirley Rogers. Rogers slipped unnoticed into the meeting, whose audience was predominantly black, and witnessed some miracle healings herself—but the highlight of the meeting was Jones's salvo at Wells's article in the *Star*. After the article ran, Jones told the crowd, he received twenty-three calls from "hatemongers" in Indianapolis. He criticized the *Star* for failing to report on the people he had saved during services, including fifteen drug addicts he took with him, he said, to California.

The next day, the *Star* ran, under Wells's by-line, a story announcing that the Indiana State Board of Psychology Examiners would be launching an investigation of Jim Jones's alleged healing powers.

> While local and state medical and law enforcement officials say they are helpless to take action against persons who claim supernatural

powers, the psychology board feels it may have legal authority to act.

The Rev. Mr. Jones's claims that he can cure "psychosomatic diseases" may be a basis for psychology board action, according to Dr. Jeannette P. Reilly of Indianapolis, a board member. . . .

A medical doctor who attended one of the two services held Friday said, "What bothers me is that people who are really sick may think they have been cured, and later be in more serious condition."

The doctor, who asked to remain unidentified, because of possible conflict with the American Medical Association, said the "cancer" he saw appeared to be "just some sort of white material in a plastic bag."

The Rev. Mr. Jones was asked to allow the "cancer" to be analyzed by a competent pathologist in order to ascertain its contents. The minister had "no personal objections," but he has to abide by the wishes of his church leaders "not to become involved in more publicity."

He also said he was afraid that the tissues would be switched on him in a deliberate attempt to discredit his power. . . .

"Although a lot of my healings are of psychosomatic cases, I've done more than any other healer," he declared. "That's why I don't want any more publicity either favorable or unfavorable," he added.

Jones said he is not opposed to medical science in any way, and that he is not able to cure all diseases. He added he has personally talked people into seeing doctors for illnesses he can't cure.

The Wells article marked the first time Jim Jones faced the prospect of a major government investigation of his activities. Unfortunately, loopholes in the law made it impossible to prosecute the Prophet of God on charges of practicing psychiatry without a license. The board was to have investigated Jones's claims that he could cure psychosomatic diseases, but the issue was clouded by the religious question of whether there are living prophets who transmit God's healing powers to the afflicted. The suggestion that Jones might have to submit one of the cancers passed during his services to a pathologist for analysis was enough to put him on the defensive. Jim Jones told Wells he was considering an end to "services in Indianapolis because of its distance from his main church," and was even thinking of "selling, or even donating" the church at Tenth and Delaware to "any legitimate agency that wants to use it to help the public."

The Wells article may have made Jim Jones think twice about returning to Indianapolis, but it didn't help Georgia Johnson get her daughters back from Redwood Valley. Georgia kept hoping that Wells would answer her rambling letter, but he never did. He kept it on his desk for a few days, then gave it to the city editor, who passed it on to Carolyn Pickering, the *Star*'s chief investigative reporter. Pickering was initially skeptical about Georgia's story, but she decided to look into it. She called Georgia and set up an appointment for an interview.

That first contact with Georgia Johnson, in August of 1972, was the beginning of a full-time investigation that kept Carolyn Pickering busy for more than a month. Pickering followed up Georgia's leads—the names of former members, the addresses of the church's property holdings, memories of the monkey-business days, predictions of the holocaust—and they all checked out. A veteran newswriter—she had joined the *Star* in 1942—Pickering welcomed the challenge of a full-scale investigation. She plodded through public records and unearthed documents that clearly proved that Jim Jones was in the real-estate business with a corporation named Jim-Lu-Mar. Jim-Lu-Mar's corporate charter was revoked June 1, 1970, Pickering learned, for failure to file annual reports with the Indiana Secretary of State. The same thing happened, for the same reason, to another Jones corporation, Wings of Deliverance, which lost its nonprofit charter on the same day.

While Pickering dug up the saga of the Prophet of God, Georgia Johnson was preparing for one last trip to California. Gwen had left the church. She was living with a famliy in Ukiah. Gwen had sneaked out the back door of Beam Board and Care on May 18, 1972, and when Georgia contacted her, Gwen told her mother she wanted to get out of Mendocino County as soon as possible. Her boyfriend—not a member of Peoples Temple—had a car pockmarked with the tiny craters of pellets, describing perfect circles of chipped paint, from the shotgun blasts it had stopped when he and Gwen were driving around together. Gwen was frightened.

After a tearful reunion in September, Gwen and Georgia set about trying to find Mickie and little Joseph. They were told Mickie was in Los Angeles and would not be back for some time. Once again Georgia and Gwen got on the road to search for Mickie, driving this time the five hundred and fifty miles to Los Angeles, hoping that in the meantime Mickie would have the sense to call Indianapolis and talk to Cecil. She did—four or five times. Georgia also called several times. Both Mickie and Georgia were in Los Angeles, and both were calling Cecil long distance collect, until Cecil finally gave Mickie an ultimatum that resulted in mother and daughter meeting. "You've given me the runaround," Cecil told Mickie. "I want you to have a definite place and a definite time, and your mother's going to be there to pick you up."

Mickie's mother and sister found her in a doughnut shop. Mickie was scared to death that they were being watched by the FBI or CIA. Georgia assured Mickie that it was safe for them to travel, that they could go back to Redwood Valley and retrieve Mickie's son, Joseph.

According to Mickie, Joseph was still in the Temple's care somewhere in Mendocino County. Georgia and Gwen inquired around and learned that little Joseph was staying with Elmer and Deanna Mertle. Georgia drove to the Mertle home; the shades were drawn, and it appeared that no one was home.

231

She drove there three or four times with the same results. Finally, she knocked loudly on the front door, but there was no answer.

Georgia was not about to give up. Walking down State Street in Ukiah, near the county courthouse, Georgia saw Grace Stoen standing on the corner by the Savings Bank of Mendocino County. Georgia sauntered calmly up to Grace to tell her the sad story of her lost grandchild. Georgia felt so badly about it, she told Grace, that if Peoples Temple did not return little Joseph within twenty-four hours, she would go directly to Ronald Reagan with her problem. Georgia meant it. Grace offered to call Jim Jones right away, then get back to Georgia at the Ukiah motel where she was staying.

Grace's call informed Georgia that Joseph could be picked up at Jim's house, and the three of them—Georgia, Mickie, and Grace—drove straight to the parsonage, where they found little Joseph nestling in Jim Jones's arms. Jones tried to persuade Mickie to leave the child with the Temple because, he told Mickie, Joseph was club-footed and would never walk. Georgia was not about to buy this line, so Jim told her she'd have to pay the Mertles a hundred dollars for taking care of the baby for a month. Cecil wired the money and the Johnsons—Georgia, Gwen, Mickie, and Joseph—made their last twenty-five-hundred-mile trek back to Indianapolis.

While the Johnsons were on the road from Redwood Valley, Carolyn Pickering was wrapping up her investigation in Indianapolis. She called Tom Eastham, executive editor of the *San Francisco Examiner;* the two had worked together before at the *Chicago Herald-American,* a defunct link in the Hearst chain. Pickering asked Eastham whether anyone on the *Examiner* had ever investigated a faith-healing minister named Jim Jones and his Peoples Temple church. Yes, Eastham replied, the *Examiner*'s religion editor, Lester Kinsolving, was at that moment in the midst of such an investigation. Eastham promised to put Kinsolving in touch with her.

Kinsolving, a flamboyant Episcopal priest turned investigative reporter, called Pickering as soon as he got the message, and the two reporters talked daily for several weeks across twenty-five hundred miles while they collaborated on the Peoples Temple story. Kinsolving needed background on Jones's escapades in Indianapolis; Pickering needed current information on Jones's California operation. They shared leads, corroborated stories, double-checked information from documents, and soon the two reporters—one in Indianapolis, one in San Francisco—had their series of articles ready for press.

Kinsolving was first out, September 17, with a front-page article in the *Examiner* headlined "The Prophet Who Raises the Dead," telling of the strange church in Redwood Valley with its armed guards, the power Jim Jones and his reputed 4,711 followers wielded in Mendocino County, Jones's claim that he had raised people from the dead, and quoting a letter Kinsolving had received only five days earlier from Tim Stoen:

Jim has been the means by which more than forty persons have literally been brought back from the dead this year. When I first came into the church I was the conventional skeptic about such things. But I must be honest:

I have seen Jim revive people stiff as a board, tongues hanging out, eyes set, skin graying, and all vital signs absent. Don't ask me how it happens. It just does.

Kinsolving charged that Stoen had gotten wind of his investigation from George Hunter, managing editor of the *Ukiah Daily Journal:*

There is little question of The Prophet's influence on the *Ukiah Daily Journal*—for when the *Examiner* inquired about the Peoples Temple and its charismatic pastor some months ago, *Journal* editor George Hunter immediately reported the inquiry to the office of prosecuting attorney—thus relaying the news to the precincts of Timothy O. Stoen, assistant prosecuting attorney and assistant to The Prophet.

Kinsolving was not amused when he attended a service in Redwood Valley and the guards at the door took away his notebook and pencil. Neither was Fran Ortiz, *Examiner* photographer, amused to lose his camera. The two newsmen did not protest having to surrender the tools of their trade, however, when they noticed on the way in at least three of the guards carrying pistols—one a .357 magnum—and a fourth carrying a shotgun. When Kinsolving inquired later about the armed guards, Temple attorney Eugene Chaikin offered this by way of explanation, in a note hand-delivered by Sandy Bradshaw of the Mendocino County Probation Department:

We have suffered threats and vandalism. Our local law enforcement agency has requested that we have trained persons carry firearms, and we have reluctantly acquiesced to the Sheriff's instructions on this matter.

Chaikin's explanation was refuted in another Kinsolving article three days later. Kinsolving read Chaikin's response to Undersheriff Tim Shea, who denied the sheriff's office made "any such request" that the Temple arm itself. Shea regarded Chaikin's written explanation of the guns as "an absolutely untrue statement."

Of the eight articles Kinsolving wrote about Peoples Temple, only four ever saw print. Kinsolving showed up for work on the morning of September 19, 1972, and encountered about a hundred and fifty Peoples Temple pickets marching in front of the *Examiner* building at Third and Market, carrying signs reading "This Is Invasion of Privacy of Religious Services" and "Government That Governs Least Governs Best." Among the pickets carrying placards was the Reverend Dave Garrison, whom Jim Jones had charmed away from the Macedonia Missionary Baptist Church. The Reverend Garrison's sign bore the words: "This Paper Has Lied. They Saw Healing Undeniable & Would Not Print." Kinsolving's boss, Tom Eastham, advised the feisty religion writer he "ought to go down and welcome them." Kinsolving replied he would go one step further. He borrowed a policeman's hat and held it upside down, walking among the protestors as if he were taking an offering.

"Brothers and sisters," Kinsolving said with dramatic inflection, "we welcome you today, and we're passing the collection." Kinsolving's theatrics backfired that evening, however, when KRON-TV, a station owned by the *Examiner*'s competitor, the *San Francisco Chronicle,* ran their coverage of the event on their evening news and "froze me with my mouth open, after they had turned the volume of my voice up so I sounded like Mount Vesuvius erupting . . . and then they faded, and here was Jim Jones sitting in a chair looking like the Angel Gabriel, talking sweet nothings in that . . . Fletcher's Castoria voice of his."

The next day, September 20, the *Examiner* ran the fourth of Kinsolving's articles and squelched the remaining four—not so much because of the Temple pickets or Kinsolving's theatrics as because of threats of litigation. "I kept pleading with them," Kinsolving recalls, still bitter. "They were already being sued by Synanon, and they were afraid, so they took the coward's way out." That fourth and final article dealt with a request by the Reverend Richard Taylor, for six years pastor of the First Baptist Church of Ukiah, for an investigation by the state attorney general's office of Peoples Temple "as well as the conduct of the church's attorney, Timothy O. Stoen, who is also assistant district attorney of Mendocino County." In his letter requesting the investigation, the Reverend Taylor described "an atmosphere of terror created in the community by so large and aggressive a group," which, he noted, "employs armed guards, contending that their pastor, the Rev. Jim Jones, has been threatened."

Taylor is an official of the American Baptist Churches of the West. He first locked horns with Jim Jones, of the Disciples of Christ, following the death of Maxine Harpe in March of 1970. At that time, the Reverend Taylor complained to Mendocino County District Attorney Duncan James about the conduct of his assistant DA, Tim Stoen, who had allegedly counseled Mrs. Harpe just before her death, and about allegations that members of Peoples Temple had ransacked Mrs. Harpe's home. "District Attorney James informed me that he had discussed this matter with Stoen," said the Reverend Taylor in his letter to Attorney General Evelle Younger, "but no action was taken other than requesting Stoen to refrain from any further misuse of his office."

One day after the last Kinsolving article, on September 21, Carolyn

Pickering published the first of her series of four exposés on the front page of the *Indianapolis Star*. As a tribute—perhaps unconscious—to the hell Kinsolving raised for his "Messiah from Ukiah," Pickering's first article was headlined, "Former City Preacher Feels Heat of Publicity in West." Two photographs accompanied the Pickering piece: the first showed the pickets in front of the *Examiner* building; the second, a pistol-packin' guard standing in the church parking lot in Redwood Valley. Pickering began with the premise that her subject was a "charlatan" whose claims of supernatural powers were "total quackery," and she let the words fly:

> The handsome, smooth-talking 41-year-old preacher who recites his Gospel attired in turtleneck sweaters and dark glasses claims . . . to have cured cancer, made the blind see and the crippled walk. . . .
>
> His congregation, mostly Negro, believes the Prophet capable of performing feats no less miraculous than the parting of the Red Sea.

In Mendocino County, wrote Pickering, "Peoples Temple has mushroomed into a virtually unmolested kingdom." She wanted to see Jones's Redwood Valley operation firsthand, but her editors wouldn't approve the travel request and Pickering had to rely entirely on interviews with former members, relatives of members, and her daily telephone calls with Lester Kinsolving. She had hoped to interview Gwen and Mickie Johnson when Georgia brought them back to Indianapolis, but the girls were too frightened to talk. They were convinced the FBI and CIA were after them, or worse, that Jim Jones's goons had tracked them down. Whoever was on their tail, they were convinced, had a tap on the phone in the Johnson home.

Immediately after the first article hit the stands, defectors from the Temple and concerned relatives surfaced all over Indianapolis. Suddenly, Pickering had no problems finding sources willing to share information, most of them frightened people who wanted help in wresting their sons and daughters from the clutches of Jim Jones. The outpouring of information and support astounded her. She was even more astounded at the Temple's response. "Within twenty-four hours after the first article appeared," Pickering recalls, "there came a flood—and I do mean a flood—of letters, telephone calls, all kinds of what I would call harassment . . . from people identifying themselves as followers and members of Peoples Temple." Pickering still finds it curious that copies of her articles were in the hands of Jones and his people in Redwood Valley so quickly.

Pickering should not have been so 'surprised; Kinsolving had warned her that as soon as her article ran her phone would be ringing like a hotline to a basement bookie just before post time, but she thought the Temple would not bother a reporter in Indianapolis, twenty-five hundred miles away from Redwood Valley. "I personally was getting a hundred [calls] a day," Pickering says, until "all I was doing was picking up the phone." Most of the callers and letter writers accused the *Star* of "publishing lies and falsehoods," Pickering recalls, "and many of them would make reference repeatedly to the fact that Peoples Temple had . . . constantly stood behind the press." Some of the calls were veiled threats that "something might happen" to her if she didn't stop printing her "lies." When it became obvious that the Temple's orchestrated program of harassment was having little effect on Pickering, Jim Jones put his chief legal adviser into action. Pickering remembers reading a letter—addressed to the publisher of the *Star*—"from Tim Stoen suggesting if the whole series was not retracted, they might sue, but we didn't retract a word, and they never sued." Pickering recalls "there was even a letter from the Reverend Jones himself to the publisher of the newspaper suggesting that [Peoples Temple] would like to contribute a monetary donation" toward "freedom of the press."

For her second *Star* article, Carolyn Pickering interviewed a former Indianapolis couple who had been with the church for seventeen years. Opal and Whitey Freestone had followed Jim Jones to Ukiah in 1965 to escape the holocaust Jones had predicted for—he said in those days—July 15, 1967. Jones's prediction for the end of the world was not quite accurate, but Whitey and Opal stayed with Peoples Temple for about three more years. Whitey and Opal had also been interviewed by Lester Kinsolving, who taped them and took affidavits, but their story never appeared in the *Examiner.* The Freestones told Pickering they had "tithed three thousand dollars to the church and gave an additional twelve hundred from an insurance settlement" for an accident during which the family car plunged down a mountainside, "fatally injuring their youngest daughter and causing permanent disability to Freestone." When, after the accident, the Freestones could no longer afford to pay the 25 percent tithe, Pickering wrote, they were told their "lives would be in danger." Opal Freestone pleaded with church officials:

> I told them it was impossible financially and I left, and we have never gone back.
>
> For two months after that, we received nagging telephone calls from Jim Jones, who told us to leave the community. He said my husband was going to be investigated for a crime.

The same article told also of a veiled threat Mickie Johnson allegedly received from Grace Stoen. Georgia was listening on the extension phone:

> The newspaper out here is harassing Jim. Your parents have signed something saying bad things about the Temple. You find out what they did and call me back. Get them to stop it. It's for your own safety, you know.

Pickering's third article, "Family Pleads With Aged Aunt Not to 'Throw Away Her Bible,'" was the story of how seventy-year-old Edith Cordell was talked into dumping the Good Book by a "Prophet" who sold her a live monkey. The fourth article told of "'Prophet' Attorney Probe Asked," the efforts of the Reverend Richard Taylor urging California Attorney General Evelle Younger to investigate Jim Jones. Pickering caught the Temple off guard with a fifth article on Jones's failure to file corporate tax returns with the state of Indiana. In fourteen years of covering federal courts, she had cultivated a cooperative source in the Internal Revenue Service. Among the allegations in the October 4 article was that "Wings of Deliverance, Inc., did not file exempt organization federal income tax returns during its five-year existence in Indiana." Pickering hoped that Jones's empire might crumble as Al Capone's did—under the weight of a tax evasion conviction—but the IRS found no hard evidence for pursuing criminal prosecution. "[Jim Jones] was very slick in the way he formed his corporations," Pickering says philosophically, "and they may very well not have had enough to prosecute him for tax evasion."

While Pickering continued to chip away at Jim Jones in Indianapolis, Kinsolving was left in San Francisco with four stories that would never be printed in the *Examiner*. The stories covered attempts by the Temple to compromise the Reverend G. L. Bedford with two Temple girls, the Maxine Harpe suicide, the "survival training" drills, and a glimpse at the Temple's burgeoning welfare scam in Mendocino County. The Temple had beaten Kinsolving down by questioning his credibility as a reporter. Jones himself alluded to Kinsolving's penchant for "negative" stories on religion in numerous interviews with the press. In a rambling interview with Ukiah radio station KUKI, Jones also hinted a libel suit might be in the works:

Now attorneys are coming to us and telling us that he's got into the area of libel. I've never sued nor have I been sued, and I don't like to think in those terms, but if it would cause him to be more careful in the future before he attacks innocent people, then we may consider such. . . . The *Examiner* has been very, very kind. The editors have offered on Sunday to give a front page story of the good works that we're doing and I think that will help to alleviate some of the fears and misunderstandings.

Jones had high expectations for the Sunday, September 24, issue of the *San Francisco Examiner*. They had been promised, Tim Stoen said, a "fair article," and that's what they got. The *Examiner* printed a transcription of an interview of Jones by two reporters the editors selected, John Burks and John Todd. Burks did his homework; before the interview, he picked up copies of Kinsolving's notes, searched the newspaper's files, and spent a few hours in research at the San Francisco Public Library, "so I went in loaded for bear."

Burks approached the Prophet of God expecting a man who was dynamic and magnetic. The man he saw sitting across the table was simple, it appeared, a "hick preacher" with a quixotic view of his powers in the universe. Jones was wearing a western-style polyester leisure suit—he "looked like a really dim bulb," Burks says—and seemed extraordinarily nervous. "I thought he was very strange," says Burks. "He was wearing his shades. He would take them off, put them on; take them off, put them on, and take them off and put them on again." Jones had another habit that bothered Burks, one frustrating for an interviewer: changing his answers. Whenever Burks asked sensitive or potentially embarrassing questions about Jones's paranormal powers, each answer the Prophet gave was radically different from the preceding answer, until Burks was totally confused about just what Jones was trying to say. Burks had had some experience interviewing slippery characters, including Richard Nixon, and he was accustomed to equivocators and back-pedalers. But Jim Jones was something else again. The Prophet kept changing his answers whenever Burks asked for clarification so that the subsequent answer was nowhere in context with the first, having moved a hundred and eighty degrees to suit what he sensed were the prejudices of his interviewer.

Burks, in his article, used Jones's own words, and he had Jones cold. Essentially a transcript, the article was headlined "Prophet Tells How He Revives Dead," and began with Jones's answer to Burks's question about what it was like doing forty resurrections:

> It's just spontaneous. I would say, "This is Jim." That's my title. No "Reverend" or anything, "This is Jim." If it were someone I didn't know very well, I'd say "pastor." I'd say, "This is pastor." But most of them had attended at least several times.
>
> I'd say, "This is Jim. I love you." When you feel something like this, what do you say? "I love you. We need you. Your family needs you. We care. I'm giving you love." It would never be any magic words. No magic little catechism or prayer. Feeling.

When Burks asked him about the holocaust, Jones denied that he had ever predicted one. "I have never prophesied the end of the world," Jones said. "Where that came from I'd be interested in finding out. I'm not that fatalistic. . . . I project the positive. If I can't, I keep my mouth shut. I wouldn't talk about the end of the world. I might as well fold up—why should I work so hard?"

At two o'clock Saturday morning, Burks's article was off the presses in the "bulldog edition" of the *Examiner*. (The bulldog edition is the first to hit the streets.) Before the presses ran second edition, Burks recalls, "Jones and his people had a chance to look at it and came by the paper, really incensed." Jones's attorneys were in immediate contact with the *Examiner*'s editors, whose heads were still spinning from dealing with the Synanon libel suit, and the editors agreed to cut substantial parts of Burks's story. The parts they cut, essentially, were the verbatim words of Jim Jones. Burks was furious. "I told [the editors]: 'Well, O.K., this is your newspaper. You can publish what you want to, but if you're going to publish the story I wrote in this edited version, my name comes off.' And it did."

The same Saturday that the two versions of Burks's story were on the newsstands, Lester Kinsolving found a way to get away from the frustrations of the Peoples Temple stories: he took his family to Berkeley to watch a University of California football game. While Kinsolving was enjoying the game, two of Jones's aides broke into his home in San Francisco. The Kinsolvings discovered the burglary when they returned home and found, on the basement door, the pane of glass next the doorknob broken. The only items missing were his checkstubs and copies of his syndicated columns, which he was writing four or five weeks in advance.

Although the burglary caused Kinsolving some momentary trepidation, it failed to dissuade him from pursuing the messiah from Ukiah. After his four articles appeared, letters poured into the *Examiner;* the bulk of them were from the Temple and full of the Temple's typical paranoid rhetoric, but a few offered praise and encouragement. One of the letters was from Brenda Ganatos, a Ukiah telephone office supervisor. Brenda thanked the paper for printing Kinsolving's exposés and charged that the press in Ukiah "presented only biased stories" praising the Temple. She and her friends had sent numerous letters about Peoples Temple, asking for some kind of inquiry or calling attention to possible abuses, to the hometown press, but to no avail; Brenda thinks the letters must have been scooped into a wastebasket. She was pleased that her letter to the *Examiner* was printed on the editorial page.

Kinsolving was pleased, too. He called Brenda as soon as he saw the letter in print. Brenda's news was disappointing, however; she informed Kinsolving that his articles had had little impact in Mendocino County because the Temple bought up most of the copies from the newsstands. Brenda had a friend who owned a liquor store, whom she called with the request to save the last three copies. They were probably the only three copies for miles around.

Brenda explained to Kinsolving how, for about a year, she had been gathering information on Jones and the Temple. Her first contact with the Temple occurred in 1967 or 1968, when the Cobb family, part of the exodus from Indianapolis, moved in next door. Initially, she was impressed with the Temple's good works; she even donated clothing. Then, usually during her lunch hour at work, she began hearing stories and rumors about the Temple's strange activities and methods—stories of threats against members who tried to break away, rumors that Jim Jones was taking over the county government, allegations that those who had received threats "were going to the sheriff's office and not getting anywhere."

Soon Brenda found herself on the telephone every night for three, four, as long as six hours, talking to local people who had had confrontations with Peoples Temple or who knew people who had. She started holding meetings in her home two or three nights a week, trying to do something, anything, to help the people she talked with and to unearth the truth about Peoples Temple. "You just felt like you were batting your head against a wall," she recalls of her early involvement in Ukiah's anti-Temple movement.

> I just felt like I had to do something. Nobody was doing anything.
> Everybody was turning their heads away, and hoping it'd go away, but
> it wasn't going away. . . . It was a really scary thing. A lot of people
> were frightened. . . . [Jones] had the whole town of Ukiah sewed up.
> [Temple members] were in the hospitals. I had to go to the hospital,
> and I was afraid. The Temple had RNs in there. All they had to do
> was come pull your oxygen or do whatever they wanted to do. So you
> kind of had this one eye open in the hospital.

There were about a dozen regulars in Brenda's group, and of that original number two were men. Then Whitey Freestone became the third man to join the group; he started attending with his wife, Opal, after Kinsolving had put him in touch with Brenda. Ukiah was full of fearless, conscionable men who didn't care much for Jim Jones and who sat in the bars bad-mouthing Jones and his Temple over their beers when they weren't boasting of the deer and pheasant they had killed. These were no-nonsense, tough-talkin' hombres who drove pickup trucks with rifle racks in the rear windows, who feared not a thing in this world but the armed encampment in Redwood Valley. They talked about Peoples Temple, they talked a lot; they never did a thing. The men in Brenda's group, however, all three of them, tried their damnedest.

They talked to Lester Kinsolving, who made several trips to Ukiah to interview the people in Brenda's group. He methodically recorded them on tape, continued to gather evidence, and, now seeing a second chance, tried to build a case on Jones that was airtight and vacuum-sealed. Word got around about Kinsolving's presence in Ukiah and apparently caused Jim Jones some concern. "We would be at someone's home," Brenda recalls, "[and] some cars would go up and down the street, and they'd stop and they'd look at our cars. We caught them looking at our cars. As soon as we walked out the door, they'd jump in their cars and leave."

Kinsolving turned the bulk of the information he had gathered over to Tim Reardon, a deputy attorney general in the criminal division of the attorney general's office in San Francisco. After he reviewed the materials, Reardon decided the investigation would be more appropriately carried out by the charitable trust division, where it was placed in the hands of Deputy Attorney General Charles Rumph. Kinsolving claims he was never informed of the disposition of the Temple investigation. Rumph, who left the attorney general's office in 1974, says he doesn't have "any independent recollection" of the outcome of the case.

Kinsolving was convinced that Jim Jones was a "maniac" and, looking back on his feelings of urgency at the time, he would have been elated to see an investigation of Peoples Temple by whatever agency came along. At one point, he recalls, he went to the Federal Bureau of Investigation with his evidence against Jim Jones. The agents he talked to, he says, were "polite and noncommittal." No investigation was, to his knowledge, ever undertaken.

Kinsolving stayed on the Peoples Temple story despite the frustrations until he quit the *Examiner* in the summer of 1973, even though not a word of his research ever saw print in San Francisco. He left San Francisco in June to cover Washington, D.C., for a group of midwestern newspapers. Even three thousand miles away, the Peoples Temple story continued to plague his mind. He managed to stir the pot only once with his syndicated column, in a report on his confrontation with Dr. Kenneth L. Teegarden, president of the denomination, and other leaders of the Christian Church (Disciples of Christ). The Disciples had accepted Peoples Temple as an affiliate in 1960, had ordained Jim Jones in 1964, and Kinsolving wanted to know what the church was planning to do about their maverick minister in Redwood Valley. The Disciples, Dr. Teegarden explained, believe in local autonomy, which would preclude the national office's taking any action. Kinsolving claims that, nevertheless, the national office in Indianapolis, Indiana, sent one of its staff attorneys out to Redwood Valley to take a look after Kinsolving's column appeared in the *New York Times*. The attorney spent only a day, Kinsolving charges, and didn't even attend services.

Kinsolving was incredulous. The Christian Church was the eighth-largest Protestant denomination in the United States. It touted itself as being strongly supportive of scholarship, while it accepted into its ranks a crazy faith healer who claimed he was Jesus Christ reincarnate. The Disciples of Christ contributed, by its inaction, one hundred and forty years of credibility to a church that worshipped a madman. To the Brotherhood, it appeared, Peoples Temple was no more than one of the four-thousand-odd independent congregations the Disciples comprised; perhaps the Brotherhood was exercising its proud claim to tolerance and strict adherence to the New Testament while Jim Jones thrived under its mantle of respectability.

Nearly two years later, during the summer of 1975, Kinsolving decided to reenter the fray when he saw a letter endorsing Peoples Temple on letterhead paper from the Methodist Church. Kinsolving was working at the time for WAVA radio in Arlington, Virginia. The program director showed him the letter from the Reverend John V. Moore, district superintendent of the East Bay (Oakland-Berkeley area) Methodist churches. The Reverend Moore, Kinsolving learned, had two daughters in the Temple: Carolyn Layton, Jones's loyal mistress and chief of staff, and Annie Moore, a Temple nurse. Kinsolving saw a story there, with definite West Coast appeal. He dashed off a memo to four northern California newspapers that were running his columns regularly: the *San Francisco Progress,* the *San Jose Mercury News,* the *Berkeley Gazette,* and the *Sacramento Union.* A fifth paper bought his columns each week but refused to run them: the *San Francisco Examiner.* When Kinsolving called its editors to complain, they dropped him completely. The editors of the other four papers, however, told Kinsolving they would be interested in a special series on Peoples Temple.

Kinsolving called the Reverend Moore and set up an interview. He was sitting at a picnic table in Moore's backyard when he confronted the Methodist leader with the letter of endorsement. Moore became incensed and ordered Kinsolving to leave, whereupon Kinsolving picked up the seven file folders he had brought with him and made a hasty departure. "I walked out with my files," Kinsolving recalls, "but I left my briefcase, which is about the worst mistake I ever made."

The briefcase arrived in Washington, D.C., via United Airlines, two days later; Kinsolving's wife picked it up at the airport for him. Kinsolving had an appointment the next day with the *San Francisco Progress* to discuss the possibility of a full-blown exposé on the Temple. When Kinsolving arrived for his appointment, he was greeted by Jones's "goon squad, headed by Mr. Michael Prokes," who threatened to sue Kinsolving and the *Progress* if his series were ever published. The *Progress* backed off, rather than risk the minimum ten-thousand-dollar cost of defending a libel action. Curiously, the three other newspapers that initially expressed interest in the series followed the *Progress*'s lead and backed out, too. Kinsolving couldn't understand why all four newspapers decided simultaneously to kill the exposé until he returned home and examined the briefcase he had left under the Reverend Moore's picnic table. Two items were missing: a letter from Redwood Valley schoolteacher Ruby Bogner, who was part of Brenda Ganatos's group, and copies of his three-page memorandum to the four newspapers detailing his proposed exposé.

After it was certain that Kinsolving's exposé would not see print, the Temple took measures to seal the lips of Kinsolving's sources. Many of them, during the latter days of September 1975, received threatening phone calls. Mrs. Bogner received a call threatening her job, her property, and her life. Nancy Busch, another active member of Brenda's group, received her call at about 7:00 A.M., Sunday, September 28:

> By the time I really got fully awake and found out what they were talking about . . . I can remember them talking about Reverend Kinsolving and how he lied about everything, and I remember thinking: "they're not telling me this; they're reading it to me,"

because of the way they were talking, more like they were reading than talking. They were telling me about Reverend Kinsolving and how bad he had been and how he really put everyone down, all the different churches and everything, and different pastors, and then they . . . started in on me about [how] I had better never give [Kinsolving] any more information concerning Peoples Temple, or something would be likely to happen to me.

Ironically, the ringleader of Ukiah's Temple enemies, Brenda Ganatos, never received a single threat; nothing "happened" to her except, as she learned later from her boss, Jim Jones went to an official in the telephone company with charges he hoped would get her fired. She kept her job.

On October 3, the Friday after Nancy Busch received her threatening call, a group calling itself "Ukiah Area Friends of Peoples Temple" placed a half-page ad in the *Ukiah Daily Journal*. The ad offered a five-thousand-dollar reward "to the first person providing evidence leading to the arrest, conviction and imprisonment" of a "few very sick people [who] have been impersonating members of Peoples Temple Christian Church and making threatening calls. This is the most insidious kind of thing, and we have had enough of it. . . . All of their leaders and staff say they will take polygraph lie detector tests or sodium pentathol to prove the calls do not come from them."

Without naming Kinsolving, the ad blames him for concocting rumors about the Temple:

> Most of the gossip which has been circulated came from the one, and only one, sarcastic article about the church by a so-called clergyman-journalist who once had a column in a daily Northern California newspaper. We can offer you proof that he has attacked or vilified nearly every major denomination in the United States, and nearly all fundamentalists (for example, the Rev. Dr. Billy Graham, Kathryn Kuhlman, and the entire Pentecostal movement). His treatment just before he left this area was the most scurrilous attack against Dr. Norman Vincent Peale, making terribly unkind remarks about his age. He tried to portray Dr. Peale as senile, though all who know him know this is not true.

The Temple closed its heavy-handed pitch by clothing itself in the sanctified robes of the Christian Church:

> Peoples Temple has seen it proven over again that the vast majority of people in Ukiah and Redwood Valley are either supportive of its humanitarian purposes and activities, or at least sympathetic. The church is affiliated with the large denomination of the Christian

243

Church (Disciples of Christ) of 1.5 million members in the United States, including such people as the family of Lyndon Baines Johnson, the FBI Director Clarence Kelley, and several Governors, Senators and Congressmen throughout our great country. We direct this notice of reward toward the small fringe minority which is using such cowardly, dishonest and criminal means to attack the church. IF THIS ELEMENT ISN'T STOPPED, IT MIGHT BE *YOU* NEXT TIME THAT IS MALIGNED.

Neither the five-thousand-dollar reward nor the additional twenty-five-hundred-dollar reward "to the first person giving proof leading to successful litigation against those responsible for . . . malicious gossip" was ever claimed. Nor were there ever any arrests or lawsuits. Lest anyone think the Ukiah Area Friends of Peoples Temple were not seriously considering a lawsuit, their letter was signed "by Eugene Chaikin, their attorney." Lest anyone think Peoples Temple was not a church to be reckoned with, the ad implied that anyone who took on the Temple would be taking on a 1.5-million member Protestant denomination, along with the director of the FBI, the former First Family, and a crew of other political knights in shining armor. Even J. Edgar Hoover had counted himself a member of the Brotherhood.

With that kind of respectability, Jim Jones shielded himself from the slings and arrows of his detractors behind the walls of a mighty fortress—or so it appeared. The mighty fortress—the Disciples of Christ—is, in truth, little more than a loose confederation of "voluntarily associated" congregations that believe in adult baptism, the weekly celebration of the Lord's Supper, the New Testament teachings, and, to some degree, the importance of Christian social action. Most Disciples congregations are politically liberal; there is within the Brotherhood, however, a large group, the Independents, who maintain a politically more conservative stance and who place a lesser emphasis on social action. Jones, of course, courted the liberal faction, or the Cooperatives.

Jim Jones made his first inroads with the Disciples of Christ in Indianapolis in 1954, when he met, through a friend, the executive secretary of the church's Department of Church and Society, the Reverend Barton Hunter. Jones was, at the time, an unordained minister who was raising money for his South Side church by selling monkeys.

Hunter was impressed with Jim Jones's high ideals of Christian brotherhood and racial equality; the two ministers became casual friends. Over the years, Hunter marveled at Jones's good works in the community: how he integrated his church, how he fed between twenty-five and thirty derelicts each day from the basement of Peoples Temple on North Delaware Street, how he got himself appointed the first executive director of the Indianapolis Human Rights Commission.

Jones told Hunter that, when he visited Cuba shortly after the revolution,

244

he asked a soldier to take him to meet Fidel Castro. There was no problem; the soldier, Jim, and Marceline all hopped into a taxi and caught up with the Cuban leader, who was touring Havana in an army Jeep. Jones claimed he had chatted with Castro while they moved about the city. "I have no reason to doubt that he literally was in contact with Castro," says Hunter. "He was obviously bright; people . . . recognized that rather clearly [and] took him seriously."

Officials of the Disciples of Christ took Jim Jones seriously enough on February 16, 1964, to ordain him as a minister after a "duly constituted ordination council carefully studied [his] credentials . . . investigated his preparation and his life, and questioned him thoroughly as to his intent and purpose." The Reverend Robert Peoples, an Indianapolis minister who was on the committee, recalls that the investigation of Jim Jones's background was not as thorough as the committee's routine report implied. The committee studied Jones's application, Peoples recalls, and called him in for an interview. "We asked about his belief," the Reverend Peoples says, "and he appeared to satisfy us." With the high recommendation and enthusiastic support of the Reverend Hunter, Jones passed easily, a matter of routine.

The Reverend Jones and the Reverend Hunter didn't cross paths again until seven years later, when Jim Jones returned to the pulpit at Tenth and Delaware for a special rally. The *Indianapolis Star* ran an announcement of the big event, and Barton Hunter decided to attend services just to see what his old friend Jim was up to. Hunter recalls he "didn't have much question but what psychosomatic healing went on at times, but I had real problems with . . . this bit of taking people out and bringing them back from the bathroom, saying that they had passed a cancer. . . . I just couldn't buy that at all." Hunter chided Jim Jones after the service about the phony healings, and Jones replied matter-of-factly, "Well, I have certain abilities. I don't know where they come from. I simply am able to cure people." Barton Hunter did not press the issue with Jones, nor did he take it up before any official body of the Disciples of Christ. Jones may have been different, even eccentric, but he was still a Christian minister in good standing, and Hunter recognized that the Brotherhood would probably never take any investigative action.

Jim Jones brought that good standing with him to California, where he and his church were affiliated almost immediately with the Northern California–Nevada Region of the Christian Church (Disciples of Christ). Because Jim Jones and Peoples Temple were already recognized in Indianapolis, affiliation with the Northern California Region was a routine matter. Church records show that the membership of the Temple in 1966 amounted to a modest eighty-six persons. By 1969, the Temple began showing signs of growth: three hundred members. By 1972, Peoples Temple tallied its faithful at more than two thousand souls.

Although no records of previous religious affiliation are available for the

245

members of Peoples Temple, it is a fair assumption—considering the intensity of Jones's sheep-stealing efforts—that most of his converts had left other churches to join his. They came from the Macedonia Missionary Baptist Church in San Francisco, from Pentecostal and Holiness churches in Indianapolis, from Father Divine's Mission in Philadelphia, from the Reverend Eddie Wilson's healing tabernacle in Cincinnati. They were Methodists, Baptists, Presbyterians, Catholics, Greek Orthodox, agnostics and atheists; they were Quakers, too. Most of the Layton family belonged to the Berkeley Society of Friends before they joined Peoples Temple in 1973. Lisa Layton, a member for fifteen years of the Berkeley group, submitted a letter terminating her membership on July 11, 1973. Her son, Laurence John Layton, she says in the letter, received his conscientious objector status "with the help of Jim Jones, pastor of Peoples Temple Christian Church." Lisa Layton adds that Laurence and his sister, Deborah J. Blakey, "and their respective spouses are members of that group. I have also become a member of Peoples Temple."

The Prophet of God also had some success, although limited, with other Disciples of Christ congregations. During the long, bitter years of the Vietnam War, the church was riven by considerable internal strife and congregations were split up and dissolved over issues of war and peace. The Reverend Robert Lemon, pastor of the Barrett Avenue Christian Church in Richmond, California, first heard of Jim Jones in 1966 through the Reverend Barton Hunter, who had the highest praise for the Temple's good works in Indianapolis. Lemon drove his family up to Ukiah for a service; they came away impressed with the fellowship and enthusiasm of the Temple family. They were no less impressed with the Temple family's pastor, who seemed to care deeply about racial inequality, the war, and other social problems and popular causes. As an act of Christian brotherhood, Lemon placed Peoples Temple on his church's mailing list.

Peoples Temple responded to Lemon's subsequent ouster over the Vietnam issue by sending the family letters of condolence and a box of homemade candies. The Lemons were deeply moved. "I never forgot that," says Adelle Lemon, the embattled pastor's wife, "because we felt really rejected and resentful and hurt and confused, and here came a sign of love from another congregation." Those who left the church with Lemon also were moved by this outpouring of love from the church in Redwood Valley, and it was only a matter of time before a few of them drove north to see Peoples Temple firsthand. A few—among them Elmer Mertle and Rita Tupper—even decided to make the total commitment to apostolic equalitarianism.

Shortly after Elmer Mertle and Rita Tupper joined Peoples Temple, their ex-spouses, Zoa Kille and Larry Tupper, confided in a former elder of the Barrett Avenue Christian Church named David Conn. Both Zoa and Larry had children living communally in Redwood Valley, and both had a difficult time buying the stories they were hearing about the perfect life there. During the summer of 1970, Conn attended a service at Jones's "Garden of Eden" north of Ukiah that confirmed all he had heard from Larry and Zoa. Conn was appalled by the faith healing and the adulation of Pastor Jim; he was astounded that the church would allow a charlatan like Jones to affiliate.

Soon after he attended the service, Conn arranged, in August of 1970, a luncheon meeting with the interim regional president of the church, Nellie Kratz, to discuss his concerns about Peoples Temple. Conn had, by that time, gathered some inside information on how Jones was pulling off his psychic stunts, and he seriously questioned the veracity of the healings. Nellie Kratz was candid; she admired Jim Jones. She had heard about him, as Robert Lemon had, through her longtime friend, Barton Hunter. She had met Jim Jones and a few Temple members at a statewide ministers' meeting and found him to be "an interesting, warm individual." Conn continued to press the issues of fear and fakery, but Nellie merely smiled and changed the subject. She finally agreed to look into Conn's allegations to determine for herself whether there was anything amiss in Peoples Temple.

Conn left his luncheon meeting with Nellie Kratz entirely unconvinced that anything would come of it, so he sat down on September 14, 1970, and drafted a four-page letter detailing his concerns and urging an investigation by the church. Unless the church knew for certain what Jones was up to, he suggested, the church could be embarrassed later "if some bad scene takes place" in Ukiah. Conn also suggested that the church plant a physician in the audience during a healing service, unbeknownst to Jim Jones, and have the physician request one of the cancerous tumors. The tumor could be examined by a pathologist, Conn reasoned, to determine whether it was in fact what Jim Jones said it was.

After talking with Conn, Nellie Kratz decided to take Jim Jones up on his invitation to attend People's Temple services. She notified Jim Jones well ahead of time that she would be coming, and he prepped his people for several days, so that what Nellie Kratz saw in Redwood Valley was what appeared to be a spontaneous expression of Christian joy. She saw people of all races hugging each other; she heard them singing together to the spirited music of the Temple's band and choir. She heard Jim Jones preach a sermon that was a call to action, an appeal to solve the nagging problems of poverty and racism. When Jim Jones introduced Nellie Kratz to his congregation, they welcomed her with thunderous applause. Nellie was deeply moved by what she saw; she was, however, concerned that Jones's followers "had an almost worshipful attitude" toward him. "I thought they were putting an awfully heavy load [on him] in practically making a messiah or a divine person out of Jim," she recalls, "and I thought that was a little more than should be expected." Despite her misgivings, Nellie was at a loss as to what to do. She was, after all, merely an interim regional president, soon to be replaced by the newly elected president, Dr. Karl Irvin. "At the present time," she replied in a letter to Conn, "I really don't feel that I have any evidence on which to act or even on which to talk to Jim."

Peoples Temple was listed in the directory of member churches as soon as it became affiliated with the Northern California–Nevada Region. That another Disciples minister or member of a distant congregation traveling north on U.S. 101 would stop at the church in Redwood Valley unannounced one Sunday was inevitable. The Reverend Russell Coatney, who succeeded Lemon as pastor of Barrett Avenue Christian Church, was vacationing with his wife and mother-in-law near Ukiah during the summer of 1972. On the first Sunday of his vacation, he looked for the nearest Disciples of Christ Church and found Peoples Temple in Redwood Valley. Coatney, his wife, and his mother-in-law, when they arrived, "were met in the parking lot by two young ladies who asked us all sorts of questions." The Reverend Coatney thought it a bit odd that he would have to be interrogated before being allowed inside the church, but he was determined to receive communion on the Lord's Day. The three visitors chose seats at the rear of the church where, as outsiders, they would attract the least attention. "As it turns out," he said, "we attracted a good deal of attention, and people were looking our way. Finally, a gentleman came back and asked us if we would like to see their old folks home. . . . We said, 'No, we came here for the purpose of worship. We don't want to go out and spend the time looking at some convalescent home.'" The Temple greeter left politely and returned a few minutes later, this time with an invitation to the Coatneys to tour the Temple care home for the mentally retarded and the vegetable garden. Coatney stood his ground, again vowing to stay at the service until the celebration of the Lord's Supper and the morning message from Pastor Jones.

The people seated near the Coatneys were staring at them. Some of the stares were downright hostile. The greeter returned a third time and told the Coatneys they would have to leave because the service was "not open to visitors." The Temple greeter was adamant; Coatney was not about to argue. Coatney could not have helped noticing the apostolic guardians standing menacingly at the entrance to the church and posted strategically inside. Coatney never saw the weapons of the guardians, but he assumed they were carrying them. He motioned to his wife and his mother-in-law that it was time to leave.

Coatney was not going to let this pass, being treated as an intruder by a church affiliated with the Brotherhood, without informing the regional office. He called the office of regional president Dr. Karl Irvin, but was told Irvin was not available. Coatney did, however, tell his story of mistreatment at Peoples Temple to Dr. Irvin's secretary, who promised to pass the information on to Irvin. Coatney told the story of being barred from services and he told of the literature he picked up at the door claiming that Jones had raised forty-eight people from the dead and had cured hundreds of suffering souls of malignant growths. Coatney recalls no response at all from Dr. Irvin; he does remember vividly the personal letter he received from Jim Jones apologizing for the incident at the Sunday service. Jones wrote that he had not been aware that Coatney's party had been barred from the service; had he but known, Jones said, the incident would never have happened.

Only a few weeks after Coatney's visit to Peoples Temple, Lester Kinsolving's scathing articles on the messiah from Ukiah made their appearance in the *Examiner.* Dr. Irvin recalls talking with Lester Kinsolving, on the telephone, "at about the time the articles came." He recalls also talking to representatives "of the Temple about those charges [in the article], and they were adamant that they were false." There was never any official investigation, Irvin says, although there was an informal inquiry. "We inquired about those charges," he says, "but we didn't set up an investigative team because we knew investigations were being done by the district attorney's office and other legal bodies, and we felt sure that in due time the information would be coming to us."

Ignited by the sparks from Carolyn Pickering's flint-tipped typewriter keys, the national Disciples of Christ headquarters in Indianapolis conducted its own inquiry into the charges against Peoples Temple. A. Dale Fiers, the denomination's national president from 1964 to 1973, called the Oakland regional office and talked with Dr. Irvin and other church officials. The consensus of the regional staff, Fiers says, was that the charges were "misleading." On February 8, 1973, Fiers issued a form letter to be sent out from the national office to those who were inquiring at Peoples Temple. "The article[s are] innacurate, prejudicial and misleading," Fiers wrote. "For one thing, the main charge that the Rev. Jones claims to be the reincarnation of Jesus Christ has been categorically denied by Jones himself." Thus ended the inquiry.

By 1973, following the purchase of the church on South Alvarado Street in Los Angeles, Peoples Temple had become two congregations; one was affiliated with the Northern California–Nevada Region, and the other with the Pacific Southwest Region. According to the Reverend Charles Malotte, Dr. Irvin's counterpart for the Pacific Southwest Region, the Los Angeles Temple's application for affiliation was approved routinely, "because they were basically a branch office, so to speak, a branch group from a recognized congregation in northern California." Malotte recalls that the Temple's application was regarded as "unusual in the sense that I don't know of any other instance" of a congregation affiliating in two regions simultaneously. Church officials in the southern region, like those in the northern region, never bothered to conduct a probe into the activities of the Temple, despite the Kinsolving articles and other press reports alleging Jones's improprieties. When officials from the southern region decided to attend Temple services out of "curiosity," Malotte recalls, they were escorted to the basement of the Temple on South Alvarado

Street, where they were given a pep talk on the Temple's good works. Malotte recalls not a single instance when regional church officials were allowed to attend one of Jim Jones's marathon services.

Despite widespread reports of phony healings, armed guards, threats by telephone and mail, body searches at the Temple doors, Peoples Temple remained under the wing of the Disciples of Christ. Tim Stoen and Bonnie Beck served on the denomination's statewide board, and the Reverend James Warren Jones remained a minister in good standing with the Disciples until his death. Had there been a groundswell of outrage against the Temple's unorthodox practices, it would have made little difference, for the bylaws of the Brotherhood have no provisions for censuring or expunging a member congregation. "Every church is an entity unto itself," explains Dr. Irvin. "It calls its own pastor. It fires its own pastor. It is a completely autonomous group of people, and whatever happens beyond that local congregation is done entirely on a voluntary associational basis." Unless Peoples Temple decided on its own to get rid of Jim Jones, there was nothing the Disciples of Christ could do about him. Meanwhile, the money kept flowing in from Temple coffers. The denomination's annual reports for the years 1966 through 1978 show $1.1 million in Temple contributions to the Brotherhood and its related causes.

Shackled by its own code of tolerance and local autonomy, the Disciples of Christ watched helplessly as Peoples Temple grew to be a large and strangely exclusive congregation. Most members of the Disciples who knew about Jim Jones tried to pretend he was just a bad dream that would somehow go away, but David Conn was determined to do something. He spoke, in confidence, to several church officials, and from all of them got the same story: that neither the regional nor the national office has any authority over local congregations. Conn kept gathering information. He had been a source for the Kinsolving articles. He talked to friends who had close relatives in the Temple. In late 1976, Conn met with Zoa Kille, an old friend and the ex-wife of Elmer Mertle; Zoa added more tales of horror to Conn's handwritten notes. One day some time later, Zoa called Conn to tell him that Elmer had left the Temple and might be willing to talk to him. Conn and Mert had known each other for years; they had both worked as chemical analysts at an oil refinery in Richmond, and had attended Barrett Avenue Christian Church, until in November of 1969 Mert quit both job and church to join Peoples Temple. Conn recalls of his meeting with Mert: "He told me the whole horror story—the beatings, phony healings, defrauding of property, threats on people's lives, the coercion on people to make up things about mothers having sex with their sons and fathers with their daughters." Conn was shocked. He convinced Mert that the best course of action was to talk to someone—someone they could trust—in the press.

Conn talked with his daughter, Eileen, and they approached her husband, George Klineman, who was at the time a stringer for *The Press Democrat* and a free-lance journalist who had sold some magazine articles. Klineman was always, like most journalists, sniffing around for new material, but when he heard Conn's story, he wasn't sure it would be wise to get involved. If Conn's allegations were true and the Temple was an armed camp of blindly loyal followers, the story surely involved some risk. Conn assured Klineman, however, that he had known Mert long enough to trust him. They contacted Mert and set up a meeting for January 15, 1977, at Mert's place in Berkeley. Other defectors would be there, too.

Despite the risks of Temple goons capable of killing and the possibility of informants in the group, ten defectors were assembled at Mert's when Conn, Klineman, and Eileen arrived. The tension in the air was palpable; Klineman could not use his tape recorder, nor even take notes, for none of the defectors was willing to speak for the record. As a reporter, Klineman's hands were tied; the only help he could offer was to write a publishable magazine article and try to sell it, and the success of that effort depended on using names and taped interviews. All the reporter could do was listen.

The meeting ended amicably after some five hours. Klineman repeated that he couldn't do much for the Temple defectors unless they were willing to be quoted, and they repeated that they were too fearful of Jones and the consequences of being found out. Jones would stop at nothing to protect himself from public exposure, they were certain, and they feared for their lives should word get out that they talked. All Klineman could do was check out the leads they gave him, and he promised them he would.

The following week, in a meeting with a Treasury Department agent for a story not even remotely connected with Peoples Temple, Klineman asked about a church in San Francisco that was arming itself and shipping weapons to South America; had the agent heard anything?

"We've heard rumblings about that," he said.

Klineman wouldn't name the group, but he did describe their modus operandi. Although the agent pressed for the name, Klineman explained that his sources were scared to death of what might happen if they were associated with an investigation. The reporter finally capitulated when the agent assured him that he would be the only one in his office to know it, and that, without it, he couldn't very well check the information. Klineman provided a few leads: the name Chris Lewis, the names of the Temple's boats, the allegations of armed guards in Redwood Valley. Within forty-eight hours, the agent called Klineman with the news that everything checked out. He'd even had a friend, a cop in Mendocino County, drive by the Temple in Redwood Valley; there were armed guards in front of the place. The agent wanted to talk to Klineman's sources. He promised to put Klineman in touch with an undercover cop who knew more about the Temple. Klineman called Mert and passed on the information that the agent was interested. Mert said he would have to talk with the others before he talked with the agent.

Five or six days later, about 7:30 P.M., Klineman received a call from the undercover cop. He told Klineman that the Temple was extremely dangerous. "You better know what you're doing, pal," he said, "or you could end up in a barrel." At the cop's insistence, Klineman met with him that same night, and the undercover cop put the fear of God into the young reporter.

Mert called Klineman the next day; he and the other defectors agreed to talk with the Treasury agent on the condition they would not be prosecuted for any illegal activities they might have performed while under the influence of Jim Jones. Klineman told Mert he'd have to take that up with the Treasury agent. Klineman would be bowing out after the second meeting, until the agent decided actually to bust the Temple, because it would not be ethical, he explained, for him to work with the government on an investigation he planned to write about. The meeting with the Treasury agent was essentially a repeat performance of the earlier meeting; same people, no tapes, but the defectors did permit Klineman and the agent to take notes.

Klineman kept his distance from the investigation, but he did maintain weekly communication with both the defectors and the agent while he continued, on his own, to gather information about the Temple. In late February, the agent told Klineman there would be a full-scale government investigation involving federal, state, and local law-enforcement agencies. Two undercover agents—a husband and wife team, the agent said—would try to infiltrate the Temple. The government planned to bust Jones the following December—ten months away. To Klineman, it seemed an awfully long time to wait, but he was frankly relieved that the Peoples Temple story was out of his hands for a while.

With the Temple story no longer his responsibility, Klineman did not have to worry—much—about what was, to him, a reasonable fear: given the defectors' original "eccentricity," the motives that caused them to join Peoples Temple in the first place, might they not be just as dangerous as the true believers? His worst fear was that they would get impatient and blow the whistle on themselves. He—and the agent—stressed to Mert and the others the importance of keeping the circle as small as possible. He had full confidence only in those closest to him—his wife, Eileen, and David Conn, who had promised not to make any moves without checking with him first.

For about two weeks, Klineman was out of touch with Mert, Conn, and the Treasury agent when, on the evening of March 23, Conn telephoned him. "I really blew it," Conn began. "I told Dennis Banks everything."

Conn recounted how he had told the Peoples Temple story to George Coker, who worked with Conn at the refinery. Coker was a Seminole and an acquaintance of Lehman Brightman, Sioux president of the United Native Americans and an instructor at Contra Costa College. Coker told Brightman that a friend at work had inside information on the Temple, and it could be embarrassing to the movement because of Dennis Banks's association with

Peoples Temple. Dennis Banks was spokesman for the American Indian Movement; his wife, Ka-mook, had accepted nineteen thousand dollars bail money from the Temple. Brightman would talk to Banks and see what he could do. Brightman had sheltered Banks from the authorities when the AIM leader was arrested for extradition to South Dakota; he had shared the stage with Jim Jones at an April 1976 rally in support of Banks. He would call Coker as soon as he had talked with Banks.

Coker received Brightman's call at 12:30 A.M. on the twenty-third. Brightman said Banks wanted to talk with Coker and his friend right away. Coker called Conn; they met, and the two of them drove to Brightman's house in El Cerrito for the meeting. Conn didn't know whether he could trust Banks and Brightman, but he was convinced he had to go through with the meeting. It was too late to back out; the Indian movement already knew who he was and what he was up to.

For two hours, Conn poured out his soul. He told Banks nearly everything he knew. He told the Indian leader about the Treasury Department investigation and the free-lance journalist who was gathering information. Fortunately, Conn did not mention any names.

Conn advised Banks to write a notarized statement disavowing his support for Jim Jones before the story hit the media and the Temple was busted by the Treasury Department. Conn suggested that Banks draft the statement as soon as possible, stash it away in a safe, and when the time came and the media began to probe the connection between AIM and the Temple, Banks could produce documentation proving that he had not been totally hoodwinked. Banks was indifferent to Conn's ideas about protecting the movement from the tarnish of Jim Jones. He pressed, instead, for additional information from Conn.

The meeting ended with handshakes all around. Conn went to bed at 3:30 A.M. believing that the worst that could happen would be that Banks would ignore his advice. Within a few hours after the meeting, however, Banks talked to Jim Jones, and Jim Jones immediately unleashed a wave of retaliatory threats against the defectors and against Conn's family. The Mertles received a hand-carried message:

Dear Cousin,
    I think I should inform you that your latest course of action is the unwisest of all. I know everything that D. Conn boasts of having. Don't you know what kind of fool he is making out of you? The public will never forgive people who are like unthinking robots when they are in fact devious liars. Imagine not giving you any credit for holding any political beliefs. You should know that one hundred will be staying back. This man can do nothing without your assistance and litigation will begin. I am not talking about just the potential of

litigation. I am talking about a decision to litigate all the way *for sure.*
So notify all your friends. You know the legal dangers of lying to the
Treasury officials and the police, don't you?

K

On March 24, 1977—approximately thirty-six hours after Conn's meeting
with Dennis Banks—Marshall Kilduff was at the meeting of the San
Francisco Housing Authority Commission. The chairman, Jim Jones, was
there with his usual entourage. Kilduff watched from the audience as
Chairman Jones collapsed "from exhaustion," Kilduff's article says, and the
official word from the Temple explaining the incident was that the Prophet
had been up all night counseling a suicidal drug addict; he had worked so hard
all night long that he passed out and fell down at the commission meeting.

While Jones was being picked up off the floor, his messengers were busy
delivering the mail. Grace Stoen received a threatening message delivered to
her parents' home. Susan Black, Conn's ex-wife's daughter, thought she saw a
prowler. The next day, Susan received a terrifying anonymous phone call. The
man who called somehow knew all about her, even the brand of food she gave
her pet rabbit. Susan's mother, Donna, went to dump the trash the following
day and noticed the can was strangely empty. It wasn't until days later that
Donna and Susan made the connection of the phone call and the empty can.
The next weird call to Donna Conn's house came from another male voice that
sounded like a poor recording made on a cheap cassette machine and played
over the telephone's transmitter:

> *Nice to be talking with you again. You were photographed on Thursday at
> two. You are right. You do have something to worry about. You
> impersonated Treasury officers to take part in illegal activities. Tell Bruce,
> Alexander, and Mike, too. We're going to burn your place down to the
> ground.*

The Mertles received another message, this time signed by "Chris,"
apparently Chris Lewis, prime enforcer for Jones:

> You know, if any of your lies ever surface, it's going to be kind of
> refreshing. You make false accusations of brutality. How would you
> like to *hear* all about yourself? The brutal acts you have done. What
> went on in your home, Liz, under hypnosis, etc. Don't you know *you*
> were never trusted? When the whole story comes out it will be shown
> in your own words and through photographs, just who were really the
> violent and sick sadists, along with other bizarre, sick behavior. I am

254

looking forward to it, it will be quite invigorating. The first time I am bothered the whole country will know of your lies and behavior.

The note went on with an elaborate plan describing how Mert could let Chris know that he and the other defectors would remain silent. Mert filed the note with the other Temple materials.

George Klineman received no notes or phone calls; apparently Conn did not divulge his name to Dennis Banks. Klineman contacted the Treasury agent. The investigation was off. The agent was apologetic, but his attitude was philosophical: "When you're dealing with people who have been part of a flaky organization like that," he said, "they're bound to be a little flaky, too." It would have been just a matter of time, he added, before one of the defectors confided in the wrong person. The undercover cop they'd been talking with had a similar view. "All you have to do now," he said, "is protect your rectum."

A little more than two weeks later, while the heat of paranoia over the Dennis Banks meeting persisted, Mert's ex-wife, Zoa Kille, opened a copy of the *San Francisco Bay Guardian* and read one of the most disgusting puff pieces on Jim Jones she had ever seen. The article had been written by Bob Levering, a journalist whose work Zoa had become accustomed to reading; it extolled the virtues of Peoples Temple, "a church that puts faith into action," and made Jones look like nothing so much as Jesus Christ reincarnate. Zoa knew better.

From the beginning, Zoa had been skeptical about the Temple. She became suspicious the minute her ex-husband told her he was living in Utopia. All she knew about the place initially was what Mert told her in his letters: it was full of pigs and goats and dogs romping freely, and it was held together by the "Christian principles of Jesus." Mert's enthusiasm and the fact that their daughters joined up soon after he did had her looking into the Temple pretty carefully. She saw Jim Jones perform his phony miracles. She stumbled on to the secrets of his revelations when she returned from a service and learned that one of her daughters, who had remained at home, had received a call from someone who wanted to know a lot of personal information. She saw her daughter, Linda, with buttocks bruised black and blue from her seventy-five whacks with the Board of Education.

Zoa wrote a letter to Levering denouncing the article. Her letter told of Linda's beating and of the other experiences that showed Jim Jones to be a fraud and sadist. She asked that her letter be printed in the letters-to-the-editor column. Her letter never ran. Other letters, praising Levering for his coverage and Peoples Temple for its good works, did run. Levering says he tried to get in touch with Zoa Kille immediately after he received her letter, but was unable to reach her. Her letter, he says, is still in the *Bay Guardian* files.

255

A couple of days after she mailed the letter, Zoa got a call from Eugene Chaikin, Temple attorney. Chaikin threatened to sue for defamation of character. Zoa politely informed Chaikin that she was not afraid of Peoples Temple. After the call, she wrote another letter to the *Bay Guardian*. "I think it was pretty chickenshit of you to give [the letter] to Mr. Chaikin to try to frighten me," she wrote. "You see, I don't fear Peoples Temple and that is why it is so worrisome to them when I speak my opinion."

She canceled her subscription.

The story of Jim Jones and his Peoples Temple is not over. In fact, it has only just begun to be told. If there is any solace to be gained from the tale of exploitation and human foible told by the former temple members in these pages, it is that even such a power as Jim Jones cannot always contain his followers. Those who left had nowhere to go and every reason to fear pursuit. Yet they persevered. If Jones is ever to be stripped of his power, it will not be because of vendetta or persecution, but rather because of the courage of these people who stepped forward and spoke out.

—Phil Tracy, *New West* Magazine,
from "Inside Peoples Temple" by
Marshall Kilduff and Phil Tracy,
August 1, 1977

IX

The Conspiracy

Peoples Temple was little more than a passing paranoia for George Klineman when Mert called him on June 11. Over the past several months, Klineman had managed to remain invisible; all the Temple knew about him was that he was some northern California reporter. Even while the threats were coming down in the Bay Area against the Mertles, Grace Stoen, and Conn's ex-wife, Klineman remained content to keep his distance. He didn't end up in a barrel, he didn't end up in a hospital, he didn't receive any of those weird, cryptic notes delivered by unseen messengers. Although he didn't even receive a threatening phone call, he had been telephone shy ever since Grace and Mert told him Jim Jones would find out about him; it would just be a matter of time. Did that mean they still believed Jones had special powers? The last time Klineman had talked with Mert, Mert was still afraid to be quoted. So was Grace, but the fear may have been more for her son, John-John, than for herself. With that kind of fear, there wasn't a whole lot the press could do for them. So the call came as a bit of a surprise.

"What's up, Mert?" Klineman greeted his caller. "I haven't heard from you in a couple of months." Klineman's initial utterances, whenever his sources called, were always marked by optimistic inflections.

"Have you seen the Barnes story in today's *Examiner?*" Mert got right down to business; no chitchat. He was enthusiastic, excited. "Jones has really blown it this time. He thinks Kilduff has all the inside stuff you have. He must think Kilduff is the reporter we talked to in December."

"Makes sense."

"Why don't you get in touch with Kilduff? Find out what he knows."

"It isn't that easy, Mert," Klineman said. "Does Kilduff really have something?"

"I don't know. Barnes doesn't say a thing about what Kilduff has. He does say a lot, though, about media people being hassled by the Temple."

"Has Kilduff talked to anyone you know?"

"Not to anyone we know," Mert reassured him.

"You mean they're freaking out before anything's even published?"

"That's what Barnes says."

Klineman, no longer quite so content to keep quite so much distance, climbed into his van and from his home in the hills drove to Sebastopol, the nearest community where there was still an *Examiner* in the racks. He dropped a couple of dimes in the slot and took the paper over to the streetlight. He found the article quickly on page 7, headlined "Yet-to-Be-Printed Story Builds a Storm." By-line, W. E. Barnes. It told of trying days at the San Francisco office of *New West* magazine. Word had leaked that *New West* was doing an article on Peoples Temple, and Jones's disciplined troops went into action. They called the office more than fifty times a day and kept the lines busy with praises for the Temple's good works, vague allusions to "serious consequences" if the article wasn't killed, and innuendoes about the integrity of *San Francisco Chronicle* reporter Marshall Kilduff, the article's author.

What did Kilduff have? Klineman searched the Barnes piece and found a hint only in the first two paragraphs, which summarized Jones's political clout. The rest concerned Kilduff's difficulties getting the manuscript into print, and the Temple's style of harassing the media. Julie Smith, another *Chronicle* reporter, once tried an article on Peoples Temple. "It was so distressing," she told Barnes. "Just this vast thing coming at you. All the letters, all the phone calls, all the murmuring from people in high places."

Among the hundreds of letters to the magazine was one that warned of possible "militant reaction" from "people of disadvantaged backgrounds." *New West* senior editor Rosalie Wright said, "I'm not ready to label that a threat, but I have to admit I feel threatened. How would you interpret militant action?"

The magazine's Beverly Hills office got it, too. One of the callers was California Lieutenant Governor Mervyn Dymally, who said he heard the magazine "was preparing an unfavorable story on Jones and he wanted to advise the editors of the man's beneficial activities." When the callers and letter writers realized that their harassment of the San Francisco and Beverly Hills offices yielded nothing, they directed their efforts to the magazine's owner, Australian newspaper magnate Rupert Murdoch. They even hassled the magazine's advertisers.

The Barnes article was enlightening on the tactics of harassment; but what did Kilduff have? Klineman would have bet that Kilduff had no more than a political web story, with press harassment for added color.

The next evening, after spending all day Sunday rereading and pondering the Barnes article, Klineman called Mert. The two men agreed that calling Kilduff could be risky. Kilduff may not have had anything at all—except perhaps a big mouth and an appetite for publicity. How did Barnes get the story? Did Kilduff call Barnes? Did *New West*? Or did Barnes wander into the magazine's office one day and find it under siege?

Mert thought *New West* planted the story to draw people out of the woodwork. If that were true, Klineman asked, would Mert and the others be willing to speak on the record? Mert said he could speak only for himself and Deanna, but he was 99 percent certain that everyone he'd been in contact with would go with their names if the magazine would stand behind them. Klineman decided to make the first contact with Kilduff. After a restless night, he got up early and picked up the phone; perhaps some of his sources in San Francisco knew Kilduff. By late Monday afternoon, a trusted source called back and told him what he wanted to hear: Kilduff had a reputation for being persistent and thorough; Kilduff, the source said, was not the kind of guy who gave up easily.

Klineman dialed the *Chronicle* immediately and the switchboard operator put him through. "Kilduff," said a disinterested voice.

Klineman introduced himself. "I just read an article in the *Chronicle* about your Peoples Temple article in *New West*."

"*Examiner*," said Kilduff. "It was the *Examiner*." Kilduff seemed uneasy.

"Right," said Klineman. "I knew that. I got mixed up."

Klineman's neck felt tight and warm; he was sure he'd blown it with Kilduff for that first sentence. The *Chronicle*, indeed. He proceeded to relate the story of his involvement, as a free-lance writer, with former Temple members and their stories. Kilduff began to show a little interest; he pressed Klineman for more information, but Klineman would say only that he worked for a northern California newspaper. Then Klineman pressed Kilduff for some information on the content of the manuscript, and Kilduff refused. Klineman gave the San Francisco reporter his phone number and invited him to call back, and Kilduff said he might and hung up.

Klineman missed the connection, damn it, an important one; *the* important one. There must be someone, he thought, who could get to Kilduff. He went through his roster of newsmen he had worked with—Ludlow. Lyn Ludlow at the *Examiner*. They had worked together before on a story about the Emiliano Zapata Unit, a terrorist group who had had a bomb factory in Rio Nido on the Russian River. Klineman had got the story; Ludlow had written it up. He picked up the phone again and tried several times to get through to Ludlow, finally reaching him at ten Tuesday morning. After they exchanged pleasantries, Klineman told Ludlow of his abortive attempt to join forces with Kilduff.

"We were so goddamned paranoid we couldn't talk to each other," he told Ludlow. "I've been sitting on this story for six goddamned months because my sources are afraid to talk on the record. But with a magazine like *New West* backing them, they'll sing; they'll tell everything they know about Peoples Temple. Everything. Could you call Kilduff and assure him I'm not some kind of a nut?"

Ludlow was one of the most respected reporters in the Bay Area and a man of few words. He thought for several moments before he answered. "I hardly know the guy," Ludlow said, "but O.K., I'll do it. I'll do what I can."

"Terrific," said Klineman, "As soon as possible, O.K.? And while I have you on the horn, I have a proposition for you. If Kilduff doesn't call back, how'd you like to team up with me on a magazine article? I have the bizarre stuff; you can get the political stuff. What do you think?"

"Thanks, but I'll pass on that one."

"You're kidding. It's gotta be the hottest story since Watergate. You know about Jones's connections in Sacramento? Washington?"

Ludlow paused, apparently to choose his words again. "I hope you know what you're getting into," he said. "It's the kind of story you'll be working on for the rest of your life. There's no end to it."

Ludlow's words echoed through Klineman's mind while he waited for the phone to ring. He didn't wait long.

It was Kilduff.

"I'm really sorry about the way I reacted on that first call. You wouldn't believe what's been going on around here." Kilduff's voice was pleasant. "What a surprise, getting a call from Lyn Ludlow. He tells me you have some information to contribute to the article."

"Well, not exactly," Klineman answered. "What I'd like to do is join forces with you. You apparently have the political information. I have the inside stuff."

The two men exchanged some cautious reporter talk. They agreed to meet at seven o'clock Wednesday—the next evening—in Occidental for dinner, drinks, and more cautious reporter talk.

Kilduff was waiting in the rustic redwood bar at Negri's, one of the local restaurants, when Klineman arrived. The *Chronicle* reporter adjusted his plastic-frame glasses and leaped from the barstool to shake Klineman's hand; he was itching to plunge into the story. "Two Heinekens," Kilduff ordered from the bartender, and they sat down at a table near the bar as Kilduff got right down to business.

"There's one person who left the Temple I really want to talk to," Kilduff began.

"Who?"

"Grace Stoen."

"The last time I talked to Grace, she . . ."

"You talked to Grace Stoen?"

"Twice."

"What?" Kilduff was mildly astonished. "I've been trying to locate her for weeks. Her ex-, uh, estranged husband, Tim, is still with the church. But I understand she broke away last year."

Kilduff had been doing his homework. Klineman asked him whether he'd heard about the mass beatings.

"Beatings?" Kilduff asked. "You know about that?"

"Do you? Tell me about it."

"No. But I guess I do now." Kilduff leaned back in his chair and laughed. He asked Klineman what else he knew, and ordered another round of beer.

They could talk. They began to fall with ease into the camaraderie of two beers and a common interest, and they could talk. Over the sounds of the pinball machines in the corner and the early evening chatter of working men, the two reporters started swapping information. Kilduff wondered why there was such a big deal about his manuscript, why the Temple was hassling him so heavily, and Klineman told him the *commedia-del-arte* tale of mistaken identities that began after the Dennis Banks incident.

"You're being hassled," Klineman explained, "because Jim Jones thinks you and I are the same person. He thinks you're in touch with my sources."

"I like it. I like it," Kilduff laughed. "But I have to level with you. I really don't have much of anything on Jones. I was hoping the Barnes article would flush people out, people with knowledge of what's really going on at Peoples Temple. Looks like the ploy worked."

Kilduff was explaining how he got the story when Eileen came in and joined them. After introductions, Kilduff continued. "I couldn't believe it the first time I saw Jones walk into a Housing Authority Commission meeting with those bodyguards around him," Kilduff said, "and he's always wearing those shades. He always has this audience of black grandmothers from the Temple who clap and cheer every time he opens his mouth. So I got curious. I began asking questions and the more I asked about Peoples Temple, the more I got hassled." Mike Prokes, the Temple's assistant minister, called him every time he talked to San Francisco politicians about Jones.

Klineman reached into a thick cardboard binder and pulled out some copies of *Peoples Forum*, the Temple newspaper, and some six-year-old clippings from the *Indianapolis Star*—the Pickering series. "Have you seen these?" Klineman asked.

"I'm sure I already have them," said Kilduff. "I have a lot of material."

Klineman was curious about why Kilduff, a *Chronicle* reporter, didn't run his Temple story in the *Chron*. City editor Steve Gavin discouraged it, Kilduff told him. Gavin was enamored of Jim Jones; Jones had turned him on to a story about the "Pink Palace," a notoriously poor housing project, and Gavin had assigned Kilduff to cover it. Kilduff's coverage earned him and the *Chronicle* an Associated Press award. Jones had provided entree to black groups that normally excluded white reporters, and Gavin was grateful—so grateful that when Kilduff attended services at Peoples Temple, he saw Gavin seated in the front row. Under the circumstances, Kilduff couldn't do the story with his own paper, but he eventually found a receptive audience at *New West*. "How about some dinner?" Kilduff finished his tale. "I'm getting hungry."

The trio crossed the street to the Union Hotel and sat at one of the tables covered with red-and-white gingham oilcloth. Between courses, they discussed a plan of action. Kilduff was to talk to *New West* about more funding to include Klineman as a collaborator. They sealed their alliance over cocktails.

George, Eileen, and Marshall finished their dinner and left the Union Hotel to head for Marshall's battered Volvo parked across the street. Marshall didn't talk much on the way to the car, except to say that he definitely wanted to meet with Klineman's sources. "I'll be in touch," he promised as he drove away.

The next morning, Klineman got a call from Rosalie Wright at *New West*. Kilduff had spoken to her as promised. Rosalie was more than agreeable; she was enthusiastic. She seemed surprisingly collected, considering the chaos that surrounded her. The night before—possibly during the dinner in Occidental—someone had forced open a second story window at *New West* in San Francisco, climbed inside, and gone through the filing cabinet. Nothing had been taken; only the Peoples Temple file had been disturbed. That evening, on the six o'clock news, George and Eileen saw the short film clip on the *New West* break-in. It showed a couple of tight shots of the pry marks on the second story, and there was a brief interview with Phil Tracy, the *New West* editor who was working with Kilduff.

Klineman now entertained new waves of paranoia. He had to know whether his name and number were anywhere in that file, perhaps on a slip of paper someone had thrown in. He tried to call Kilduff, but there was no answer, not at home nor at the office. He finally called *New West*.

"Yeah." The voice on the other end of the phone was the voice he had heard only moments before on the news. "Tracy."

Klineman introduced himself and asked Tracy what was in the file.

"D-Don't worry about it," Tracy replied in a thick New York accent. "The only thing in the file was Kilduff's—uh—manuscript, and he—uh—he doesn't have a damn thing." Tracy was writing sentences in his head before he spoke; that was the habit of a seasoned reporter who's faced a lot of deadlines. The lag time between thought and sentence caused him to stammer; it was characteristic, and this was not the first time Klineman had heard it.

"Look, I—uh—I—I—I don't want to talk about the file," Tracy said. "Whoever broke into here might—uh—m-might have planted a bug in one of our phones."

"Right."

There was a tentative plan for Kilduff and Tracy to meet with Klineman and his sources the next day at Mert's place in Berkeley. Klineman and Tracy both knew about the meeting, but they didn't mention it—not on a hot phone.

Mert called just after dinner to confirm the Saturday meeting. The instructions were to park on the street near the rest home Mert and Deanna were running and knock on the front door. They would be taken out to the house in back. "Oh, and bring flowers for grandma. Don't forget you're visiting a rest home. We're under surveillance; I'm sure of it. I've seen 'em on the street, and there's no telling when they're going to be here."

"How about a box of quilts for grandma?" Klineman offered. "I could have one quilt folded on top, and my camera gear underneath, O.K.?"

"I'll be watching the street when you arrive."

Klineman called Kilduff to tell him the plan for Saturday: He would call Kilduff at 6:30 P.M. to give him a telephone number; once he and Tracy arrived in Berkeley, they were to call that number for directions to the meeting. When Klineman suggested Kilduff bring a bouquet of flowers, Kilduff reacted predictably; it was silly, but he'd go along with it. Klineman was wary. Kilduff and Tracy were still not convinced of the dangers.

When George and Eileen arrived in Berkeley, they stopped at the Chevron station at Gilman and San Pablo to call Kilduff and give him Mert's phone number. "Oh, and by the way, did you remember the bouquet?"

"I don't want to get into that cloak-and-dagger stuff," said Kilduff.

"Look," said Klineman, "I just don't want you guys coming in with notebooks and tape recorders, O.K.? You're going to be walking through a rest home to get to Mert's house, and you should have something for grandma, get it? Mert says there's a damn good chance the place is being watched, so I don't want you to look conspicuous."

"O.K., George, I get it, I get it. Phil has a box for his tape recorder. I have a bag for my notebook."

"All right. See you in about forty-five minutes."

George and Eileen drove across Berkeley to the neighborhoods where the streets are lined with trees and checked the addresses. They found the brown-shingle building on the left side of the street and Eileen eased the Volkswagen between two parked cars. "That's it," she said, and started to get out of the car, but George restrained her. They sat for a moment and looked up and down the street. "O.K.," Klineman said. He picked up the box from the back seat. They walked unhurriedly toward the rest home, arm in arm, carrying quilts and goodies for granny. They were about halfway there when Klineman saw a car approaching out of the corner of his eye. He turned his head slightly. The car was something out of the fifties, and the driver appeared to be wearing a fur-lined cap with earmuffs. The car made a U-turn in the middle of the block. It passed the couple again. The driver was Mert.

"It seems to be clear," he said. "Go ahead inside."

They were greeted at the door by Deanna's mother, Mary Gustafson, a pleasant, elderly woman. She took them through the parlor, past a half circle of the silently aged, who stared as they passed, and out the back door. She pointed to a house in back. "Just knock on the door."

Deanna ushered them quickly into the living room. Another knock had Deanna on her feet again; it was her son, Eddie, with the news that there was

264

a strange car out front. The driver was taking down license numbers. Deanna called the Treasury agent; he called his friend in the Berkeley Police Department, who promised to have a squad car cruise by. Mert, meanwhile, had gone out front to take a look. He returned minutes later and told the group that the woman in the brown compact car started it up and drove away as soon as she saw the cruiser.

Good. If Tracy and Kilduff had pulled up while that spy, whoever she was, was sitting there, they could have blown the cover on the meeting. Everyone in the Bay Area who watched the news had seen Phil Tracy's unmistakable face, his bushy hair and tinted glasses, the evening before.

After Grace Stoen and Walt Jones arrived, and then Linda Mertle, the group was complete except for Kilduff and Tracy, and Dave Conn. Now Klineman could discuss with them some of the ground rules for interviews. They were to understand clearly what Kilduff and Tracy were offering them; they were to be sure of what they were going to say before they went on the record. "I'll be standing with you," he assured them. "My name's going in that article, too."

Kilduff and Tracy called, on schedule, from the Smokehouse, a hamburger place at Telegraph and Woolsey. They arrived only minutes later. As Klineman watched them cross the street, he was relieved the woman in the brown car hadn't made a return visit. Kilduff was inconspicuous enough in his conservative dress, but Tracy was another story, with a huge medallion dangling on a chain around his neck and those weird yellow-tinted glasses. They had remembered their packages for grandma.

Klineman greeted them at the door and took them into the kitchen of the rest home in front, where they discussed ground rules and the importance of impressing the sources with the now-or-never reality before them. Klineman had already done his best to build the group's confidence in Kilduff and Tracy. The reporters had to be a team to pull it off. "Shit, yes," said Tracy. "Yer goddamn right we're a team."

Klineman led them to the house in back, where Deanna was waiting at the door. Klineman handled the introductions. When he introduced Grace Stoen, he watched Kilduff's face for a reaction. Grace was beautiful. Kilduff was speechless. He extended his hand and Grace smiled shyly.

Dave Conn arrived. Everyone except the *New West* reporters knew him from the meeting of January 1977. Klineman explained that Conn was the first "outsider" Mert called to tell his story of the Temple. Dave remained silent while George described the Dennis Banks incident.

Tracy took over. He began a long-winded stammering rap that sounded like a lecture for a journalism class, a lecture on the responsibilities of sources, the responsibilities of reporters. He outlined libel laws and court decisions. He chain-smoked Chesterfields, droning on like a talking law book for the blind. George looked at Kilduff; Kilduff was fidgeting. Tracy was using the oldest ploy in the reporter's bag of tricks: a long-winded, boring speech can be a dam restraining a flood of stories eager to be told, and when the speech ends, the people with the information are bursting to spill it.

Grace spoke first. Her attorney, Jeff Haas, advised her not to talk to the press without his being present. He was unable to come to the meeting, so he helped her draft a statement. Tracy asked her to read it. It sounded like a legal brief that carefully outlined Grace's fears and her disenchantment with Jim Jones. She told about the last time she saw her five-year-old son, John-John, before Jim Jones took him to Guyana. There were tears in her eyes. "I just want him back, that's all." Grace would not consent to a taped interview.

Linda Mertle broke the ice. She had to leave in a few minutes and she wanted to get the interview out of the way. She sat on the couch with Tracy and told of her seventy-five whacks with the Board of Education. Before she left, Klineman took her picture.

Walt Jones was next; he hesitated at first, shrugged his shoulders, and followed Tracy into the kitchen. During his two-hour interview, Walt told of turning county money intended for care homes over to Peoples Temple, to the tune of a thousand dollars a month. While Tracy was interviewing Walt, Deanna brought out some tapes of Jim Jones and played them; it was the first time George and Eileen had heard his voice. Jones spoke in circles, it seemed, with rapid-fire run-on sentences uttered with a hypnotic midwestern timbre in his voice. Kilduff listened for only a moment, then walked away. "You could go crazy listening to that voice," he said.

The elder Mertles were next. Elmer explained to Tracy why they changed their names to Al and Jeannie Mills. While they were in the Temple, Jim Jones made them sign blank sheets of paper in the lower-right-hand corner. Above their signatures were typed incriminating statements. Their interview lasted until three in the morning.

Monday morning, Tracy called to ask Klineman to do some research in the Santa Rosa office of the California Department of Public Health. He wanted everything Klineman could get his hands on concerning the Temple's state-licensed care homes in Mendocino County. Klineman walked into the office early the same afternoon.

"May I see your public records on care homes in Mendocino County?" he asked.

"You want to see public records on CARE HOMES IN MENDOCINO COUNTY?" the clerk asked back, raising her voice on the last five words for the benefit of her coworkers.

Klineman wondered what the hell was going on. Had they been expecting him? He forgot for a moment he was in the office where Jones's wife, Marceline, worked as an inspector of nursing homes.

"We can't open all the records on Mendocino County because some of the information is confidential," the clerk said.

"What do you mean, 'confidential'? I thought state inspections were a matter of public record."

"There is material in the files pertaining to some of the patients in care homes, and that information is confidential," the clerk said. "If you could give me the name of a care home, I could remove the confidential documents from that file."

"O.K. I'd like to see the file on Happy Acres."

"You want to see the file on HAPPY ACRES?"

The other clerks were listening to the conversation. Klineman wasn't sure what was going on, but he didn't like it much. The clerk took him to a room with several desks, pulled out the file, and removed the forbidden pages. Before she handed him the file, she asked him to fill out a form requesting the documents.

"What do you do with the forms?" he asked.

"We keep them on file."

"Who looks at them?"

"Nobody, really."

"O.K. Let me get out my pen."

As the clerk looked over his shoulder, Klineman filled in the form with a phony name. The phone rang and the clerk left the room. The file was on the table. When the woman returned, Klineman handed her the stack of materials and she made copies. He complimented her on the beauty of the redwood office with its potted plants. He kept on talking all the way to the door. No request form of his would ever grace her files. It was in his pocket.

Soon after he arrived home, Klineman got a call from Mert. Mert wanted to get his materials back from the Treasury agent; he wanted *New West* to have them for documentation. Klineman suggested Mert call the agent first and he would do the rest. Mert called back a few minutes later and said the agent was more than willing to return everything. "He says the materials are of no use to him," said Mert.

"Good," said Klineman. "I'd rather see Treasury out of the picture anyway, now that *New West* is on to the story."

Klineman and the agent met the following day at a truck stop in Cotati. While the agent was handing Klineman the box of the defectors' materials, a woman's voice crackled over his car radio with the message that George was to phone Eileen immediately. The agent waited in the car while George called home. Eileen said Tracy wanted to talk to him right away. Tracy wanted to know whether there was any way he could interview the Treasury agent. Klineman didn't think so. He returned to the agent's car and conveyed Phil Tracy's message.

That evening, George and Eileen went through the box of Mert's materials and itemized the sixty-plus items it contained: power-of-attorney documents, Grace's notary book, threatening letters, instructions, photographs smuggled from the Temple, even a bottle of Jim Jones's Blessed Annointed Oil. Although the materials helped substantiate the stories from the Berkeley meeting, the reporters still were not home free. Tracy called again and gave Klineman the phone number of Ross Case in Ukiah. Case was one of the several former Temple members who called *New West* after the Barnes article. Tracy wanted Klineman to interview Case right away.

The next morning, Klineman called Mert to learn the names of any former members in the Ukiah area who might be passing information to Jones. Mert gave him four names. Ross Case was safe—Mert was certain—because he left the Temple in the early sixties. Klineman reached Case on the first try.

"Ross Case speaking."

Case's voice threw Klineman off for a moment. It was the resonant voice of a fundamentalist minister, melodic and assured, extremely gentle.

"This is George Klineman. Phil Tracy told me to call you."

"Yes. We have a group of people here I think you would like to talk to."

Case's voice was calming, but Klineman was not entirely convinced; he might have been walking into a trap. After they set a meeting for the next night, Klineman asked who would be coming. Case ran down the list of those who would be there. None of the names matched any of the four Mert said were risky.

"There's one more person who might show up," Case said.

"Who's that?"

"Danny Pietila."

Danny Pietila was one of the four names on the list.

That evening, George and Eileen drove to Tracy's apartment with the materials from the Treasury agent. They spread out the piles of paper on the dining room table. Kilduff devoured every word; Tracy stacked everything in subject piles.

"You think there's enough for an article?" Klineman asked.

"We aren't home free yet," said Tracy. "Maybe we will be by tomorrow when you get back from Ukiah. By the way, I got a call from your Treasury source today. He didn't tell me his name or his agency—only enough to convince me he works for the government."

By noon the next day George and Eileen were on the road north to Ukiah. They were not quite sure what to expect; Mert told them Pietila's parents were still in the church and they were risking a leak with today's interview.

At the courthouse in Ukiah, they pulled copies of the church's articles of incorporation, deeds of trust showing gifts of property to the church, notices of reconveyance. On the ledger in the county recorder's office was a listing for amended articles of incorporation for Peoples Temple of the Disciples of Christ. The document showed that Peoples Temple was reorganized in 1974 from "a non-profit corporation" to "a California corporation" with the authority to buy and sell property, along with the usual capitalist benefits and privileges.

At 4:15, George and Eileen left the courthouse and headed for Ross Case's house. They were about twenty minutes late; the group was waiting. Klineman assured them that others who had left the church—he couldn't yet reveal their names—were speaking to *New West*, and he invited them to tell briefly about their involvement with Peoples Temple. Danny Pietila spoke first. He told of humiliations and beatings, so many he'd lost count. Danny's story sounded genuine, but Klineman was still wary.

Ruby Bogner was the first witness to go on tape. She was a schoolteacher in Redwood Valley. There had been a sudden influx of children to her school, children from Peoples Temple, who kept falling asleep in class because they were kept up at night until all hours. Black children had been taught to hate white children. When she complained to school officials, Temple parents started showing up in committees wearing dark glasses.

Danny was the next to go on tape. Klineman decided to get him out of the way early, before he heard the others, just in case Mert was right and Danny was passing information.

"Could you spell your name for the tape, please?"

"P-I-E-T-I-L-A."

"Age?"

"Twenty-two."

"Occupation?"

"I'm a drummer."

"What do you mean, you're a drummer?"

"I play drums in a band."

"Are you saying you make your living playing drums?"

The kid was perplexed. He didn't understand why he should have to be grilled like that after he volunteered to provide information. It was exactly the reaction Klineman wanted to see.

Later in the interview, Klineman asked Danny which Temple members he would say hello to on the street.

"Jack Beam?"

"No, I wouldn't want to run into him."

"Elmer Mertle."

"No. He's still in, isn't he?"

"Grace Stoen?"

"No way. Grace is still in, too, and she's head counselor. I'd never want to run into her."

It was already past nine o'clock before Birdie Marable's story was on tape. Eileen had been taking notes on the others in the group. They wrapped up the session with an interview of Ross Case and called it a night.

269

The next day at *New West*, Klineman and Tracy sat around Tracy's office with the boxes and bags full of materials from Ukiah spread around their feet, waiting for Kilduff while Tracy related the latest gossip. Rosalie Wright had gone to Police Chief Charles Gain to see about carrying a concealed weapon; she'd moved temporarily, taken her kids into hiding. Tracy was certain a spy from the Temple had been lurking outside the office the day before. As Marshall arrived, Tracy was busy recreating the scene for George and telling how he waited for the guy to get close to the front door before he leaned out the window with a camera. "I got you, motherfucker," he shouted, pretending to snap frames as fast as he could flick his thumb. The three of them spent a couple of hours reviewing the materials; they were finally home free. They celebrated with a Mandarin dinner out on Clement Street.

Tracy would write the first draft from that mountain of materials; there was not much more for Klineman to do. During the lull, he scheduled an interview with a spokesman for the Coors beer boycott, something he'd been postponing for two weeks. He was talking with a boycott leader who had worked at the Coors brewery, at Charlie's Park-In on Lombard Street, when a waitress approached the table.

"Are you George Klineman?" she asked.

"Yes."

Again, it was Eileen, calling with the message that George should phone Phil Tracy right away. Klineman wrapped up his interview and called Tracy. Tracy wanted him to pick up a list of property transactions to research in Ukiah. Klineman drove to the office on Pacific Avenue and waited. Tracy emerged looking like one of Jim Jones's work-wracked zombies; he hadn't slept for three days. He wasn't sure where to begin. He handed Klineman the list and said to call him at *New West* in Beverly Hills as soon as he finished the research.

Those were the last few details Tracy needed. He negotiated and renegotiated with *New West*'s managing editor, Frank Lalli, for more space in the magazine. Kilduff flew down to see the final manuscript.

Within a week, the magazine was on the stands. The threats and reprisals Klineman had been expecting did not materialize; it was so damned quiet, it was spooky.

On August 1, Marceline Jones resigned her job as an inspector of nursing homes for the state. On August 3—via radio-phone from Guyana—Jim Jones resigned his post as chairman of the Housing Authority Commission.

Then came the media barrage.

Examiner, Sunday, August 7: "Power Broker Jones."

Examiner, Sunday, August 14: "The Temple: A Nightmare World."

New West, August 15: "More on People's Temple: The Strange Suicides."

United Press International.

Newsweek.

The New York Times.
Television.
Radio.
Investigations.
Lawsuits.
Radio.
Investigations.
Lawsuits.
Jim Jones never came back.

I know some of you are wanting to fight, but that's exactly what the system wants—they want to use us as sacrificial lambs, as a scapegoat. Don't fall into this trap by yielding to violence, no matter what kind of lies are told on us or how many.

Peoples Temple has helped practically every political prisoner in the United States. We've reached out to everyone who is oppressed, and that is what is bothering them. We've organized poor people and given them a voice. The system doesn't mind corporate power for the ruling elite, but for the first time we've given corporate power to the little man and that's an unforgivable sin. And that's the whole problem in a nutshell.

> —The Reverend Jim Jones, speaking
> via telephone relay from Guyana,
> July 31, 1977

X

The Promised Land

Estelle Bedford knew about Jim Jones from way back in 1968 when he stole some sheep from her husband's church. Her husband, the Reverend G. L. Bedford of the Macedonia Missionary Baptist Church on Sutter Street, was among the first of California ministers to lose members to Jim Jones, and the memory of that episode stayed in her mind with somewhat less warmth than the air over San Francisco that night in 1977 when she was shopping for groceries. On the sidewalk in front of the Safeway store, she chanced upon two elderly women, black and in tattered clothes, begging for money. One of them stopped Mrs. Bedford. "Help the poor," she said.

"What poor?" asked Mrs. Bedford.

"The poor in Guyana."

"The poor in Guyana? You're here," Mrs. Bedford reminded the woman.

"I want you to help the Temple."

"What temple?"

"Jim Jones's Temple."

"Honey," said Mrs. Bedford, "you ought to be ashamed of yourself. . . . You're out here cold and raggedy. I know you're cold. . . . You stop begging for Jim Jones. That's all you're doing."

Mrs. Bedford saw the women in front of the Safeway, again and again, "every week for a long, long time," she says. "Not only that store—all around." All around the streets and sidewalks, the stores and corners of San Francisco, little old black ladies and revolutionary adolescents held out cans for spare change for "the poor" and "for starving babies," all in Guyana, all in The Promised Land where Jim Jones retreated only days before the *New West* article hit the newsstands. Jones's departure was not as abrupt as it might have seemed; he did speak of his plans to the Reverend Cecil Williams, pastor of Glide Memorial Methodist Church.

"The day that he left the Bay Area to go to Guyana," the Reverend Williams recalls, "he called me from Los Angeles. I hadn't heard from Jim in some time, and he called me and said, 'I'm leaving. I want you to know that I'm leaving.'"

"Why are you leaving, man?"

"It's just too much for me at this point. There's too much coming down at this point."

Williams, who had shared the pulpit and the podium with Jim Jones many times, advised his friend to stay and stand up to the charges soon to be made public. "You're running, Jim," Williams said. "Don't run."

"They really need me in the mission," Jones countered. "I'm going down to work in the mission."

"Jim, you are running."

"I'll be back," Jones promised.

"Jim," said Cecil, "you ought to stay here, man. Whatever it is you need to face, face it here."

Jim Jones would face whatever he needed to face, to be sure, only not immediately; the Temple circulated rumors that his return was imminent, though, and with his defiant return he would "take off his sunglasses and unleash his powers on the world." Former members doubted that he would ever come back to the United States. The weight of the charges in print was too formidable for Jones to carry in a Second Coming, and the press was not about to stand idly by and watch his ascent. The Prophet's burden was made heavier yet by the reports—covered widely in Bay Area newspapers—that "several government agencies," including Treasury and the San Francisco District Attorney's Office, were investigating the Temple's activities. One government agency under whose aegis Jones could feel secure, for it was not about to investigate him or his church, was the office of the mayor of San Francisco. Although Supervisor Quentin Kopp had requested a probe of the Housing Authority Commission's chairman after having read the *New West* article, Mayor George Moscone said his office was "not equipped for such an investigation." Furthermore, the mayor said on July 27—only days after the article appeared—that *New West* showed "no hard evidence the Reverend Jones has violated any laws."

If Moscone's disclaimers didn't lighten Jim's load, they certainly did nothing to increase it. Of more help to the Prophet of God was the meeting on July 31, 1977—despite ample evidence that exposed Jim Jones as a charlatan, a beast, a brute, a liar, a usurer, an extorter—at Peoples Temple in San Francisco. His loyal supporters in the community gathered under the same roof to extol Jim Jones and his good works, to pledge their continued support. Among the speakers on this august occasion were two state assemblymen, Willie Brown and Art Agnos, and other local and national dignitaries of the left: The Reverend Cecil Williams of Glide Church; President Joe Hall of the National Association for the Advancement of Colored People; American Indian Movement leader Dennis Banks; gay activists Howard Wallace and Harvey Milk. Said Assemblyman Willie Brown:

> When somebody like Jim Jones comes on the scene and talks about Angela Davis, for example, and the Black Panther party having a right to survive and function, and constantly stresses the need for freedom of speech and equal justice under law for all people, that

absolutely scares the hell out of most everybody occupying positions of power in the system. . . . I will be here when you are under attack, because what you are about is what the whole system ought to be about!

Came Art Agnos's echo:

I am proud to stand with you. I have seen you wherever people have needed help. It is clear you are effective; people who are not effective are not attacked.

Enthusiastic support was voiced in the editorials of two newspapers, the *Sun-Reporter* and the *Ukiah Daily Journal*. The publisher of the *Sun-Reporter*, Dr. Carleton B. Goodlett, wrote in a rambling editorial denouncing the *New West* article:

We have from time to time investigated the complaints that persons have lodged against Peoples Temple. On the basis of repeated in-depth investigations, we say, as one with strong commitments to the role of religion in the lives of men: We have found no fault with Jim Jones's religious philosophy or the activities of the Peoples Temple.

Despite the fiery rhetoric of these champions of the oppressed—the politicians, the publishers, the editors—the under-the-table word among the people of the left was, according to Berkeley leftist Ted Vincent, subtly different:

Don't you stick your neck out to support Jim Jones. Don't attack him. . . . Don't get involved. . . . Be cool on the matter because we all know he does a lot of good works . . . [but] you're gonna get hooked because he does some bad things. It really does happen.

It really did happen to the family of Steve Katsaris. Katsaris is the director of the Trinity School in Ukiah, a private school committed to special education. His daughter, Maria Katsaris, was active in Peoples Temple. Steve read the article in *New West*. "I was devastated," he says. "I knew all these people. I knew Grace Stoen. I knew the Mills." Shortly after the *New West* article appeared with its devastating allegations, Steve's daughter, Maria, called him long distance overseas from 41 Lamaha Gardens, the Temple's headquarters in Georgetown, Guyana, to ask him whether he had read the piece. Steve replied that he had and Maria cautioned her father not to believe a word of it; it was, she said, "all a bunch of lies."

"Maria, if it's all lies," Steve replied, "Jim should not be down there. He should come up here and face his accusers."

Maria told her father that Jim Jones had "two perforated eardrums" and that the "doctors won't let him travel."

"Jesus Christ, Maria!" Steve was normally calm and rational, a former Greek Orthodox priest. "This thing is so severe and so critical, the papers are doing nothing else but writing about it! If he can't fly with two perforated eardrums, he ought to take a slow boat to Florida and come across the country by train."

Because it was only an earache that kept Jim Jones in Guyana—the story was circulated widely—a ray of hope was cast on the speculation that Father would in fact come home, back to the United States and San Francisco, and lay waste his critics as soon as he recovered. That hope was dimmed on August 2, when Jim Jones resigned from the Housing Authority Commission via radiophone from Guyana. Harriet Tropp received the message in San Francisco and it was delivered to Mayor Moscone on Housing Authority stationery the following day:

> It has become increasingly apparent that the needs of my congregation in Guyana necessitate my ongoing presence there which would require my absence from the city for extended periods of time.
>
> Because I believe that San Francisco deserves and demands strong and effective leadership from one who can give full commitment to the job, I am today submitting my resignation as a member and Chairman of the Housing Authority so that you may expeditiously fill that vacancy.
>
> As you know, I have wanted to resign for months, finding the responsibilities of a city official essentially incompatible with my duties as a pastor of a large congregation both here and in Guyana.

Several days passed without further word from Jim Jones, without a single indication of his plans for the future. Rumors abounded; some former Temple members interpreted Jones's silence as an omen that he would surprise the world with some bold move or, perhaps, just lay low until he could slip back into the United States to lead "The One Hundred"—his mysterious cadre of terrorists and assassins—in a bloodbath of vengeance against his enemies. Their fears were not irrational, for Jones's enemies were by now formidable: in addition to the defectors and the government agencies engaged in the imagined conspiracy, there were the journalists; they were hitting Jones with what Chronicle columnist Herb Caen described as "a ceaseless media barrage these days." As to Jim Jones's plans, the first inkling appeared in Caen's August 18 column, wherein he reported that Jones

> . . . wants to come home and answer the charges being leveled at him and his Peoples Temple, but his lawyer, Charles Garry, is advising against it. "Garry thinks Jim would be chewed up by the media," says

Jones's aide, Mike Prokes. Nevertheless, Prokes goes on, "Jim is dying to come back," from the South American country of Guyana, where he is running a church-backed mission. "This campaign against Jim," suggests Prokes, "is orchestrated at the highest level, perhaps FBI or CIA. We know the FBI became interested in Jim years ago, when he was an outspoken civil rights advocate in Indianapolis. It seems significant that whereas Peoples Temple is 80 percent black, 90 percent of those making these wild charges are white. We know many of them to be provocateurs and conspirators in the past. In my opinion, some of them are being paid.". . . The 45-year-old Jones communicates almost daily with his Peoples Temple staff via short-wave radio. Several ham operators who have picked up his transmissions tell me "he seems to be speaking in some sort of code." Prokes laughs. "Typical," he says. "Sometimes the connection is so bad that he is unintelligible but—code? Really."

Caen's ham radio sources were not exaggerating; Temple communications between Guyana and San Francisco were conducted in a kind of code that might have been devised by a Boy Scout working toward a merit badge in cryptography. Transcripts of the broadcasts reveal that Jim Jones's mind was on such worrisome people as "Morris" (Marshall Kilduff) and "Rich Man" (George Klineman). Jones himself was "Victor"; Charles Garry, "Philip." "Gratitude" meant money. One radio transmission has Jones reminding his lieutenants of the obligation for "expressing gratitude to Osgood." Much to the chagrin of "Morris" and the others who were listening in, the three-dot columnist's eagerness to get the story out forced the already paranoid Temple leadership to work out other code systems for messages whose meanings, now, may never be known.

Cryptic though some of Jones's messages may have been, other messages came through loud and clear. Nearly every Sunday during the first year in Guyana, the Reverend Jim Jones continued to perform, via radio transmissions, his miraculous healings and revelations. These performances were something apart from his daily broadcasts between six and seven o'clock in the evening; they were Sunday specials that were piped right into services. "I remember when he first went over," says the Reverend Dave Garrison. "Every Sunday he would call back here . . . [on] ham radio . . . and he would heal several members in the church. He'd tell you who was at the church and call them out." One of his more miraculous achievements over the airwaves—announced in a brochure mailed to past contributors—was the healing of his wife, Marceline, of cancer of the right lung.

While Jones soothed the faithful in San Francisco with miracles and the press continued to chip away at him, the loyal remainder in the city were gearing up for a mass exodus to The Promised Land. The first report that the Temple was clearing out appeared July 31, 1977, in a *San Francisco Progress* article by E. Cahill Maloney. She and Temple defector Linda Mertle toured the ghetto to look at residences on Fillmore, Fell, Divisadero, Sutter, and Steiner streets that had once served as Temple communes. Maloney reported that the cramped flats and apartments "appear to be emptying out fast." Even the Temple's secondhand store on Divisadero Street, Relics 'N' Things, had a "Closed" sign on the front door. By mid-August, widespread press reports told of huge stacks of plywood shipping crates at the rear of the Temple on Geary Boulevard, all stenciled *Peoples Temple Agricultural Mission, Port Kaituma, Guyana, S.A.* Beside the crates were pallets loaded with tires and farm equipment, 300 fifty-five-gallon drums full of perishables, and hundreds of boxes containing personal belongings. The faithful worked day and night, nailing up the crates and loading them onto two flatbed trucks that left early in the morning for Miami harbor, where the Temple maintained a berth for its two seagoing vessels, *The Cudjoe* (later renamed *The Marceline*), and *The Albatross.*

To all appearances, a massive desperation move was in progress to the project that had become, because of press exposure, more a sanctuary than a mission—but the farm had not always been regarded in that light. There was a time, shortly after Jim Jones founded the agricultural mission in 1973, when it was being touted not as the last safe place for the warriors of apostolic equalitarianism but as an oasis of love and caring, far removed from the crime-ridden cities and ideal for teaching young people the values of brotherhood and equality, a school for redirecting wayward youth like Danny Pietila and Robin Wages.

During the summer of 1974, Danny and Robin were so tickled by the rub of love that Jim Jones told them they were "the second most disruptive force in our family." Other young people in the Temple were following their example and were flagrantly loving and rubbing without prior clearance. Danny and Robin got the full treatment; the Temple's leaders tried shaming them, humiliating them, beating them with belts and boards, encouraging them to pursue instead homosexual relationships, but the bond was unbreakable. Father decided the second most effective alternative for Danny and Robin was to send them to The Promised Land for rehabilitation. Jim Jones approached Danny and Robin one day and pulled two hundred and seventy-five dollars cash from his wallet. He handed them the money and told them to drive to Miami, where they were to climb aboard the next boat to Guyana. Danny followed Father's orders and drove his blue Toyota and his Robin all the way across the continent. They stayed on board *The Cudjoe* and waited for it to weigh anchor and head for South America. After two weeks they jumped ship. They hightailed it to South Carolina; Danny was eighteen and Robin close to sixteen years old, and with a little persuading they got Robin's mother to sign consent papers and when they left Carolina they were as married as two people can be.

To the young couple who found paradise enough in each other's arms, the lure of the tropics was eminently resistible. From South Carolina they moved back to Ukiah, in violation of the Temple's rule prohibiting defectors' living within five hundred miles of California. The violation prompted a couple of threatening phone calls, and the worst that happened to Mr. and Mrs. Pietila was Jim Jones's making them repay every dime of the two hundred and seventy-five dollars. It was a small price to pay, considering the alternative.

The alternative was to stay on *The Cudjoe* until it sailed. Had Danny and Robin so elected, they'd have been part of the first contingent of Peoples Temple pioneers who cleared the first thirty acres of Jonestown in October 1974. These first settlers, according to a 1977 progress report on the mission, numbered eleven; they worked outdoors during the day and slept in a "bark cottage" at night. Their work was made possible only after some careful research, begun the year before when the church board first conceived the idea of establishing an overseas mission. According to a statement by Linda Sharon Amos, it was in 1973 that Tim Stoen reviewed the laws and political affairs of several nations, one of which was Guyana, and advised the board of his findings. Stoen's participation entailed considerably more than a long-distance study; he and Mrs. Amos and Johnny Moss Brown traveled to the South American country for a firsthand investigation of its "laws and regulations and their probable [e]ffect on the mission development." The team related their conclusions to the board and selected Guyana as the site for the Peoples Temple Overseas Mission. Stoen aided further with some of the legal problems of resettling the Temple members, helping them dispose of their personal property in the United States, and applying for and acquiring passports. By late 1973, the Temple was nearly ready to break ground after numerous discussions and negotiations between Temple leaders and Guyanese officials in the Ministry of Agriculture and National Development.

Jones's introduction to Guyanese officials was sanctioned by two letters from U.S. congressmen of opposite ends of the political spectrum. One of the letters of introduction, dated November 20, 1973, was from Congressman Don H. Clausen, a glad-handing conservative Republican from what was then the First Congressional District; stretching from Sonoma County to the Oregon border, Clausen's district included Mendocino County. His letter was addressed to Forbes Burnham, prime minister of the Cooperative Republic of Guyana:

It is my pleasure to introduce to you an outstanding humanitarian, Reverend James W. Jones. He is the pastor of Peoples Temple Church and will soon be visiting your country to seek permission to establish a missionary human service work there. He and his people have shown themselves to be extraordinarily responsible, industrious and compassionate—working to serve people in what ever way they can.

Jones's other letter of introduction to Burnham, dated November 26, 1973, was from Congressman George E. Brown, Jr., an antiwar Democrat who represented California's Thirty-Eighth Congressional District, with offices in Colton. Congressman Brown said of Jones's flock:

> . . . They are highly industrious, work well with other groups, and do good without seeking recognition for it.
> This past August I was with Rev. Jones and 660 of his people in Washington, D.C., where I saw them systematically picking up the litter left by others all over the Capitol Hill area. The *Washington Post* was so impressed they wrote an editorial commending the group as "the hands-down winners of anybody's tourists-of-the-year award."
> Any courtesies you could extend to the Rev. Jones and the members of Peoples Temple would be deeply appreciated.

The congressmen's kind words undoubtedly helped persuade officials of the former colony of British Guiana, which since May 26, 1966, has been an independent socialist nation, to allow the Temple to make formal application to lease 27,000 acres in the jungle near Port Kaituma, between the Kaituma and Barima rivers. The lease provided for an annual rental fee of twenty-five cents per acre for the first five years and negotiable rates for each of the following five-year periods for twenty-five years. Two Temple trustees, Eugene Chaikin and Archie Ijames, signed the application and agreed on behalf of the Temple to invest a million Guyanese dollars in the agricultural project over the first two years. The Temple was permitted to begin settling the land in 1974. In February of 1976, the government granted a lease on 3,824 acres, in keeping with the government's program of encouraging development of the tropical hinterlands, which are populated sparsely by the native Amerindians. The rest of the population—90 percent of an estimated 810,000—lives in a flat coastal strip whose widest portion is only forty miles from the shore. The rest of the land is dense, steaming jungle, largely inaccessible except by travelers on foot, wielding machetes.

Jim Jones was virtually unknown in Guyana until December of 1974, when he brought his faith-healing roadshow to Georgetown, the national capital. The Temple bought a front-page ad in a Georgetown newspaper announcing a December 29 service at Sacred Heart, a Catholic church, and touting Jim Jones as "the greatest healing ministry through Christ on earth today. . . . This full Gospel deliverance ministry has been widely acclaimed for its humanitarian works. God has blessed Pastor Jones with all nine gifts of the

Holy Spirit and thousands have been healed of every kind of affliction." About a thousand people jammed into the church and spilled out onto the street for the afternoon service, which featured miracle healings of cancer and arthritis.

The size of the crowd, however, was not an index of the service's success. According to an account in the *Guyana Chronicle,* "a substantial number of the people attending were Catholics," who were under the mistaken impression that "Bishop" Jones—a title he conferred upon himself in Guyana—would perform a special Mass. The Catholics were furious when they saw Jones's faith-healing exhibition; such theatrics, they believed, had "desecrated" their church. An embarrassed spokesman for the Roman Catholic Church in Georgetown said church officials were unaware ahead of time that "Bishop" Jones would be doing healings at the service. The miracles at Sacred Heart Church raised a nasty uproar that the local press covered with gusto. Jones and his staff responded by issuing the most apologetic statement ever released in Peoples Temple's brief history:

> The Peoples Temple in Guyana intends to be an agricultural mission. Our only interest is to produce food to help feed our hungry world in whatever way best suits the people of Guyana. . . .
>
> We love the [United States]. Good changes towards a more perfect democracy are being made there. If we cannot serve Guyana, then we will have no reason to remain. Certainly, we are not interested in your land. We just want to utilize it to help serve the people and have no other interests in it.
>
> We will gladly prove that to you, by withdrawing and letting good Guyanese people carry on with or without connections to our denomination of 2,000,000 members in the U.S. including Congressmen, members of all political parties and Governors.
>
> We can easily live in North America. We will leave on a good note. If you don't feel we can serve well or if you do feel we can serve, just write to us and let us know or write to the government.
>
> We have no desire to leave this wonderful country, but we have no desire to impose on your people.

After the faith-healing fiasco at Sacred Heart, Jones and fifty of his followers returned to San Francisco while an unsympathetic Guyanese press continued to hammer away at the "self-styled bishop" from California who planted shills in the audience for phony cures. In San Francisco, the returning pilgrims didn't even mention the disastrous events in Georgetown; Jones told them to keep their mouths shut—even about the agricultural mission being developed in the hinterlands. "For a while," says Selma Vincent, a Berkeley leftist who joined the church in late 1975, "they didn't even talk about Guyana. We weren't sure where [The Promised Land] was."

For several months, Jim Jones let his followers play a guessing game about the location of The Promised Land. He said it was in the jungle: people immediately thought Africa or South America. Then he let slip, "South America"; that eliminated from the game an entire continent. Finally, he said, The Promised Land was in a socialist country; then, a socialist country whose population was about 35 percent black, and whose primary tongue was English; the more astute members deduced that The Promised Land was in Guyana.

At several meetings, Jones described The Promised Land as having some unique characteristics. The Reverend Dave Garrison recalls how Pastor Jones explained that The Promised Land would be one of the few safe places on earth in the event of a nuclear holocaust. "Instead of going to the cave," Garrison says, "he had discerned a place over in South America [where] the trees reached one hundred feet up in the air and would filter out all the breezes that came through." The trees, Garrison was told, would protect Jones's followers "regardless [of] how many H-bombs they drop here." Protection from the holocaust, Garrison recalls, was one of The Promised Land's strong selling points. "That's one reason why so many of them flocked over there," he says. Another reason was that The Promised Land promised refuge for all the Temple's blacks when the Fascists took over the United States and would almost certainly confine and torture black people when the race war that Jim Jones often prophesied became a reality.

Vicky Moore was worried about the Fascists, too, but she viewed The Promised Land as a copout. "It seemed like a very nice place," she says. "For a while, I wanted to go, and the more I thought about it, the more I thought, Hey, I don't want to run away from where I'm needed. It didn't last very long that I wanted to go to Guyana." Vicky's father, Archie Ijames, had visited the Guyana mission in 1974. He was so upset by his treatment there that he quit Peoples Temple. The Reverend Archie Ijames, assistant pastor, ranking black in the Temple hierarchy, got down to the tropical farm and butted heads with major-domo Joyce Touchette, who oversaw the colony in the early days, and she treated him "like a child." Archie was furious. Rosabell caught the next plane for San Francisco. Archie followed a few days later with all the indignation he could muster and fifty thousand dollars of the Temple's money to start a new life. He and Eugene Chaikin had buried the money under a government building in Port Kaituma. When Archie returned to San Francisco, Rosabell told him that Jim Jones had called for volunteers to do him in. The Temple also put pressure on Archie about the missing money, but Archie blamed it all on Chaikin. Jones kept putting pressure on Archie and Rosabell until they eventually rejoined the Temple—on the condition that neither of them would ever have to return to The Promised Land.

When Jim Jones spoke of the paradise down in the jungles of Guyana, his descriptions were as selective as a travel agent's sales pitch. He spoke of how the even temperatures stayed between sixty-five and eighty-five degrees in the interior, and of how the nights were cooled by gentle trade winds from the Atlantic; but he neglected to mention the high humidity and the torrential downpours that sometimes lasted for ten straight days. He neglected to mention the prolific mosquito population, the thousands of snakes—some of them huge boas—that slithered silently through the trees and the dense underbrush, the noisy, mischievous crowds of monkeys, and the Amerindians, noble savages who were said to cart away everything that wasn't nailed down, chained up, or secured under lock and key.

The Amerindians' penchant for pilfering justified the posting of twenty-four-hour security guards around the encampment. As new arrivals soon learned, however, the job of the guards was as much to keep Temple members in as to keep invaders out, in case anyone tried to escape from paradise. Despite Jones's lofty claims, the Peoples Temple Agricultural Mission was a hard labor camp not unlike Devil's Island, the legendary penal colony six hundred miles down the coast and off the shores of French Guiana. Whatever their motive—fear or dedication—the early Temple pioneers worked hard from dawn to dusk to cut a ten-mile road from Port Kaituma into the settlement, to clear the land for the buildings and the crops. They did most of their work by hand, through 1974 and until July of 1975, when the Temple moved in some U.S. government surplus heavy equipment—including a crane, two Caterpillar tractors, and a dump truck. Over the next few months, shipments brought three large farm tractors, a fifteen-thousand-dollar sawmill, a six-thousand-dollar diesel generator, mechanic's tools, a machine shop, corrugated iron roofing, restaurant equipment for the communal kitchen, medical supplies, and a large cache of firearms. The firearms were, according to former members, hidden in crates of clothing and other innocuous items shipped from San Francisco and Seattle.

Along the way in developing the tiny colony were setbacks that drove the settlers to work ever harder to attain their goal of self-sufficiency. The chickens that were to provide eggs and meat all died during the 1975 rainy season, and the rains washed away the fragile layer of topsoil left from clearing the forest, leaving under the rivulets and puddles an unfertile clay loam. The settlers burned out their prized diesel generator with improper wiring. Their fifteen-thousand-dollar sawmill was equipped for softwoods and could not handle the iron-hard greenheart trees felled to clear the settlement; the pioneers were forced to rely primarily on rough-cut crabwood from a distant mill site along the Wiani River.

Father was impatient for progress. He wanted Jonestown—so named by Guyanese officials—quickly to become a model of self-sufficient communal living that would be the envy of the Third World. His impatience was colored by a desperation to prepare a haven against the day when he and his followers had nowhere else to go. Work days increased from twelve to fourteen hours, from fourteen to sixteen, then were followed by marathon "catharsis sessions." Those who failed to complete their assigned tasks or who expressed doubts about the ultimate success of the mission were berated by the others and made to wear a yellow hardhat as a form of dunce cap. For more serious charges, offenders might also be forbidden to speak for several days, or assigned additional work hours, or have their heads shaved. Those who were careless about their tools or their clothing were compelled to pay the cost of the items, not with money, since all their money was taken when they reached Guyana, but with forfeited meals, assessed at one dollar each, until the value of the broken hammer or hoe was attained.

Father visited his jungle plantation frequently, although rarely for more than a few hours. When he was in Guyana, he spent most of his time at the residence the Temple rented in the capital at 121 Third Street in a section of the city called Alberttown. The home's most regular resident was Paula Adams, a member of the Temple since 1971 and one of the first group, along with Debbie Touchette (Archie's youngest daughter), to move into the Third Street address in January of 1974. The members in the Georgetown home had several duties. Vicky Moore recalls a planning commission meeting in San Francisco—sometime before she left the Temple in April 1976—where Jim Jones discussed "the strategies to be used on the political uppities of Guyana." One ploy to be used, Vicky recalls, was sexual compromise. "Paula Adams was specifically given directions," she says, "to have a sexual affair with this political person in Guyana in order to control [him] or get political influence with him." Although Vicky cannot recall the name of "this political person," Paula Adams has admitted she was seeing Guyana's ambassador to the United States, Laurence E. Mann. "It has been reported that Ms. Adams made tape recordings of her sexual encounters with Mann," notes a May 1979 *Congressional Report*. "Transcripts of some of these tapes were apparently made for Mr. Jones and periodically turned over to high officials in the Guyanese government."

On the whole, though, Guyanese officials had no inkling that there were any improprieties at all about the forward-looking, left-leaning church from North America. Their impression was, clearly and distinctly, that Peoples Temple was a highly respected organization in the United States, and that it had, through Pastor Jim Jones, direct links to the White House and other institutions of federal government. Guyanese officials were given, to bolster Jones's credibility, not only the two laudatory letters of introduction from congressmen but also firsthand experience with Jones's political clout on the Potomac's banks. A May 1979 State Department report reveals that:

In late December 1976, Lieutenant Governor [Mervyn] Dymally of California visited Guyana accompanied by Jones. The two men met with Guyanese Prime Minister [Forbes] Burnham and other senior

285

Guyanese officials as well as with the Chargé of the Embassy, Richard A. McCoy. In the course of the meeting with the Chargé, according to the latter's reporting telegram, Jones raised the concern of the Guyanese Government officials about CIA involvement in Guyana. [Jones] also mentioned a meeting he had with Mrs. Rosalynn Carter and Vice President-elect [Walter] Mondale in which he had been assured that the Carter Administration would not interfere with the domestic affairs of Guyana. He expressed the intention of passing this message to Prime Minister Burnham.

Prime Minister Burnham, who heads the predominantly black ruling party, the Peoples National Congress, was undoubtedly relieved to hear those assurances. Guyanese officials' concern with CIA activity and interference in Guyana's domestic affairs was not without foundation; it had been a CIA-fomented strike that eventually toppled the fledgling nation's first home-rule government, headed by Dr. Cheddi Jagan.

Jagan, a Marxist-Leninist, rose to power under the banner of the People's Progressive party, which consists primarily of the descendants of East Indian indentured servants, who represent 55 percent of Guyana's population. Guyana's blacks, roughly 35 percent of the population, are descended from African slaves brought to the colony in the seventeenth and eighteenth centuries by the Dutch, who alternated with the British in controlling the area until 1814, when the Dutch officially ceded it to the United Kingdom. The blacks, although a sizable minority, found their party in power after 1964 as a result of a coalition with the more conservative United Force, the party representing the minorities of Chinese, Portuguese, and East Indian middle-class business interests.

Considering the long history of tensions between the East Indians and the blacks, the high unemployment rate, the widespread poverty (annual income per capita was $588 in 1975), and the risky business of having nationalized American-owned firms, Jones's good tidings of noninterference from the new administration in Washington were the kind of news that in ancient times caused kings to heap praises on messengers. Apparently the CIA was not going to upset Guyana's apple cart and would leave in the hands of the government the former Demerara Bauxite Company, which was nationalized in 1971 after the government had reached a compensation agreement with ALCAN (Aluminum Company of Canada), the previous owners. Guyana was the world's fifth largest producer of bauxite, the ore that yields aluminum, the ore that accounted for 52 percent of Guyana's export dollars. Between former owners ALCAN and Reynolds Metal, Guyanese officials were understandably jittery about their nationalized bauxite industry, and Jim Jones's promises of noninterference by his good friends in the White House were more than adequate to assure his welcome in elegant style.

Jones, in his turn, courted his hosts in equally elegant style. In February of 1977, the Temple purchased 41 Lamaha Gardens, which became its "permanent" Georgetown headquarters. The building was a two-story yellow stucco house in an upper-middle-class neighborhood, which sported a covered balcony on the second story where the tenants found relief from the muggy heat; and a neatly kept yard was protected by a waist-high fence. The house with its lattice accents was ordinary in every way except for the roof-mounted aluminum mast that supported the ham radio antenna—for communications with Jonestown and California—that reached high above the neighboring rooftops looking for all the world like a television antenna in a city without TV.

The new headquarters at Lamaha Gardens was comfortably furnished; one could entertain there, without embarrassment, the most influential of Georgetown's citizens. Among those who attended the Temple's gala parties there was Pat Small, a former liaison officer with the Guyana Foreign Affairs Ministry. "[Jones] used to have these big open houses where you would find the doctors, the lawyers, the judges there," she says. "You could have drowned yourself in liquor, all types of liquor. You name it, it was there." During the gala evenings, she recalls, there were showings of an impressive film of the Jonestown settlement that included some footage of the Reverend Jones at the wheel of a tractor, tilling the jungle soil.

That was probably the only time, or one of the few times, the populist pastor actually dirtied his hands at Jonestown, but for the public relations mileage it got, the pose for the film was well worth the blackened fingernails. The more usual PR measures were invitation-only tours of the settlement for Guyanese officials and for American visitors like Mervyn Dymally. Such visitors would invariably come away favorably impressed. And well they should have been; according to a progress report to the Guyana government—dated summer 1977 but in fact prepared weeks earlier—the noble experiment at the jungle mission had attained an impressive degree of self-sufficiency with a population of about 520 persons. That figure may or may not have been accurate, for the population figures are elusive; U.S. embassy officials never bothered to take head counts, and embassy figures conflict with Temple figures. According to the embassy, there were "fifteen to twenty persons" living at the commune on March 13, 1975, when Ambassador Max V. Krebs made his visit. By May 1976, when Wade Matthews, deputy chief of mission, visited the compound, the embassy reported "some forty individuals." Beginning in April of 1977, after Jones got wind of the Treasury Department investigation when David Conn talked to American Indian Movement leader Dennis Banks, the population swelled considerably, according to embassy records:

On March 31, 1977, the Embassy learned from the Guyanese Foreign Minister that the Peoples Temple in San Francisco had decided to move 380 of their members to Guyana April 3 by two chartered planes. . . . In his request for Guyanese Government approval of this planned immigration, Jones reportedly had stated that the prospective immigrants "represent some of the most skilled and progressive elements of his organization and as such are most vulnerable to state repression on the part of American authorities." He also was said to have exhibited an envelope which, he claimed, contained a check for $500,000 that he intended to deposit in the Bank of Guyana to help settle the intending immigrants. He also spoke of his intention to transfer all or most of the Peoples Temple assets in the United States to Guyana.

Subsequently, the Guyanese Government granted the necessary permission for the immigration. While the record is not clear, it appears that the 380 intending immigrants travelled to Guyana in groups of 40 or 50 in the next several weeks.

The embassy figures are in direct conflict with Temple figures provided to Guy Wright, a columnist for the *San Francisco Examiner,* who wrote on June 9, 1977, that there were 151 people at the agricultural mission, including 135 "misfits from the streets of San Francisco" and "a staff of twenty-one." Wright's description of the commune, based on his interview with Jones, paints the place as a utopian correctional camp:

> You'll find a purse snatcher feeding pigs, a shoplifter hoeing corn, a transvestite driving a tractor, a prostitute and a couple of dope addicts in the sewing shed making their own clothes.
>
> They are succeeding remarkably well, according to the Rev. Jim Jones, pastor of Peoples Temple on Geary Street and originator of this unusual experiment in human salvage.
>
> "What I see is turning me into an environmental determinist," he said. "We take incorrigibles—people no one could handle. Down there they straighten themselves out. With the dramatic change in environment comes a dramatic change in the person."

Countering rumors that Jonestown was a hard-labor camp, Jones told Wright:

> Everyone works but no one is forced. . . . Pretty soon after they arrive the work ethic just makes a comeback. No one is forced to stay either. But not one person has requested to come home.

Such glowing reports of life at Jonestown were repeated time and time again—in Temple brochures soliciting donations, in Temple newspaper *Peoples Forum,* in communications with the government of Guyana. That summer 1977 progress report, issued to Guyana's Ministry of Agriculture and National Development, was one of the few reports that detailed the project's major successes with its claimed 170 varieties of plants. According to the report, the Temple farm enjoyed success with eddoes, a tropical tuber; sweet potatoes and bell yams; bitter and sweet cassava, staples cultivated mainly for the starchy, milk-white juice in their roots; several varieties of bananas, totaling two thousand pounds each month; cutlass beans, which when formed into patties and fried, the Temple claimed, tasted just like pork sausage; and a wide variety of garden vegetables and fruits, including papaya, boulangers, pinto and bora beans, tomatoes, and cucumbers. Showing promise for the future, according to the report, were other vegetables and fruit and nut trees. The only livestock raised there were chicken and pigs, both largely unsuccessful.

Although the settlers' farming techniques may have left much to be desired, their imaginations were active. They used some Robinson-Crusoe ingenuity to overcome the obstacles the jungle posed. The communards built a cassava processing plant from two iron pulleys, a three-cornered file for a grater, a five-horsepower electric motor, a tub lined with a plastic feedbag, two truck wheel rims, a ten-ton hydraulic jack, buckets for catching the juice, and other odds and ends. When the mission needed a method of planting seeds more efficient than bare hands, the jungle farmers improvised an ingenious device that could be pulled by a tractor:

> Using odds and ends from around the project site, like bicycle sprockets and chain, we created a mechanical planter that enabled us to plant 5 acres in an 8-hour day. We have since then converted our spring-tooth cultivator into a planter that covered the 5 acres in 3½ hours, using 1 driver and 4 other people. This job previously took 20–60 workers 3 to 5 days to complete.
>
> Here's how we did it: We reset the cultivator tines to match the furrows made by the wheel. Then we made a seat of boards that sits on top of the cultivator, large enough to hold four people at one time. Three-foot hoses are connected to the tines at one end, and to funnels made with cut-off plastic bleach bottles at the other end. The seeds are dropped through the funnels and the hoses to a pan set on the tines, from which they are dropped to the furrows. Another tine then follows to cover the furrows.

By far the most successful enterprise at Jonestown was the sawmill, which turned out the color-coded lumber for the prefabricated town that housed a thousand people; the system it supplied built the town in only a few months. "The system is so efficient," says the Temple's progress report, "that an 8' x 20' wall frame complete with windows and door can be completed in 15 minutes; a 12′ x 8′ wall frame complete with windows and door can be completed in 10 minutes, rafters can be completed in 5 minutes. An entire 12′ x 20′ house, rafters included, can be framed in 12 hours by a crew of three!" The sawmill was in operation twenty-four hours a day shaping the rough-cut crabwood into boards, trim, and siding. Nearby was a cabinet and furniture shop for manufacturing doors, stools, shelves, baby cribs, benches, and cupboards.

By the summer of 1977, Jonestown consisted of twenty-five prefab cottages and four dormitories, of simple single-wall construction like the cabins of a Boy Scout summer camp, elevated on stilts and painted in shades of beige, gray, blue, and green. Arranged in clusters, they encircled a central plaza that included a huge open-air pavilion that resembled a livestock barn at a county fairgrounds; a children's playground with a swing set, monkey bars, and a partially buried truck tire painted red and gold; two rustic school buildings that served grades one through seven; a dispensary, a day-care center, an ammunition storage shed, a central office and a ham radio shack. Several hundred yards away from the pavilion stood the medical clinic where Larry Schacht, a medical student who had not quite finished his internship when he was summoned to Jonestown, two nurse practitioners, and six registered nurses cared for the health needs of the community. Towering above the corrugated steel roofs were the radio antenna and a guard tower with a windmill that never seemed to work. The communards camouflaged the guard tower with brightly colored ocean scenes and a children's slide, lest visitors get the impression that Jonestown was anything like a prison camp.

All paths in Jonestown eventually led to the pavilion, where Dad—Jones had left "Father" behind in San Francisco—would exhort his followers to leave off their selfish ways and labor even harder in their common interest. The paths—some covered with asphalt, some with wooden slats—meandered past neat rows of banana bushes, broad-leaf almond trees, tin-roofed bird feeders on seven-foot poles, and dormitories with names like Harriet Tubman Place, Mary McLeod Bethune Terrace, Jane Pittman Gardens, Sojourner Truth Apartments. A path leading from the pavilion, past the ammunition shed, dead-ended at a three bedroom cottage that, by Jonestown standards, was palatial in its appointments: the home of Jim Jones. Dad's home was more spacious than any of the other quarters. It had a refrigerator stocked with catsup and other condiments, bottled salad dressing, Pepsi-Cola, meat for his self-diagnosed hypoglycemia, vitamins, and an array of drugs—uppers, downers, and painkillers—that filled most of two shelves on the door. The house had a front porch, screened in with mosquito netting, where Dad would sit with his two live-in mistresses, Maria Katsaris and Carolyn Layton, to while away the hot, muggy days. Jones's wife, Marceline, lived elsewhere in Jonestown. The house was set off at a distance of several hundred yards from the nearest cluster of cottages, which, unlike the big dorms, were identified by numbers instead of names.

Surrounding the encampment was dense and treacherous jungle, a sea of undulant green that stretched for miles in all directions in which Jonestown was a tiny island of would-be civilization, fighting daily to repel the uncontrollable vegetation. Through this unbroken growth a man might walk the twenty-five miles to the Venezuelan border as an ant might grope its way through unmowed meadow. In the other direction, one hundred and fifty miles to the south, lay Guyana's only major city, Georgetown, where the U.S. embassy maintained its fragile presence. Ten miles north and east of the encampment was Port Kaituma, a tiny community whose acknowledgments of the twentieth century included a burnt clay airstrip and a funky bar called the Weekend Discotheque, and twenty-four miles to the south and west was Matthews Ridge, accessible only by trail. Both the road and the trail were patrolled.

The guards kept the communards confined within the settlement and prevented outsiders' wandering in. According to Pat Small, the only Guyanese citizens allowed into Jonestown were government officials invited by Jones for guided tours and soul-music extravaganzas. Jonestown residents were prepared well in advance of these visits with specific instructions on what to say, if they were to say anything, and how to act. Only the thoroughly tested and most loyal were entrusted with speaking parts in these charades, and only after they had carefully rehearsed their lines.

The shroud of secrecy that kept from outsiders the truth about Jonestown's day-to-day life became an opaque blanket after the *New West* exposé hit the stands in July of 1977. While the Temple's propaganda mill in San Francisco continued to churn out the sweetness-and-light stories about the modern-day Garden of Eden, the authors of the exposé watched and waited to see the article's effect, speculating that the Temple's walls would come tumbling down, that Jones would stay in Guyana, and that his deserted followers in California would seize the day to begin their lives anew. Phil Tracy had hit Jones with a solid one-two punch in the first article by calling for government investigations of the beatings, the irregularities in property transfers, and the Temple's claim that courts, probation departments, and other government agencies had released to the Temple's care "disturbed or incorrigible youths" who eventually ended up in Guyana; and by reporting the rumors, which the Temple categorically denied, that Jones's "closest followers are planning to relocate in Guyana any time soon."

Shortly after the *New West* articles appeared, San Francisco District attorney Joseph Freitas announced that his office would conduct an investigation of Peoples Temple. His investigators confirmed in mid-August that about four hundred of Jones's followers had packed their few worldly goods and

291

moved to The Promised Land. The investigators said they based their estimates on interviews with between fifty and sixty members, some of whom had relatives still in the church. Stories were aired of Temple members abruptly quitting their jobs—those who worked outside the church—and, late at night, boarding buses bound for Miami. Once in Miami, the departing refugees checked into cheap motels, eight or more to a room, and awaited passage to Georgetown from Miami International Airport. In Georgetown, they were shuttled to Lamaha Gardens and packed into the house's five bedrooms. During the day, they were ordered to beg on the streets of the city for money and food, supposedly for the Jonestown mission. Only a small portion of what they collected went to the jungle outpost; most of it was used to fill the day-to-day needs at Lamaha Gardens.

Periodically, new faces would appear among the Temple beggars as one group left for Jonestown and another would settle into the Lamaha Gardens headquarters. The departing group would leave Georgetown aboard the *Cudjoe,* sail north along the Atlantic shore for about twenty-two hours, turn into the Kaituma River, and disembark at Port Kaituma. Some few might make the journey on a chartered plane, a matter of only two hours. At Port Kaituma, the settlers were met by the Temple's ten-wheel dump truck, which carried them ten miles through the jungle to Jonestown.

Although the hasty emigrants were told not to tell their relatives where they were going, word trickled out. Despite the relatives' pleas, there was no way to dissuade the frightened faithful from their goal. Blacks had been told that The Promised Land was their only refuge from the concentration camps that were their certain destiny in the United States; whites, that their names were on secret CIA enemies lists because of their association with Peoples Temple. Without the protection of Jim Jones, the CIA was sure to track them down and torture and kill them. Backing up the fears of the government's bogeymen were Father's "connections"; anyone who balked at making the trip would be "taken care of" after a simple phone call. Some of the recalcitrants were given beverages sweetened with powerful tranquilizers and stayed drugged throughout the trip.

Stanley Clayton was not one of the recalcitrants; although he had a reputation for being one of the Temple's most uncooperative members, no one had to sweeten his drinks with tranquilizers to get him to go to Guyana. Temple leaders wanted Stanley to ride the buses to Miami with the rest of the emigrants, but Stanley was going to fly. He had never flown before, and he had enough money to pay his own way. He was street-wise, black, and twenty-three years old. He had grown up in Oakland and done some time for armed robbery. He had a way of saying no that everybody, including Jim Jones, respected. So when Stanley said no, he was not going to go on the bus, and no, he was not going to turn over his eighty dollars pocket money, nobody messed with Stanley Clayton.

A friend who had flown before told Stanley that the drinks served on the plane made flying "easier," so Stanley drank as much of the good airlines Scotch as the flight attendants would serve him. He was celebrating his trip to The Promised Land, and when he got to New York on the first leg to Miami he was feeling no pain. He accosted complete strangers to tell them of the "vacation" he was taking in Guyana. It would be a vacation, Stanley was sure, because Jim Jones had once told him that all the rules against drinking and smoking, loving, and dancing at the discotheque on Divisadero Street were "temporary." Once everybody got settled in The Promised Land, Jones told him, there'd be drinking and partying every night. Stanley also looked forward to living in a country that was run by black people.

In Georgetown, Stanley lived and worked his first three weeks in South America on *The Lafayette*, a salty old vessel the Temple had rented to haul wood to Jonestown. While the boat was docked at the capital for those three weeks, Stanley and his Temple buddy, Cleve Newell—a street-savvy brother from LA—partied by night and spent the days recovering by partying some more. They could drink Demerara rum all night long and work the next day because their work was simply guarding the lumber on the boat. During those times when they felt energetic, they would pitch in and help the Guyanese workers load the crabwood on to the boat's creaking deck.

The Lafayette was to leave for Jonestown on August 23, Stanley's birthday—his twenty-fourth. He and Cleve bought a couple of bottles of rum for the trip. They started early. They were already drunk when they arrived at the dock at 2:30 P.M., and there were a couple of dozen new arrivals from the United States waiting to board the boat. One of the passengers was seventeen-year-old Dorothy Buckley, who had a reputation in the San Francisco Temple as a woman of easy virtue; when she sidled up to Stanley, inured as he was to the aroma of spirits, he could still smell the rum on her breath. Dorothy was on her way to freedom at last and she "wanted to enjoy herself," says Stanley. "Dorothy Buckley, she just couldn't let loose of her li'l hot self. I say hot 'cause she's gon' all the way out of her way to really put on a show, and really get somebody fired up." Dorothy finally enjoyed herself with a Guyanese crewman in one of the cabins under the deck.

The trip from Georgetown to the lagoon on the Kaituma River near Jonestown took about thirty hours, Stanley recalls. The meals on the boat were of biscuits and butter, nothing else. People in Jonestown had to be awakened to greet their friends and relatives when the boat arrived late at night. One of the first people Stanley met was his old drinking and pot-smoking buddy, Robin Gieg. Robin warned Stanley to toe the line in Jonestown. "Stanley," said Robin in a fearful whisper, "if you got any cigarettes throw 'em away. Man, you think the flo' over dere was somethin', you ain't seen nothin' yet."

Sure enough, word of Dorothy's exploits aboard *The Lafayette* was bruited about Jonestown and Jim Jones called her up on the floor. "Where's that bitch at?" Dad shouted. "Goddamnit, I want your ass up here!" The crowd shouted Dorothy up to the floor to face Dad's wrath. "Out there fuckin'," he said with disgust. "You can't even come from one country to the next without opening your goddamned legs! What made you do that?"

"'Cause I thought I was free," Dorothy replied shyly.

"Who told you that?" Dad asked.

"Stanley Clayton."

Stanley denied he told Dorothy she was free, at least not in those words, but Jim Jones sentenced him to a week of hard labor with the "hardhat crew." Dad in his mercy later commuted Stanley's sentence to five days.

Stanley's initial enthusiasm about The Promised Land was typical of those who chose to settle there and begin a new life. There were many, however, who had no choice. Among the emigrants were 267 children, twenty-two of them under temple guardianships, who were taken to The Promised Land by their guardians. Those who went with their mothers almost invariably did so without the approval—or even the knowledge—of their fathers. Often these departures occurred despite court-ordered visitation rights and child support payments. Bill Bush—the Berkeley hairdresser who once flashed a knife at Jim Jones in what was probably the first and only such incident that was not staged, whose wife, Beverly, ran the Temple's secondhand stores—last saw his son, Billy, during the summer of 1977. On October 12, 1977, Beverly wrote to Bill. "As you probably know by now," she wrote (he didn't know), "I was fortunate enough to be able to come here to Jonestown, Guyana, S.A. It's so beautiful here! Billy and I are going to be staying here indefinitely." She described briefly the flora and fauna—the chicken frogs, which, she said, "are as big as cats," and the colorful toucan birds—then made a request, universal among ex-wives but something less than reasonable in a self-sufficient commune: "Billy could use some money. If you would like to send it, you can send the regular check. I'm sure it can be cashed." Bill recalls that, "for more than a year," he sent money orders and personal checks for child support to the Temple's post office box in Georgetown. The checks came back to him canceled by the Georgetown branch of the Bank of Montreal. Bill suspected all along that Billy wasn't seeing a dime of that money, that it was probably ending up in church coffers, so he started slipping five- and ten-dollar bills in Billy's letters, hoping his son would pocket the cash and maybe get out for a hamburger now and then; Billy loved hamburgers. Instead of sending a child support check to Guyana, Bill started depositing money in a trust account. He notified Beverly of the new arrangement; she never replied.

There was little chance that Beverly and Billy would return. After Jones was exposed in the media in 1977, the chances of anyone, except his most trusted aides, from Jonestown ever setting foot on United States soil were remote. Jones's fear that something might happen to him was great enough to keep him in his private enclave; he rarely ventured out, even to Georgetown. He confided in his closest aides that the United States was forever out of the question unless he wished to spend the rest of his life in prison. He may have been right, considering the number of government investigators snooping around San Francisco, Ukiah, and Los Angeles, asking questions and chasing down leads about the Temple's nefarious operations. Five investigators from the San Francisco District Attorney's Office spent a thousand hours looking into charges of homicide, child abduction, property extortion, arson, battery, kidnapping, the use of drugs for personality control, and the diversion of welfare funds to Guyana. DA Joe Freitas told the press his chief prosecutor, Robert Graham, was "anxious to make a case" on these charges, but no indictments were forthcoming.

The investigation attracted the attention of Laurence Mann, Guyana's ambassador to the United States. Mann claims he called Freitas's office in August and was told the investigation "was closed." Freitas was, in fact, tight-lipped for several weeks about the progress of the probe; not until mid-November did he begin telling reporters who inquired that there was "insufficient evidence" to prosecute Peoples Temple. Freitas neglected to mention that on August 28, 1977, he had received a secret report, never made public, on the status of Graham's investigation. After listing the allegations against the Temple and noting the difficulties he was having finding evidence, Graham concluded:

> Except with respect to the alleged arson [of the San Francisco Temple on August 23, 1973], the Special Prosecutions unit is converting the Peoples Temple inquiry to inactive status. We will, of course, continue to talk to anyone who can provide us with or lead us to hard evidence of criminal acts in San Francisco. Otherwise, we are moving on to more promising investigatory areas.
>
> Obviously, nothing in this memorandum should be read as approving of the practices of Peoples Temple, many of which are at least unsavory and raise substantial moral and noncriminal legal questions.

Freitas's investigation reached a dead end. It wasn't the only one. On August 19, U.S. Customs agents conducted a "random search" of ninety crates the Temple was shipping to Guyana via Miami. Customs had hoped to find firearms or other contraband in the crates, but turned up only personal belongings.

The Treasury agent who had interviewed Temple defectors Grace Stoen, Elmer and Deanna Mertle, and Walt Jones—among others—filed an interim report to the State Department on August 26 about his investigation. Among the allegations in the report, based on the agent's interviews, were that the

295

Temple had smuggled firearms out of the country in false-bottomed crates and in personal luggage, and that Jones was establishing a "power base" in Guyana. The agent noted that conducting an investigation of Jones's activities in California was difficult because of the charismatic leader's "contacts" with politicians, especially in San Francisco. At the time the report was filed, U.S. Customs also informed Guyanese Customs, through the International Criminal Police Organization (INTERPOL), of the possibility of arms shipments, but random searches in the port of Georgetown also turned up nothing. Whenever guns were to be shipped to Guyana, Jones's aides were given a complete description of the containers they were shipped in, the baggage claim numbers, and any other pertinent information. Jones's aides would be sure to claim the gun-bearing containers when they arrived at the port in Georgetown, using various schemes to ensure that the inspectors did not examine the containers too closely. One simple ploy was to send one or two of Jones's young, slender courtesans down to the port of entry to flirt with the baggage inspectors. An undated memorandum written by Linda Sharon Amos, the Temple's "public relations" director in Georgetown, and obtained in Jonestown by an Associated Press reporter, indicates there were efforts to woo the inspectors before the weapons shipments:

> Two men from customs came and danced with Karen [Layton] and me (they dance very close) and were absolutely obnoxious. But we were friendly to them, and one of them was there when the stuff came through customs.

Despite the presence of an arsenal in Jonestown, the Temple's record with Guyanese Customs officials remained clean, thanks to efficacy of the smuggling ploys. Guyanese Customs finally got around to notifying INTERPOL of the unsuccessful searches on January 31, 1978. The information was passed, in turn, to U.S. Customs. According to State Department documents, U.S. embassy officials in Georgetown were unaware of the smuggling allegations until they heard them from local Guyanese officials and members of Peoples Temple. The embassy never did get a copy of the Treasury agent's August 26 report to the State Department.

The embassy was aware—only because it was receiving news clippings from northern California papers—that large numbers of Temple members were moving to Jonestown; the knowledge was further confirmed when, according to the State Department, an unnamed Guyanese official "indicated concern that the large influx of Peoples Temple members might pose problems for Guyana." That official's concern grew out of an August 22 telephone call to Richard A. McCoy, who was then the embassy's vice-consul, from Joseph Mazor, a San Francisco private investigator who said he represented the parents of seven children at Jonestown. Mazor claimed that he had been granted in California, on behalf of the parents, court orders demanding that the children be returned to the United States, and that he would soon be granted court orders for the return of twenty more children. McCoy advised Mazor he would have to take his case to the Guyanese courts, which would ultimately have to decide whether the California court orders had legal standing and whether they could be enforced against Peoples Temple.

The embassy was aware of the exodus; so were relatives of the emigrants, their employers, the government of Guyana, the press—everyone, it seemed, except the Temple leadership in San Francisco. Their official line was to deny that the movement of nearly four hundred people from one continent to another in a matter of a few weeks could be described as a "mass exodus." "Even though there are nearly a thousand [in Jonestown] now," said the Temple in a press release, "and more want to go, we are absolutely not pulling out of San Francisco or California." The Temple leadership—those who remained in San Francisco—also denied that the huge rummage sale in Redwood Valley, in the middle of August, was a sign that anyone was moving. So also was mere coincidence the evidence, as shown in public records in Mendocino, San Francisco, and Los Angeles counties, that Peoples Temple was hastily selling its properties.

Among the properties up for sale were the Temple-operated care homes, which defectors claimed were pumping thousands of dollars each month into the Temple's bulging coffers—estimated, then, and conservatively, at better than $12 million. J.C. Ortiz, an investigator for the California State Department of Health, began looking into the allegations of misuse of public funds in August of 1977, following publication of the exposés on Peoples Temple in *New West* magazine. In a six-page confidential report completed almost a year later, Ortiz concluded:

> There is evidence which indicates that irregularities do exist within board and care homes operated by members of the Peoples Temple. These irregularities include the embezzlement of resident funds, which has been referred to the Medi-Cal Investigation Unit. I currently feel that to continue this investigation without the aid of the United States Bureau of Special Consular Services would involve extensive time and money, as well as duplication of investigative services.

The report recommends that the "investigation be closed and that we extend help and cooperation to those federal agencies currently investigating Jim Jones and the Peoples Temple." Apparently because it was impossible to interview key witnesses in Guyana, the investigation—like those of DA Joe Freitas and the Treasury agent—reached a dead end.

Despite Ortiz's recommendation that the investigation be dropped, there were enough allegations in print, beginning with the *New West* magazine exposés, to keep all of the state department of health's invetigators busy for months. According to a 104-page April 1980 report by John B. Moy, a deputy attorney general who was assigned to investigate charges of "malfeasance, misfeasance or nonfeasance" on the part of health department officials, the sad truth was that the Peoples Temple investigation was treated as a political hot potato because of Jones's political connections, and was passed from department to department within the agency with no action. One of the officials in the agency who refused to act on the allegations in the Ortiz report and in the press was Mari Goldman, who headed the department that oversaw foster homes. Prior to working for the state department of health, Ms. Goldman worked in the office of Lieutenant Governor Mervyn Dymally, one of Jones's political allies.

The only health department official named in the Moy report who pressed for a Temple investigation was Muriel Evens, a staff attorney. Evens told Moy she "was dismayed by the allegations that foster children were being removed from California to Guyana, as well as the allegations of fraud and murder" in the Ortiz report. Ms. Evens kept pressing for an investigation, but her efforts also reached a dead end because health department officials agreed with Ortiz that there was no need for the state to get involved when investigations were already underway by federal agencies.

That dead end was getting crowded. The California Secretary of State's office launched an investigation that never really got off the ground into some allegedly falsely notarized documents; neither did an investigation by the Mendocino County Department of Social Services. A San Francisco Police Department investigation into allegations, by an informant, that the Temple planned to purchase a cache of rifles, shotguns, and dynamite was never pursued beyond a second interview because "there was no further information to go on," according to a December 15, 1978, *San Francisco Examiner* article by James A. Finefrock.

Those Temple defectors who had provided leads to investigators, who had freely given hours of interviews, who had tried, despite their fears, to rescue others suffering under Jim Jones's reign of terror, were deeply disappointed by the apparent lack of interest and the actual lack of progress and—in some cases—the downright ineptitude of government probes. They were glad— delighted—that Jim Jones was out of the country, probably forever; but they were worried, too, that reprisals would begin as soon as the heat was off. Whether Jones returned or not, he still had the power to make their lives miserable, for they were now easily identified as his real enemies, having spoken out in the press. They could never rest easy; they had resigned themselves to the ever-present nightmare that at any moment the "Angels"— an elite and highly secret "hit squad" Jones had designated one night at a planning commission meeting by circling the room while all eyes were closed and tapping the shoulders of the chosen few—would swoop down with their terrible swift sword and kill them, all at once or one at a time. The press offered hope. As long as Jones was kept on the defensive, the defectors believed, as long as other defectors continued to step forward to tell their stories, Jones would be too busy preparing his defenses to strike back.

The press sometimes has a short attention span. When it became apparent that Peoples Temple stories could no longer crowd plane crashes and oil prices out of the headlines, and as long as Jim Jones remained in South America refusing to communicate with anyone except his attorney, Charles Garry, and his loyal lieutenants, the press could no longer find much drama in the continuing saga of the eccentric preacher. The only avenue through which the defectors could seek redress of grievances against their former master was the courts.

Ironically, the first threat of litigation, although from a Temple defector, was not directed at Peoples Temple or Jim Jones, but at *New West* magazine and the *Mendocino Grapevine,* a weekly newspaper published in Ukiah. Against these publications, Tim Stoen—who had quit the Temple on June 12 after returning from a visit to Jonestown—announced on August 22, through a Ukiah attorney, that he was planning to file libel suits totaling $18 million. Stoen's attorney, Patrick Finnegan, told Steve Hart of *The Press Democrat* that Stoen singled out the two publications because "they were the source of most of the stories that were damaging to Tim Stoen." He stressed, however, that the threatened legal action was "not even directly related to the Peoples Temple." Stoen managed to create some front-page thunder and some speculation about the Temple's next move, but he never carried out his threat.

Two days later, Stoen's estranged wife, Grace, went before San Francisco Superior Court Judge Donald King for a temporary order granting her custody of her five-year-old son, John Victor Stoen. Tim had left the child in Jonestown, he told Tim Reiterman of the *San Francisco Examiner*, in February of 1978, "because there were guards on him. I knew Jim Jones was going to be attacked in the press and I believed I could serve as an agent of reconciliation when he came back. I expected I could get John in return." Despite objections from Jones's lawyer, Charles Garry, Judge King granted the custody order in Jones's absence.

The minor blitzkrieg of legal gambits resumed six days later when the Mertles—Elmer, Deanna, and daughter Linda—filed a $1 million lawsuit charging Jones and Peoples Temple with fraud, false imprisonment, and assault. Elmer and Deanna, who changed their names to Al and Jeannie Mills because of the many incriminating documents they signed while they were members, and Linda claimed in the lawsuit that the Temple had falsely imprisoned them with "threats of force and coercion" and had bilked them of their property.

The lawsuits could be dealt with by attorneys; the press attacks, by ignoring them or counterattacking with the usual Temple propaganda; but the threat of a visit to Jonestown by a relative was something Jones would not tolerate. Jones learned in late August from his twenty-four-year-old mistress, Maria Katsaris, that her father, Steve Katsaris, intended to fly from Washington, D.C., to Georgetown "in a few weeks." In an earlier telephone conversation with Maria, Steve had already made it clear that he thought Jones should return to the United States to answer the charges against him and that he did not believe Jones's earache was adequate justification for staying away. He had hinted also that he could believe the monstrous allegations in print; he knew most of the people quoted in the *New West* article, having been their neighbor in Mendocino County for several years. A man of conscience and compassion, the former cleric was bright, perceptive, and articulate—hardly the attributes a charlatan like Jim Jones liked to see in people curious about what he was up to.

Steve had no idea of the extent of Maria's involvement with Peoples Temple, not even when she left with the second mass exodus in late June of 1977. He had no idea she had been entrusted, as the Temple's "head of banking," with hundreds of thousands of dollars in cash. He had no idea she was one of Jim Jones's live-in mistresses. When Steve made his call in late August to tell Maria he'd be visiting "in a few weeks," he expected that Jones would be made uneasy—look at all that unfavorable press and those snoopy government agencies—but he had no idea of the depths of paranoia his threatened visit would stir.

Steve realized, given what he knew about Jones, that Maria might have been in danger in Guyana, and his visit might shake her security more than he wished. He devised an excuse for her to get away. He called his ex-wife, Maria's mother, and asked her to call Maria. "I really don't know what's happening," he said, "but I'm concerned about Maria. I've had a history of kidney problems. Maria knows this. So why don't you call Maria—I'm sure they're going to be listening in on an extension—and at the end of your conversation, just casually drop the information that I'm going to have surgery?"

Maria's mother made the call. In the next few days, Steve received several letters from Maria. In one of them, Maria said she would like to see her father before he had his surgery, and that letter was so vastly different in tone and character from the others she had written from Guyana that Steve was convinced Maria had smuggled it out of Jonestown and mailed it herself. Steve tried to contact Maria again at Lamaha Gardens, but he was told she was in Jonestown. He called the Temple in San Francisco and spoke to the radio man, Tom Adams, who was in touch with Jonestown every evening. "I want you to phone my daughter," Steve said, "and tell her that I'm going to be there on the twenty-sixth." He gave Adams the flight number and arrival time. "I know that Maria probably needs a lot of things since she intends to stay there for a long time," Steve added. "Have her say what she wants and I'll take it down to her."

While Steve awaited the reply from Jonestown, Jim Jones was coiled and ready to unleash his powers on the world. Certainly no one thought Jim Jones would retreat to his jungle hideout and forever after be silent; but few people expected his communications with the outside world to be quite so theatrical as they became. At a press conference called by Jones's attorney, Charles Garry, in San Francisco on September 8, 1977, ostensibly to answer the charges leveled against his embattled client, Garry was called to the telephone just as the conference was getting under way. Garry returned moments later to announce—in solemn tones—that the call was from a Temple official in Georgetown. There had been an incident at Jonestown. Garry said that the caller informed him that someone had tried to shoot Jim Jones "just four minutes ago." Jones escaped unharmed, Garry said, and added that the shooting incident followed close on the heels of a similar attempt to assassinate his client only two days earlier. "Three persons came on the project two days ago," Garry said. "When they left there was a shooting." The Temple later identified the assailants as "three white men" who were not connected with the church.

After the phone call, Garry proceeded to weave a web of conspiracy against Jim Jones involving "an organized, orchestrated, premeditated government campaign to destroy a politically progressive organization." As proof such a conspiracy did exist, Garry introduced Indian leader Dennis Banks, who told of his March 23 meeting with David Conn at the home of Lehman Brightman, president of United Native Americans. In an affidavit he handed out to reporters, Banks claimed that "Conn said . . . he was working with the U.S. Treasury Department, with an [Internal Revenue Service] agent, and with two men from the San Francisco Police Department." Banks, who was facing extradition to South Dakota for sentencing on convictions of assault and inciting a riot, charged that Conn had tried "to make a deal" with him. Conn, he claimed,

> . . . did not talk about my extradition. He read material that was disparaging to Jim Jones. He went on for some time. Finally I interrupted Conn. I asked him what all this stuff about Jim Jones had to do with my extradition. Conn asked me, "Well, you took money from the church, didn't you?" He said that my association with Peoples Temple could reflect very badly on my extradition. He then asked me to make a public denunciation of Jim Jones. He assured me that if I made such a denunciation, the rulings on my extradition would go in my favor. . . .
>
> Conn was obviously making a deal with me, and I was being blackmailed. Conn let me know that besides working with Treasury

agents and other government agents, that he was already working with ex-members of Peoples Temple, such as Grace Stoen, and that he had people who would talk against Jim Jones.

Banks acknowledged that the Temple had put up nineteen thousand dollars bail for his wife, Ka-Mook, who was being held in a federal prison in Kansas. "There's no way I could denounce Peoples Temple after they raised money for my wife," Banks told reporters.

Most press accounts of the incident also carried Conn's denial of Banks's charges; Conn claimed that his only motive for meeting with the Indian leader was to warn him that continued association with Peoples Temple could discredit the Indian movement. Conn also denied that he was working for the Treasury Department and that he even mentioned the subject of extradition to Banks. It was true that Conn, Klineman, and the defectors had met and spoken with a Treasury agent, but that agent—had he been willing to go public—would have denied, truthfully, any prior knowledge that Conn was going to meet with Banks. Surely he'd have shared Banks's perplexity—as did Klineman—about what motivated Conn to meet with Banks at all, given Banks's closeness to Jim Jones.

The absence of any logical motive for letting word get back to Jones that defectors were talking fed Jones's paranoia as effectively as a direct FBI raid might have. The government conspiracy theory was a flimsy web, but there were frayed threads enough for the Temple to build a circumstantial case linking Conn with his old friend Elmer Mertle, Grace, Stoen, *New West* magazine, Klineman, and the Treasury Department. *Peoples Forum,* the official organ of the Temple, screamed the news across the front page:

CONSPIRACY!
BLACKMAIL, BRIBES, FALSE TESTIMONY, FACE-
LESS ACCUSERS, & MEDIA-MANIPULATION
HAVE CHARACTERIZED A CONTINUING PLOT
TO DESTROY PEOPLES TEMPLE & JIM JONES
The pattern of a conspiracy against Peoples Temple has begun to emerge. The attempt to coerce American Indian Leader Dennis Banks into denouncing the Temple in exchange for immunity is only the tip of the iceberg. The charges and sensationalistic publicity about the Temple have come as a result of a well-coordinated effort to get individuals, both ex-members and others, to supply damaging testimony against the church, in some cases for various favors. This kind of plotting is not unfamiliar to those who have experienced efforts by reactionary elements to destroy individuals and organizations that are deemed a threat to their interest.

302

The weeks preceding and following the Garry-Banks press conference were busy weeks for attorneys. While Garry was gathering the ammunition for the "conspiracy" charges, Grace Stoen's attorney, Jeff Haas, was pressing the custody issue concerning her son, John Victor Stoen. Although Grace had been granted a temporary custody order in San Francisco Superior Court on August 24, the order had no legal standing in Guyana, where John-John resided with Jim Jones. During the first week of September, Haas flew to Georgetown hoping he could persuade the courts there to issue a similar order. When Haas arrived in Georgetown, he met with Richard A. McCoy, the chargé of the embassy, who assisted him in making the necessary contacts with Guyanese officials.

Although McCoy was unconvinced that anything was amiss at Jonestown—he had visited and was favorably impressed—he assisted Haas in his contacts with the Guyanese judiciary. Haas obtained a favorable ruling from a Georgetown court summoning Jones to appear to explain why John Victor Stoen was in his custody. Haas flew to Jonestown with a marshal from the Guyana court to serve the summons. He was met by a "very hostile" group of Temple members who claimed Jones was not around. Later that same day, Haas met a group of Guyanese immigration officials who were surprised that he hadn't made contact with Jones; they had spent the entire morning with him.

Haas went to court a second time and obtained a court order permitting him to serve the summons on Jim Jones by posting it on three buildings at Jonestown and handing copies to Jones's aides. Haas returned to Jonestown accompanied again by a marshal of the court. They tried to post the notices on the buildings, but angry Temple members tore them down and threw them back into the marshal's Jeep. The Temple's flagrant disregard for the laws of Guyana angered the Guyanese judiciary, who responded with a ruling on September 10, by a justice of the Guyana Supreme Court, that ordered the arrest of John Victor Stoen, who was to be brought into the custody of the court, along with a summons ordering Jim Jones to appear to show cause why he should not be held in contempt.

Jones learned of the ruling and flew into a fearsome tirade. According to Deborah Layton Blakey, who was, at the time Jones received the court order, a high-ranking Temple official in San Francisco, she and Terri Buford—Jones's public relations adviser in the same city and a journalism graduate from UC Berkeley—"were instructed to place a telephone call to a high-ranking Guyanese official [Deputy Prime Minister Ptolemy Reid] who was visiting the United States and [to] deliver the following threat: unless the government of Guyana took immediate steps to stall the Guyanese court action regarding John Stoen's custody, the entire population of Jonestown would extinguish itself in a mass suicide by 5:30 P.M. that day." It was the wronged-martyr ploy taken to the extreme; Blakey says Jones called this tactic the "crazy-nigger approach." To cover all bases, Jones had his aides place similar "crazy-nigger" calls to high-ranking Guyanese officials, according to information Deborah deciphered on the Temple short-wave radio. The ploy worked, at least temporarily.

According to the State Department, the warrant for John Stoen and the summons for Jim Jones remained unsigned as of September 17, "apparently because of intervention by Guyanese government authorities." When McCoy learned of the efficacy of Jones's ploy, he sent a "formal note" to Guyana's foreign minister expressing concern "over the apparent intrusion of Guyanese government authorities in a case that was solely a matter for the courts to decide." Four days later, the foreign minister informed the embassy that the Guyana government would act on the court order. Jim Jones was never summoned to appear. John Victor Stoen was never placed in court custody.

While attorney Jeff Haas was learning firsthand about the merciless bite of Guyana's judiciary and attorney Charles Garry was spinning the web of conspiracy against Jim Jones, Steve Katsaris was patiently awaiting a response from his daughter in Jonestown. On September 9, the day after Garry's press conference, Temple radioman Tom Adams called Katsaris to tell him that poor radio reception made it impossible to reach Maria. Steve was worried about his daughter's safety; he had read in the newspapers the story of the alleged assassination attempt on Jim Jones. Steve picked up the phone and tried to sound casual, unconcerned.

"You keep trying," he told Adams, "and I'll be down there the twenty-sixth. There's still a couple of weeks. Let me know."

Steve was awakened at four o'clock the next morning by the ringing of his telephone. Four o'clock phone calls are not a frequent occurrence in the Katsaris home; Steve was certain that his aged mother was dying or that Trinity School was burning down. With the adrenaline already pumping through his veins, he picked up the receiver and heard a quiet, serene voice: "Mr. Katsaris, you don't know us. We're part of the group that left Peoples Temple. We hear that you're planning to go down to Guyana. You shouldn't do that. Please don't do that."

The caller hung up. Steve hadn't uttered a word.

Nearly twenty-four hours later, this time at three o'clock in the morning, Steve was again awakened. The caller was a woman who spoke in a whisper: "Uh, look, if you're still planning to go down there, don't go. That's a strange group. A lot of things could happen." Steve tried to talk with the woman, but she hung up.

The next night about the same hour, the voice was that of a young black man: "Look, you live out on a ranch all by yourself. You could be burned down. I wouldn't mess around with Peoples Temple." Again, before Steve could say anything, the voice clicked off.

When Steve's phone rang again the fourth night, he wasn't at all certain what to expect. Tom Adams was calling from the Temple in San Francisco. Maria was on the radio from Jonestown; Tom said he would be patching her into the phone system in moments. Maria tried to speak to Steve, but there was a high-pitched squeal that obliterated her words. "I can't hear you!" Steve shouted into the phone. "I can't hear you!"

Maria's voice came through a few phrases at a time, alternating with the squeal. That squeal, Steve thought, sounded exactly like the effect of another radio transmitter jamming the one Maria was on; he'd heard it before while flying. There was a pause, then Maria's voice again.

"Don't come down now," she said. "It's not appropriate. . . . Come down in December . . . when a group of prominent clergy . . . will be visiting." Maria sounded stilted, as if she were repeating coached phrases between the squealing interruptions.

"Well, look, honey," replied Steve, "it won't be convenient for me to come down in December. I don't want to come down with a group of prominent clergy. I'm going to be in Washington in a couple of weeks, and I'll come down then."

"The government doesn't want visitors down here."

"Why, Maria?"

"Because Jim Jones has been shot at in the jungle," she answered. She continued to sound as if she were reading cue cards.

"Maria, you know I'm not going to shoot at anybody," Steve said matter-of-factly. "Besides, I'm going to be in Washington, and I'll have some friends of ours in government take me around to the Guyanese embassy, and I'm sure they'll clear me for travel down there." He continued, nonchalant. "I'll meet you in Georgetown," he said. "I don't need to come out to the project."

There was a pause. In a few moments, Maria was back on, saying that she wouldn't be in Georgetown on the twenty-sixth; she'd be on Temple business in Venezuela. Steve remained unruffled. Nothing Maria presented as an obstacle was going to be a problem at all.

"I'll meet you in Venezuela," he offered.

"I'm only going to be there a few days."

"We'll just have dinner together one night, then."

"I'm going to be there with my fiancé."

It was the first time Maria had disclosed the fact that she was engaged.

"For God's sake, what fiancé?" Steve asked.

"Oh, you would like him."

"Well, does he have a name?"

"Larry . . ." The last name of the lucky lad was lost in the radio transmission.

"Well, what does he do?"

"He's the doctor down here."

"Well, honey, I'd be delighted to meet you and your fiancé for dinner in Venezuela."

There was another pause. A few moments later, Maria returned to the microphone, yelling. "DON'T COME DOWN! DON'T COME DOWN! I WON'T BE ABLE TO SEE YOU! DON'T COME DOWN!"

Never in the past had Maria become hysterical, never had she shrieked and screamed at her father; they had always been close and loving. They had always been able to count on each other's affection. Steve was worried.

"Maria, if you can hear me, just hang on, 'cause I'm coming down. I'm going to use every diplomatic, legal avenue open to me to come down. *Just hang on.* I don't know if you can hear, but hang on. . . ." The radio transmission went dead.

The next morning, Steve got in touch with his attorney, Barry Wood. Barry had known Jim Jones back in the days when the Redwood Valley preacher served on the board of the Mendocino County Legal Services Foundation; Barry Wood was the director. Wood advised Steve to send a telegram to Jones detailing the difficulties he had communicating with Maria and advising Jones that he, Katsaris, would be arriving in Guyana on the twenty-sixth of the month on his attorney's advice. Steve sent the telegram and waited several days. Jones never replied.

Steve flew on to Washington, D.C., and met an old school chum, Art Mendakis, chief of staff for the Congressional Subcommittee for Inter-American Affairs. Steve told Mendakis the story of Maria and her involvement with Peoples Temple. Mendakis offered to take his old friend around to the State Department, the Guyana embassy, and Vice-President Walter Mondale's office. At the State Department, Steve told the story to Frank Tuminia, who headed the Guyana desk. Tuminia confirmed he had heard "some strange reports" about Jonestown. At the Guyana embassy, Steve checked with Ambassador Laurence Mann's aides to determine whether Maria was telling the truth when she said that Guyana was not welcoming American visitors. Steve was told he didn't even need a visa if he wasn't staying longer than two weeks. Steve then went to the vice-president's office and told his story to John McFeeney, Mondale's military adviser, and McFeeney promised he would cable the embassy in advance of Steve's arrival in Georgetown.

On September 26, Steve flew out of Washington and by midnight had landed at Timehri International Airport. He checked into the Pegasus Hotel—an eight-story cylindrical building that resembles the Capitol Record Tower in Hollywood—at two o'clock in the morning. Six hours later, Steve walked into the U.S. consulate, knowing that McFeeney's cable from the Office of the Vice-President of the United States had preceded him. He approached the desk of Richard McCoy not with his hat in his hand but with supreme confidence. "I'm going to get my daughter," he thought, "and I'm going to leave." He had been told McCoy was the contact at the consulate who was in charge of all matters concerning Peoples Temple.

"I've been expecting you," said McCoy, a fortyish, no-nonsense bureaucrat with a barbershop haircut and dark plastic-frame glasses. His desk was tidy. As is the custom in Georgetown, he wore a lightweight shirt-jacket instead of a suit and tie.

"You got the cable," said Steve, anticipating that McCoy would comment on the communiqué from the vice-president's office.

McCoy did not reply. Instead he handed Steve a handwritten transcript of a radio message from Jonestown that Paula Adams had delivered to the embassy. The message read:

> I'm Maria Katsaris. I'm twenty-four years old. I'm engaged to be married. I'm very happy down here. I've had a traumatic childhood. I don't wish to see my father again.

McCoy quickly explained that he had told Paula Adams he could not officially accept the transcript because anyone could have written it. McCoy said he had advised Adams to bring Maria to the embassy, have her identify herself with her passport, and tell him directly her objections to seeing her father. McCoy had promised Adams that if Maria herself told him she did not wish to see her father, the embassy would cable Steve immediately and give him that message. Adams said a face-to-face meeting was not possible; Maria, she said, did not want to see her father under any circumstances because he was a "sexual deviate" and had "sexually abused Maria" when she was a child.

Steve was stunned. "Jesus Christ, McCoy," he said, "something's wrong! My daughter didn't send that message. My daughter could never say anything like that. I'm really worried. Why are they going to these crazy extremes to keep me from seeing her?"

Steve asked McCoy to accompany him to Jonestown. McCoy refused; he had just been there the previous week. Besides, he was too busy. Steve was desperate to see his daughter and, with this latest news, more than ever concerned about her well-being; McCoy's attitude irked him. He would charter a plane, Steve told McCoy, if McCoy would call Lamaha Gardens to make arrangements for Steve's solo visit. The official got on the phone and talked to Paula Adams. Adams refused to arrange a meeting with Maria because the problem was "a family matter."

Although McCoy advised Steve not to go to Jonestown uninvited because he could be arrested for trespassing, Steve was determined. Steve asked McCoy if there was a way he could bypass Lamaha Gardens and communicate directly with Jonestown. McCoy told him the main post office in town had a government-provided short-wave radiophone available for public use, and advised Steve to try that. Steve tried for two days, but there was "too much

307

traffic" on the primitive communications system for him to get a message through to Jonestown. Steve did manage to contact a charter service at Ogle Field, a tiny airstrip on the outskirts of Georgetown, and the pilot agreed to fly Steve up to Port Kaituma the following day, September 28, at eight o'clock in the morning. Steve drove out to the airport at the appointed hour. He found the plane but not the pilot. He waited on the airstrip several hours. The pilot never showed.

Steve returned to the consulate the next morning and told his latest tale of woe to McCoy, who advised him to go back to Washington and buttonhole as many government officials as he could get to listen to him. "Jim Jones carries a lot of clout down here," McCoy explained. Steve took the next plane out of Georgetown and arrived in Washington on September 30, where he spent the next two weeks talking. He talked to Frank Tuminia of State, Guyana's ambassador Laurence Mann, the International Human Rights Commission, and aides to Senator Hubert Humphrey, Congressman Don Clausen, and Congressman Philip Burton. Everyone who heard Steve listened intently to his story: none of them could promise any action.

While Steve was in Washington, a deluge of letters hit the State Department, several members of Congress, and the U.S. embassy in Georgetown. The letters were from Temple members and all of them discussed the Stoen custody case. At two court hearings, on September 23 and October 3, a new issue surfaced to cloud the case. Jim Jones's attorneys argued for inclusion in the proceedings of an affidavit by Joyce Touchette. "Grace Stoen gave me notarized parental consent and power of attorney dated March 1976," said Touchette in her affidavit, "in which she and her husband, Timothy Stoen, consented for John Stoen to be taken to Guyana to live and be cared for under my guardianship or custody." Jones's attorneys submitted the signed document to which Touchette refers. The judge examined the document and reversed the earlier ruling that John Victor Stoen was to be placed in court custody. The judge also reversed the order summoning Jones to appear, although the arrest order was left pending—as was the entire custody case.

Steve Katsaris returned to California in mid-October and contacted Al and Jeannie Mills to set up a meeting with them, Grace Stoen, and other Temple defectors. Because of Steve's daughter's close connection with Jim Jones, the Millses were initially reluctant to arrange such a meeting, but Steve assured them his only purpose was to learn as much as he could about Maria's role in the Temple. At the meeting, besides the Millses and Grace Stoen, were Neva Sly, the estranged wife of Don Sly, and Mickey Touchette, daughter of Charles and Joyce Touchette. Steve's innocent, attractive daughter—whose classic Greek features might have graced an ancient urn—was utterly loyal and devoted to Jim Jones. Early on, the group told Steve, Maria was greatly feared in the Temple because of her penchant for reporting even the slightest transgressions of Temple rules to the planning commission. She rose quickly through the Temple ranks, they said, especially after she started sleeping with Jim Jones—her first lover—sometime in 1974. Steve learned that Liz Forman, the classroom aide at Trinity School who first interested Maria in the Temple, had left the Temple in 1976.

The defectors put Steve in touch with Liz Forman. She told Steve more about Maria's role in Peoples Temple. She told him that Maria sometimes had "two hundred thousand dollars or more in her room, stacked all around in piles," and that Jones entrusted Maria with that money on flights to banks in Caracas, Trinidad, and Panama City. She told Steve about an undated suicide note Maria had written and signed; should Maria ever defect, and were the Angels to "take care of her," the note would be placed on Maria's body. She told Steve of statements both she and Maria had signed alleging that Steve was a "sexual deviate" who had "molested children at Trinity School," which was staffed by "dopers and homosexuals," and was "involved in a gigantic welfare fraud scheme."

Armed with new information on the Temple's modus operandi, Steve flew back to Washington and conferred with Ambassador Mann. After hearing Steve's story, Mann promised he would insist, to Jones, that Maria have a face-to-face meeting with her father. While Steve was in his office, Mann called Georgetown and repeated his insistence to a high-ranking Guyanese official. Two days later, Steve got a call from Mann, who was in Georgetown. Mann told him a meeting was in the works. "I've just spoken to Bishop Jones by short wave," Mann said, "and he says of course you can see your daughter. He encourages the closest ties of children and their families. When can you be down? Can you be down Tuesday?"

Steve was there on Monday, November 7. On Tuesday, Mann dropped by the Pegasus Hotel to inform Steve he had been in touch with the Temple and that it would not be possible to bring Maria to Georgetown until Wednesday. Steve got the same story for Thursday and Friday. Mann called again on Saturday and assured Steve that Maria would be in Georgetown at four o'clock that afternoon. Four o'clock passed without word of Maria. At five o'clock, Mann called Steve's hotel with news of another delay. Mann, who admitted he was getting "miffed" with the Temple's delaying tactics, said he had been told that Maria was in Georgetown but could not meet her father for dinner because she "was not feeling well from the trip." Steve was miffed, too. He called Lamaha Gardens immediately and asked to speak to his daughter. A woman's voice asked him to hold on; ten minutes later, a man's voice came on the line and said, "Maria is not here. She's out to dinner." Steve simply left the message that Maria should call him when she returned.

Steve waited in his hotel room all night for the phone to ring. At 7:15 the next morning—Sunday—Paula Adams called. Maria would be able to see Steve in forty-five minutes, she said. Steve called Richard McCoy and asked him to come along to the meeting, which was to be held at the home where Ambassador Mann slept with Paula Adams when he was in Georgetown. McCoy agreed; he was already at the house when Steve arrived, and so were Ambassador Mann, Paula Adams, Carolyn Layton, two men from the Temple who were never introduced, and Maria.

Steve had been told to expect Maria to be much thinner than he remembered her, but she did not seem to have lost much weight. Her complexion, however, had become sallow; it seemed to belie her reports, in her letters to Steve, of Jonestown's healthy environment. Under her eyes were dark circles from lack of sleep—a badge of merit within the Temple, evidence of true dedication. Steve tried to make eye contact with Maria, but her eyes seemed not to focus and she kept avoiding her father's glance. Steve walked over to hug her and she "sort of just turned her face to the side; not that she didn't want me to kiss her, but she just couldn't look at me."

Steve wanted to sit across from Maria, but Carolyn Layton directed her to sit next to him, presumably to avoid eye contact. Steve touched Maria on the arm; she was rigid. Before he could utter a single word, she launched into a tirade. "Because of you," she said to her father, "Guyana has been blackballed in the International Human Rights Commission. You are a member of the CIA. I've seen proof that you're in league with a right-wing congressman to destroy Peoples Temple." She went on and on in a voice that was nearly hysterical while Steve strained to appear calm and controlled. After a few moments Maria, like a tape recorder with old batteries, ran down and stopped talking.

Ambassador Mann expressed some surprise at Maria's allegation that Guyana had been "blackballed" by the International Human Rights Commission. "I haven't heard that," he said. Maria had no response. Steve zeroed in gently and asked Maria whether she was aware he had tried to meet with her the previous month. Maria said she was. Steve asked her whether she was aware that Paula Adams had told McCoy "that the reason you didn't see me is [that] I was a sexual deviate, a child molester, and [had] abused you sexually?"

"That is a subject we shall not discuss," said Maria, sounding again like a tape recorder.

"For God's sake, child," chimed the ambassador, "your father's come down here. It's a subject you have to discuss!"

"That is a subject we shall not discuss," she repeated.

Ambassador Mann was incredulous. "If one of my children said that about me," he said, "and refused to talk about it, I would be hurt to the point of death."

"That is a subject we shall not discuss."

Steve tried another approach. "I've heard some things that worry me," he said. "I want you to listen to me. I'm worried that you've signed an undated suicide note, that they've threatened to kill you. Is that true?"

"What is your source of information?" Maria demanded.

"God, Maria, that's not important. Just tell me. If it's not true, I won't worry. If it is true, I want you to trust that we can give you protection."

"If you do not reveal your source of information," Maria answered dispassionately, "that is a subject we shall not discuss."

The meeting went on for two hours with nothing more than rote responses from Maria. Steve assured her there would be an emergency passport and an airline ticket waiting for her at the U.S. embassy any time she wanted to leave. Toward the end of the meeting, Steve began to worry that if Maria did show signs of breaking, the Temple might kill her, so he eased his questioning and gave the impression that the Temple had won. He told Maria he was convinced that she was staying in Jonestown of her own accord, that she was old enough to decide on her own what she wanted to do with her life. He added that he loved her and would forgive her for everything she had said about him. Maria had no response. Steve got up and left. He returned to his hotel room, packed his belongings, and caught the next flight to Washington, where for the fourth time he spent a week "knocking on all those goddamned doors."

The press reports on Peoples Temple had eased considerably by November of 1977. What began as a·flood in July had subsided to a trickle. The Temple's image was losing some of its tarnish; it was regaining its credibility as a force in San Francisco's leftist community, even starting to regain some of the leftist leaders it had befriended in the past. The Temple was definitely on the comeback trail when, on November 13, the *San Francisco Examiner* carried a front-page article by Tim Reiterman on the tragic story of the Houston family. The story centered on Sammy Houston, an Associated Press photographer for forty years, whose family had been torn apart by the involvement of his son, Bob Houston, in Peoples Temple. The article told how, in October 1976, Bob was crushed and mutilated under the wheels of a flatcar at the San Francisco railyard where he worked; how Sammy's two teenaged granddaughers, Patty and Judy, left the Bay Area in August of 1977 on what was purported to be a Temple vacation to New York. The next time Sammy heard from his granddaughters, a few weeks later, they were sending him letters from the Temple's agricultural mission in Guyana. Sammy decided to speak out, he explained to Reiterman, because he was scheduled to have his cancerous larynx removed and would not be speaking much longer.

The Sammy Houston story enraged Temple leaders; they had believed the heat was off. "The article in the San Francisco *Examiner* was the last straw in months of an organized, well-financed campaign designed to destroy the very fabric of this community's most effective advocate of Third World, minority and progressive struggles," wrote *Peoples Forum*. Three days after the article appeared, the Temple set up an early morning picket line in front of the *Examiner* Building. Marceline Jones led the pickets. They carried signs

311

accusing the *Examiner* of "McCarthyism" and "printing lies." The Temple claimed there were five hundred demonstrators; other observers estimated the crowd at one hundred and fifty. The highlight of the day-long demonstration was Marceline's carrying, by hand, a letter to Reg Murphy, the *Examiner's* executive editor. The letter read in part:

> We deny all the distorted allegations, half-truths, innuendoes, and outright lies made against us. We, the undersigned, represent the members of Peoples Temple who demand that an apology is in order. If reason does not succeed, then we will begin litigation.

The *Examiner* never apologized, and the Temple never sued.

The Sammy Houston article attracted the attention of Democratic Congressman Leo Ryan of San Mateo, who had known Sammy and his family since the 1960s. Leo Ryan was at that time an English and social studies teacher at Capuchino High School in San Bruno with a penchant for inspiring students to make something of their lives. Bob Houston had been one of his students. When the Capuchino High School band was invited to participate in the 1961 inauguration of President John F. Kennedy, Leo Ryan was the faculty sponsor. Sammy had been assigned by the Associated Press to help cover the event. He and Ryan roomed together in Washington. Not only did the two become good friends during their brief stay in the nation's capital, but Ryan believed afterward that he owed Sammy a favor. Sammy had photographed Ryan walking down Pennsylvania Avenue with a large group of Capuchino High School students on either side, and the photograph was reproduced widely in West Coast publications. Ryan, at the time mayor of South San Francisco, was aspiring to a higher elective office, and he believed that Sammy's photograph helped him win a seat in the State Assembly. Less than four years later, Ryan was elected to Congress—the first Democrat to represent that district in a hundred years. In 1968, Ryan won the nomination of both Democratic and Republican parties.

When Congressman Ryan read about his old friend Sammy in the November 13 *Examiner,* he was deeply moved. He was conducting, at that time, what he called "in-home visits" nearly every week. Ryan shunned the large public meetings other congressmen held in their home districts and preferred instead to meet for a half hour at a time in the homes of his constituents. Ryan asked Joe Holsinger, his chief of staff in California, to schedule an "in-home visit" with Sammy Houston as soon as possible.

Sammy had already undergone the surgery that removed his voice box when Ryan and Holsinger visited his house. Sammy communicated on a chalkboard while his wife, Nadyne, filled in details of the narrative. Ryan watched and listened, and when Sammy finished the story, Ryan put his arms around his old friend and told him, "Sammy, I promise you, no matter what happens, I'll do everything I can to get your granddaughters back for you." Everyone in the room—including Ryan, who stood six feet two and towered over the others—cried.

Steve Katsaris was not aware of the congressman's meeting with Houston in California when he returned from his frustrating visit to Washington, D.C. One of Steve's first stops in California was the home of Al and Jeannie Mills. They informed Steve that Tim Stoen had decided to surface after months of silence and join his estranged wife, Grace, in her custody battle for their son, John Victor Stoen. Steve met with Tim and other Temple defectors who had relatives in Jonestown, and they began talking about forming an organization to bring their loved ones back to the United States. Some of those in the group had never been Temple members but were, like Steve, grief-stricken that their sons and daughters, or mothers and fathers, sisters and brothers, had followed the cult to Guyana. Sherwin Harris, ex-husband of Linda Sharon Amos, suggested calling the group Concerned Relatives. His daughter, Lian, was in Guyana with her mother, and he was concerned about Lian's safety.

Members of Concerned Relatives agreed that unless there was constant pressure on government to do something, Jones would keep their relatives incommunicado in the jungle for as long as he wished, brainwashing them into believing they would be killed if they returned to the United States. They also feared that Jones, in a fit of madness, would talk his followers into committing the ultimate act for the cause: a mass suicide. Pressure on government seemed the only route to take. The press had done its best, had done a thorough job of exposing Jones, but it seemed to have run out of steam and the Temple was again finding room to operate. With the demonstration at the *Examiner* Building and the constant barrage of information regurgitated from the Temple's presses on the so-called conspiracy to destroy a "progressive" organization, the Temple seemed to be regaining some of its former influence. At the least, the Temple appeared to be making a comeback as a persecuted cult that continued to flourish despite general disfavor created by the press. Countless exposés had been written about other cults—the Moonies, the Scientologists, the Hare Krishnas, the Children of God, Synanon—but to little avail. Not only did these cults continue to flourish, but some of them had joined together in a move toward mutual self-preservation by forming a group called Alliance for the Preservation of Religious Liberty (APRL). Although there is no evidence that Peoples Temple ever joined APRL, there is evidence of a minor alliance with Synanon, the communal drug rehabilitation project that evolved into a paranoid and heavily armed cult similar in many ways to Peoples Temple. Receipts obtained from the Temple show that Synanon donated to the Temple large quantities of food service items—everything from paper plates to food chests to cartons of spaghetti—from its warehouse at Oyster Point south of San Francisco, on December 12, 1977. There was another large shipment on December 15 consisting mostly of kitchen utensils—dishes, loaf pans, and appliances. Both receipts have the notation "For use in Guyana only." Again on December 20 there was another donation, of paint and sunscreen lotion, and another on March 10, 1978, of clothing, shoes, rubber boots, and sports equipment.

Like Synanon, Peoples Temple was, at least in the posture it assumed, the wrongfully persecuted social cause. Despite the Temple's hysterical output of propaganda about conspiracy theories, the media seemed not to be interested, and the frustrated members in San Francisco again took to the streets on December 24 and 27 with placards and sandwich boards. The demonstrators, reported the January 1978 *Peoples Forum,* were

> . . . determined to convey what *really* lies behind the anti-Temple publicity that has inundated San Francisco. Articles vindicating the Temple have seldom appeared anywhere but on the back pages of the obituary columns. Placards, street parades and demonstrations seem to be the only way we can get the truth out to people. We are not sure anybody is listening or that many care. We would not be surprised if we were short-lived.

In a letter from Jonestown, Jim Jones, too, echoed the mood of doom and desperation. The letter was printed in the same issue of *Peoples Forum:*

> I will be back one day. But just as others who have been courageous enough to stand up and speak their minds in America have paid the final price—whether revolutionary as the first Americans who believed in liberty or death, or whether nonviolent, like Martin Luther King—I also expect to die for my beliefs. And in these days you don't have to be as great a man as Martin Luther King to die for taking a stand. Often I wish I could be there with you, but I had no choice. . . . I am not about to let us be used as an excuse to bring hardship down on the people of the United States. . . .

For members of Concerned Relatives, the hardship was the inability to communicate freely with their loved ones. The relatives knew all too well that whatever Jim Jones said, the opposite was probably true; that whatever he blamed on others was a projection of his own motives and behavior. Members of Concerned Relatives had no problem accepting the truth of the preacher's psychological aberrations, but convincing the people with the power to do something—congressmen, State Department officials, other government leaders—did present problems. On Steve Katsaris's fifth trip to Washington, D.C., he had an opportunity to enlighten another political leader on the subject of Peoples Temple, a leader with whom he had not yet met. Steve found himself in the plane sitting across the aisle from San Francisco Mayor

George Moscone. Steve poured out the entire agonizing story, recounted all his frustrations in trying to regain his brainwashed daughter, Maria, while Moscone listened. When Steve was finished, Moscone turned to him and said, "Gee, Steve, I'm sorry to hear this, and I'll say a lot of prayers for Maria."

Steve met Tim Stoen in Washington and together they lobbied Congress and the State Department. For a week they tried to talk someone in government into taking action against Jim Jones, then Tim had to fly to Georgetown to join Grace in another round in the custody case before the woefully slow Guyanese judiciary. Before they could appear in court—armed this time with a joint custody order signed by a San Francisco judge—Guyanese immigration officials informed them their visas had been canceled and that they would have to leave the country within twenty-four hours. The Stoens went to the U.S. embassy with their problem and were told the arbitrary expulsion order had been issued by a "high-ranking Guyanese official." The embassy protested the expulsion the following day "in a formal diplomatic note" and the government rescinded the expulsion order.

Even though the court took no action on the custody case, the presence of Tim and Grace in Georgetown caused Jim Jones tremendous consternation. On January 16, Temple representatives delivered to the U.S. consulate a copy of the February 6, 1972, affidavit signed by Tim Stoen in which he acknowledged "under penalty of perjury" that he had asked Jones "to sire a child by my wife, Grace Lucy (Grech) Stoen, who had previously, at my insistence, reluctantly but graciously consented thereto." When Stoen learned that the document was in the hands of the embassy, he insisted that he was the natural father and that Jones asked him to draft the document as a sign of unwavering loyalty to the cause. Stoen admitted he acted "foolishly" in drafting the affidavit, which he assumed had been destroyed years before.

Jones's emotional fervor over the Stoen case was evident during an official State Department visit to Jonestown on February 2, 1978. The two visiting officials, Frank Tuminia of the State Department's Guyana Desk and John Blacken, the embassy's deputy chief of mission, both reported, according to the State Department, that Jones kept ranting about conspiracies against the Temple and that one member of the group around him vowed the communards "would die before giving up the child." Both officials concluded, as had others before them, that no one was being held against his will at Jonestown.

The press in the United States neglected to pick up news of the paternity dispute until February 21, when Jones told his side of the controversy to *San Francisco Examiner* reporter Tim Reiterman in a surprise telephone patch from Jonestown. "I am the father," Jones told Reiterman. "I have taken a statement [in support of his paternity] from one parent under penalty of perjury. I have sworn statements from hundreds of people." Jones further claimed he was in the delivery room at Santa Rosa Memorial Hospital when John Victor Stoen was born. Stoen countered the claim by producing a "Consent to Admission of

Expectant Father to Delivery Room" as proof that he was present at the birth. The attending physician, Dr. John Bodle, said he believed that the man in the delivery room was Tim Stoen, but that he would "find it difficult to swear in a court of law after all these years."

John Victor Stoen, according to Jonestown survivors, lived in Jim Jones's cabin and was convinced that Maria Katsaris was his mother, that Jim Jones was his father. John believed that Grace Stoen was the most evil, destructive person on earth. When Grace was in Georgetown, Stanley Clayton recalls, Jones called a "white night"—a general alert—in Jonestown. Everyone was summoned to the pavilion and ordered to encircle the commune armed with rifles, cutlasses, and other weapons. "It didn't make any fuckin' sense," says Clayton. "She's in Georgetown, and here we were standin' out there with cutlasses and shit, waitin' for Grace Stoen to come here. I mean, it didn't make any fuckin' sense to me."

While the communards mobilized for the imminent arrival of the most dangerous person on earth, a Temple delegation of Marceline Jones, Terri Buford, Jack Beam, and Deanna K. Wilkinson lobbied the halls of Congress. The Temple's strategy, apparently, was to attempt to discredit Stoen, who had made an effort with Congress less than a month earlier. The delegation extolled the virtues of Jonestown while they tried to dissuade congressmen from assisting the Stoens with letters of support for their custody battle. As soon as the delegation left Washington, letters poured in from Temple members on both continents. President Carter received letters supporting Jones from Assemblyman Willie Brown, Angela Davis, San Francisco Supervisor Harvey Milk, and several prominent black leaders.

Desperate to attract attention and support, the Temple made a grandstand play on March 14 with a letter signed by Pamela Moton that was addressed to every senator and congressman in the United States, a total of 535 pieces of mail. The letter was an omen of what was to come:

> We at Peoples Temple have been the subject of harassment by several agencies of the U.S. Government, and are rapidly reaching the point at which patience is exhausted. Radical Trotskyite elements which defected from our organization when we refused to follow their violent course have been orchestrating a campaign against us. Two of these, Michael Cartmell and Jim Cobb, were actually discovered making ammunition several years ago. . . . To date, several agencies have been attempting various forms of harassment. First was the Social Security, which tried to deny legitimate beneficiaries of their rights by cutting off all checks that were coming to Guyana. Through the intervention of various government officials, we were able to have this reinstated as it should have been.
>
> Now, however, we see that the IRS and the Treasury Dept. and

even the Federal Communications Commission, are trying to initiate ways to cut off our lifelines. The FCC has suddenly decided to pursue a very minor complaint that was registered a year ago. It is clear that the intention is to disrupt our essential medium of communication, amateur radio. . . . We cannot believe that you would want to see this, nor would you in any way condone such an organized effort to "starve out" hundreds of U.S. citizens, who are seeking to live in peace and be a credit to the U.S. elsewhere. These same agencies and elements in the press would seek to destroy any progressive thinking individual. . . .

We receive letters weekly from Russia, as well as from people in other parts of the world who have heard of the project, offering advice and assistance. In fact, several overtures have been made from Russia, which sees our current harassment as a form of political persecution. We do not want to take assistance from any people nor do we want to become an international issue. We also do not intend to be starved out by having our legitimately earned income cut off through the efforts of Trotskyite people and embittered malcontents. We have no political aspirations whatsoever. Jim Jones has spent the last 8 months working to develop the project in Guyana. We wish to continue to do so unmolested and unhampered.

The letter ended with a not-so-subtle warning:

. . . It seems cruel that anyone would want to escalate this type of bureaucratic harassment into an international issue, but it is equally evident that people cannot be forever continually harassed and beleaguered by such tactics without seeking alternatives that have been presented. I can say without hesitation that we are devoted to a decision that it is better even to die than to be constantly harassed from one continent to the next. I hope you can look into this matter and protect the right of over 1,000 people from the U.S. to live in peace.

The letter was so completely ignored that it wasn't even mentioned, much less reproduced, in a May 1979 report, 782 pages long, to the House Committee on Foreign Affairs on the tragedy of Peoples Temple

The letter caused great consternation among members of Concerned Relatives, who were well aware of the implications of the "decision that it is better even to die." Less than a month later, on April 11, Concerned Relatives countered the death threat with the delivery of a fifty-page document— "Accusation of Human Rights Violations by Rev. James Warren Jones Against Our Children and Relatives at the Peoples Temple Jungle Encampment in

Guyana, South America"—to Peoples Temple in San Francisco. The document accused Jones of a long list of violations of human rights, including the suicide threat, physical intimidation, mind-programming, confiscating of passports and money, prohibiting telephone calls and any other contacts with "outsiders," censoring mail, extortion by threats to cut off communications to relatives outside Jonestown, and preventing children from seeing their parents. The document also accused Jones of stationing guards around Jonestown to prevent escapes, depriving people of food and sleep, imposing hard labor conditions, and employing "other coercive techniques commonly used in mind-programming." Jones, they accused, was an absolute and cruel leader who kept his kingdom in line with the threats and execution of brutal punishments, who ordered his guards to kill anyone who tried to leave his jungle domain.

The twenty-five Concerned Relatives, who had a total of thirty-seven loved ones at Jonestown, demanded that Jones explain publicly the meaning of the collective "decision . . . to die," remove the guards around the compound, return all passports and money, allow one-week visits at the expense of the relatives in the United States, permit the writing of uncensored letters and the private reading of letters from the United States, and abide by court orders issued in the United States.

Backing up many of the charges was a four-page affidavit by Yolanda Crawford, a black woman who was appointed to the Temple's planning commission in the mid-1970s. Yolanda was not a part of Jones's inner core, but she was aware of what was going on. She had been in Jonestown from April 1, 1977, to June 29, 1977. Yolanda claimed that Jones was, in addition to violating the human rights cited in the Concerned Relatives document, telling his flock "the Ku Klux Klan is marching in the streets of San Francisco, Los Angeles and cities back east," and that there was "fighting in the streets, and the drought in California is so bad, Los Angeles is being deserted."

Yolanda charged that all mail had to be "cleared" by Temple secretaries before it went to the post office. Before she was allowed to leave Jonestown, Yolanda said,

> I was forced to promise him I would never speak against the church, and that if I did, I would lose his "protection" and be "stabbed in the back." Furthermore, Jim Jones ordered me to sign a number of self-incriminating papers, including a statement that I was against the government of Guyana, that I had plotted against that government, that I was part of the PPP (Peoples Progressive Party), which is the opposition party in Guyana, and that I had come to Guyana to help the PPP. Jim Jones said the reason for signing those papers was to discredit me if I ever decided to leave the movement "and talk." Also, before leaving Guyana, I was ordered to fabricate a story and sign it

stating that I killed someone and threw the body in the ocean. I was told that if I ever caused Jim Jones trouble, he would give the statement to the police.

At the San Francisco Temple yard where the shipping crates were still being assembled, Hugh Fortsyn—designated spokesman for the San Francisco Temple and an associate pastor—received the Concerned Relatives' allegations one afternoon when Steve Katsaris handed him a copy through the Temple yard's chain-link gate. Although Jim Jones did not reply to the charges against him, six days after the Temple received the Concerned Relatives document he ordered a phone patch from Jonestown into Charles Garry's office in San Francisco. Garry had indicated he would hold a "press conference" in his office to answer some of the charges. What reporters found at Garry's office was a radio-telephone performance by the Jonestown communards speaking over the microphone, one by one, to tell how happy they were to live in a socialist paradise. Not one of them had any desire to return to the United States under any circumstances. Each of them repeated the phrases of the witness preceding. All of them had to decline offers from their relatives for tickets home because they were happy and because their relatives were moral degenerates. "I'll set the record straight once and for all," said Maria Katsaris. "I'm not being held in captivity. That's totally absurd. The statement by Mr. Katsaris is an insult to myself, Reverend Jones, Peoples Temple and Guyana." Marceline Jones threatened to sue for "defamation of character" unless there was a complete retraction of all the "lies" about the Temple. Said another member, whose name was lost in the radio transmission: "We are staying here. We are staying here. We are staying here."

Concerned Relatives struck back in May by marching around the Federal Building in San Francisco while they continued to lobby with congressmen, state officials, and anyone else in a position of authority who would listen to them. In mid-May, Steven Katsaris filed a $15 million libel and slander suit against the Temple for the false charge that he had molested his daughter, Maria.

The verbal and legal battles between Peoples Temple and Concerned Relatives and the enormity of the charges hurled by both sides caused Jones's earliest and most loyal supporters in the fourth estate to wonder whether there might not be some truth to the plethora of allegations. Kathy Hunter, wife of the managing editor of the *Ukiah Daily Journal* and author of several puff pieces on Jim Jones and the Temple dating back to their 1965 arrival from Indianapolis, had an especially difficult time coming to terms with the paternity dispute between Tim Stoen, once highly regarded as Mendocino County's assistant district attorney, and the Reverend Jim Jones, the persecuted Christian martyr from Redwood Valley. The two men had impressed Mrs. Hunter equally; she found herself unable to ally herself with

319

one side or the other. After she talked to Tim Stoen, Mrs. Hunter concocted a story on February 27 that drew analogies to Greek tragedy. She wrote:

> There are no heroes or villains in this tragedy built upon human frailties—only two desperately driven men fighting for the mind and body of a boy they both claim as their son. The mother of the child, Grace Stoen, stands in the wings awaiting the outcome of the drama which began when she first committed herself to a man dedicated to a cause and who marched to a different drummer.

Mrs. Hunter decided in May she would fly to Guyana on her own (she had an open invitation from Prime Minister Burnham) and take a look at Jonestown firsthand. She would go there, she decided, with "an open mind."

Her initial contacts with Temple representatives—on May 18, the day after she arrived in Georgetown—were cordial. By Friday, May 19, Mrs. Hunter was beginning to be put off by the "broken phonograph record" of CIA conspiracies against the Temple. "I became irritated," she wrote later in *The Press Democrat*, "and the conversation deteriorated to the point where I finally got up from the table and told them I was becoming very upset, that they were beginning to sound as if they were giving me the same delaying routine as had been given others who attempted to contact Jim and their relatives at Jonestown." Mrs. Hunter went to her room to "cool off" and ten minutes later there began a series of false fire alarms at the Pegasus Hotel. By Saturday, the alarms were going off every few hours. Each time, the hotel was evacuated. Mrs. Hunter was placed under round-the-clock security guard. By Sunday, the hotel's management had to put out two fires that had been set outside Mrs. Hunter's second-floor room. On Monday, Guyanese immigration officials ordered her out of the country. She protested, but she was told she would be on the Wednesday plane to New York "whether I liked it or not." By Wednesday, her nerves were shattered by the terror she experienced in Georgetown, and she was retching uncontrollably. Pat Small, the lower-level liaison officer with the Foreign Affairs Ministry who had attended a public relations party at Lamaha Gardens, was Mrs. Hunter's constant companion during the ordeal at the Pegasus. Mrs. Small stayed with the fifty-eight-year-old reporter until she left on Saturday, May 27, on a flight from Georgetown to San Francisco. "I have heard about the things that go on with the Peoples Temple from some of the Guyanese people," Mrs. Hunter told Tim Tescone, a reporter for *The Press Democrat*, "and it's enough to curl the hair on your teeth."

The Temple countered Mrs. Hunter's story with a lengthy news release denying all her allegations of harassment in Georgetown and accusing her of being part of a "monstrous conspiracy." Her visit to Guyana, the Temple charged, was "another attempt to make us the prey for sensational news to destroy us because we are a nonviolent socialist church with belief in brotherhood and equality. . . . If the media wants a story from us, they will have to be objective and separate themselves from this smear campaign which is entirely based on politics."

The Temple's overinflated conspiracy theory started to burst at the seams in mid-June, when two newspapers, the *San Francisco Chronicle* and *The Press Democrat*, ran articles about the defection of Deborah Layton Blakey, a member of Jones's inner core. Blakey had gone to Jonestown in December of 1977 with the understanding that she would not have to stay longer than two months. As soon as she saw the armed guards—fifty of them—forming two rings of "security alert teams" around the compound, Deborah decided she wanted to get back to the United States. The opportunity for escape finally came in mid-May, when she was sent on Temple business to Lamaha Gardens in Georgetown. On May 12, she went to the U.S. embassy and asked to be returned immediately to the United States. While she was at the embassy, Blakey signed a statement, which she gave to Richard McCoy, declaring she was "afraid that Jim Jones will carry out his threat to force all members of the organization in Guyana to commit suicide if a decision is made in Guyana by the court to have John Stoen returned to his mother." Blakey left Guyana on May 13, Jim Jones's birthday. On the plane to New York, she talked further with McCoy, who was on his way to a State Department conference in Washington. She told him about the physical abuses at Jonestown, the armed guards, and the smuggling of weapons. McCoy advised her to contact a federal law-enforcement agency when she landed in New York.

McCoy advised Blakey against talking to the press, but she decided to talk anyway, hoping she could somehow stop Jones before there were corpses rotting in the jungle. She told reporters the same story she had told the embassy. She was convinced, she said, that Jones would follow through his plans for a mass suicide and, not being willing to die for the cause, she left the compound to try to do whatever she could to prevent the tragedy. Blakey talked to three reporters: Tim Reiterman of the *San Francisco Examiner,* Marshall Kilduff of the *San Francisco Chronicle,* and George Klineman of *The Press Democrat.* Kilduff's article, "Grim Report from the Jungle," ran June 15; Klineman's, "Escapee Tells of Suicide Plan at Rev. Jones Outpost," June 19. Reiterman didn't write an article.

For all three reporters, Deborah's story posed a problem: there was no one to corroborate it. Knowing what they already knew about Jim Jones, it was impossible for Klineman and Kilduff not to believe Deborah's account of trouble in paradise. Klineman argued that Deborah, as one of Jones's most trusted aides, knew what she was talking about, but his editor shook his head in disbelief. He thought the idea that a thousand people might voluntarily kill themselves for their leader was just a little farfetched, especially when the story came from only one source. With no one to back up Deborah's allegations, neither Klineman's nor Kilduff's paper printed her descriptions of the brutal punishments Jones was using to keep his followers in the fold. She told how Jones no longer used the Board of Education on recalcitrant members; the common punishment, she said, had become beatings with bare fists. She saw one woman beaten so badly that "one eye was black and blue and bleeding, and her face was all puffed out of shape." The woman was punished, Deborah said, for having sexual relations with a Georgetown pharmacist without first procuring drugs for Jim Jones.

Deborah told of public "knucklings," a painful torture in which guards ground their knuckles into the victim's temples "for several minutes." Those being disciplined, she said, had to restrain themselves from showing pain lest they be punished again. Jim Jones taught his followers that a stoic expression in the face of pain was "proof that they love socialism and wouldn't buckle under torture when questioned."

Deborah said she saw one member punished with Steve Jones's pet boa constrictor. Jones had the snake brought to the stage, she recalled, and ordered the reptile wrapped around the necks of members who broke the rules "until they turn purple." As soon as the snake was removed from the offender's neck, Jones required a smiling, "Thank you, Dad," and a penitent kiss for the snake before the sin could be expunged.

Jones, Deborah said, had gone completely mad. He was constantly brooding about his "rightful place in history" and his death. At least once a week, she said, he would call a "white night." Blaring sirens would awaken everyone in the compound, early in the morning while it was still dark, and fifty armed guards would move from cabin to cabin summoning stragglers to the pavilion. "During one 'white night,'" said Deborah in an affidavit she wrote when she returned to San Francisco, "we were informed that our situation had become hopeless and that the only course of action open to us was a mass suicide for the glory of socialism. We were told that we would be tortured by mercenaries if we were taken alive. Everyone, including the children, was told to line up. As we passed through the line, we were given a small glass of red liquid to drink. We were told that the liquid contained poison and that we would die within forty-five minutes. We all did as we were told." The red liquid was nothing more than unsweetened strawberry Fla-Vour-Aid, a Guyanese product similar to Kool-Aid, but Jones didn't tell his flock that the alert was a hoax until after the poison was to have taken effect. The alert was a "loyalty test," Deborah said, but Jones "warned us that the time was not far off when it would become necessary for us to die by our own hands."

At one "white night," Deborah said, she "watched Carolyn Layton, my former sister-in-law, give sleeping pills to two young children in her care, John Victor Stoen and Kimo Prokes, her own son. Carolyn said to me that the Reverend Jones had told her that everyone was going to have to die that night.

She said that she would probably have to shoot John and Kimo and that it would be easier for them if she did it while they were asleep."

Deborah said "life in Jonestown was so miserable" that she had become "indifferent as to whether [she] lived or died." During her first month in Jonestown, she said, she was assigned to work in the fields from 7:00 A.M. to 6:00 P.M. every day. The tropical sun was so hot, she said, "you get blisters on your body." Everyone worked under the watchful eyes of guards, who often hid in the jungle along the edge of the compound, keeping track of who was working and who was not. The only break during the day, she said, was an hour for a lunch that usually consisted of rice-water soup. "There was rice for breakfast . . . and rice and beans for lunch," she said. "On Sunday, we each received an egg and a cookie. Some very weak and elderly members received one egg per day." The food, she added, improved "markedly on the few occasions when there were outside visitors." Before each visit, she said, "Jones would instruct us on the image we were to project. The workday would be shortened. The food would be better. Sometimes there would be music and dancing."

The twenty-five-year-old former church financial secretary, who estimated the communards were signing over sixty-five thousand dollars in Social Security checks each month, charged that Temple propaganda about the farm being self-sustaining was simply not true. There was too little food produced to feed the mission's population, she charged. "In February 1978," Deborah said, "conditions had become so bad that half of Jonestown was ill with severe diarrhea and high fevers. I was seriously ill for two weeks." Jones bought inferior rice that was infested with weevils and maggots. The bad rice was the fault of the CIA, Jones claimed; he also claimed the CIA had stolen the church's money and supplies, and had seeded the clouds so that constant rains would ruin the crops.

When Deborah left The Promised Land in May, Jim Jones was a ranting, raving paranoid. The CIA had tape recorders hidden in the trees, he said. Mercenaries lurked in the jungle, waiting for the right opportunity to rape, torture, and slaughter everyone at Jonestown. Jones harangued his flock for six hours a day on an intercom system that stretched throughout the compound. He read his own version of the news, which invariably included stories of government corruption and CIA plots in the United States. "Charles Manson is one of our most misunderstood people," he said one day, hinting "there was more to Manson" than had appeared in print. He spoke of his deep admiration for Ugandan dictator Idi Amin, with whom he claimed to have had some "connections." He praised the Red Brigades for the murder of Italian prime minister Aldo Moro. He spoke endlessly of death and of what it means to die or to kill for a cause.

Jones backed up his dreams of killing for the cause with an arsenal consisting, Deborah said, of between two and three hundred rifles, twenty-five pistols, and a homemade bazooka. "There was a group assigned to take care of the children," Deborah said. "Then there was another group assigned to take care of those people who spoke out against Jones. . . . Everybody who was going to kill anybody had someone assigned to them as well."

Jim Jones was absolute ruler in the colony. He decided matters of punishment, policy, marriage and divorce, said Deborah. Unless marriages were "arranged" by Jones—as commonly occurred—couples had first to get approval from the "relations committee" for a relationship to proceed on a three-month trial basis. For the first three months, the couple was allowed to talk together but could show no physical signs of affection. If the relationship did not conflict with the goals of the cause, the couple was allowed to live together for six months—as long as the relations committee approved. Couples lived in cabins with fourteen bunkbeds crammed inside. Each couple was given one bunkbed and all the privacy possible behind hanging sheets.

There was no privacy for getting dressed in the morning. The showers accommodated twenty bathers at a time. Men and women sat side by side to move their bowels while others behind them waited in lines to take their turns in time to get out to the fields by 7:00 A.M.. There were, of course, no sanitary facilities in the fields. There was no water unless workers brought their own containers. With Jones's voice blaring most of the day over the loudspeakers and meetings in the pavilion nearly every night, there was little privacy even of thoughts. Life at the jungle farm was "so structured," Deborah said, "you had no freedom to yourself, no time to be alone."

When Dad learned on his birthday that Deborah had defected, he called a meeting in the pavilion that dragged on for twenty-eight hours. He rambled on and on about the meaning of betrayal. Periodically, he took a vote on how many were willing to die for the cause; anyone who voted no was brought to the floor to face Dad's wrath. "He'd ask for a vote every few hours," recalls Harold Cordell, who went to Jonestown in January 1978. "Meals were brought into the pavilion. Groups were allowed to go to the bathroom in the company of armed guards." Not everyone in Jonestown was immediately willing to die; some preferred any kind of life over death. Each of the nonconformists was dealt with separately until, after twenty-eight hours, the colony reached a unanimous vote. "I raised my hand," Cordell recalls. "I felt if we stopped arguing with him, we could all go to bed."

After Deborah left Jonestown, Dad was perpetually morose and brooding. Often the depression and anger would be replaced, in Dad's heart, by melancholy; he would speak of his selfless mother, Lynetta, who had stuck with him to the end. Lynetta died December 9, 1977, of a heart attack, according to a handwritten death certificate signed by Larry Schacht, the Temple's "doctor," and Joyce Beam Parks, a Temple nurse. She lay in state for two days in the pavilion. The members had to file by her remains and pay their respects while her son eulogized her as the mother of the cause, the true socialist. She was buried in a fruit orchard on a gently sloping hillside overlooking Jonestown.

Lynetta's death didn't upset Jim Jones nearly as much as Deborah's defection did. He took immediate steps to prevent anyone else escaping—or thinking about escaping. Tom Kice tried it. The guards held a loaded gun to his head while Jim Jones tested his loyalty. Tommy Bogue tried to escape, too; like Kice, he was caught in the act and returned at the point of a shotgun. Jim Jones set off the siren and called a meeting right away. Someone in the audience suggested Bogue be placed in shackles and handcuffs, so Donald Fitch, the commune's blacksmith, was ordered to pound out a set from chains and scraps of iron. Bogue had to keep wearing his shackles and handcuffs for more than a month. The idea caught on; others who tried to flee were led back to the compound in front of shotguns and bound with the same restraints.

Children owed the cause the same allegiance that adults did. Children who misbehaved or tried to run away were as brutally disciplined as adults. At night, recalcitrant children would be lowered on a rope into a deep, hand-dug well. Two adults hiding down in the well's dark bottom tugged at the child's legs and dunked the child into the water. The name of this punishment was "Bigfoot," and the screams of its victims could be heard through the camp.

The children were treated as adults in other Jonestown activities, too. In eliminating ageism, Jones applied his rules to everyone, young and old. Everyone old enough to write had to write regular confessional letters to Dad. Most of the letters were apologetic and self-flagellating. Fourteen-year-old Michael Heath confessed:

> I am chauvinistic towards sisters because I don't like taking instructions from sisters. I am elitist because I get extra things and I get mad when other people get things I don't have at the time.

Wrote Shirley Hicks:

> I became a rebellious bitch because I could not see my son like I saw other people seeing their children whenever they wanted. I gave my son to you, Dad and I know you will do what's right.

Wrote "Pops" and "Moms" Jackson, 108 and 103 years old:

> Dad, this is from our hearts. For six years you have been our father and our brother, and we love you. We have tried our best to prove this to you and the Peoples Temple, not by words alone but deeds and fellowship and this will continue until death do we part.

325

Wrote a guilt-ridden teenager, Willie Malone:

> I'm very sensitive and let little things upset me too easily. I get highly upset. I have a very bad temper. There is no excuse. You control your temper and you have an explosive temper also. This is my worse problem. Sexually, I'm not interested in anyone at the moment. I can jack off and get the same feeling as a fuck so that doesn't bother me at all. I am sexually attracted to a lot of brothers and would rather fuck one in the ass than get fucked. It doesn't bother me at all. . . . I have feelings about going to the states for revenge against people. Other than that I don't think about it much. Jumbo Jacks are far from my mind. I think about getting high too much. I think about getting drunk a lot.

Gerald Parks had the courage to speak out against conditions at Jonestown, although most of his letter reveals that he was no less guilty than those less courageous:

> I don't like living like this. Everything in me rebels against it. I don't think it is right for someone else—no matter what he believes or stands for—to enslave minds and bodies. I don't believe in sticking my head in the sand and hiding from the problems. Neither do I believe in exchanging one problem there (in the USA) for another here (in Jonestown). . . .
>
> I do feel guilty about my responsibility towards the starving oppressed world. If this isn't enough to make you commit suicide, then I don't know what is. . . . I feel like the devil reincarnated or something evil beyond help. I even thought I might be Judas Iscariot here again. I could go on and on, Dad, but that makes me feel really selfish to do so knowing what's happening all over the world. Hope you will not think bad of me.

The last six months at Jonestown were the worst. Public beatings became increasingly brutal. Jones took to strolling the compound with a short-barrel .357 magnum in his hip pocket. He would have the seniors line up on the stage to help with discipline by beating offenders in the face with their canes. The beatings were severe enough to warrant treatment at the colony's much-touted medical facility, of which, officially, Marceline Jones was in charge; but the clinic was definitely the domain of "Doctor" Larry Schacht, who had been with the Temple since the late 1960s when members found him wandering the streets of Berkeley, hanging around Telegraph Avenue in a drug-induced stupor. The Temple helped Schacht to clean up his act and sent him to medical school at the Universidad Autonoma in Guadalajara, Mexico, for three years of medical studies. He completed his studies at the University of California, Irvine, in June 1977 and had just begun his internship at UC Medical Center in San Francisco when Jim Jones ordered him to Guyana. Although he failed to complete his internship, Schacht could still call himself Doctor—but only in Jonestown.

Schacht often brooded about his lack of a license to practice, and his love assignations with Jones provided only temporary relief; he often sunk into fits of depression. More than once he threatened to kill himself, shouting and slamming his fist on the examining table. Once a nurse had to restrain him from throwing himself on a machete. According to Leslie Wilson, the medical facility's twenty-one-year-old "gynecologist," Schacht took great pleasure suturing wounds without anesthetic; the pain of the sewing, he said, was preparation for the tortures ahead when the fascists, the mercenaries, and the CIA conquered Jonestown. Schacht laughed at his patients' injuries; he laughed at their complaints. He kept them waiting during examinations and treatments while he thumbed through medical texts trying to fill the gaps in his training or his memory. He hated his patients. He hated his work. By all accounts, he hated himself. He grew increasingly withdrawn, until he was the only person in Jonestown who took his meals alone.

Schacht supervised, during the final months of Jonestown's existence, the final solution—short of death—for potential escapees. Those who could not be reached through humiliation and violence were sent to the "Extended Care Unit," a mini-hospital equipped with an array of mind-altering drugs like Thorazine, Valium, Haldol—tranquilizers potent enough to render an angry bull as harmless as an obedient puppy. Inmates of the Extended Care Unit were drugged to insensibility, no longer able to think for themselves, then the nurses and guards would periodically parade the zombies around the compound as a mute warning to anyone else contemplating escape.

The combination of fear and tight security was effective; it kept everyone in the fold after Debbie Layton left. Jones certainly did not want anyone getting loose who might corroborate Deborah's account of life at Jonestown. Because Deborah had no one to back up her story, the Temple felt free to operate with efforts to discredit everything Deborah said. Deborah's mother, Lisa, and her brother, Larry Layton, still loyal to Jones, refuted all the charges for the press via short-wave radio.

Attorney Charles Garry called George Klineman two days after the reporter's article on Deborah Layton Blakey's account of life in Jonestown ran in *The Press Democrat*. Garry complained of "inaccuracies" in the article. The attorney's chief objection was to Deborah's allegation that "When Charles Garry was in Guyana, he was given the best cabin there. The food was better. There was dancing and partying." Garry pointed out that Deborah hadn't arrived in Jonestown until December, two months after his visit, so there was no way she could have known firsthand what went on during his guided tour of "paradise." Garry's razor-sharp perception failed to demolish Deborah's credibility in the reporter's eyes, however. When Klineman broached the subject, Garry admitted there were armed guards at Jonestown; the security system was, in fact, his idea. "While I was there," Garry said, "I set up the security system because Jim Jones had been shot at. I worked out the system where there was a twenty-four-hour watch on the gate." Garry added that he had "encouraged" the Temple "to get weapons." Klineman asked Garry if he knew where the Temple got the weapons. "No, I don't," Garry said. "I did not inquire. I assume they bought them somewhere like people do in this country." Garry had no comment about the suicide threat. "I don't know where she's coming from," he said of Deborah.

The two published accounts of Deborah's life in Jonestown may not have had any noticeable effect on the governments of the United States and Guyana, but the tales of the atrocities did have an effect on worried relatives back home. Jim Cobb, a San Francisco dental student and active member of Concerned Relatives—he had a mother, two brothers, and three sisters in Jonestown—filed a $23 million lawsuit against the Temple on June 22, charging threats to the lives of his family, harassment, and libel. Cobb also charged in his lawsuit, filed in his behalf by Tim Stoen, that the false allegations about him—that he was a "radical Trotskyite," that he "stole guns and rifles," that he "plotted to blow up a bridge," that he "forced young men and women to bow before him and kiss his genitals"—were circulated by a top-secret group in the Temple called the Diversions Department, headed by Terri Buford. Threatening letters, he claimed, were written on "typewriters at various public libraries throughout the San Francisco Bay Area, or upon typewriters obtained secondhand and then discarded into the ocean or bay." Cobb further charged the mass suicide threat would inevitably result "in the death of minor children not old enough to make voluntary and informed decisions about serious matters of any nature, much less inane proposals of collective suicide."

Another relative, Clare Bouquet—a San Mateo teacher whose twenty-four-year-old son, Brian, was in Jonestown—read the Kilduff article and for the first time suspected that her son might not be safe where he was. She went into action immediately. She wrote letters to Prime Minister Forbes Burnham, Ambassador Laurence Mann, President Carter and Secretary of State Cyrus Vance, Congressmen Pete McCloskey and Leo Ryan. She asked Kilduff what she could do to further an investigation of Jonestown; Kilduff put her in touch with Tim Stoen. Clare Bouquet's first contact with Concerned Relatives was her July meeting with Tim Stoen. In early August, she told her story to Congressman Ryan and his chief aide, Jackie Speier. Ryan promised Clare he would investigate conditions at Jonestown, but not until after the November elections. Clare hardly expected such a positive and immediate response; the best she expected to hear was that the congressman would take the matter under advisement.

Ryan wanted to start preparing immediately for the trip. The first step, he said, was to have a meeting with others who had relatives in Jonestown. That meeting—which set the stage for the November trip to Guyana—included Steve, Anthony, and Elaine Katsaris, Tim Stoen, Clare Bouquet, Leo Ryan, and Jackie Speier. Ryan promised the group he would go to Jonestown and see the conditions there himself.

While plans were underway for Ryan's trip to Guyana, the Temple struck back on two fronts. On the legal front, Charles Garry filed a $150 million lawsuit charging Tim Stoen with compromising the "attorney-client confidentiality" he maintained while he was attorney for the Temple. "One wonders if he divulged to his present client [Steve Katsaris] what he had advised his former client," said Garry in one of his briefs. On the "diversions" front, the Temple appeared to be busy in Ukiah again. Reporter Kathy Hunter complained to police that two black men walked into her house on June 25 and forcibly poured a bottle of bourbon down her throat. A week earlier, she had reported that someone had broken a window in her home, near where she sat watching television. She was receiving threats, too, she said, including an ominous warning: "Jim knows what you're doing. If he goes down, you and all your family will go down with him." The Temple countered Mrs. Hunter's charge of a "three-week reign of terror" with an offer on August 1 of a five-thousand-dollar reward "to anyone who provides information leading to the arrest and conviction of any person or persons" responsible for harassing Mrs. Hunter.

The Ukiah journalist was still recovering from a bad case of jittery nerves when she received a phone call from a man who identified himself as "Mark Lande." Mrs. Hunter was wary at first, but "Mark Lande" convinced her that he was a reporter for *Esquire* magazine. He was putting together an article on Peoples Temple, he said, and he wanted to interview her sources. Mrs. Hunter talked to two of her sources, Birdie Marable and Steve Katsaris, and both of them agreed to interviews. "Mark Lande" showed up at the appointed hour for the interviews on October 2. Mrs. Hunter called Steve for his interview at three o'clock.

Steve's lawsuit was still active and he was still the official spokesman for Concerned Relatives when he met the "reporter" from *Esquire*. The reporter said his name was Mark Lane. Steve knew he had heard the name before, but he couldn't connect it with a context of events. He finally asked the reporter where he might have heard his name before. Lane volunteered, "Maybe you've read my book, *Rush to Judgment*." That answer refreshed Steve's memory enough to associate the name with conspiracy theories; Lane was a specialist on conspiracies. Steve became a bit suspicious about the attorney-turned-author's intentions. Katsaris's attitude was one of willingness to help Lane "or anybody else who would write an article on Peoples Temple," even someone who had made a career out of materializing conspiracies. Steve consented to a taped interview of about fifteen minutes' duration.

Neither Katsaris nor any of the others was aware when they talked to Lane that he had already accepted thousands of dollars to represent the Temple, that he had visited Jonestown, and that on September 19 he held a press conference in Georgetown to charge that there was a U.S. government conspiracy to destroy Peoples Temple. Lane told reporters there he would, "within ninety days," file lawsuits against the United States Attorney General, the Department of State, the FBI and the CIA.

The day after his interviews in Ukiah, Lane surfaced at a press conference in San Francisco to repeat the charges and to add to his list of conspirators the names of other agencies—the Treasury Department, the Internal Revenue Service, and the Postal Service—he planned to sue on the Temple's behalf. Lane said he had visited Jonestown under the auspices of the Citizens Commission of Inquiry, a private nonprofit investigative organization formed originally to look into the conspiracy theories around the assassination of President Kennedy. Lane, a director of the organization, said he got involved in the Temple investigation when the northern California chapter of CCI asked him to look into the allegation that the Temple had a "concentration camp" at Jonestown. Lane countered the "unprincipled attacks" in the media with an eyewitness description of a collective paradise. There were seventy people on the medical staff at Jonestown, he said, and people who had been wandering aimlessly most of their lives were happy for the first time. "There is no place in America where they could be helped," he said.

Lane was careful not to give any specifics about the government conspiracy against Jonestown, although he did suggest a thin motive. The U.S. government, he said, is "terrified of twelve hundred Americans who are saying very openly, 'We've heard the present talk about human rights in every other country. We left the United States of America to find human rights for ourselves.'" As Lane moved from press conference to conference, from radio talk show to speaking engagement, the plots against Peoples Temple became ever more sinister. He even hinted he had uncovered a plot to assassinate the Reverend Jim Jones.

Mark Lane's sudden appearance on the Peoples Temple bandwagon surprised everyone, but no one so much as Charles Garry. One day there was Mark Lane speaking as if he were Jones's attorney, and Garry didn't even know Lane was on retainer. Garry had spent most of a year checking out the Temple's conspiracy theories and had to conclude there was "no conspiracy by the U.S. government."

When Lane appeared and started rekindling the conspiracy fires, Garry's worst fear was that he was "going to be faced in a courtroom with some of this shit he'd been talking about." Garry called the Temple in San Francisco and said he was resigning as counsel unless Lane bowed out. Temple officials assured Garry that Lane was only donating his time. While Garry fumed, there were—unknown to him—meetings in Washington to plan Congressman Ryan's upcoming trip to Jonestown. Garry, who was living at the time in Ryan's district, was not apprised of the trip until more than a month after talks began with the State Department. The government officials neglected to inform Garry of Ryan's planned visit; they assumed Jones's attorney was Mark Lane.

Lane's media blitz on the Temple's behalf offered much talk and little substance, but the attorney was sufficiently adept at titillating America's interest in plots and conspiracies to attract some attention. "Lane's work has had the best response I have seen as far as community pull," wrote top aide Terri Buford in a confidential memo to Jones, "and with the exception of Garry the response has been good." Buford told Jones in her memo that she had taken her name off all the Temple's secret bank accounts. She suggested the Temple could divert some of the heat away from itself by branding her a "provocateur" and blaming her for "the stuff that the church is presently in trouble for." She said she expected to be called "traitor," although she indicated she would continue to feed information to the Temple. She left behind, apparently, all the Temple's intelligence files, which had been kept in a cramped closet where she slept. She put her keys in the refrigerator and left a note for Jean Brown with the memo to Jones attached. About a month later she surfaced again—this time as one of Mark Lane's clients.

Terri's departure from the fold aggravated Dad's self-diagnosed terminal condition. Some days he was dying of cancer. Other days he was having heart problems. His prostate gland was acting up and he needed a catheter to urinate. He was in constant pain, he said, and required oxycodone tablets just to keep going, uppers to stay awake, downers to go to sleep. He miraculously survived fevers of 106 degrees. Two witnesses to his poor health were U.S. Consul Douglas V. Ellice, Jr., and Vice-Consul T. Dennis Reece when they visited Jonestown on November 7, 1978. They had been informed beforehand that Jim Jones was ill, having recently suffered a heart attack, and at the lunch break during their visit, they were told that Jones "had a temperature of 105 and was not feeling well." Jones joined the officials for lunch wearing a surgical mask because "he had a cold and did not want to spread germs." Jones had to be assisted to his chair by two of his aides. He appeared to be unsteady on his feet. He arrived for lunch just as the Jonestown Express was finishing its rendition of "America the Beautiful" while hundreds of communards sang with hands over hearts. Jim Jones took off his surgical mask when lunch was set before him and consular officials couldn't help noticing that he was not perspiring, despite his high fever. In their official report of the visit, Ellice and Reece observed "during their various conversations with him before, during and after lunch that the Rev. Jones's speech was markedly slurred. During his luncheon conversation with Mr. Ellice, Rev. Jones tried at one point to spell a word that he did not want a nearby child to hear. He was unable to spell the word correctly and gave up in apparent confusion." Despite Jones's strange behavior, the report's conclusion was nearly identical to other reports on life at Jonestown, the results of prearranged visits:

> . . . At no time did the officers . . . see any barbed wire, any guards, armed or otherwise, or any other physical sign that people were being held at Jonestown against their will. Nor did any of the conversations by the consular officers with Peoples Temple members at Jonestown reveal any indication that the inhabitants of Jonestown were receiving anything less than normal Guyanese standards of food, clothing, shelter, and medical assistance.

The report failed to mention whether Jones or any of his aides spoke of Congressman Ryan, who had sent Jones a telegram November 1 announcing his intention to visit Guyana and the Peoples Temple Agricultural Mission. In the wire, Ryan was frank about the "anxieties" expressed by some of his constituents who had relatives in Jonestown. Ryan stressed, however, that he had also "listened to others who have told me that such concerns are exaggerated." Ryan said he would be joined on the visit by Congressman Ed Derwinski, an Illinois Republican.

Jones's initial response—through the U.S. embassy in Georgetown—was that he simply would not allow Ryan and his party into Jonestown. Jones was within his rights to refuse because the colony was on private property in a foreign country. Jones expressed, through his aides, further reasons for his reluctance to admit the congressman and his party: Ryan would "be arriving with well-developed prejudices" against Peoples Temple; and Ryan had shown "bad faith" by allowing an NBC-TV news crew to accompany him. According to the State Department, NBC became interested in the trip immediately upon learning that Ryan was going. The following day, attorney Mark Lane fired off a letter to Ryan objecting to the short notice given for the trip, which was to take place in mid-November. "You should understand that Jonestown is a private community," Lane wrote, "and that while they appear willing to host your visit there under certain circumstances, courtesy requires that arrangements be made in advance of your visit." The timing was wrong, Lane said, because he would be testifying before the House Select Committee on Assassinations during the balance of November. Lane gave Ryan a not-so-subtle warning that pressing the issue of a mid-November visit "might very well result in the creation of a most embarrassing situation for the U.S. Government." Lane noted that "two different countries, neither one of which has entirely friendly relations with the U.S., have offered refuge to the twelve hundred Americans now residing in Jonestown. Thus far the Peoples Temple has not accepted either of those offers but it is their position that if religious persecution continues and if it is furthered through a witch hunt conducted by any branch of the U.S. Government, that they will be constrained to consider accepting either of the offers."

Lane's blustery letter did nothing to dissuade Ryan from his plans to visit Jonestown. While Ryan's California staff met with Concerned Relatives, his Washington staff worked out last-minute details with the State Department. On November 10, Ryan wrote Lane a letter informing him that the congressional inquiry would proceed on schedule, whether Lane was there or not. Ryan chided Lane for his threat that the trip could embarrass the United States government, and the inference that the inquiry was a "witch hunt":

> . . . I am truly disappointed with your use of the phrase "witch hunt" in connection with an open and honest inquiry of the United States House of Representatives into the welfare of American citizens presently living in Jonestown. The committee asks no more of Mr. Jones than any parent does whose son or daughter is away at school or whose mother or father resides in a distant convalescent home or hospital.
>
> No "persecution," as you put it, is intended, Mr. Lane . . . [and] your vague reference to "the creation of the most embarrassing situation for the American government" does not impress me at all. If the comment is intended as a threat, I believe it reveals more than may have been intended. I presume Mr. Jones would not be supportive of such a comment.

Despite Mark Lane's efforts to scuttle the inquiry, Ryan forged ahead as if there were no obstacles, as if Lane did not exist. As he had explained to the NBC news crew the evening before—November 9—he had long ago "learned not to be afraid anymore."

Ryan and the newsmen—Don Harris, a forty-two-year-old NBC News reporter widely praised for his coverage of the war in Southeast Asia; Bob Brown, a thirty-six-year-old cameraman who had joined NBC in April after years of freelancing for the major networks; Bob Flick, an NBC News producer; and Gordon Lindsay, a British free-lance writer—discussed the advisability of packing handguns. They decided against the idea because the weapons would, if discovered, only fuel Jones's paranoid fires of CIA conspiracies—or, worse, lead to an armed confrontation. To plan ahead was difficult without knowing whether Jonestown was an armed concentration camp or paradise on earth; all the travelers could get from the State Department was that Jonestown was a "benign" religious community in which none of the embassy officials who visited had observed guards or weapons. The

State Department neglected to send Ryan the report of the November 7 visit, when Jones appeared for lunch wearing a surgical mask and acting as if he were drugged. Ryan was not at all sure what he might be facing in Jonestown, but he made the newsmen a firm promise: anyone who wished to leave Jonestown would leave with him—assuming, of course, the delegation got inside the compound in the first place.

Plans for the trip were already final when Charles Garry became involved. Garry first learned of the congressman's trip to Jonestown in the November 8, 1978, *San Francisco Chronicle*. Two days later, Ryan aide Joe Holsinger dropped by Garry's office to share some of the correspondence the congressman had received from Mark Lane. Garry was furious. He called the San Francisco Temple with an ultimatum: "You transmit to Jim Jones that unless Lane is pulled out of this in its entirety, I'm withdrawing as the attorney for the Temple as of the thirteenth." The next day, Garry received a call from the Temple in Georgetown informing him that Jones was "semicomatose" and had a fever so high he had to be "packed in ice." Temple officials relayed to Garry the request from Marceline that he postpone his decision to resign until Jones was feeling better. "Horseshit!" replied Garry. "Marcie Jones knows who I am. She's been working with me, and if she can't make the decision, I can. I'm not going to represent the Temple anymore. As of Monday, I am through." Monday passed without word from the Temple and Garry assumed that Jim or Marceline or both had decided to stick with Lane.

Monday, November 13, was the delegation's last day in Washington before Ryan, Concerned Relatives, and the press left for Guyana. There was a last-minute briefing at the State Department. Congressman Ryan spoke briefly of his intentions for the trip and Deborah Blakey described conditions in Jonestown. The next morning, the entourage was on the plane for Georgetown. Representing Concerned Relatives were Clare Bouquet, Carol Boyd, Jim Cobb, Sherwin Harris, Nadyne Houston, Anthony Katsaris, Steve Katsaris, Howard and Beverly Oliver, Wayne Pietila, Grace and Tim Stoen, Bonnie Thielman, and Mickey Touchette. Representing the press were Tim Reiterman, a reporter, and Greg Robinson, a photographer, from the *San Francisco Examiner;* Ron Javers of the *San Francisco Chronicle;* Charles Krause of the *Washington Post;* Gordon Lindsay, free-lance writer researching an article for the *National Enquirer;* and the NBC News crew: reporter Don Harris, cameraman Bob Brown, sound man Steven Sung, producer Bob Flick. Accompanying Ryan were his chief aide, Jackie Speier, and James Schollaert, a staff consultant to the House International Relations Committee.

Ryan's plane was already in Georgetown when, the following day at noon, Charles Garry arrived in his office after a morning in court and picked up the message that Jim Jones wanted him in Jonestown immediately. Garry canceled all his appointments for the next five days and caught a plane to Kennedy Airport in New York. The plane to Georgetown didn't leave until three o'clock the next day, Thursday. Garry was going through security en route to the loading gate for his flight when he ran into Mark Lane. Lane introduced himself and shook Garry's hand. Garry bristled. Lane mumbled something about being held over in Washington on the James Earl Ray case, but said nothing about going to Georgetown. Garry said nothing. He called his office in San Francisco about Lane's having the same destination, but Garry was persuaded to continue to Jonestown and, once and for all, straighten out his relationship with Jim Jones. The two attorneys sat on the same plane. They represented the same client. They spoke not a word to each other all the way to Georgetown.

Some months I've tried to keep this thing from happening, but I now see it's the will—it's the will of the Sovereign Being that this happened to us, that we lay down our lives in protest of what's been done.

—Jim Jones, November 18, 1978

XI

White Night

The obstacles started as soon as the plane carrying Ryan's delegation landed at Timehri International Airport just after midnight on November 15. Ron Javers, the bearded, dapper reporter from the *Chronicle*, was detained in customs because he had no entry visa. The Guyanese authorities stamped Javers's passport "Not Permitted to Land," apparently oblivious to the fact that no one else in the press party had an entry visa either. Bob Flick of NBC stayed with Javers while the rest of the party waited more than an hour for the customs inspectors to go through their luggage, fighting off the drowsiness from the flight and the warm, muggy air of Guyana.

Congressman Ryan was able to go on to Georgetown ahead of the others; U.S. Ambassador John Burke, at whose home Ryan would be staying, was at the airport when the plane arrived. The rest of the party—except for Javers and Flick—hailed cabs in front of the airport and were driven to the Pegasus Hotel, where they had reservations. The ride took about a half-hour along a two-lane paved road, one of the few modern roads in all Guyana, and after the long flight and the wait at the airport, the twenty-six-mile journey to Georgetown seemed hardly a delay at all since there would be showers and beds waiting at the other end. When they got to the Pegasus at three o'clock in the morning, Steve Katsaris went to the front desk to announce their arrival and get their keys. The clerk politely informed him no rooms were available; all the reservations for Concerned Relatives had been canceled.

Most of the group spent the night in the hotel's lobby, although a few left with Tim Stoen to get rooms at the Tower Hotel, about a mile away. Steve and Anthony Katsaris took up Gordon Lindsay's offer to share his room until the reservations problem was straightened out. The lights in Lindsay's room weren't out twenty minutes when the phone rang and the desk clerk told Lindsay there had been a mistake; he should not have been allowed in the country, and an immigration official would be waiting for him in the lobby in fifteen minutes. Lindsay went downstairs; the immigration official never appeared. An immigration official gave Tim Reiterman and Greg Robinson similar treatment, with the difference that he did appear. The desk clerk summoned the *Examiner* newsmen to tell them there was a problem with their visas. The official would be there in an hour. Three hours later, the baggage inspector who had checked in Reiterman and Robinson at the airport showed up in jeans, T-shirt, and orange motorcycle helmet. He demanded their passports and, with a stroke of his pen, shortened their stay from five days to twenty-four hours.

Javers, meanwhile, was still being held at the airport, and Flick was still staying there with him. Late that morning, Congressman Ryan called Javers and assured him he was doing everything he could to ensure that the reporter would be allowed into Guyana. News of Javers's detention had reached the United States, where Congressman Philip Burton, a San Francisco Democrat, was pounding the halls of the State Department demanding immediate action. Finally, about noon, Javers was cleared through the Ministry of Immigration and allowed to stay five days. The remainder of the press contingent was cleared by four o'clock Wednesday afternoon.

The Concerned Relatives, fourteen in their group, were given rooms at the Pegasus Hotel late Wednesday morning. Anthony Katsaris awoke to the sound of an impassioned orator in the street outside the Pegasus, somewhere below Lindsay's window.

Wednesday afternoon, the Concerned Relatives piled into three cabs and went to 41 Lamaha Gardens, where they were met by an obese woman wearing a muumuu, standing at the gate and seeming to match, in every detail, the description of Patty Cartmell. The woman told the group to get back in their cabs because they were not welcome. "We don't want to have anything to do with you," she said. There were two other women in the front yard with the fat lady, but their presence intimidated the relatives no more than the fat lady's words. The relatives approached the gate and courteously asked the women if they would contact their families at Jonestown. Anthony stepped up to the fence and asked the woman in the muumuu to tell his sister, Maria, that he was visiting from California. "She told you she didn't want you to come down!" the woman snapped.

Anthony feigned indifference to the woman's answer; he did not want to show anger and thus give the Temple an excuse to prohibit his seeing his sister. "That's none of your business," he said as politely as possible. "I'm here to see her, and if you'd relay that message, I'd appreciate it."

The woman replied she would not accept any messages except through the U.S. embassy. Other relatives talked to the women behind the fence. They got the same answer.

When the relatives returned to the Pegasus, they learned that the embassy had received a petition, signed by six hundred Jonestown residents, objecting to the visit. "Many of us, the undersigned residents of Jonestown, Guyana, have been visited here by friends and relatives," the petition read. "However, we have not invited and do not care to see Congressman Ryan, media representatives, members of the group of so-called Concerned Relatives, or any other person who may be traveling with or associated with any of those persons." Congressman Ryan, who had spent most of his day with embassy officials, said the petition did not discourage him and indicated he had a plan of action.

Ambassador Burke hosted a dinner at the embassy Wednesday evening for Congressman Ryan, Jim Cobb, and Bonnie Thielman. After the dinner, Ryan decided to follow up a hunch that the people at Lamaha Gardens might be willing to talk with him. He hailed a cab with Charles Krause of the *Washington Post* and together they rode out to the Temple's Georgetown headquarters. Krause waited in the cab while Ryan got out, opened the front gate, and knocked on the door of 41 Lamaha Gardens. "Hi," he said. "I'm Leo Ryan. I'm the bad guy. Does anyone want to talk?" Ryan had a "not unfriendly" meeting for about forty minutes. Perhaps a dozen Temple loyalists were there.

Thursday at two o'clock, Ryan and the Concerned Relatives met with Ambassador Burke at the embassy for a briefing on Jonestown. Burke was a heavyset, reserved man who boasted frequently of being "an Irish bachelor" and who never lost his self-control. For the briefing, chairs were set in neat rows and a slide projector sat on a table near the back of the room. Burke said he would be showing some slides of Jonestown taken by Deputy Chief of Mission Richard Dwyer. Some of the relatives protested; they had not come to see a slide show. Burke was determined; they watched the slides. After the showing, the relatives moved the chairs into a circle and, one by one, told their stories; a few of them were too choked with tears to finish. Burke, meanwhile, Clare Bouquet recalls, "didn't show any emotion at all. He was businesslike. He didn't appear to be moved."

That evening, Steve Katsaris suggested to Anthony and Grace that they sit out on the front lawn of the Pegasus and listen to a stir-crazy orator deliver his State of the World message from across the street. Some friends of Steve's drove up and chatted with the three of them for a few minutes, then left, only to return moments later to tell them the Temple van was parked down by the seawall, perhaps a block away from the hotel, with a group of the Temple's young men standing around it. The relatives decided to talk to the Temple members. Steve and Anthony walked ahead along the boardwalk in a slow stroll, ordinary tourists walking off a dinner, and Sherwin Harris and Clare Bouquet followed, casually, almost five minutes behind them. No one hurried.

The Temple van was parked where Steve's friends said it would be, but it was deserted; Steve and Anthony continued strolling until they came upon a group of young men, mostly black, with their backs to the boardwalk and looking out to sea. From their failure to notice the strollers' approach, Steve suspected they were the Temple group.

"Hello," said Steve, breaking the ice.

They turned around, leery and guarded. One of the men in the group asked whether Steve and his son were Americans. Steve explained that he was in Guyana to see his daughter, who lived in a place called Jonestown. "Ever heard of it?" Steve asked.

One of the men replied that all of them lived in Jonestown. The group warmed a little; they seemed almost friendly until Steve asked whether any of them knew his daughter, Maria. They became guarded again. Steve and Anthony singled out the man who seemed to be the leader of the group—a black man who later identified himself as Lee Ingram—and started talking directly to him. The group was in Georgetown to play basketball, Ingram explained, and he was the coach. Ingram was also the husband of Sandra Bradshaw Ingram. Sandy Bradshaw used to work for the probation department in Mendocino County. She was in San Francisco.

Five minutes passed with this small-talk. Sherwin Harris and Clare Bouquet joined the group, and soon Grace Stoen was there, and she recognized Stephan Jones and put her arms around him. Grace's eyes filled with tears as she explained to Stephan that the only reason Concerned Relatives had come to Guyana was to see their loved ones. All she wanted to do was see her son, she said. Stephan agreed her request was not unreasonable; he said he would do what he could to persuade his father to let Grace spend some time with John Victor in Jonestown.

Jim Cobb joined the discussion. He teased Lee Ingram about coaching the basketball team. "You don't know how to play basketball," Cobb said. "What you trying to pull?"

From her fourth-story window, Mickey Touchette spotted the group and recognized her brother, Al, whom she hadn't seen in four years. She ran all the way up the boardwalk and as soon as they saw each other, Al and Mickey embraced.

The relatives talked with the basketball team for two hours, until Ingram said it was time for the team to return to Lamaha Gardens. Al and Mickey tried to keep talking, but they had to cut it short; it was time to go.

By the time the relatives got back to the Pegasus Hotel, the others of their group were already halfway through dinner with Congressman Ryan. The relatives viewed the meeting at the seawall as an encouraging sign. If Stephan Jones were to talk with his father as he had promised Grace he would, there was a chance the rest of the party could go to Jonestown, too. While the relatives were talking, several of them noticed members of the basketball team—who had been so hurried to cut short the talk and return to Lamaha Gardens—were hanging around in the Pegasus, keeping a watchful eye.

At 1:30 in the morning of the next day, November 17, Steve Katsaris received a phone call that furthered his contingency plans to retrieve Maria in the event the Concerned Relatives were barred at the Jonestown gate. He,

Don Harris, and Gordon Lindsay had enlisted the cooperation of a pilot from Trinidad to provide a plane and fly them—and the rest of the NBC crew—into Jonestown. Katsaris's plan was to have the pilot

> . . . come with his airplane to the Port Kaituma strip. I then felt that between Anthony and me we could probably steal a vehicle [in Jonestown] and then throw Maria into it and make off with her. I had taken some pretty powerful tranquilizers with me, and if Maria didn't want to come, I was going to inject her.

The early morning phone call from Trinidad barely confirmed Katsaris's hopes, however; the Caribbean flyer's cooperation was merely "tentative."

The backup plane was unnecessary. After a 7:30 breakfast with Ambassador Burke, Congressman Ryan returned to the Pegasus Hotel to discuss the best way to carry out the journey to Jonestown. Despite the petition with its six hundred signatures and the hard hearts of the Lamaha Gardens staff, Ryan was determined to fly in, with or without permission. Attorneys Garry and Lane—now willing to speak to each other—had arrived at the hotel, and the group conducted negotiations until late morning. From time to time, various members of Concerned Relatives left the hotel lobby to keep scheduled meetings—of about twenty minutes each—with Consul Doug Ellice, during which the consul explained the embassy's diplomatic paralysis owing to the First Amendment and the Privacy Act. As the relatives returned to the hotel lobby, the congressman was successfully parrying the attempts of the attorneys to dissuade him. First, Garry and Lane wanted no one to go up to Jonestown; then they softened their posture somewhat and suggested that perhaps Ryan alone could go. Ryan would have none of it. He insisted that the press accompany him—their presence would be his best protection—and the attorneys countered by refusing to allow any of the relatives to go. When Ambassador Burke called Ryan at about a quarter after eleven with the news that the plane was available and waiting at the airport, Ryan became firm: There were nineteen seats; Ryan's staff, the press, the officials, and the two attorneys required only fifteen. There were four seats left for the relatives. Ryan advised Katsaris and his group to select the four who would fill those seats.

Garry and Lane made a last stab at influencing the process by stipulating that, of the relatives, none who were involved in a lawsuit against the Temple should go. This stipulation found general agreement, although it eliminated Steve Katsaris and the Stoens, and the relatives caucused immediately in the hotel lobby to elect their representatives. A few of the relatives were still scattered about, or gone to their appointments with Ellice, but most of the original party of fourteen were there. They selected Jim Cobb (although he was involved in a suit) and Beverly Oliver, both of whom knew several

342

Jonestown inmates and both of whom, significantly, were black; Jones had made much of the fact that the majority of the Concerned Relatives were white. Anthony Katsaris was selected; his father could not go according to the attorney's stipulation, and Anthony was the only one who might get close enough to Maria to take her out. If Maria defected, given her position in the Temple, others would surely follow. One seat remained, and it was decided the seat should go to one of Ryan's constituents, to fortify the legal tie-in; Carol Boyd lived in Ryan's district, and it had been her father who was first to enlist the congressman's interest and aid after the death of Carol's brother, Bob Houston.

When Richard Dwyer showed up at the Pegasus Hotel at noon—the departure time Ryan had estimated in the phone conversation with Burke—Lane and Garry and others of the Peoples Temple group still had one more card to play: they were going to Lamaha Gardens to radio Jonestown and would return to the Pegasus not at noon but at two o'clock. Dwyer informed Ryan's delegation that such a delay would mean that the plane could not take off until after three o'clock, would arrive at Port Kaituma at 4:30 or 5:00 P.M., and have no time to wait, having to leave Port Kaituma before the six o'clock darkness made takeoff impossible. Ryan told the Temple bunch to meet them at Timehri Airport if they wanted to talk again.

Apparently the lunch-hour excursion to Lamaha Gardens was more than simply a ploy by the attorneys to delay the flight. Garry contacted Jim Jones by radio to advise him that Ryan's determination was ironclad. He was bringing the press with him to test whether Jonestown was as open as was claimed. Ryan's strategy was simple: should admission to Jonestown be refused, he would approach the entrance to the encampment and ask to be let in; if Jones refused, the media would be there with cameras and tape recorders going to show the world proof that Jones was lying. Garry relayed this strategy to Jones with the admission that Ryan had "won the media battle," and with the advice that—on this point, anyway—Jones had best capitulate.

There was further delay at the airport. Lane and Garry were late. Linda Sharon Amos had to come along to the airport with them, with a small group of others from the Lamaha Gardens headquarters. An official of the Guyanese Ministry of Information, Neville Annibourne, had been assigned at the last minute to accompany the group, and occupied one of the relatives' seats. Annibourne, according to his own story in the *Guyana Chronicle*, "looked upon the trip to Port Kaituma as a pleasant interlude from the hurly-burly of the city." The Guyanese government's by-now legendary sensitivity to the plight of their guests was again manifest; Anthony Katsaris recalls:

. . . at the last minute, this Annibourne guy wanted to go with us, which would have meant there was only three spaces for us. And he didn't seem to have any empathy for the fact that he was bumping

343

people off our plane. . . . I was kind of pissed because it didn't seem to me he was too sensitive to the fact of how upset, an emotional thing, this was to all of us. And he kind of showed up with this idiot grin on his face, and he got on the plane and he was just smiling away. I gave him a few dirty looks, but they didn't seem to register.

With the plane's engines warming up and everyone in his seat, Carol Boyd found she had no seat; she had to get off the plane—in tears. The plane began its taxi down the runway. Ryan made the pilot stop and open the door again. Steve Katsaris got behind Carol and gave her a boost up through the plane's door, where Leo Ryan's hand grasped hers and pulled her in.

Grace Stoen and Mickey Touchette were standing beside Steve as he boosted Carol into the plane, and as the door closed and the plane taxied away, Steve says, they jumped up and down with glee. "Don't talk to me now," he told the two women. "I'm concentrating on sending positive thoughts to the pilot: 'Take off. Keep going. Take off. Keep going.'" Steve had been concentrating as well on his instructions to Anthony:

> "Don't tell her to get on the plane, but at the last minute, when everybody's saying good-bye, put your hand on [your sister's] hand. Tell her, 'Look, now's the time; it's safe. These people in the television crew will give us protection.'"
>
> I'd talked with Don Harris and Bob Flick and said, "Hey, if by any chance Maria wants on that plane, Anthony may need some muscle, OK? Could you guys get in the way if any Peoples Temple people try to stop her from getting on the plane?" Don Harris and Bob Flick both laughed. By the way, those guys were pretty tough characters. They'd filmed wars all over the world. And we were apprehensive about walking downtown in Georgetown, but they weren't.
>
> And Bob Flick says, "Hey, if Maria wants to get on, they're not going to touch her." And Don Harris says, "And I'll see that it's all photographed."
>
> So I said to Anthony, "Look, don't worry . . . they'll protect you."

Steve, Grace, Mickey, and the others waved the twin-engine DeHavilland Otter down the runway, finally, with its cargo of twenty souls: the pilot, Guy Spence; Congressman Leo Ryan and aide Jackie Speier; Richard Dwyer from the embassy; newsmen Don Harris, Bob Flick, Bob Brown, and Steve Sung from NBC, Tim Reiterman and Greg Robinson from the *Examiner,* Ron Javers of the *Chronicle,* Charles Krause of the *Post,* and freelance Gordon Lindsay; Concerned Relatives Jim Cobb, Beverly Oliver, Anthony Katsaris, and Carol Boyd; Temple mouthpieces Charles Garry and Mark Lane; and the Guyanese Ministry of Information official, smiling Neville Annibourne. The time was 2:15 P.M. The pilot from Trinidad never showed up; there was no need.

The flight from Georgetown to Port Kaituma took an hour; the plane banked first over the muddy Demerara River and pressed to the northwest above the deep green jungle, forty shades of green interrupted occasionally by light-brown streams and rivers, where mists rose without pause during the day and caused the landscape below the twin-engine Otter literally to steam. Jim Cobb looked down from his window. "I couldn't believe anything could grow that thick," he says. "Just an—expanse. So we went all the way out there, and it's obvious by the time you get to Jonestown, that you're *way* out there."

As the Otter approached Port Kaituma, pilot Guy Spence radioed the airstrip. It was too wet for landing after the recent rains; the plane would have to turn back. "Jesus," thought Anthony, "another obstacle!" Someone suggested they circle the encampment; perhaps they could get some photographs. Spence banked the craft and steered toward Jonestown, buzzing the low buildings and, Maria Katsaris later told Anthony, "scaring these little old ladies." Spence steered back to Port Kaituma. "I'm going to go in low and take a look at the runway," he announced. Then: "There's nothing wrong with the runway." The landing gear stirred a little mud as the plane touched down. "It rains here all the time," said the pilot.

The debarking party was greeted by a group of people from the Temple— Jim McElvane was there, easily recognizable for his size and scowl; he stood at least a head taller than most men and had decided, years earlier, never to smile—and by a contingent from the local constabulary who frightened the hell out of Anthony. One of them carried a shotgun, not as if it were a lethal weapon but as if it were a "pool cue," Anthony recalls, and the man wore no hat or badge, no uniform to mark his authority, just a loose-fitting, short-sleeved shirt, loose slacks, sandals; he appeared to be one of the Jonestown group, except for that shotgun. Only through conversation did the visitors learn he was a cop. Both Bob Flick and Anthony Katsaris recall that it was the policemen, not the Temple representatives, who informed them they were not welcome at Jonestown. There were two of them—the deputy, "younger than I was," Anthony says, and his boss, Corporal Rudder, "dressed the same way; you couldn't tell." The policemen's function was, apparently, simply to inform the visitors of the constraints the police had to honor, why, in short, they couldn't help them any more than the embassy could with its hands tied by the Privacy Act.

The welcoming party from Jonestown seemed, by contrast to the cops, hospitable. They permitted, after some small talk, a small group to mount the dump truck—a big, ten-wheel, heavy-duty vehicle painted yellow—to go talk with Jim Jones. Only the officials and attorneys were allowed to enjoy the jarring ride along the Jonestown road: Congressman Ryan and Jackie Speier, Lane and Garry, Dwyer, and smiling Neville Annibourne. The others—the press and the relatives—had to wait in the shadow of the plane; they were not permitted to go into town nor to wander from the airstrip. Somebody sent a local kid to pick up a case of beer to help kill the time. When he returned, the beer was warm. Down at the extreme northwest end of the runway sat a disabled Guyana Defense Force plane guarded by a group of four disinterested soldiers, but they might as well have been in another world.

They sat on the burnt clay runway for more than an hour. The beer was gone before the dump truck returned at six o'clock with bearers of good tidings: everyone could come to Jonestown—press and relatives—except that British writer, Gordon Lindsay. Lindsay had written an article Jim Jones did not like, and Jones said Lindsay was not welcome to visit Jonestown. Anthony helped Lindsay load his bag back on the plane, and Lindsay returned—angry but subdued—to Georgetown when, moments later, Spence revved up the engines and took off for the capital.

The others—twelve in all, now—climbed aboard the dump truck without any help from the welcoming party and tried their best not to appear anxious, to make small-talk with their hosts. Ron Javers tried to ask a few innocuous questions of big Jim McElvane. McElvane came back, "Look, man, I've been around a little bit, so don't try to interview me on the sly." Anthony Katsaris asked whether McElvane remembered meeting him at Liz Forman's house in Ukiah. "Yeah." Others tried to make conversation, lightweight and low-key. McElvane didn't smile. By the time the truck reached Jonestown, the sun had set and the rainbows that had brightened the flight from Georgetown had long since disappeared. The clouds overhead were low and threatening.

At 6:58 P.M. Pacific Standard Time, a ham radio operator in the United States was talking via the airwaves with Al Touchette from Jonestown. Touchette's message was that if anything happened to him (Touchette), the ham operator was to notify Jim Randolph at the San Francisco Peoples Temple; Touchette gave him Randolph's name and number. An article in the *San Francisco Examiner* for December 5, 1978, says:

> According to [ham operator] Marshall, Al also told him there would be trouble at Jonestown and mentioned Rep. Ryan and group in that context.

If there was going to be trouble, there was certainly no hint of it when the delegation with Congressman Ryan arrived at the Temple outpost. One of the first things the passengers in the dump truck saw as they turned off the public road on to the Jonestown road was a little guard hut bearing a sign with instructions for the locals about what to do if they were in need of medical attention. The Peoples Temple Agricultural Mission was equipped to handle their problems, and the clinic was open every Sunday. The chain that often blocked the road was down, and the truck passed easily into the muddy, rutted road that wound for three miles into the compound. When the truck was pulling in, Anthony spotted his sister, Maria.

346

. . . And I said, "Hey, Maria!" And she turned around from the group of people she was talking to, and kind of waved and said, "Hi, Anthony," and went right back and went on talking with those people. It was kind of strange.

The hosts pointed proudly to the up-to-date facilities they had erected in the clearing—the sawmill, the children's playground, the living quarters. Off in the distance were the chickens and pigs; over to one side, a group of women were doing laundry. Several electric lights were burning. Night had already fallen by the time the truck pulled to a stop.

Marceline Jones greeted the visitors as they descended from the back of the truck. "You must be hungry," she said. "The food is waiting at the pavilion." Marcie and a crew of kids who followed her around led the guests to the central pavilion, where long tables were prepared for the visitors. Jim Jones sat at the head table, against which two others had been pushed to form a U. Beside Jones sat Leo Ryan, talking quietly and settling down to a dinner of hot pork sandwiches, greens and eddoes, and coffee and tarts. Jones wore a red, short-sleeved sport shirt, khaki pants, and the ever-present sunglasses, behind which beads of sweat formed on his forehead and cheeks. As the guests settled into their places, women circulated pouring coffee.

Anthony Katsaris lagged behind the rest of the group. He went over to Maria, as soon as he got off the truck, to give her a hug,

. . and the whole time it was just like dealing with a statue . . . She was really wooden. And we stood there for a minute and had real small talk; it was hard for me to get anything going. Anything I said got a one-word answer.

When Anthony and Maria joined the others at the tables, he tried to give his sister "a lot of stuff . . . that Mom sent down." Maria's response was, "I don't want them taking my pictures; I don't want the press around me at all!" As if in answer to Maria's fears, Marceline announced over the public address system that the press would respect the wishes of all the Jonestown campers; if they didn't want their pictures taken, it was necessary only to raise a hand. Maria sat with her hand up and repeated to her brother, "I don't want them taking my picture." When the food was served, she asked Anthony, "Are you sure you want to eat dinner here? Haven't you heard how we poison all the food? And how we serve stewed people, human meat? . . . That's what the press is reporting."

As the dinner progressed, conversation became more and more difficult. An eight-piece band, the Jonestown Express, played its amplified soul music at a deafening level. The band's repertoire included the Guyanese national anthem and a stirring version of "America the Beautiful," but the real show was old-fashioned blues, modern soul music and contemporary rock, a touch of gospel—even a female comic who was dubbed "Jonestown's Own Moms Mabley"—all performed and presented with enviable professionalism. Nearly everyone loved the entertainment—everyone except Anthony Katsaris:

> It was getting kind of disgusting, because it was about what I figured would happen, because after all the delays . . . we're delayed some more . . . and soon after we see our relatives they start this loud music, which makes it really hard to talk to anybody.

After dinner, Leo Ryan enjoyed a cigarette while the show continued. Everywhere, people were snapping their fingers, clapping their hands, moving to the band's stirring boogie. Anthony Katsaris saw several middle-aged people he had seen in the streets of Ukiah years earlier, with hair cut short over their red necks, bopping to the music as if they were inveterate blues addicts at a Friday night fish fry. "Look at that man's face, just look at his face," said Krause. The man was in a trance. All around were "gray-haired Okies" in overalls, rocking out with their black brothers and sisters, in a programmed wooden shuffle. Marceline made an effective emcee. Across the table from Anthony and Maria Katsaris sat Neville Annibourne, smiling back at Anthony and saying, according to Anthony,

> "Everything's all right now, isn't it? Here's what you wanted. You get to see your sister. See? Isn't everybody so happy here?" And I'm looking around, and I'm seeing all these blank stares on people, and things just don't seem right.

Jim Jones made the rounds, shaking hands and smiling at the visitors, followed by his own photographer. As they approached Anthony and Maria, Anthony knew the reason that Jones wanted photographs of them was to show the world that people were free to visit their relatives, that his sister, Maria, was not truly a prisoner. Anthony raised his hand, as Maria had earlier. Jones's expression registered his disappointment at Anthony's signal; his handshake was quick and limp.

Leo Ryan continued to talk with people at his table. After about forty interviews, the congressman stood on the stage and took the mike. "I can tell you right now that by the few conversations I've had with some of the folks here already this evening that . . . there are some people who believe this is the best thing that ever happened in their lives." The people cheered for twenty minutes. When the music resumed, spirits everywhere in the encampment seemed high. The print media crew were allowed to stroll among the people. Often, however, when a reporter would approach a group of members appearing to chat casually, they'd move from where they were resting and regroup elsewhere. As if on signal, another member would approach the reporter and say something like, "Hi! Isn't the music good?" and try to steer the reporter back toward the center of the pavilion.

The party appeared to be a success. Now and then strange complaints would slip into Jim Jones's occasional speeches—things like, "I wish I had never been born at times"—and he would complain of his 103-degree fever, adding, ". . . in many ways I feel like I'm dying. Who knows what stress can do to you?" Jones brightened considerably when Maria Katsaris fetched little John-John Stoen to show him to her brother—Anthony says John-John "was one of the neatest kids I ever saw. He was really outgoing . . . intelligent, and it didn't seem to faze him at all that all these people were around"—and John-John ran over to Jim Jones and sat beside him. "This is my son," said Jones, and, grasping the boy's face to show his teeth, added, "Here. Show 'em your teeth." To the people observing, Jones asked, "Don't those two teeth look like my teeth?" Anthony Katsaris remembers the incident clearly: "He was showing the kid off like a piece of cattle," Anthony says. John-John believed he came from Maria's womb. Jones was certain he was John-John's father, and in response to a reporter's question, reiterated his vow never to turn John Victor Stoen over to Tim and Grace Stoen. Yes, Jones admitted, he had had an affair with Grace, of which John Victor Stoen was the fruit, but only because Tim and Grace had insisted. The line of inquiry eventually led to questions concerning sex in Jonestown: Was normal sex permitted? What about the allegations that no sex was permitted, or that only homosexual activity was encouraged? Harriet Tropp's answer: "Bullshit. All I have to say is, bullshit. People do fuck in Jonestown." Jones himself admitted that people in Jonestown were required to take counseling before marrying, but, as evidence that life there was normal in every way, he pointed out that thirty-three babies had been born there. The party definitely appeared to be a success.

There were a few islands of discomfort, however. Anthony Katsaris had difficulty talking with Maria in any way that was other than stilted or rehearsed. Her responses were inexplicably defensive. While Jones was showing off John-John "like a piece of cattle," Anthony tried to get Maria to talk of her assumptions about what he had read in the press. "Aren't you guys worried about PR, your public relations?" he asked.

"What do you mean by that question?" Maria countered.

"Why treat the press poorly, if you want good press?" Anthony asked. Anthony recalls further:

And everybody kind of focused in, like, "Why are you asking that question?" Jim McElvane came over and he goes, "Why are you asking that kind of question?" And I just said [to Maria], "Hey, I'm here to talk to you, and I don't want to talk to all these guys." And she goes, "I can say anything I want. I can say anything I want when I'm

349

sitting here, with everybody here—or somewhere completely different, like standing out there."

The power of Maria's logic was overwhelming; Tony agreed to go "out there" to continue their conversation. In the frustration of trying to get Maria to make some kind of sense, Tony gently grasped his sister's arm. "Maria, come on. Wait a minute. I got something I want to say. It's important." Maria stiffened. She screamed for the security guards to come help her. Tony let go her arm and backed away, and Maria stopped her screaming. Tony broke down and cried, "freaked out," with tears streaming down his cheeks, and he gave his sister a hug born of months, years of frustration, and Maria said, "Well, don't worry about it. Don't worry. In the church, here, we're very open with each other's feelings, and we don't mind people crying. It's OK." She patted Tony gently on the shoulder.

The party was winding down. The music stopped at ten o'clock. NBC newsman Don Harris approached his producer, Bob Flick, and showed him a piece of paper one of the Jonestown residents had slipped to him. Harris had stuffed it into his boot so that it would not be found. It was a note requesting help in getting out of Jonestown. Harris got it from Vernon Gosney, a young white man who was in Jonestown only because he had been threatened with death if he refused to go there. Gosney had been forced to leave his sick wife in a coma in a hospital in Santa Rosa. He had heard nothing from her since arriving in Jonestown.

Only the attorneys, Mark Lane and Charles Garry, and Congressman Ryan and his aide, Jackie Speier, and Dwyer and smiling Neville Annibourne were welcome to spend the night in Jonestown. The others—eight members of the press and four Concerned Relatives—had to go somewhere else. The dump truck's motor was already warming when Anthony Katsaris heard his name over the public address system. He had to be paged; it was time to go. Marceline Jones comforted Anthony as he left the pavilion. "There, there," she said in her best Mary Worth inflections. "You'll be able to come back out tomorrow. You'll see things are OK." Anthony argued that he'd like to stay right there; perhaps he could just lie down on a bench in the pavilion or something. "We've made arrangements," answered Marcie. "There's no room for you here."

On the road back to Port Kaituma, Anthony struck up a conversation with one of the Temple members riding in the back of the truck—a young man about Anthony's age named Wesley Breidenbach—about their common interests. Anthony was interested in science and nature, and so was Wesley. They spoke of trees, and Wesley identified trees Anthony had never seen before. They talked about the stars in the skies near the Equator. They discussed some of the local wildlife. "It was a pleasant chat," Anthony recalls. "It was like talking to someone who was in the Peace Corps." When the

350

relatives were dropped off at Port Kaituma, Anthony had made, if not a friend, at least some human contact.

Accommodations at the Weekend Discotheque in Port Kaituma were not at all pretentious. Mike, the owner, offered the two women in the group the use of the bedroom, and the men could use the floor of the living room and the "dance floor" in the discotheque. The dance floor was a small platform raised about six inches from the floor around it. When Bob Brown carried a tray of rum and cola for the press party, he tripped on the elevated stage, breaking the rum glasses and falling on his face. Bob Flick mocked him amicably for it: "I'll never forget the night that Bob Brown broke all the rum, that wonderful night in the tropical paradise." Anthony Katsaris sat in a chair, feeling a little distant from the apparently carefree newsmen who had no relatives, no emotional ties, at Jonestown, yet feeling also that

> . . . I wanted to, I was really interested in staying up all night listening to them carrying on. All these guys were like—like they're kind of "hard core," like Bob Brown was real macho . . . a nice guy, but always in charge. So it was doubly funny when he fell over. And Greg Robinson, the photographer, was getting kind of drunk, too, and he, like, he had a kind of innocence about him, and these guys were belly-laughing and he was, like, giggling, and they were kind of ribbing him, a little bit. . . . It was really interesting to watch them.

Anthony was too tired to stay up, though, despite the attractions of the newsmen's gaiety and the disco's half-dozen reggae records. He went upstairs to sleep. Sometime later, he heard several of the newmen coming back from somewhere, laughing and bumping into things, making much of removing their muddy boots before entering the house—except for Bob Brown; in situations like this, Brown said, he slept with his boots on.

The truck was scheduled to arrive at 8:30 in the morning. It appeared about two hours later. By the time the group arrived again in Jonestown, it was after eleven, and the plane was scheduled to leave Port Kaituma that afternoon. Because of the lateness of the hour, the guests declined the Temple's offer of breakfast, preferring instead to make a tour of the compound.

Earlier, Jackie Speier had accepted a breakfast, but she insisted on eating what all the Jonestown residents ate and she stood in the chow line with the others, according to Stanley Clayton, one of the cooks. Because the visit made the day a special occasion, bacon was served with the morning meal. Ms. Speier declined her portion and passed it instead to one of the seniors. Apparently the old woman had never had bacon, or hadn't tasted it in a very long time, for the eagerness with which she accepted the meat from Ms. Speier "caused a scene" among the other Jonestown residents. Although, after the scene, breakfast was out of the way, Clayton knew "I had a heavy day ahead of me." The meal to be served was to be grilled cheese sandwiches—which, Clayton says, had "never, never been done before in Jonestown." Clayton was uneasy; "the word has start flashing around that there were two people that wants to leave Jonestown" with Leo Ryan, and Clayton realized from the expressions on the faces of the people in the kitchen, "now, we took gripe." Stanley Clayton kept on working.

Marceline Jones led a tour for the benefit of the press and the visiting relatives. The NBC crew were taping near the nursery area, where, according to Anthony Katsaris, "Marcie was just going on in these glowing terms, of all these wonderful things they were doing with the kids, and this and that, and I thought, 'This is a mistake.'" Bob Flick of NBC observed that the tour at that point "wasn't going too well; it became apparent that we were just being led around, and we weren't going to see what we wanted to see, so we started to split up, and people went different directions."

Although the curious newsmen and relatives went off in different directions, Stanley Clayton remembers the security guards stationing themselves at strategic places around the pavilion area to guide members—mostly the seniors—back toward their cottages and dorms. The pavilion area was cordoned off effectively simply by the guards' presence. "They didn't want people walking up that way," Clayton says, "because too many people were walking up there saying, 'I want to leave.'" It was becoming apparent that the classroom, the nursery, were just showplaces—bright cabins designed to give an impression of joyful daily living. To some reporters, it seemed odd that, when Jonestown was purported to maintain a normal schedule, school was being held on a Saturday. A group of reporters wandered over to Jane Pittman Gardens, a dormitory for a number of Jonestown's seniors. The doors were closed and the windows shuttered.

Muffled coughs could be heard from inside, but the reporters' first knocks on the door got no response. One newsman hooked his fingers under the edge of a window shutter; an unknown hand within held it shut. The Temple guards insisted that the privacy of the seniors be respected; many of them were terrified of strangers, having suffered rape and violence back in the U.S.A. The newsmen appealed to the attorneys, Lane and Garry, who intervened on their behalf—they had promised the media people that they could see everything about Jonestown—and soon Jane Pittman Gardens was opened to the snoopy crew.

Inside were scores of double- and triple-tiered bunks with maybe two or three feet between the tiers. Many of the old women who normally occupied the place scurried out the back door. Those who remained assured the reporters, in a subdued and spiritless monotone, that, yes, they were very happy. Edith Parks approached Bob Flick and Don Harris and told them she wanted to get out of Jonestown, that her whole family wanted out. Flick recalls:

. . . I told her that we, it wasn't our mission, as it were, but she could talk to the congressman. Don and I walked her back to the open-air compound . . . and I introduced her to Jackie Speier, and then we went back to what we were doing. We wanted to go over and look at some of the houses.

With everyone exploring the premises, talking with members, looking at some of the houses, lunch was surprisingly orderly and organized, if informal. The grilled cheese sandwiches that Stanley Clayton and his associates had prepared that day were served not in the usual chow line nor at tables in the pavilion, but by workers carrying trays. Mark Lane declined his sandwich, he said later at a press conference. "I brought along some cough drops," he said, "which have a lot of sugar in them. I sure as hell wasn't going to eat the cheese sandwiches." Lane neglected to explain his reasons to fellow attorney Charles Garry.

Stanley Clayton did not drug or poison the grilled cheese sandwiches; he just did his job. In the kitchen, he and his coworkers talked of the growing tension from the defections. To himself, Stanley admitted that he, too, wished to leave. He knew already that Richard Clark had got away—clean—earlier in the day with Leslie Wilson and her son, Jakari, and maybe a half dozen others by going on a "picnic," in pursuit of which they followed the old railroad tracks behind the encampment all the way to Matthews Ridge. Word reached the kitchen crew that the number of defectors had grown from the two of the previous night—Vern Gosney and Monica Bagby—to six, then to fourteen; that's why the guards encouraged people to stay home, stay away from the pavilion. Entire families wished to leave with the Ryan delegation—the Bogues and the Parks—although Patricia Parks, Edith's daughter-in-law and wife of Gerald Parks, was not totally persuaded until sometime late in the afternoon when she saw some of the security guards bringing out the rifles. That was, to her, a sign that the situation was serious. Stanley heard the word about all these defections and got busy with the evening meal, again—by Jonestown standards—an epicurean delight: black-eyed peas, collard greens, and nearly a half ton of smoked, boneless pork, which represented something like five times the normal daily meat ration.

Stanley Clayton was busy. Anthony Katsaris was worried. He knew nothing of the intended defections, for his sister was the only person he talked with or thought about in Jonestown. The family had always been close, open, willing to talk together; now, Anthony had to enlist the aid of his new friend, Wesley Breidenbach, to get any message at all across to Maria. Anthony asked Wesley whether he would, should Maria continue to be so distant, "tell her a couple of things for me?" Yeah, Wes would help. Anthony wanted to tell Maria, "I'm not down here to destroy Peoples Temple or do anything like that. I'm just down here because I'm concerned about her. And I love her."

It was hard for Anthony to talk. He stood and gazed into an uncertain distance; Wes stood by his side. "I kind of felt close to him," Anthony says, "because I'd talked to him before." Anthony stood near his friend Wesley to watch Don Harris interview Jim Jones. Jones was despondent, angry, hurt by the defections; his shoulders slumped as he sat in his chair and a frown of petulant resignation turned his mouth. His biggest worry seemed to be that, once the defectors left, they would go back to the United States and tell lies about him, his Peoples Temple, his jungle paradise.

> Everyone is free to come and go. The only thing I feel is that every time they go they lie. What I thought was keeping them here was the fear of the ghetto, alienation, the fear of industrialized society. I must have failed somehow. I want to hug them before they leave.

During that interview, Congressman Ryan approached Anthony Katsaris. He saw the pain in Anthony's face and told him, "I know you're upset, but I just think you should know that history is being made here today."

To keep track of the history as it was being made, the U.S. embassy in Georgetown posted an officer at the Lamaha Gardens headquarters of the Temple to monitor communications with Jonestown and to assist in relaying messages to the embassy. When the embassy monitor learned the frequency being used for the short-wave link to the jungle outpost, he went home to use his own radio. He could assure that the messages passed between Lamaha Gardens and the embassy were accurate, although there was little to arouse suspicion; most of the measures had to do with the logistics of accommodating the growing number of Temple defectors. To provide transportation for the departing Jonestown residents, a second, smaller plane was dispatched along with the Otter. With all the defectors adding to the original passenger list, the five-passenger second plane was hardly large enough. Ryan and his group decided to have the defectors leave on the first flight out.

As the group was heading toward the dump truck for the jaunt to Port Kaituma, there was a commotion. The Bogue family, the Parks family, Vern Gosney, Harold Cordell, Monica Bagby, and Chris O'Neill were on their way to the truck with the visitors, and Anthony Katsaris was taking up the rear when, he recalls, "there's somebody carrying their kids about ten or fifteen feet ahead of me, and this woman comes screaming after them, 'They're going to steal my babies, they're taking my children!' . . . [Al Simon] decided to go and take the kids [and] he hadn't told the wife, I guess." Marceline appeared and calmed things down. Jackie Speier reminded the attorneys that, since the dispute between Al and Bonnie Simon was an issue of child custody, they, as the Temple's attorneys, should settle it. According to Anthony, the attorneys "were kind of around, but they weren't really doing much." The Simon family returned to the pavilion with Congressman Ryan, Dwyer, and the attorneys.

The truck sat for nearly a half hour with most of the defectors aboard; Ryan and Dwyer and their aides were going to remain behind to arrange for more people to go.

Anthony Katsaris took advantage of the time to say a last good-bye to his sister; he wanted to say something to her that would communicate the feeling welling in his breast, something like, "Couldn't you at least give me a hug here, because I don't feel like I'm ever going to see you again." Instead, he gave Maria the cross that their father had given him back at the hotel in Georgetown. "This is from Pop," he said.

"I don't want it," Maria answered.

"Put it away. Keep it. It's yours. You don't have to look at it right now." He walked away to climb on the truck. Maria tried to give the cross back, but Anthony was now too far ahead of her. She threw it at Tim Reiterman. "Tell Steve I don't believe in God," she said, and took off running.

There were troubles getting the truck to move. It backed into a muddy rut and nearly bogged down. The passengers were certain the inconvenience was an indication that Jones did not intend to let them go; while they were resigning themselves to the inevitable, the tractor pulled the truck from the mud and set it back on the road. Fears were, temporarily anyway, somewhat allayed, but the defectors kept urging, "Let's go. Get started. Come on, let's go."

From the direction of the pavilion there came a scream and a yell, followed by a cheer. Members who had been standing around, seeing the defectors off or doing their chores, turned and ran toward the pavilion. The reporters jumped off the truck and joined the running crowd. At the pavilion, Leo Ryan stood with blood all over his shirt, but the blood was not his own; it had belonged to Don Sly. Sly walked up behind the congressman while he was talking to the people, pulled a knife, and pressed it against Ryan's throat. "Congressman Ryan," Sly announced, "you are a motherfucker." Then Charles Garry and Mark Lane grabbed Sly and wrested the knife away from him; Garry carried out his attack on Sly with some gusto, he recalls, because he had Sly nearly turning purple. In the fracas, the knife cut Sly's hand, and Sly's blood covered Ryan's shirt. Sly was normally more adept at handling knives. Ten years earlier he had taken one from Bill Bush in Redwood Valley, when Bill flashed it at Jim Jones.

Jim Jones looked on without change in his expression. Ryan had earlier told him that he was going to report that the terrible rumors about Jonestown were unfounded, that people were in fact free to leave if they wished, and that there were no grounds for a congressional investigation. Jones's only question after the thwarted knife assault was, "Does this change everything?"

"It doesn't change everything," Ryan assured him. "But it changes things."

It changed Ryan's plans. He had planned to stay behind at Jonestown to let the defectors and the press return on the first flight from Port Kaituma; he,

Dwyer, presumably Lane and Garry, would take the plane when it returned. Now, however, Ryan boarded the truck along with all the others, and left behind, of the visitors, only Lane and Garry. The passengers were upset about the blood on Ryan's shirt; the explanation that it was not his blood did little to calm them. As Mark Lane was urging the driver to move, one final defector ran to the truck and climbed up the back end, carrying a small bag and protesting that Jim Jones was crazy. His name was Larry Layton. The others warned Ryan not to let him go, he was too close to Jones, he might be dangerous, but Ryan stood behind his promise to take with him whoever wished to leave. Layton stayed on the truck.

According to Anthony Katsaris, Leo Ryan was persuaded to move to the front of the truck to ride in the cab, although he protested that he really didn't require any special comfort. When the truck reached the guard hut at the Jonestown gate, Anthony says,

> . . . We stopped there and this guy came out and walked around to the back of the truck, and about that time I got a little scared—but I was real naïve. It would have been—in the light of everything they did to us—it would have been easy for them just to have walked out of that guardhouse with guns and kill everybody on the truck right then and there. But I wasn't really thinking that. I was just thinking I want to get out of here. And the guy walked around the back of the truck and goes, "All right. Everybody move." Mrs. Oliver said, "Oh . . . he's just looking to make sure his kids aren't on there." . . . There were a couple of people in the [guard hut]. I think they were on the radio.

Anthony couldn't know what the guards may have been transmitting or relaying with their radio. In Georgetown, the transmissions began coming in code by late afternoon and, according to the State Department report, "shortly thereafter went dead."

After the knife attack on Ryan, Marceline continued her role as Jonestown's calming influence and advised the residents to return to their cottages, helped along by the guards. After Ryan left, Stanley Clayton says, "the mist was just so dark at the time that everybody was just in a chaos. Unnormal things was occurring." Marceline's soothing voice comforted the residents as they returned to their cottages. She promised that evening there would be a general meeting to discuss the day's events.

Over in the school, the attorneys sat with Jim Jones, trying to have a discussion. Harriet Tropp whispered in Jones's ear every time Garry said anything to him. ("I can't stand that," Garry says.) Jack Beam, Jim McElvane, and Tim Carter were all within earshot as Jim Jones admitted to Garry, "Charles, all is lost." He went on to explain that not all the people who left were defectors. "Every gun is gone from this place," Jones said. "They've taken every gun with them." Maria Katsaris came to Jim Jones and bent over to whisper in his ear. "One word was said," Garry recalls. "It took less than half a second. . . . And he pulls back and he says, 'You and Lane will have to go to the east guest room. These people are so angry at you that your lives would not be safe." Jones spotted a crumpled cigarette wrapper on the floor; he got up from his seat and carried the wrapper to an ash can.

Fifteen minutes after Marceline made her comforting announcement, a group of security guards came into the kitchen again, Clayton recalls, and counted the number of people there, then left without a word. Within another twenty minutes, the public address system was on again. This time the voice belonged to Jim McElvane, calling the general meeting. At the pavilion, says Charles Garry, "People began to trickle in by the hundreds." Garry thought there was going to be a "critique" of the value of the weekend's experiences, but "Jones was not interested in that." Jones told Lane and Garry to go on to the guesthouse. Once there, Lane and Garry saw "two young men with guns at the ready." The two men told the attorneys, "We are going to die for the revolutionary suicide as an expression of protest against fascism and racism. . . . There's nothing better than to die for the revolutionary suicide as an expression of protest."

The attorneys were dumfounded, but Lane kept enough presence of mind to suggest, "Charles and I will write your story." They hugged the guards and the guards turned around and left. The attorneys turned around and walked to the jungle and hid.

Stanley Clayton waited in the kitchen, continuing to fetch hot water and prepare food—as a cook he was usually exempt from the meetings—and he imagined that the people were just sitting around mumbling, complaining, waiting for the meeting to start, and wondering whether this meeting, like so many in the past, would keep them up all night. Clayton could only surmise that, as the moments passed, Jim Jones was lecturing the people and encouraging them, for he heard from where he stood only intermittent cheering—until he heard a cheer louder and more frantic than the others. Stanley recalls:

> You could hear . . . there was one person. She flipped. I mean, she just lost her mind. Her name was Shirley Smith. She stood up and just come on: "Leave my Jim alone! Leave my Jim alone! Goddamn, you have to kill me!" She's going completely out. She's uncontrollable. Her mind just snapped. . . . She was just movin' around the crowd, and she just didn't have any control over what she was doing. She had completely went insane behind this, and she was making such a sexual move, moving her body the way that most of the young men were actually trippin' off on that, and not really connectin' the aspect

of her mind, how she was actually—because there was about four or five people came over there tryin' to hold her and they, she refuse to be hold. So they took her away, down toward the dormitories, and they put her in one of those houses. And she just never did come out of it. So then they—she was down there for about fifteen minutes— they brought her back down, and took her back to the nurse's office and gave her a shot. The word was that they had gave her a shot of cyanide at that time.

Shirley Smith had written a letter to Dad back in July. She told Jim Jones, "I know I still follow you because you have the gift to protect me. I like to look strong but I know I'm weak."

At the Port Kaituma airstrip, Congressman Ryan called a press conference at the little shed midway down the field. The plane had not yet arrived. Bob Flick recalls that there "was a lot of confusion. The [dump] truck and the tractor and trailer were there," across the runway and several yards nearer the end. Some of the Temple loyalists were milling about with the defectors, apparently seeking the girlfriend of one of their group, when Dwyer decided to walk into Port Kaituma to get protection for the defectors from the local police. He returned shortly with three cops in a small truck; one of the cops carried a shotgun. The defectors and their relatives applauded the arrival of Dwyer with the police, knowing that now their escape from Jonestown was all but complete.

Stanley Clayton was still in the kitchen, hearing things secondhand from people who would wander back there and tell what was happening up at the pavilion. What was Jim talking about? The kitchen help wanted to know.

> . . . Like the word was: we gonna die. And Stan say, "Well, not me. I'm not dying. I don't believe in killing myself because people want to leave here. I ain't killin' myself!" I said it out loud. . . . No one said anything. I had a backup. . . . I was tellin' you about Laurice; she agree wit' me that she wouldn't die, neither. And then there was another sister named Karen. She said she wouldn't die, neither. She say, "Just 'cause those people want to leave? Shit! Why should we kill ourself? Fuck that!"

Perhaps it was because Stanley and Karen and Laurice were in the kitchen that their attitude was so distinctly different from the attitude at the pavilion, where nine hundred people were assembled from all over the camp to hear Father's loving exhortation:

> I've tried my best to give you a good life. In spite of all that I've tried, a handful of our people, with their lies, have made our life impossible.

There's no way to detach ourself from what's happened today. Not only are we in a compound situation; not only are there those who have left and committed the betrayal of the century; some have stolen children from others and they are in pursuit right now to kill them, because they stole their children. And we are sitting here waiting on a powder keg. . . . You can't steal people's children. You can't take off with people's children without expecting a violent reaction. . . . If we can't live in peace, then let's die in peace.

Joyce Touchette and Larry Schacht, the good doctor, came in the kitchen to get a large white bucket; Stanley says he usually used it to carry hot water to the stove. Dr. Schacht was carrying "a li'l brown container," says Stanley; he doesn't say what it contained. He heard from outside loud cheering.

At the pavilion, Jones continued his lamentation while Loretta Cordell and Deanna Wilkinson started the organ with a few slow chords: the choir began to sing "Because of Him." Jones said:

We've been so betrayed. We have been so terribly betrayed. . . . One of those people on the plane is going to shoot the pilot—I know that. I didn't plan it, but I know it's going to happen. They're gonna shoot that pilot and down comes that plane into the jungle. And we better not have any of our children left when it's over, because they'll parachute in here on us. . . . With so many, many pressures on my brain . . . there was just too much for me to put together. But I know now what he was telling me. And it'll happen. If the plane gets in the air, even.

The plane was still on the ground at the Port Kaituma runway. It arrived only minutes late, while Congressman Ryan was answering questions about Don Sly's knife attack. With the twin-engine Otter was a smaller, single-engine, five-passenger Cessna, the only additional plane the embassy could provide on short notice. The two aircraft sat about thirty feet apart on the runway, and Jackie Speier was moving back and forth between them, carrying a clipboard and helping to decide who should go first and on which plane. There was no argument that the defectors should leave on the first flight, with as many relatives as possible; the sixteen defectors would require nearly all the Otter's seats. Anthony Katsaris volunteered to wait for the second flight. He helped Leo Ryan carry one passenger's trunk to the steps of the plane. There had been some question as to which plane Larry Layton would occupy; when the defectors mounting the Otter were being searched, he got out of line and went to the Cessna. Jackie Speier stopped him for just a moment, but he argued that the congressman had promised he could leave with the first flight out.

Jim Cobb said something about searching Layton—"He's too high up to defect"—but everyone was in such a hurry to leave, according to Anthony Katsaris, that they said, "Let's go. We gotta go." Katsaris and Ryan picked up the trunk again to carry it to the larger plane. Anthony noticed that the dump truck had left the runway; the tractor and trailer had crossed and were parked only yards away from the Otter. Some of the men from the Temple jumped off the truck and shooed away the Port Kaituma locals who had come to watch the takeoff. They took the policeman's shotgun away. Anthony Katsaris remembers hearing two or three shots before diving under the plane and crossing over behind the wheel before a bullet went through his wrist. Ron Javers was standing near the right wing of the Otter when he got it in the shoulder and went down. On either side of him were Congressman Ryan and Don Harris of NBC News. They fell immediately after Javers did. Under the opposite wing lay Greg Robinson, near a tire that also caught one of the bullets, his body doubled over.

Near the cargo hatch of the Otter, Jackie Speier hung on to the edge of the hatch with one arm; her other arm and one leg were soaked with blood, nearly shattered. Anthony Katsaris lay on the ground near her, his bloody arm up over his head; perhaps that posture saved him from further wounds, from death. Don Harris had warned him only seconds before to pretend he was dead; then Harris crawled away to his own death. Inside the Otter, Edith Parks yelled at her grandchildren "Look what they've done to your mother!" Their mother, Patricia Parks, lay on the ground at the foot of the aircraft's stairs. Her brains had settled in Harold Cordell's lap.

Bob Flick had been standing on the ground under the pilot's window, discussing schedules and planes, when the shooting began. He hit the ground. The smaller craft had already begun to taxi down the runway and had stopped near the disabled Guyanese Defense Force plane. He remembered that the soldiers at that end of the runway had automatic weapons. As he ran toward them, he recalls,

> . . . I saw, as I approached the disabled plane, one of the soldiers tracking me with his weapon. . . . And I ran around the tail of the plane, and another soldier was standing there with an automatic weapon at the ready. And he told me to stop. I told him we were in deep trouble and needed help . . . and I said, "If you're not going to help us, at least give me your gun." And he refused.

Neville Annibourne explains the soldier's behavior in an article for the special edition of the *Guyana Chronicle:*

> The soldiers when asked why they did not come to our assistance said that it was a difficult assignment because the majority of the people were white and they did not know who was shooting at whom.

*   *   *

As Flick was returning to the Otter—without weapons—he paused near the door of the smaller Cessna when the pilot of that plane shouted, "Everybody out!" No one got out, and Flick continued. The passengers in the smaller plane were understandably reluctant to move. Larry Layton had whipped out a pistol and fired a few shots, wounding Monica Bagby and Vern Gosney. Dale Parks pushed Layton out of the plane and wrested the gun away from him, but when Parks tried to shoot him, the gun jammed. Those inside refused to open the door again.

To make sure the wounded near the Otter were dead, Tom Kice, Joe Wilson, and Albert Touchette walked over to some of them with a shotgun and stuck it in the faces of Leo Ryan and Greg Robinson and blasted away. Bob Brown kept his camera going, filming the slaughter and walking backward until he reached the tail of the Otter, where a shotgun blast splattered his face against his camera. Steve Sung saw it and took a severe wound of his own— severe enough that the gunmen didn't try to finish him off, assuming that he was dead.

Inside the Otter, Beverly Oliver sustained wounds to her feet. The Bogue kids, Tom and Teena, kept their wits about them while they crawled along the floor to close the door of the plane. "If those children hadn't shut that door," said their mother, Edith Bogue, ".Those gunmen might have gotten on the plane—and we'd all be dead now." Neville Annibourne was unharmed; so, miraculously, was Harold Cordell. Cordell had been with Jim Jones for twenty-five years and would have been a prime target for the killers' anger. Because he had been around Peoples Temple for most of his life, Cordell was able to identify some of the gunmen; but Jim Cobb observed carefully just who did what, and later provided the Federal Bureau of Investigation the names of the attackers. Tom Kice was the man so handy with the shotgun that blasted the faces of Leo Ryan and Don Harris. He had some help from Bob Kice, Joe Wilson, and Al Touchette in shooting victims in the head. The other killers were, according to Cobb's statement, Ron James, Eddie Crenshaw, Ron Talley, and the young man who had befriended Anthony Katsaris, Wesley Breidenbach. Stan Gieg was driving the tractor.

Stan Gieg had the tractor moving out as Bob Flick ran back to the Otter from the end of the airstrip. Inside the Otter, pilot Guy Spence had the motor running, but the plane couldn't move because of the tire flattened from the gunfire and the many bullets in its left engine. The engines were needed, however, to provide electricity for the radio while Spence sent out his SOS to Georgetown. On another frequency, radios in Georgetown—at Lamaha Gardens and at the embassy monitor's home—listened to messages from Jonestown, all in code. The coded messages—reproduced in the *Washington Post*, January 29, 1979—informed the members at Lamaha Gardens that the time had come. Lamaha Gardens radioed back a simple question: "How? We have no weapons." The coded response was translated: "K-N-I- . . ." The

361

radio went dead. The "K-N-I- . . ." was used to cut the throats of Linda Sharon Amos and her three children.

The tractor-trailer headed back to Jonestown.

Over the loudspeakers at Jonestown could be heard the choir singing:

> Because of Him
> This world has hope again

while Keith and Stanley Wright went into the kitchen where Stanley Clayton observed, "They had two suitcases, and they were lookin' sad. They were saying, 'We gon' die. That's why we over here burnin' up all these files.' . . . And they were just takin' things out of the suitcases, lotta documents and everything . . . and throwin' 'em into the fire where we cook at." Stanley couldn't believe it was really happening, and he damn sure wasn't ready to accept it, not even when he saw Marceline Jones, crying, being escorted back to her cabin by her adopted son Lew Erick. Lew Erick looked up and saw Stanley and his coworkers in the kitchen.

"What are you doing here?" Lew asked.

"Joyce told us to stay here and cook," Stanley answered, invoking the authority of Joyce Touchette, the camp's majordomo.

"No," Lew replied. "We want you all over in the pavilion. Everybody, over in the pavilion."

Jones was still holding forth.

> So my opinion is that you be kind to children, and be kind to seniors, and take the potion like they used to take in ancient Greece, and step over quietly; because you're not committing suicide—it's a revolutionary act. We can't go back; they won't leave us alone . . . and there's no way, no way we can survive.

Dad's voice began to crack with the last phrase—a pause, a sigh, then, "no way we can survive." He asked if there was any dissent. Dissenting opinions could be freely voiced, he told his people, reminding them in the same breath that if any of the children were left, they would surely be butchered. Stanley joined the rest of the crowd as one dissenting voice, that of a woman named Christine Miller, was raised. Christine didn't feel it was necessary for all of them to die simply because a few had defected; Jim Jones would not be swayed.

> I don't know what else to say to these people. But to me death is not a fearful thing. It's living that's cursed.

The crowd sent up a cheer of affirmation: "Yeah! Yeah!"

362

I have never, never, never, never seen anything like this before in my life. I've never seen people take the law and do—in their own hands and provoke us and try to purposely agitate mother of children.

Dad's voice finally cracked; near crying, he added,

There is no need to finish us. It's not worth living like this. Not worth living like this.

By this time the choir had stopped singing the lyrics and, to the accompaniment of Loretta Cordell's organ, voiced only the saccharine chords to "Because of Him," the final lyrics of which modulated into Dad's tearful utterances:

Because of Him
This world, this world has hope again
Because of Him
This world has got a good friend
. . . It's so wonderful to care,
To love, to give, to share—
Oh, let us show today
How to live in the same way . . .
Because of Him . . .

But the music grew increasingly faint as the crowd shouted down Christine Miller's protestings. Dad continued his efforts to persuade Christine to his way of thinking, however, merciful to the very end. Christine argued that she didn't "see it like that. I mean, I feel like that—as long as there's life there's hope. That's my faith." Dad disagreed:

Well, some—everybody dies. Some place that hope runs out; because everybody dies.

A chorus of voices again shouted unanimous agreement: "Yeah!"

I haven't seen anybody yet didn't die. And I like to choose my own kind of death for a change. I'm tired of being tormented to hell, that's what I'm tired of. Tired of it.

More applause.

To have other people's lives in my hands, and I certainly don't want your life in my hands. I'm going to tell you, Christine, without me, life has no meaning. I'm the best thing you'll *ever* have.

363

At this, nine hundred roared their approval of Dad's position and their condemnation of Christine Miller's. Stanley Clayton recalls:

> A mass of people was harassin' her throughout this. One lady, she just cussed her out, called her all kind of bitches and shit, and she said, 'You gon' die. You gon' die right along wid us, 'cause I'm gon' make you die.' And from there different people just got on her case, and after that, it drew a silence.

Somehow the faith began to crumble, quietly, subtly at first; here and there crying and moaning could be heard, only to be answered with angry shouting. "Everybody hold it," said Jones. "We didn't come—hold it. Hold it. Hold it," he repeated.

> Lay down your burdens. I'm gonna lay down my burden. Down by the riverside. Shall we lay them down here by the side of Guyana? No man didn't take our lives. Right now, they haven't taken them. But when they start parachuting out of the air, they'll seek some of our innocent babies. I'm not—I don't want . . . They've got to shoot me to get through to some of these people. I'm not letting them take your child. Can you let them take your child?

"No! No! No!" the members bleated. Jones almost whimpered, "Please, please, please, please, please, please, please," slowly and quietly, as if to no one who was visible at the pavilion. A middle-aged black man came front and center and Dad surrendered the microphone to him. "I'm ready to go," the man shouted; he was already in tears and he spoke his piece as if already overcome with the glory of revolutionary suicide. "If you tell us we have to give our lives now, we're ready—all the rest of the sisters and brothers are with me."

The truck returned from Port Kaituma. There was a cheer as the heroes returned. Tom Kice and Johnny Moss Jones—another of Jones's adopted sons—approached the pavilion, and Johnny whispered something to Jim Jones. Jones took the microphone again:

> . . . The congressman's dead. Please get us some medication. Simple, it's simple, there's no convulsions with it. It's just simple. Just, please, get it—before it's too late. The GDF will be here. I tell you, get movin', get movin', get movin'. . . . Don't be afraid to die. You'll see people land out here. They'll torture our people. They'll torture our seniors. We cannot have this.

Loretta and Deanna played random chords on the organ—not recognizable as a hymn or anthem, but somber as the music in a funeral home.

Let's make our peace. . . . How many are dead? Aw, God! Almighty God! Huh? Patty Parks is dead? . . . It's just too late. It's too late. The congressman's dead. The—many of our—are dead. They're all laying out there dead.

A woman took the microphone, pleading, "Give Dad something so he won't have to go through it—and I'm satisfied. I'll be satisfied. . . . I want to thank you for everything. You—you're the Only. You're the *Only*. And I appreciate you." Hundreds of clapping hands affirmed her appreciation. Jim Jones urged the doctor and the nurse to hasten with the potion:

Please, can we hasten? Can we hasten with our medication? You don't know what you've done. I tried. . . . There'll be more. But we've got to move. Are you gonna get that medication here? You've got to move. Approximately about forty minutes.

Stanley Clayton remembers the scene clearly. When Jim Jones gave his orders to hasten with the medication, some volunteers went to the back of the radio shack, where the medical professionals had brewed their lethal brew of Fla-Vour-Aid, tranquilizers—Valium, Thorazine, Largactil, and Haldol—a painkiller (Demerol), Phaerengen (an antihistamine to promote absorption of the chemicals into the bloodstream), and potassium cyanide. Potassium cyanide, when ingested, invariably causes excruciating pain, and works within seconds or minutes. Presumably the other drugs were mixed in with "Dr." Schacht's potion to minimize suffering; they all work after fifteen or twenty minutes when taken orally. Anyone swallowing a mixture of these drugs would have died in agony and enjoyed the effects of the tranquilizers at least ten or fifteen minutes after they had given up the ghost. The tub of this potent brew sat near the radio shack, to which the only access was a narrow pathway. Stanley recalls,

. . . There was too much of a congestion, so they brought it to the front end of the pavilion, behind where Jim Jones sat. They had tables, and they had the drum, and they brought it behind where he sat, and he ordered for all the babies to come up first. He wants the babies to go first. . . . Some mothers start. They volunteered. I didn't see the first mother, but I seen mothers who volunteered their babies to go. I seen nurses went to different babies and pulled the babies from they mothers' arms and held the babies. They poured stuff down babies' throats. . . .

After seeing that, I seen . . . mothers was arguing with nurses about their babies' going, that they wanted to go with their babies. . . . The nurses that was giving the babies this stuff was arguing . . . that they wasn't allowed to go with them.

Marceline Jones, returned to the pavilion, did not like what was happening, not at all. She tried to persuade Jim to back off it; she even wrote him a letter; she weakened, gave up, and left the pavilion, again in tears. Jim Jones, in his great mercy, permitted the mothers to die with their babies, and, according to Stanley Clayton, ". . . if a daddy want to go with their babies, let 'em go." Dad, Father, Pastor Jim, reassured his flock even as he hurried them to the slaughter. "They're not crying from pain," he said. "It's just a little bitter-tasting."

The bitter taste had babies screaming with a growling, mechanical retch in their voices as their limbs stiffened and twitched. Dad was getting impatient. "It's hard only at first," he assured them. He jumped down from his throne, above which was a carefully hand-lettered sign reminding, "Those who do not remember the past are condemned to repeat it," and pulled his people, one by one, to the line of sheep awaiting their slaughter. Stanley Clayton recalls that Jim Jones admonished everyone to embrace—"Get up and tell each other how much you loved one another. Give people confidence that this is an easy death, just like going to sleep. Go out easy; don't go out so hard. Let it be known that we was good to the end."

Stanley Clayton's Jonestown wife, Janice Johnson, "She came to me early. She asked me when I was gon' go. I told her I was gon' hang on. . . . I was tryin' to tell her with my face to hang on, too. We were sort of face-reading." They embraced. Janice went off embracing others in the crowd; Stanley was afraid to speak his true intention, lest someone overhear—although he was still not thoroughly convinced that what was happening was "real or what, because of where I stood in the pavilion." He couldn't believe it. Stanley was standing way in the back of the pavilion; he remembers that people were crying, some were rebelling about joining the line. Jim Jones convinced Stanley of the reality of the situation when he "start comin' out to people, reaching to 'em, telling 'em to come on. 'It's not going to hurt. It's your friend. Hurry, because I don't want to see you tortured. The GDF will come in here—they'll be here in a little while. We ain't got too much time. Hurry.'" Jim Jones was walking among the people, Stanley says, pulling them out of their seats while he was surrounded by guards armed with shotguns and pistols. There were other armed guards inside the pavilion, outside the pavilion, around the crowd, around the perimeter of te clearing, concentric rings of guards too numerous for Stanley to count.

While Jim Jones urged the stragglers to join the line, he got a little help from Jim McElvane up front on the mike. McElvane had had experience with age-regression experiments and counseling in Los Angeles, before he joined Peoples Temple, and he brought his experience to bear on the mass suicide:

[I had] so much to do before I came here. So let me tell you about it. It might make a lot of you feel a little more comfortable. Sit down and be quiet, please. One of the things that I used to do, I used to be a therapist. And the kind of therapy that I did had to do with reincarnation in past-life situations. And every time anybody had an experience of going into a past life, I was fortunate enough through Father to be able to let them experience it all the way through their death, so to speak. And everybody was so happy when they made that step to the other side. . . . You've never felt so good as how that feels.

After McElvane's inspirational message, other members approached the pavilion's stage and offered testimonials. One woman spoke of how Dad has "suffered and suffered and suffered . . ."

. . . and I'm looking at so many people crying. I wish you would not cry. I've been here for one year and nine months. And I never felt better in my life. Not in San Francisco, but until I came to Jonestown. I've had a gorgeous life. I've had a beautiful life. I don't see nothing that I should be crying about. We should be happy. At least I am.

The living applauded the woman's testimonial; the band began another tune. Another woman took the mike:

. . . Good to be alive today. I just like to thank Dad, 'cause he was the only one that stood up for me when I needed him. And thank you, Dad.

There was another woman, and a man, and others offering testimonials to the beautiful life Dad had given them. Dad continued to urge them to hurry to their deaths. Whole families now were permitted to die together. Friends kissed and embraced and said their last good-byes while Stanley Clayton helped a couple of other people pick up seventeen-year-old Thurmond Guy from the ground where he had fallen. Stanley recalls:

. . . He stumbled and hit me and he went down to the ground. . . . He started doin' this convulsin' and shakin' and his eyes started rollin' around in his head. At that time I said, "It's real. This man is really killin' us, and I ain't goin' through there. Ain't no way in the world I'm gon' kill myself." He was already in convulsions, just tremblin'; he wasn't screamin'. He was breathin' real hard, makin' a very harsh sound. He was spittin' up his spit—no blood, just spit.

Stanley helped the others carry Thurmond Guy back out of the way of the pavilion and lay him in a clearing in the back, face down. For some reason,

Stanley said, the nurse said it would be easier that way. He didn't ask how she knew.

> And after being in that area—I mean it's a sad thing, all these bodies right here. There's no life. People are just—you're hearing this weird sound, their voices are, I mean, everywhere you look people are dying, people that you used to laugh and play with, right there in front of you. Thurmond was a brother. And so . . . I started lookin', tryin' to figure out a way out. At that time . . . I knew I wasn't gon' go up there, that I would be one of the last.

One tub of the punch was not enough, says Stanley. The first was brought to the front of the pavilion, down on the boardwalk behind Dad's throne. The second was placed at the opposite end so that two lines could be formed and people could be served their portions with double efficiency. Then, Clayton recalls, there was a third tub brought out, about thirty minutes later. For those who were reluctant to swallow their doses, nurses circulated with syringes of the disposable plastic variety; they would jab the arm of someone who chose to remain seated, then—in accordance with their medical training—throw out the used syringe and inject the next person with a fresh, sterile one, presumably to prevent infection.

Jim Jones was impatient with the hesitancy of his followers and with their complaining.

> Lay down your life with dignity. Don't lay down with tears and agony. It's nothing to death. It's like Mac said, it's just stepping over to another plane. Don't be this way. Stop this hysterics. . . . We must die with some dignity. We have no choice. . . . Children, it's just something to put you to rest. Oh, God!

The cries of the children became louder, more agonized. Dad frowned on the lack of control. The attorneys, Lane and Garry, hiding by now in the jungle not far away, remember hearing Jones's next utterance; they were tempted later to assign it some cosmic significance:

> Mother, mother, mother, mother, mother, please. Mother please. Please. Please. Don't do this. Don't do this. Lay down your life with your child. But don't do this. . . .
> Free at last. . . .
> Children, it will not hurt. If you'd be—if you be quiet. If you be quiet . . . Death is a million times preferable to ten more days in this life. If you knew what was ahead of you—if you knew what was ahead of you, you'd be glad to be stepping over tonight.

"During that whole process," says Stanley Clayton, "I was more or less like just movin' back and forth in different directions, lookin' busy." Stanley knew he was popular with several Jonestown residents; the last thing he wanted was for an affectionate brother or sister to hail him and offer to die side by side. So he kept busy, walking around pretending to examine corpses, looking for Janice Johnson, observing the activity around him. He observed the armed guards—some of them anyway—responding to Jones's order to report to the radio shack to turn in their guns, then assemble in a neat line to take their doses. Stanley "was getting harassed between quite a few people" who called him to join them in death. There were now about fifty people in line, he recalls, and he had to say to "every other person, it seems," that he had to stick around—"You know, they want me to hang loose for a while."

Stanley continued his search for Janice and did not find her among the corpses; he hoped that perhaps she'd made it away, to the jungle. "Finally, I got away from that," he says, "and so at that time I put a strong determination that I had to leave right then and there."·Stanley had more than a strong determination; he had a plan. He passed right by the table where the poison sat, carrying two sheets—"looking busy"—as if he had been assigned, officially, to cover the dead with them. One sheet was for covering a corpse; one sheet was for covering Stanley. He would live by feigning death—so he thought until he overheard, as he passed the table, Lew Erick Jones telling Billy Oliver to walk among the dead and dying and shoot the ones who were not yet dead.

Stanley kept walking.

He abandoned the sheets and headed toward the kitchen, was questioned by a guard, and turned toward the cottages. The guard followed him. Stanley—still on official business—opened the door of a cottage. Inside were two people counting bullets. The guard entered the cottage to question the bullet counters. Stanley didn't. In the bushes, he met another guard—a woman with a crossbow—and told her he had to count the number of people still alive. She drew her crossbow, only to put it aside to embrace Stanley for their final good-bye.

Yeah. Good-bye. Hug and kiss. Stanley hugged and kissed final good-byes through seven guards until he found himself in front of the school. He told the guard there—the last guard he saw—that he was going in to say good-bye to whoever was in there. "O.K.," said the guard, and Stanley Clayton went into the school.

So I was greatly relieved. Even if he said I couldn't go in there, I was gon' go in there, 'cause that was my way out and I seen that. And it wasn't nobody gon' stop me 'cause I know he can't run. . . . And I know how to snake-run, and the fact was that that was in my mind of doing, if it done came to that.

369

From the pavilion came the sounds of the last rattling testimonials. Although now his audience was small, a young black man was moved to say

> . . . that my—my so-called parents are filled with so much hate and treachery. I think you people out here should think about who your relatives were and be glad about, that the children are being laid to rest. And I'd like to say that I thank Dad for making me strong to stand with it all and make me ready for it. Thank you.

There was no cheering. A woman took the mike.

> Everything we could have ever done, most loving thing all of us could have done—and it's been a pleasure walking with all of you in this revolutionary struggle. No other way would I rather go than to give my life for socialism, communism, and I thank you, Dad, very, very much.

The organists, Loretta Cordell and Deanna Wilkinson, seemed to take inspiration from this freedom-fighter's dying words. They changed from their improvised *marche funebre* to the majestic chords of some obscure anthem. Someone groaned to the music in a lost falsetto, then was silent. Dad whispered hoarsely:

> Take our life from us. We laid it down, we got tired. We didn't commit suicide, we committed an act of revolutionary suicide protesting the conditions of an inhumane world.

The organ, all alone, marched out chords of triumph and pomp that grew rather quickly sour, weak, resigned—then faded into silence.

"I was just down on the ground laughing about it," Stanley Clayton recalls of his stumbling. "It was funny. Here I am trying to save my own life and I fall on my ass. But then I get up again and I'm runnin', 'cause I'm puttin' my feets down as fast as I can put 'em down there—and all of a sudden I falls again. I say, 'Well, hell! You know, Stan, you must *want* to die!'" Stanley got up and kept running, and he kept tripping now and then on the roots or bumping his head on the branches of the "soda-pop" trees—so named because the Jonestown residents would let the fruit of the trees ferment to make their own "soda pop," which they sneaked out into the fields in old plastic Clorox bottles when they wanted to get drunk under the noses of the duty-bound guards. Stanley was glad for the trees, glad to be in the jungle, but he was scared. He feared

> . . . an attack by a cat or a snake, but I'd rather give a struggle than say, "Well, I'm gon' take this stuff and go to sleep." If I die, they gon'

370

have to kill me. If I'm gon' get eaten up tonight, this tiger or cat or whatever, he gon' enjoy hisself. He gon' have plenty meat for the winter.

So Stanley kept running and ducking, tripping and hiding, scratching his body on branches and thorns and bumping into trees. The jungle, even on the periphery of Jonestown, was dark and black, so black that "these little light bugs that flashes . . . scared the shit out of me." He was afraid the insects' lights might be the flashlights of the Jonestown guards. He had figured out how to function in the dark, in the silence, how to tell animal sounds from human. "I was jungleized to know the difference," he says.

Stanley found a huge fallen tree and hid behind it

> . . . and waited a period of time. I heard a victory, three yells and cheers that scared the shit out of me, actually, 'cause it sound so fuckin' loud. It sound like it was a thousand people. It didn't sound like it was a hundred people, or fifty people. It sound like it was a thousand folks and it scared the shit out of me. . . . You know, wonderin' if this cat done actually pulled one these stunts on us again . . . and here I am out here.

But Stanley's memory of Thurmond Guy reminded him that this white night had been no drill. The cheering was exceptionally loud, he reasoned, because it was for Jim Jones's great achievement, and because it was final. Stanley was right:

> It was quiet after that. No sounds or nothin'. It was real quiet. You can sense sound out there. I heard shots . . . after the cheer. I was on my way out after this, 'cause I say it was quiet, very quiet, and it came to me that it might just be all over with.

When he heard the four shots, however, he ran back into the jungle, fearing that he might be the target. He ran and crawled, scratched himself again and again, slogged through mud, until he was lost. He tried to get comfortable. He stood up and walked again, more from boredom now, he says, than fear or discomfort, until he found a trail. It led him to the hill behind Jonestown.

> As I looked in I could see, like, the cottage area is dark. There weren't no lights on. And over by the pavilion, the pavilion lights are on. The radio lights are on, and so forth. And the only thing that's runnin' is the generator. It's the only sound that's goin' on. . . .
>
> I'm gonna crawl in, cruise on in here, see, 'cause I got to get to that other side. I got to get to the road so I can get out of here. . . . The road is on my mind.

371

With Stanley's obsession for reaching the road grew his realization of what Jim Jones had done; and with the realization grew his rage. "Why the fuck he do all this shit for? Why the fuck he bring us way over here then turn around and kill us?" He passed the latrine and stopped to use it. He mapped in his mind the best course for his exit. He found himself soon beside his own cottage and went inside and rummaged through his box of clothes for some fresh jeans, a T-shirt, and a clean scarf for his head. He walked from the perimeter of the encampment to its main, central road, then remembered, "I came over to this country with a passport. . . . I need a passport to get out." He turned back and headed toward the office, where the passports were kept. All was quiet.

> I went through the seniors' residence, where the seniors stayed. They had came in there and they just left the seniors just where they were—sittin' or layin'—and just gave 'em a shot. . . . I assume they gave 'em shots because of the fact I seen needles. They took sheets and laid 'em over their heads.

In the office, Stanley locked the door behind him and turned on the lights; he wanted the building to look just like the building down the road, which was still lighted.

> I kind of froze in my stance and waited to a time I felt that it was good. Then I went toward the passport drawers and got my passport. And as I shut the door back, that's when I heard the last shot. . . .
> I assume that's when Jim Jones shot himself.

Again, Stanley froze. Absolutely still, motionless, he listened. He listened for movement; there was none. He listened for voices; there were none. He heard nothing. Had there been any movements, any voices, he would surely have heard them; he stood only fifty feet from the pavilion.

Finally, Stanley found the courage to move a little. He looked to the right and to the left. He looked up toward the pavilion; nothing. He looked down toward Jones's house; nothing. Nothing anywhere but hundreds of bodies. No motion. No sound except the engine of the generator.

"Then I said, 'Here I go!'"

The dogs were standing in the driveway. They started barking when Stanley approached. Stanley ran. He ran down the hill and hid for a moment behind the generator. No one was following. He ran again, all the way to the gate, the guard hut, and on to the Port Kaituma road.

> It was just a great feeling when I got there that I just wanted to jump up for joy—'cause I made it, and I didn't let him do it, kill me the way he wanted to. And I felt good about that.

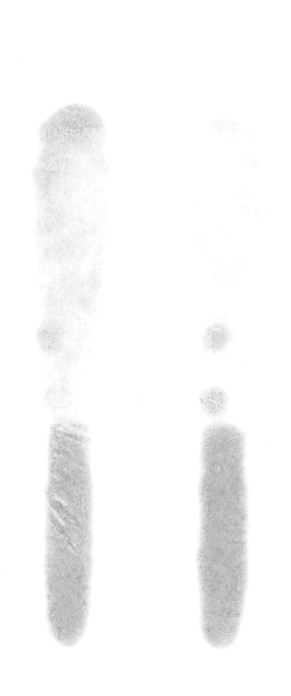